Of Problematology

Of Problematology

PHILOSOPHY, SCIENCE, AND LANGUAGE

Michel Meyer

Translated by DAVID JAMISON

in collaboration with ALAN HART

The University of Chicago Press

Chicago & London

Michel Meyer is professor of philosophy at the University of Mons and the University of Brussels. He has served as visiting professor at the University of California, Berkeley. Among his previous books are *Meaning and Reading* (1983), *From Logic to Rhetoric* (1986), and *Rhetoric, Language, and Reason* (1994).

The University of Chicago Press, Chicago 60637
The University of Chicago Press, Ltd., London
© 1995 by The University of Chicago
All rights reserved. Published 1995
Printed in the United States of America
04 03 02 01 00 99 98 97 96 95   1 2 3 4 5
ISBN: 0-226-52150-8 (cloth)

Library of Congress Cataloging-in-Publication Data

Meyer, Michel.
    [De la problématologie. English]
    Of problematology : philosophy, science, and language /
Michel Meyer; translated by David Jamison.
        p.   cm.
    Includes bibliographical references and index.
        1. Philosophy.   2. Language and languages—Philosophy.
3. Science—Philosophy.   I. Title.
B77.M4913   1995
100—dc20   94-46783
                                                         CIP

Orginally published as *De la problématologie: Philosophie, science et langage*, © Pierre Mardaga, éditeur.

Contents

Preface

Why inquire into questioning today? What is there in the current crisis of philosophy which leads us to this interrogation? These questions, which motivated Plato, Aristotle, and Descartes, not to mention more contemporary philosophers like Heidegger and Wittgenstein, are an integral part of the thought which I have termed *problematology* and which consists of the study of questioning. This study has developed from a dialogue with tradition as the necessity of the thinkable—as the positivity of the philosophical in its relationship to historicity.

But by the same token, this book is also its own limitation. It is in fact preparatory to the even more fundamental task of articulating this radical interrogativity from itself, on the sole basis of its own interrogation, to reach the systematics of the principles of thought. For once we admit that questioning must be questioned, then we need to know how it works and how it constructs a new rationality.

As a consequence, this work is both ambitious and necessarily modest. It is ambitious because it concerns itself with getting us past a crisis of immobility in philosophy by adopting a new approach. It is modest in that, above all, it presents an analysis of tradition and its aporias. In spite of this limitation, problematology appears constitutive as to language and the scientific method, and a philosophical theory articulating them both is here put forward.

Introduction

The Nature of Philosophy

This is a book of philosophy in the classical sense of the term. By that I mean that it is in the great tradition of the quest for the fundamental, that is, of radical questioning. As Descartes reminded anyone who might have forgotten their Aristotle, ". . . 'to philosophize' strictly refers . . . [to] . . . the search for first causes or principles . . . I think that everything I have just said would be accepted by all people of learning."[1]

But let us not be misunderstood: that type of inquiry has disappeared. The impact of recent history is that it has given prominence to groundless individual projects, and, by allowing debate to proceed from the unconscious or special interests, has little by little cast doubt on the validity of the discourse of this so-called foundational subject.

This implied the death of the subject on which philosophy had relied since Descartes. As a consequence, philosophical attention has been directed to language and discourse. These are the two great intellectual characteristics of our age which have thus completed the movement—begun in the last century by Nietzsche, Marx, and Freud—by which the subject came to be deprived of a foundational role.

Philosophy has therefore reflected the quickening pace and destabilization of History, to the point of making its own evolution dependent on what's fashionable or what problems are raised by current issues. It is "the age of the feuilleton," so accurately described by Herman Hesse in *The Glass Bead Game*. Serious thought has been sacrificed to the diffuse, to the transitory. We pass from the old salons of yesteryear to the grand salon of today, where the cultivated elite of the democracies meet, and we owe this to the media, better adapted to the size of this

1. René Descartes, Preface to *Principles of Philosophy*, in *The Philosophical Writings of Descartes*, trans. John Cottingham, Robert Stoothoff, and Dugald Murdoch (Cambridge, Eng.: Cambridge University Press, 1985), vol. 1, p. 179.

new audience. In so changing, philosophy has ended up renouncing itself, so to speak, in favor of superficial topics, exhibiting a lack of rigor
which has made possible the most esoteric word games. Inevitably,
there was nothing at the base of philosophical inquiry which could
guide it, either in its questions or its answers. It is clear that after
Descartes less emphasis was placed on research into principles, precisely because thought was based on the Cartesian starting point, that
is, on self-consciousness. Kant's contribution was such that his immediate successor, Fichte, to better establish that contribution, had to base
his philosophy on the search for a first principle to guide a new way of
seeing.

Today, with the death of the Cartesian foundational subject, things
are different. It is no longer possible to philosophize without beginning
again at the starting point; indeed, the problem now is to establish a
starting point. What better shows the scattershot method of present-day
philosophy than that, for want of a guiding principle, one no longer
knows what questions to ask, or how to answer them with some rigor?
As a result, many a philosopher occupies himself with anything he
wants and discusses it however it suits him best, thereby chasing after
the only guarantee still available: the endorsement of a wide public, or
failing that, the support of academe, which quite often has simply preserved the philosophical record rather than enriching it. Nothing was
left for so-called serious philosophy but to take refuge in the proven
stability of the past, to turn itself into pure history of philosophy. This
retreat, on the whole, has had the same result as the previous approach.
It led to the fragmentation and splintering of philosophy, which had
heretofore been (and always should be) characterized by unity and systemization. Now, everyone speaks of "his" favorite writer: this one
"prefers" Leibniz, another Locke or Hegel, as though such preferences
didn't need to be justified beyond the simple fact that our specialist
teaches them. To be sure, a certain degree of serious inquiry is guaranteed by the existence of the great works; but why are they great, and
how do they still speak to us? Should we study them in and for themselves, as if it were self-evident to do so? Don't we need to question
them and articulate what they say to us in regard to the problems we
endeavor to resolve, problems on which we seek their advice and to
which they could offer answers? In such a situation, an ad hoc range of
options is indefensible. To make such a choice is to fall back upon the
notion that we can pose any question and "philosophize" simply by
appealing to its history. One hides behind the institutionalization of
answers to justify the failure to raise problems solely on the ground of
Reason.

This fragmentation of thought is truly the antiphilosophical attitude par excellence, despite its appearance to the contrary, at least insofar as philosophy is intrinsically a systematizing discipline. Philosophy should respond to periods of chaos not by echoing them, because that would amount to philosophy's adulterating itself, but rather by trying to make sense of that which, because of fragmentation and discontinuity, seems to be meaningless. Philosophical fragmentation is a contradiction in terms. It is as though we were to believe that at a given time, all of society's structures existed independently from one another, with no general rationality behind them, but rather were subject only to internal, sui generis rules.

In short, the history of philosophy cannot suffice in place of philosophy, even though philosophy cannot do without reference to its past. It is a matter of subordination, and therefore of an orderly approach to the questioning of the texts whose truth and worthiness have to be discussed as well as reconstructed. That we are fundamentally concerned about the history of thought cannot be allowed to be an alibi for not thinking, in spite of the illusion that understanding of a given text can provide; hence the seriousness of academic research, which philosophical fashions have never had, a seriousness which can lead us to believe that such an attitude is grounded on a de facto consecration of self-sufficiency. If we think about it, this reductionist attitude (philosophy as nothing more than the history of philosophy) cannot account for itself philosophically without going beyond itself as pure history. Even more to the point, the concept of philosophy as history of philosophy leads to its own refutation, if one takes care to formulate the proposition. Indeed, this very formulation is not itself part of the history of philosophy.

What does this train of thought mean at its base, if, despite everything, we try to make it precise? Simply, it presupposes that no basic principle exists, that such a principle cannot be found, and therefore there is no point in seeking after it. That is all the more serious since, as I have pointed out, we no longer develop the post-Cartesian situation, where we capitalized on a tradition of acceptable (and accepted) foundations, which has been found to be a justification for a search for a first principle. The German tradition had its own Descartes in the person of Fichte. In any event, how can we put as our guiding principle the negation of all guiding principles? One cannot philosophize by putting forth as self-evident the claim that philosophizing like that is still philosophizing. To question an author refers us to some questioning necessity which is external to him and which at best he can confirm. That, in turn, compels the radicalization of questioning, which results in its objectivization, and this, in turn, amounts to making it the object of philosophy.

Whether or not we adopt a historicized approach in regard to the goal, we may safely say that to philosophize has always meant to question, to "problematize." It is necessary, then, to be able to separate the questions we need to pose from the others, as well as to recognize the answers as distinct from the affirmations which need to be rejected or left aside. One thinks of Socrates here, but this has always been a concern of philosophy. Kant's *Critique of Pure Reason* is rooted in the same preoccupation. "Human reason," he writes at the very outset of the preface to his first edition, "has this peculiar fate that in one species of its knowledge it is burdened by questions which, as prescribed by the very nature of reason itself, it is not able to ignore, but which, as transcending all its powers, it is also not able to answer." [2] The knowledgeable reader will have recognized in this demarcation of questions, as in the quest for a resolutional criterion that should call upon an explication of the demarcation, the founding articulation of the *Critique* which underlies its internal complexity. We find this same approach to questioning in empiricism, for the same reason, that is, to determine whether an abundance of philosophies and controversies is a sign of the poverty of thought rather than its wealth, in the sense that this abundance signifies a certain arbitrariness, a certain haziness, which will force us to recapture the essence of philosophy by some search after systematicity. When we read the introduction to *A Treatise on Human Nature*, we find our present situation depicted:

> Nor is there required such profound knowledge to discover the present imperfect condition of the sciences, for even the rabble without doors may judge from the noise and the clamour which they hear that all goes not well within. There is nothing which is not the subject of debate, and in which men of learning are not of contrary opinions. *The most trivial question escapes not our controversy, and in the most momentous we are not able to give any certain decision.* Disputes are multiplied, as if everything was uncertain. Amidst all this bustle, it is not reason which carries the prize, but eloquence; and no man needs ever despair of gaining proselytes to the most extravagant hypothesis, who has art enough to represent it in any favourable colors. The victory is not gained by the men at arms, who manage the pike and the sword, but by the

2. Immanuel Kant, *Critique of Pure Reason*, trans. Norman Kemp Smith (London: Macmillan, 1929), p. 7.

trumpeters, drummers, and musicians of the army. (Emphasis added)[3]

One could have believed, in reading this work which so anticipated our contemporary media-philosophy, that Hume was going to seek that which would allow, as he said, the giving of answers to the most current questions by inquiring into the questioning process itself. But that would mean forgetting that the starting point remained for him, as for his predecessors, the (human) subject, or, to quote him, "human nature." For Locke, this rooting occurs at the level of understanding, and for the same reasons:

> We should not then perhaps be so forward, out of an Affectation of an universal Knowledge, to raise Questions, and perplex our selves and others with Disputes about Things, to which our Understandings are not suited; and of which we cannot frame in our Minds any clear or distinct Perceptions . . .[4]

Today, the evidence of the Cartesian self as Archimedean foundation and its various Kantian or empiricist avatars has disappeared with the death of the subject. As a consequence, it becomes necessary to inquire into questioning itself if one wishes to understand what questions to ask and how to discriminate between those questions which are insoluble and those which have answers.

This undertaking appears clearly, at this point, to be the natural task of philosophy, but beyond methodological motivations or the need to take account of historical change, can it still be affirmed that herein lies philosophy's demand for principles? In any event, we should not lapse yet again into the usual language based on individual viewpoint and subjectivism, whose discourse arises from the death of the subject. If asking about questioning forces itself on philosophy, then it is necessary to be able to *ground* this approach and not simply confirm this particular question as one among others of equal worth, and, for that reason, legitimately opposable.

Therefore it is essential to inquire into what is originary, into what pertains to what is first, into that which may be conceived as foundational, before embarking on a specific mode of questioning of whatever sort. Now, that which emerges first in the inquiry as to what is first

3. David Hume, *A Treatise on Human Nature*, ed. Anthony Flew (New York: Collier Books, 1962), p. 171.

4. John Locke, *An Essay Concerning Human Understanding*, ed. Peter Nidditch (Oxford: Clarendon Press, 1975), bk. 1, chap. 1, p. 45.

is questioning itself, through whatever question is posed. That is why questioning is indeed the principle of thought itself, the philosophical principle par excellence. To be able to answer from the beginning about the beginning itself, as is our goal, it is necessary to be able to form an answer on the beginning itself, an answer which, whatever it *could* be, brings us back to the underlying question, therefore to questioning itself. It is impossible to have a first answer worthy of the name if that answer does not confirm the primacy of questioning. Otherwise that initial answer would defeat its nature as "first answer" by becoming a contradiction, since the answer presupposes something it would not assert, all the while claiming to be primary.

Philosophy is radical questioning insofar as it has for its principal theme questioning itself. The Greeks would have called this, literally, *problematology,* if they had been able to conceive of questioning. However, they were unable to do so, and we shall see why.

Philosophy instead has become something else, repressing, so to speak, the questioning which is its driving force, its real principle. A swift survey of history should suffice to convince us that questioning has never been the central theme of philosophy. Yet philosophy would never have developed nor been able to survive without resorting to questioning in practice. This is how questioning, by failing to thematize itself, was displaced and directed towards objectives outside itself. What have been the consequences of this nonthematization of radical questioning for its own sake?

The autonomization of answers as propositions was made inevitable, since the discourse emanating from questions was no longer able to be thought of in direct connection with those questions, but rather was considered in itself, as though it had existed in itself and was studied by, if not for, itself. The autonomization of answers has had the effect of allowing answers to be thought of as propositions; truth was their essential characteristic. The idea of resolution became subordinated to what I will call the *propositional model* of reason. By that I mean the model for the analysis of propositions which developed, little by little, from Plato and Aristotle: for Plato, a unified, dialectic, scientific link, later split by Aristotle into nonscientific, dialectic rhetoric on the one hand, and logic on the other.

What Plato and Aristotle had in common was that the propositional link, be it weak, as in dialectic or rhetoric, or strong, as in logic, was assimilated to justification, insofar as it both establishes and validates the truth of a proposition. This concern for justification is the inevitable result of a discursivity which only defines itself through the result of its own activity, considered inessential. Therefore it does not deserve mention or else can be characterized as purely psychological and subjective. Thus it was against the yardstick of the result, justified as result, that discourse measured itself, little caring whence or how it emerged, caring only about what enabled a result to be asserted as *such*, hence to be justified in its own autonomous truth, in its truth which it made it autonomous. That is why I have spoken of a propositional model of reason, but not one of language. We tend today to see a proposition as a linguistic entity, or, if necessary, a logical or at best a semantic one. But that is the result of our thinking about language as, historically speaking, a recent enterprise undertaken as an end in itself, which the Greeks, as has just been said, could not possibly have known. For them, *logos* was the term used indiscriminately to describe both reason and discourse. The propositional model, placed under the standard of justification, is inevitably the expression of the capacity for giving reasons, which must be constraining. This is why philosophy became science, before even having to distinguish itself from it. The cognitive, epistemological concern of philosophy depends precisely on justification as the paradigm of Reason. This is quite clear in Plato, for whom science deserved a specific approach through logic, which eventually gave rise to Aristotle's theory of the syllogism.

For a long time, philosophy has not been able to pass itself off as science, nor has it been able truly to disassociate itself from it. This is the origin of the ambiguous status of the concept of "sought-after science," which Aristotle called metaphysics or primary philosophy. Indeed, the propositional model aligns science and philosophy by placing them on the same level along a continuum of justification. This is a consequence of the nonthematization of radical questioning of philosophy. Philosophy nevertheless *is* this question. By repressing itself towards an object other than itself, and at the same time radicalized at the level of questioning practice and its correlative conceptualization, the object is necessarily thought of as general; it is Being, if you will. That explains why philosophy, quite the opposite of science, must proceed to adopt a global view, whether of objects or of beings, fixing its attention not on this or that phenomenon, nor even on a class of phenomena, but on the objectivization of the object, on the phenomenalization of the phenomenon, on the beingness of beings. It is this which will make an object of the object, a phenomenon of the phenomenon, that will make things what they are. But the propositional model endures because it always focuses on justification, on "what makes this be." Science is concerned with particular objects, and metaphysics with the object in general. Since both of them are philosophical, as seen above, it follows that we can call the latter primary philosophy, because from it we derive science as more or less clear and autonomous, under the form of *regional* ontologies. General ontology, therefore, is primary philosophy. But since the rules of science seemed to be applicable to all philosophy (unless it was the converse, as was true at the early time of scientific development), metaphysics could not be really and fully disassociated from science.

It was with the Renaissance that the difference, if not a nascent opposition, between science and philosophy first appeared, an opposition which has become radicalized in our time. Or, if one attempts to rejoin the two, as in the eighteenth century, one must already speak of the growing impossibility of a primary philosophy (or metaphysics). Science progresses; philosophy—at least primary philosophy—marks time. But as Kant claimed, the clear reality of a divorce imposes itself. Philosophical questions have been absorbed bit by bit by science, and others have become, little by little, unsolvable problems which have persisted in their unsolvability since the dawn of time.

Thus the different nature of science and philosophy, made even sharper by the evident retrogression of the latter, has eventually imposed itself as the problematic *par excellence*. But philosophy continued to be unaware of itself as problematology. It has been unable to think of itself according to another model, especially one which would do justice to its own specificity, one which would allow, or—even more— prefer a mode of discourse which would express the problematical rather than a mode which reabsorbs it each time into a solution which then suppresses it. Philosophy yields answers which, when examined closely, are really not solutions in the sense of the propositional model of language, or of science—that is, of Reason. Philosophical questions, putting aside the radicality which they effectuate and embody, are aimed at objects other than themselves, and therefore determine philosophy as ontology, making it the rival of science, with all the consequences that have already been underlined. And yet, there is a difference, one which plays itself out in the concept which supports questioning both in science and in philosophy. Rather than having at our disposal a problematology that takes account of this difference, we have found only a multiplicity of scattered propositions, susceptible of being true or false and therefore opposable or comparable to other propositions. In this analysis we run up against science's reality and efficacy, characteristics which are lacking in philosophical systems. In reality, the latter refer to a problematization worked through propositions which are specific, in the sense that they are *problematological*. That is, they express problematization at the same time that they answer a question. This double nature of answer and problemato-logical expression makes abundantly clear that, in philosophy, to pose a problem *is* to resolve it, since problematizing is the goal of philosophical discourse. Given that, it is absurd to be surprised that philosophy perpetuates its problems, for in doing so, it actually is answering them. That is one way in which philosophy distinguishes itself from science, which eradicates a problem once it has resolved it. Thus, what is seen as weakness in science becomes a rich resource for philosophy. There is more: the fact that a philosophical problem involves its formulation as an answer shows clearly that philosophy must posit its problems within a problematization that, in a certain sense, suppresses them as answers at the same time that it preserves them as problems. If it is understood that it is impossible to detach an answer from the problem to which it pertains, that constrains philosophy to presuppose nothing but the fact that it presupposes nothing. This is a classical definition, to be sure, which can be found, for example, in Hegel. But it was already considered the supreme necessity for thought by Plato, in his search after an *anhypothetical* principle, one which would place philosophy above the sciences, for example, geometry, which can only start from hypotheses.

All this suggests that philosophy should be its own object, and that it undoubtedly always has been, in a roundabout way, since questioning itself has never been in question. Therefore it has been done indirectly, through ontology and not problematology. As a result, philosophy has had to support an unbearable competition with science, made even more absurd by the fact that the two are not even on the same level, at least from the point of view of answers. Metaphysics thus has been rejected and then more or less disassociated from philosophy, which continued to relate itself to science, since science also answers and resolves problems. Kant, for example, consecrates this division between philosophy and science against a metaphysics which he then discards, as he grounds it in its inevitable questioning, itself rooted in the nature of reason. These two theses are equivalent in that each mutually implies the other. However, philosophy, which, as we have seen, cannot exist without a primary philosophy because it is essentially metaphysical (based on some ultimate principle), has been heading towards the ontologization of its questions to the point of reaching the kind of profusion and variety which characterizes the most changeable of fashions. Hence the betrayal of philosophy, the need to restore to it a principle and remove its ontologization, realizing that its deepest reality is not only in questioning, but in *radical* questioning, if we want it not to be altered into some kind of occult answer.

When we say that philosophy needs to be its own object, that may seem an absurd notion, or, if one accepts the idea, an already ancient one. The meaning of our claim here is extremely precise, and, I hope, clear. It is not a matter of defending the thesis that philosophy must turn itself inside out, asking itself incessantly what it must and what it can do, and after that directing this effort into some positive content of thought. Rather, what I mean is more immediate. Philosophy is its own problem in its possibilities as well as its very existence. Whether we like it or not, it is a historical fact. Therefore, philosophy must inquire into the resources of problematization at large to apply them to itself. That thought is its own problem is a historical observation. We must be aware of it: asking questions in philosophy inevitably brings our attention to problematizing, philosophically and therefore radically (that is, without any presuppositions). "Philosophically" means that we are not going to stop at the question of questioning, as expressing the present embarrassment of thought, but that we are going to put this question for itself and from itself and thereby unfold the answer. What we still need to know, then, is whether such an interrogativity gives rise to some principle, whether it is foundational. Thereby we move from the historical to the metaphysical (in the truest sense of the word) level, and that will give a sufficiently clear value to philosophy's reflection on its own existence. This will be a double value which allows us to re-think the philosophical in relation to its requirement of fundamentality (after having perceived the historical aspect of this requirement).

If philosophy has thus torn loose from its own foundation through multiple and specialized thematizations, need we say that it has erred, until now? In fact, it is not a matter of forgetting or erring, but of historical impossibility. Past philosophies are not errors, because it was in the nature of the questions they confronted not to be thought of as such but to be resolved, not to be posed as queries but to be posed as a first step in a resolutional process. As a consequence, solutions do not call themselves solutions, but instead describe *what is* the solution, and that is another thing entirely. The question deletes itself in the answer, which does not describe itself as answer, but asserts what it has to say without saying that it asserts it. It is normal that an answer would not describe itself as an answer, and, in so doing, does not refer back to whatever question, be it radical or not, to raise the issue of radicality as a problem.

An answer is naturally affirmative of something other than what it is itself, of the foundation that makes it an answer. Philosophy, in not having paid attention to questioning, has been unable to do more than reconfirm itself as an answering process, and because of that, it has been ignorant of its nature. The distinctive characteristic of philosophy's specificity proceeds from the fact that there would always be a multiplicity of possible answers, since a problem is never exhausted but instead is posed again and again, giving rise to other solutions, and so on. This structure is due to the fact that philosophical answering is problematological: it poses an answer which is problematized, and that which is problematized is, by the fact that it is so, solved by problematological answering. The latter is, of course, problematization, and, as with any question, does not have only one possible answer. Most of the formulations of a philosophical problem ("What is freedom?") call for legitimately multiple systems where a problem is put and thereby finds itself conceptualized. At the same time that it is defined, it is resolved by the system itself. The question of freedom, for example, will appear differently to Kant and to Marx. The terms of the question will be different for each, because each of the two philosophies approaches human freedom in its own way, and sees the notion, and deals with the concept at issue, in the light of its own conceptual apparatus. Philosophical problematization is necessarily global, and therefore self-enclosed due to the problematological nature of its answering, *hence*, self-involved, differentiated question and answer. Problematization which contains within itself a proposed or suggested differentiation will therefore give an answer to the question it poses. That is why Marx and Kant, to continue with the example, offer solutions to the problem of freedom, such as, and insofar as, they have phrased it, but *cannot* possibly be exhaustive in their answers precisely because the answer of each is *purely* problemato-logical. By contrast, there is another type of response, called *apocritical* in Greek, which both solves and suppresses a problem.

Philosophy, however, teaches us that problems do not disappear. Must we conclude therefore that there is a fundamental split, a basic failure which would by its existence render philosophy a vain exercise, even though we sense it to be an existentially necessary one? If we follow the problematological approach, the answer is clearly negative. Similarly, there is neither a progression nor a cumulative approach within answers, as in science, for the simple reason that the nature of the answers is different and will not tolerate a reduction to "propositionalism." A problematological answer has the peculiar nature of bringing the unthought out from thought, of setting forth alternatives, of creating a realm of relationship and meanings. It is in that way that the solution it raises must be understood. It is not a solution in the ordinary meaning of the term. An apocritical answer closes the inquiry, represses the problematical, and detaches itself from the question rather than digging into it, exploring it, and bringing it to light. An apocritical answer is the basis for another question, and another after that. Questions disappear, answers accumulate in the apocritical.

The illusion that philosophy should measure itself against this standard evidently depends on the fact that its questions have not been understood problematologically, hence the criticism that has been leveled against philosophy from science's viewpoint. By constantly posing questions in a nonproblematological way, philosophy has not questioned questioning, but has instead turned elsewhere, placing itself in competition with science, which, by the way, it has nonetheless made possible.

It is the plurality of possible answers in philosophy which reveals such a specificity, and this situation is purely historical. Historicity forms a pair with questioning, understood problematologically; that is, both are fundamental, and philosophically so. History alone shows that problems persist even in the answering process; they persist despite, and yet because, they are different in content. Therefore, the philosophical imposes itself as answering only *a posteriori*, and only in the historicized perspective placed by philosophy on itself. If we avoid the reading that historicity implies, it is clear that questioning has repressed itself as primary and has not understood itself to have done so. As a result, there will be an incapacity to think of questioning as such, and questioning will be reduced to a psychological and linguistic manifestation, while the fundamental philosophical nature of questioning (because it is the foundational aspect of the philosophical) will escape philosophical thinking completely. The succession of answers in philosophy will therefore always appear as both unsupported and unsupportable propositions because of their irreconcilable nature, which renders them mutually opposable, even if purely dialectically, as in Hegel. They will be the free expressions of separate individualities. We can refer to Spinoza or Locke, for instance, because we can see in their philosophy no more than the reflection of a creative genius, and not primarily an *answer* to be considered historically. What we need to know, and this will be the subject of our first chapter, is why problematology has only today become possible. Indeed, given that philosophy has had to fight off the double blow against it from the nihilistic forces of science and the rapid pace of history, whatever the epoch, it could not have behaved otherwise. History gathers all those forces of dissolution and renders all the more evident the lack of an originary as a deficiency that now becomes a problem. The truth of interrogativity comes through at a level and in forms specific to the repression, hence the expression of this interrogativity remains omnipresent at the core of intellectual activity. That is why philosophy has for a long time seemed like a free-for-all of great personalities opposing one another, when in fact there is in that nothing but the phenomenalization of History, which suppresses itself in its imposing originary, though variable, problematicity. That is why there is an appearance of autonomy and arbitrariness in philosophical systems, which is only a sign of the repression of questioning that becomes autonomous through answers which are not thought of as answers. Freedom, in this sense, is nothing more than philosophy posing as autonomous in relation to the repression of self-reflected but historically, incessantly displaced questioning: hence formalized by or within something else. This freedom, therefore, should be considered as the correlate of History, as an *answer* to that which it allows or requires. Freedom is, then, the necessity of History as the repression of questioning as such: it is necessarily philosophical in its expression. The illusion consists of seeing in freedom a simple extension of itself, rather than seeing in it a possibility implied from elsewhere, one which could easily be missed; hence the freedom in the reflection of necessity. Briefly put, autonomy in regard to History is itself historical. It faded away little by little after the nineteenth century for intrinsically historical reasons born of the rapidity and perception of change. The historical integrated itself into the philosophical as a requirement of the self-reflected necessity of thought. But philosophy will lose itself due to the lack of ability to reconceptualize itself fundamentally into an articulation with the historical, because both are centered on questioning. Philosophy's renunciation of a role as primary philosophy, which Kant accomplished in a certain sense, doomed philosophy to the impossibility of thinking of principles. It will then be by the Hegelian version of historicity that this impossibility will acquire credibility.

The debate between primary philosophy and secondary or derivative philosophy refers to the difference between metaphysics and physics, between philosophy and science. The underlying notion is that philosophy could be other than primary. In fact, it cannot be anything else, but only insofar as it is first radical questioning, oriented toward first principles. But what is philosophy when it forgets or rejects this concern for radicality? Then it places itself on the same level as any scientific ontology, focusing on one or another specialized research area. At that point, philosophy is the real loser, because its ways of questioning produce the type of answers that exclude indisputable truth and its correlative technical efficacy. Referring to human subjectivity, we may note that literature is often more accurate than philosophy at emphasizing the particular and suggesting whatever universal it exemplifies.

In summary, the debate described herein, whether one likes it or not, suggests the dissociation of the metaphysical from the philosophical, the latter absorbing the former, rendering thereby "pure reason" as metaphysics increasingly sterile.

Can we save philosophy by such an amputation of the metaphysical? Nothing is less sure. The dilemma is, as it always has been, unsolvable because of the propositional model. Philosophy could place itself with science to give itself an exemplary efficiency. In so doing it would copy a method but lack the basic ability to apply it. Philosophy would be in any event secondary and subordinate to science. What could it affirm about the world in a truer way than science? We could perhaps support the proposition that philosophy is better at considering the presuppositions and the unspoken foundations that underlie science. But what would be the sense of such an enterprise? Science is quite capable of moving forward without such philosophical results, which, if they are aiming at explicating scientificity itself, are really redundant and useless. On the other hand, if it is a question of justifying the scientific model of reason as the only meaningful *logos*, that effort, being internally unscientific, is self-defeating. The metatheoretical debate about foundations is always internal within science. Or else, and this is the second possibility, philosophy can set itself apart from science, and metaphysics will be what differentiates them: it will be philosophy insofar as it is heterogenous. But this second version of the distinction between philosophy and metaphysics is equally untenable. The propositional model of reason dooms the discursive mode of metaphysics to failure, because this model sets the standard for all possible discursivity. Metaphysics will be equated with primary philosophy, but only *in reference* to a type of discursivity which embodies in and by itself all the virtues expected from discursivity in general. Briefly put, it creates a foundation where no foundation is needed. Indeed, what exactly does it make foundational?

The requirement of a principle in philosophy—a requirement which characterizes philosophy as such—should not be reduced to a model which it cannot account for and which, in fact, dooms it to failure. It would be contradictory to find in the notion of a principle, the foundation of things or of discourse about things. This very idea presupposes an unfounded content for the notion of a foundation which it could thus impose without having questioned it first. And if one questions it, one must fall back on the primacy of questioning. That the first principle has been ontologically conceived through the agency of discourse as *ratio cognoscendi*, or via the real itself as *ratio essendi*, stems from an a priori propositionalism. Indeed the aim is always to justify as true a group of propositions which can only be supported as justifications by the basic justifiability which ties one proposition to the next, where each serves as the principle for another.

Thus, it is within the propositional model, which makes justification the essence of the *logos*, that principles have been "questioned," rather than proceeding in the opposite way and trying to discover whether it is in the nature of the question of principle-as-requirement to engender a *logos* which ignores questioning.

This metaphysical reversal of Plato and Aristotle will be the task of our inquiry. The reestablishment of philosophy as meta-physics, thematically defining such a metaphysics as problematology, and no longer as "something beyond (physical) being," will require a new theorization of the *logos*. It will require opening our minds to another model of thought, not of justification, but simply of rationality. The giving of reasons—and we always give reasons when we philosophize and carry on critical inquiry—must involve the problematological inference. That is to say, it must articulate discourse on the questions which account for it. Science and the scientific method become just one modality for this inference, not its only possibility nor its whole measure. But the inferential modality belongs to problematology, and for that reason, one may truly speak of a philosophical foundation. This conceptualization of science excludes both the competition and the monopolization of rationality by science. The scientific method is part of the general theory of problem solving, but it is included there in a very specific way. It will no longer be possible for us to think of science separately, nor for science to think of *itself* separately.

The foundation of philosophy no longer consists of ontologizing the principle upon which science should depend and therefore seeing science as depending on metaphysics as in "Descartes' tree," with the absurd but inevitable consequence that "an atheist cannot be a geometrician." We can think here of Kant, because he initiated the great schism of contemporary thought in this respect. The foundation of philosophy, for him, no longer consisted of the validation of science. In *Critique of Pure Reason,* we can find a "starting point in the laying of a ground for metaphysics" (Heidegger). But this possibility results from an ambiguity which inheres in the Kantian attitude itself. Science, for him, is a given where the issue is not one of validation, but where it is necessary to deduce what makes it valid. This deduction allows us to regress to the foundation of knowledge and make this deduction the model of all possible knowledge. That is the significance of this transcendental method: through the "Transcendental Deduction," philosophy captures the cognitivity which it will apply to itself for the sake of its own future progress. Whether we like it or not, philosophy derives its substance and the conditions of its progress from the scientificity it uses in analysis. This is only possible after having purified the metaphysical. Will there be a new metaphysics emerging from its foundation, or will we simply have to conclude its impossibility? In the end, is it a matter of liberating metaphysics from scientific referents and, in so doing, finding for metaphysics a proper status? But how can this be done starting from science itself? Isn't the metaphysical in fact impossible, since it has only been able to exist through science from which it must, but cannot, detach itself? Isn't a philosophy which would seek to be metaphysical impractical, paradoxical, and condemned from the start with regard to science at the very level of the principle which governs its method, which it cannot—but has to—adopt? Seen thusly, metaphysics is impossible. Did Kant really break new ground, create a truly new point of departure, when he dissociated it from science? Or did he instead condemn it purely and simply in its traditional form, not to grant it an opening to its traditional unthought foundation, namely Being, but instead to favor the development of science serving as a method for refundamentalization and authentication? Isn't the latter option what has been called the "Copernican revolution," where the allusion to true science as new ontology gains the upper hand over the so-called underlying truth of the old ontology? The ambiguity arises, as I have been saying, from the fact that metaphysics is possible if science is possible. The possibility of science comes from the Transcendental Deduction, which, itself, guarantees the objectivity of this intellectual demarche and also serves as a model for a possible future metaphysics. The Transcendental Deduction is indeed the locus of the a priori synthesis, of the progression of the mind in its unicity, beyond any form of science. For Kant, this foundation is the transcendental point wherein the faculties of our minds engender a synthesis which should free metaphysics from its old "objects."

For Kant, the quest for foundations is, by his own admission, a problematic, but still an empty problematic, unthinkable other than as a deficiency with respect to scientific assertoricity. What Kant calls the problematic is not a positivity in itself but a reality awaiting its justification, a structural flaw or deficiency; it is a negative concept. The foundational is of the order of the faculties: it is deduced analytically in a regressive deduction, which, even though it consists of the truly philosophical, nonetheless derives its strength and substance from science. The foundation, therefore, emerges from the old ascending-descending movement operated by philosophy upon science. That roots both of them in the transcendental, deductive, analytical capacity of mind.

In spite of all this, a deduction so conceived places the fundamental in a justificatory model of reason, which is the source of the "*quid juris,*" the question "by what right?" which emerges as the privileged or even the sole issue to be considered. Metaphysics submitted to the "Copernican revolution" by pulling away from the science which inspired it, rather than deducing it purely and simply, as in Descartes. This shows the relationship which exists between them. The possibility of metaphysics making itself autonomous in regard to science was a real difficulty for Kant and has been since his time. This situation is inevitable as long as we want to find in the foundational that which can validate science and justify its results, whether or not it also has repercussions for philosophy.

This Kantian heritage will bear heavy consequences. On the one hand, it has generated a so-called scientific philosophy, which consists of upholding a model of scientific rationality as the only viable alternative. It is the "metaphysic of understanding," if we are not afraid of speaking in contradictory terms. On the other hand, the Kantian heritage produces opposite results in that we can find in metaphysics a philosophy dissociated from scientificity, where, even for Heidegger, the task was to seek out its unexamined bases. For want of a proper problematology, metaphysics tends to become ontological. Rather than confronting the propositionalism of the justificatory model, it avoids the challenge by a truly unfounded appeal to poetics. This so-called new metaphysics distinguishes Being from *all* that previously had been referred to as *being*, but which is in reality the same thing. Although *being* different, it is no less definable as an ontological neantization. That is to say, it once again defines itself in relation to what is not primary, but can be such only in a complementary fashion, as if it were possible to retrieve the fundamental as the Nothing in what is not fundamental.

The price which primary philosophy has paid for modeling itself on justification, whether or not it has operated on the basis of the synthesis of human faculties, is its own dissolution. The negative ontology of Heidegger, where "being is that which is not said," is the Nothing of what is, is the contemporary manifestation of this model. We will again encounter this philosophical nihilism when we speak of Wittgenstein (chapter 1).

When we affirm the necessity of rediscovering the sense of the fundamental, it is necessary to understand that philosophy can only be primary, or it does not exist as philosophy. If this is to be true, then philosophy must question what is first. "First" means here that philosophy proceeds by a radical questioning into first things, without being concerned with what follows, and, even more, in total indifference to what might follow. It is not a matter of reducing such a quest either to a scientific one or to any other. The question that is raised deals with what is primary as such, *as* being the first or originary question, that is, as an end in itself. Philosophy is primary for the unique reason that it first poses the question of *what* is first, without reducing the principle brought to light in its answer to *what* it is the principle *of*, to that in regard of which it could be defined as a principle. And what is more primary in questioning what is primary than questioning itself? Anyone who would doubt this would still be questioning.

There is no such thing as a model or secondary essence which underlies our questioning: it is alone unto itself. To put it another way, questioning is the only meaning for the foundation of philosophy. This ventures far from the traditional idea of the foundational, in the usual sense of the meta-physical. There is no longer reference to a nature or a being as basic nor to a corresponding discourse to be made legitimate. The principle can no longer be the *a posteriori* constructed object of a reality which itself would be at base the primordial term so that the principle would perforce become "meta." To bring back meaning to the idea of a philosophical foundation no longer means searching for the foundation of *some thing*, which would therefore determine it as a thing. It is instead to accept the fundamental as a question and pose it as a question. It will be a fundamental question inasmuch as there has been no prior one, and inasmuch as it stands on its own without other support. Questioning is thus practiced in its intrinsic originary nature. In this way, philosophy will find anew its dignity and worth in virtue of the *radically new* thematization which our historical situation imposes on human thought. The foundation is to be questioned, and this necessary questioning suffices to create its meaning. Certainly, all that is put in question is not enough to bestow philosophical meaning upon it. But it is certain that if philosophy wants to succeed in resolving its problems, it is essential that it begin by inquiring about problematization, and more especially, that it inquire into philosophical problems. This brings us back to the necessity of instituting a *logos* founded on the difference between question and answer, and not to rely on propositionalist indifferentiation.

The special task of philosophy is found in the radicality of its interrogativity. When it again becomes foundational, philosophy will pose, as a radical question, the only question which can respond to this demand: the radical question is the question of what is radical, and the answer cannot be other than that which is radical in this very question. What is first in this questioning of what is first is questioning itself. As a result, primary philosophy can only be thought of as problematology. It might accurately be said that philosophy needs to *think about itself* rather than being *thought about*, because through the radical questioning which is reflected in its fundamental nature, philosophy takes its own practice for its object. Going beyond this situation is the radical task for philosophy, to be accomplished internally, through itself and by itself, and is, by necessity, metaphysical. Human thought has to be able to assume its own existence as questioning of itself. Then, thought will be by its nature foundational, because it will depend on nothing else in putting forward its first truth as saying what is first. *Of Problematology*, therefore, as the first part of its subtitle indicates, philosophizes on the philosophical. And why these other themes, *science* and *language?* First of all because it is essential to reject the propositional model of reason, as we find it expressed, with mutual support, in language theory and in scientific analysis. Problematological regrounding requires a new language where the assertoric derives from problematization, and not the reverse, a language which lets the problematical exist within the assertions which express it. In this way, we can relocate the philosophical in relation to the scientific in a larger rationality which will reveal both their complementarity and their differences, rather than expressing the science-philosophy relationships in a conflict-oriented discursivity based on indefensible criteria.

Thus our title, *Of Problematology: Philosophy, Science, and Language.* It is time we restored philosophy to its natural function, which is metaphysical, thanks to problematological conceptualization, if we want to arrive at an understanding of how thought takes root and grows. It is high time to abandon the sterile philosophical arguments which have, as said earlier, been a part of the Kantian heritage. Both positivism and ontological metaphysics, renewed by a difference bearing the same name (i.e., the ontological difference), reflect a contradiction as insurmountable as it is inadequate, especially between science and philosophy. Both conceptions depend on the propositional model, a self-justificatory model, because insofar as it *only* admits justification, as in positivism, it destroys itself as philosophy. Or else this model functions as the straw man for the metaphysics of the ontological difference, because it still functions on the level of ontologization but accepts no model of *rationality* other than justification in its assertive meaning, which it precisely rejects, thus plunging into irrationality as its only alternative.

Should we continue to accept this false dilemma, which has provided only false solutions, and which has succeeded only in presenting us with impossible alternatives, because it lacks the philosophical reconceptualization of the basis of the foundational, which is the fundamental question? A science and a metaphysics which oppose one another are badly conceived. The rupture of the philosophical is the ineluctable consequence, as we have seen. But what is misconceived, at base, is that there can even be opposition between the two, because that would mean that they are being compared at the level of *results*. It is inevitable that if the only intellectual tools one has available are those offered by a philosophy of justification (which has dominated human thought ever since Plato), the result will be a philosophy which concerns itself with propositional verification as the only test of truth. Our concern here will be to present a new vision of the *logos*, and, at the same time, an answering which will make answerhood possible *as such*. To that end, language and thought must be investigated. By the same token, we must rethink the rationality of science side by side with that of philosophy and not external to it. Philosophy will then be really primary, but in a new sense which is neither Cartesian nor Kantian.

Nowadays philosophy is more problematic than ever, riddled as it is with internal divisions and sliced apart by cutting criticisms coming from the social sciences, or from such fields as psychoanalysis. Problematization is the positive expression of this state of affairs. The questioning of questioning is a response to our very history, a way of understanding and pursuing it, of putting in check the nihilism which is coming from all sides, a nihilism which is the easy, but least philosophical, solution. If questioning is the only point of departure possible, if it is necessarily so insofar as it is the answer to the foundational question of what is truly foundational and free from all presuppositions, still, nothing forces us to ask such a question. A response to a historical state of affairs is like all responses: autonomous with regard to the problem which generated it and explains it. One may, therefore, quite easily fail to problematize the problematizable, or to interrogate interrogation. Philosophy remains the very expression of our liberty to the extent that it frees itself from any historical conditioning and thereby creates a tradition that is sui generis.

But if we *refuse* the quest for the fundamental as fundamental, we fall into a contradiction. For that which is fundamental whenever one asks what is fundamental, and that which will always be presumed in any possible answer, is simply the fact that one questions. One might also say that it does not make sense to search for principles, and even to refuse to do so. There again, what happens fundamentally is that we still question, and we end up confirming a fundamentality which we deny or which we have sought to put to proof. To the question, "Why seek after some ultimate principle?" (which seems to suggest some vacuity in the problem), one can only answer that, in posing such a question, one has already answered it. The principle is put in question by posing such a question. One could still say that the principle is a metaphysical chimera of the kind that contemporary and future philosophy must rid itself of once and for all, just as we get rid of anything meaningless. But are we not also faced with a question or position of principle, if not a petitio principii which has as a consequence that we always answer the question of the originary, even if indirectly, by not asking it? Are we not thereby presupposing that which makes sense, or even that the originary is resolved within the confines of a theory that is necessarily more fundamental about meaning and nonmeaning, a theory which would itself give sense to what the so-called originary is? At the extreme, one could argue that the claim that the question of what is originary is meaningless, implies a conception of what is a meaningful question. This claim itself is nonsensical and internally contradictory, since it provides an answer to that question. The assertion is self-defeating because it resolves the question, in spite of itself, so to speak. It destroys itself by the sole fact of its being posed. Even if not posed, it is answered. This might appear paradoxical, but is only apparently so, insofar as not posing the question is already a way of providing an answer to it, a way of deciding about it in some way. What is left, then, is the ultimate recourse to a language which cannot confront this paradox and expresses it as it is by a language of "traces" or "absent presences," a language which permits its adherents to affirm anything at all because it forbids being taken literally for what it says.

In sum, the question of the originary is at the origin of every intellectual enterprise, even if it is only implicitly presupposed. If one wants to save the effort of posing it to go one step further, which science often does, this still does not prevent one from reconstructing the organizing presuppositions of the conduct and method of others' thoughts, even if it is done externally, in overview.

What we can legitimately contest is that philosophy can proceed in this way, deciding the question of the originary without even asking it, deciding it solely by focusing on its answers, as science or human actions demand, more out of a simple concern for efficiency than because of some a priori impossibility. Let us go further: since this question of the originary is at the origin of every possible *answer*, it is inevitable that one poses it, even if, de facto or de jure, one denies doing so. Hence our approach here, putting the matter explicitly as a question. But what is not contestable is that one can always not pose the question *explicitly;* that is, pose it to *oneself*. There is an undeniable element of freedom in this, which is characteristic of questioning. We are free not to take into account the problematization of philosophical discourse in its very possibility and to make the philosophical independent from the historicity which characterizes philosophy, by repressing the historicity of our questioning from questioning itself.

A *pure* philosophical approach follows from this, but it would seem that is no longer tenable today, even though it is intrinsically, philosophically, *possible* without any contradiction. To philosophize is to create; it is to put into play an autonomous act—autonomous because it is free. Philosophical questioning at work in the answers which have resulted from it, since they are problematological, has led to a plurality of compatible solutions. But there is a loss to thought if the necessity of answering in regard to the originary as an affirmation of questioning does not reflect the freedom of its birth. This synthesis of necessity and freedom is actually related to the theoretical and the historical, respectively. For it is the theoretical which conditions, not the historical, since there is always the possibility of the latter's not being accounted for in a theoretical structure. The historical can be thought of as a conditioning factor only if one acknowledges that it poses alternatives, that is to say, *questions*, which allow at least two opposite readings: an answering, or ignoring the question (which is yet another way of answering). The paradox of a History which initiates causal links through the freedom of reacting negatively to them can only be resolved in terms of questioning. If we perceive that we are free to respond to the problems of History, to History *as problem*, then we still are under the influence of History, and complete its effect by the freedom shown regarding it. In short, History asks for an answer from us, and the problematics which it imposes on us are experienced even as the possibility of not posing them, of displacing or even denying them as part of a theoretical construct which, nevertheless, would still answer them. The problem-solution relationship is such that there is this possibility of not posing the problem and, by that, answering it. The inherent feature of all problematization is that it contains within itself the freedom not to reflect it. We cannot claim *our* philosophizing to be the only way possible, or that it *has to be* undertaken, but it necessarily is one which, as an expression of freedom, allows us to think about philosophizing and to make explicit its many possibilities. Historicity is recovered in what it makes possible, and therefore imposes, because of the detachment of theoretical results from the *possible* which characterizes the effectiveness of History. The transcendental is none other than the historical negation of the historicity of the thinkable. Historicity so expressed is the repression of History, which means that the theoretical emerges *as such*. The autonomization of answers, which deny themselves even as they are affirming what they affirm, that is, *something else*, is historicity, that is, the internal structure of questioning. It seems, then, to be autonomous, nonhistoricized, and History becomes external to it, to the internal structuring which it must carry into effect in order to *be*.

Nonattention to problematology and the failure to think of thought as the difference between questions and answers are facts of History. Even when History finds some such problematization necessary, this necessity is only theoretical, for, historically, the alternative remains, and problematological nonthinking, or aproblematological thinking, are both still possible. But such a *possibility* is only problemato-logically thinkable as such because the possible is not an autonomous category. It is answering itself which defines the possible as an alternative, as a choice, and as a free multiplicity. The possible is to the theoretical what freedom is to the historical. In the denial of philosophy as problematology there is the very freedom to ask as one wishes, which is put into practice; doing so always confirms what problematology affirms about questioning. Philosophy might decide and *can* decide not to question questioning. This is necessarily a possibility whenever there are questions, but our hypothetical philosopher thereby confirms what he ignores or claims to deny.

The contemporary difficulty with what a philosophical problem means, indeed with the very task of thought, which will be the subject of our first chapter, suggests that we seek a standpoint to address the notion of a problem. In so doing, we can fall back on the idea of method in philosophy. What is the value of method in a discipline like metaphysics? If it is to show that not all points of departure have the same status, that has already been done by showing the role of questioning. If it is to conceive of questioning from an external model copied, for example, from the sciences, that is no longer possible. The new view which we have argued in regard to the relationships between science and philosophy is not so much an external point of departure, but rather a consequence of something more profound which we have to take up again and develop concerning the necessity or non-necessity of a method in philosophy.

The question is vast, and we will return to it later when we speak more specifically of science. But one thing is certain: the relationship between philosophy and method introduces into reasoning a circularity which is unacceptable. Broadly, we can say that method is needed to solve a philosophical problem, but justifying the choice of method, if not its first principles, requires a metaphysic, an ultimate principle which grounds it by instantiating it. We can think here of Descartes, who, from science and method, went on to metaphysics. The difficulty is that to arrive at a first principle for this metaphysics, there must already be an inferential method, not to mention the resultant deduction. This is the source of the split between analysis, which controls method, making it possible to reach a first principle (the *Cogito*), and synthesis, which is constitutive. Several consequences, unacceptable in my opinion, follow from this rupture. Method is one and indivisible; what can be deduced analytically must be able to be developed by synthesis. We can see this clearly in Descartes' *Replies to the Second Set of Objections*. This suggests that what one wanted to differentiate can be differentiated only inessentially, and metaphysics assumes the method it is supposed to be founding. The split between the metaphysical and the methodological is a rhetorical device trying to separate what cannot be separated. Spinoza, and then Hegel, condemned this distinction and supported the proposition that method must fall within metaphysics, and no longer could be thought of as a mere means to arrive at an autonomous end. But does method, as a concept, still have a meaning in philosophy?

And there is more: the first principle of metaphysics, that is, the *Cogito*, in the case we are considering, is first only to the degree that we accept the independence of the metaphysical from method. We arrive at this pinnacle thanks to method. *Primary* philosophy once more is situated within a domain where what follows it defines and guarantees it. What is meant by the method is the scientific method; it sets off the true from the false by a chain of reasons which justify the former by eliminating the latter. It is science which defines what is ontologically primary, by means of the divine understanding, which soon doubles the *Cogito*. Even if the principle of the *Cogito* is methodologically first, it is so as an intermediate point within a global *perspective*, a framework, which alone counts when all is said and done. In the case of Descartes, it is a demand for method, that is, science, which commands the (or a) metaphysics: metaphysics is not undertaken independently.

Because method cannot justify itself, metaphysics must then do it. But it can do so only in a circular way, at the cost of an ontological subordination to a scientificity to be established (Descartes) or which is already accepted (Kant). Such a concept of method cannot establish a philosophy that is authentically *first*. Such a philosophy refuses to impose itself by a simple denial of its secondarity, which, in fact, traditionally underlies it. The result is a refusal of any form of "meta"-obedience.

Having rejected the idea of method in philosophy, we still have the question of a point of view which will allow us to treat the questions that are raised. This is preeminently a problematological problem.

Let us take up our inquiry again, to search for what can meet the methodological requirement in a *truly* primary philosophy, a need which is a substitute for the notion, classical since Descartes, of method.

If we pose the question of the originary which is at the very foundation of every interrogation, the primary answer, the only one possible (and which emerges apodictically), is to affirm questioning as this originary. Any other *answer* would be self-defeating. By the very fact of questioning questioning, the out-of-the-question arises as declaring this questioning for what it is. The *fact* of asking the question explicitly provides us access to go beyond it, to that which suppresses it. As a consequence, we are able to progress. This *method* for moving from question to what is out-of-the-question as an *explicating* reflection of the question, establishes the answer. This procedure can be found again and again throughout the history of philosophy, certainly in Descartes, as we shall see, but also, for example, in Hegel. It is unimportant here to know whether or not the answer preserves the question which it overcomes. This "method," as I have already said, will not be thought of as such because it has no minimal or unique conditions other than the differentiation of question and answer. There will thus be a derivation, a displacement of the "methodological" in what has been classically understood as method: the delimitation and justification of truth as such. We will have occasion to study this derivation later. What is striking is that the mode of problematological inference, though put into practice, will be theorized according to a twisted model of method which leaves no place for this *problematological difference*, the question-answer difference. Therefore, there will be a divergence between theory and practice, with, as a consequence, a failure adequately to perceive the specific mechanism of the philosophical inference. The philosophical inference is then projected onto another type of deduction, which it is supposed to ground, but which, in fact, is differentiated from it at the *factual* level, as for example in the *Meditations*.

The problematological difference is the necessary and sufficient criterion. It specifies when one is no longer in the problematic which is recognizable as such, and that one can set the problematic apart from the answer, which can also be identified *by the observation of the difference within the same process*.

What, then, is the question to put in place of the problem of "method?" How does this problematological difference function in philosophy, to be sure, but also in other intellectual activities, for example, in science? If, in philosophy, answers flow from the *fact* that one asks oneself a question, the same is not true in science. There, an answer, contrary to philosophy, becomes autonomous, since the goal of the resolution is not to problematize something, but to suppress all problematization in regard to that something. Since the movement from question to answer is not satisfied with the mere formulation of this problem, intermediate links are needed, and this constitutes, properly speaking, scientific method. Because of an inability to clarify this distinction, the Transcendental Deduction in Kant, for example, is to be judged in reference to scientific deduction, and will be seen as circular and incapable of proving anything. Therefore it is not in conformity with what we usually mean by the term "deduction." On the contrary, it may be a true deduction as problematological inference, as we will see later on, or it will be misunderstood in its philosophicalness, even if the outcome is conceded, given that people have called Kant "a great philosopher." To understand this deduction accurately, it is necessary to think of this deduction problematologically. The Transcendental Deduction is not a true deduction, in the logico-scientific sense of the term, but Kant had no other way of conceptualizing it. This did not prevent it from being a correct inference, in my view, in that it established a problematological differentiation, though unreflected as such.

To describe this differentiation, I prefer the term "rigor" rather than "method." Philosophy can neither use experiments to verify its claims, as in natural science, nor through formalization is it able to confirm the true and eliminate the false, notwithstanding the fading promises of the seventeenth century. What remains for it if not the necessity of endowing itself with its own necessity, not arbitrarily, but by putting into practice from the very point of departure the *necessity* of its point of departure? Putting the cards on the table in this way puts before those who want to play the game a list of its rules and at the same time makes clear that not playing is one of the game's possibilities. Games derive their rules from the fact that it is necessary to have rules, a necessity that is philosophically well established and primary.

O_{ne}

What Is a Philosophical Problem?

1. Intellectual Nihilism in the Contemporary Era

Distrust and skepticism about philosophy have always come as much from within philosophy as from outside it. Indeed, distrust of philosophy and philosophers ultimately will be seen to have been one of the major characteristics of twentieth-century thought.

The doubt expressed about philosophy's capacity for solving problems has been joined to the usual list of criticisms about its lack of general utility. The numerous critics are a prestigious group, since they come from the universities, where the emphasis is on what is instrumental and functional. The proclaimed triumph of analytical thought, which carves up its subjects to better understand them, is inevitably nonphilosophical. While some scientists are able to think about science from a philosophical outlook, they often forget that their viewpoint is rooted in particular interpretation drawn from their own field. Consequently, they attempt to pass off as valid generalizations what are instead scientific considerations, arbitrary in their basis and limited in their validity.

Be that as it may, it is certain that the attack on philosophy, whether skeptical or dogmatic, is nothing new. We may note in passing that those societies which are relentless in their denigration of philosophy are often those in a period of decline. There is a simple reason. The abandonment of critical and rational thought, which drives people into the embrace of diverse sects and new religions, feeds on the destructuring of thought in all its aspects as well as on the lack of structure in corresponding ways of life.

The rejection of philosophy has rarely been other than an indication of decadence, insofar as it reveals a growing skepticism towards systematic thinking, in fact a skepticism about thought itself. But that fragmentation of thought anticipates even greater disruption, leading to an increasing search into compensating unfounded visions and intuitions, before arriving at pure and simple obscurantism and intellectual charlatanism.

Is that our present situation? Certainly, philosophy has always had to confront skepticism of all kinds. So this can be said to be merely a new version of an old story. We will leave it to the reader to answer the question, one that History will resolve in any event.

In what way can we speak of a specific *contemporary* situation?

The history of ideas reveals an increasing incapacity of philosophy as it has confronted the prodigious developments in the sciences since 1900. The natural sciences come immediately to mind, but the main offensive does not come from them. It is the emergence of the social and human sciences that has been biting off pieces of the traditional problematics of philosophy; the other sciences have long been independent and autonomous.

Philosophy has been dispossessed of its principal Subject, and hence of its very foundation, by Marx and Freud. After all, how could the subject be truly foundational when language speaks through it and when it is alienated from itself at the level of its own drives and interests? With Nietzsche, our ultimate values were uprooted. Literature took as its theme the problem that philosophy did not know how to resolve. All of postromantic fiction is a response to the fragmentation of the subject and therefore of the stabilizing and unifying form the subject imposes on the world. The great formal creations after Proust confirmed the impossibility of the subject's finding that privileged position it appears to assume in everyday life as it is expressed in everyday language. As discursivity became ideologized, philosophy itself fell under suspicion. With the present collapse of ideologies, nothing is left of philosophy but its critical function, now skeletal in form and defensive in tone. In short, philosophy itself has become skeptical. Whether ideology is preeminent or rejected, philosophy is sentenced always to be on the wrong side.

Thus, it is not surprising that the so-called "human sciences" were substituted as the new positivity in philosophy. The feeble discourse of consciousness gave way to the science of the unconscious, just as idealistic discourse that integrates history turned itself into a kind of sociology, economics, and a science of the past as early as the *Manuscripts of 1844*.

Philosophy could only see itself as being entirely called into question, or at least as incapable of resolving its own problems by itself. With the early development of logic machines, moreover, it became questionable whether reasoning was even understandable if it could not be rendered mathematically, and whether human thought itself still belonged to philosophy.

That is why the philosophers of the early twentieth century inquired into the possibilities of philosophy, into what philosophy could and couldn't say (Wittgenstein), and into its necessary end as consecration of silence.

Heidegger's thought is instructive in this regard.

2. The Question of Being, or, the Impossible Thinkable

What is the historical significance of Heidegger's thought?

Unquestionably, Heidegger's thought represents a new stage in the process of self-problematization. While problematization was unable to think of itself as such, still, the vocabulary of questioning was more present here than ever, clearly showing the growing historical nature of the problematological dimension of the twentieth century. What prevented Heidegger from conceptualizing it? The answer *might* be that it was his overriding concern for ontology. The inevitable consequence of this was the criticism of science, a criticism whose a priori effect is to eradicate any possibility of competition between philosophy and science.

Despite everything, however, such an analysis remains superficial, because it does not take into account the specific import of what Heidegger presents at the level of ontologization of the philosophical.

Traditionally, ontology poses questions about everything that exists, therefore about Totality. Science tells us what exists. The ontological distancing now operates by placing us at the level of Totality. The question is about whatever is, inasmuch as Totality cannot *be* just like any other element of that Totality. The difference is an ontological one. To understand Totality, it is necessary to be able to place some limits around it, to delineate it, and, since there can be nothing beyond Totality, Nothingness becomes the only place where the metaphysical is still possible. The renunciation of being, of "that which is" in the proposition "all of that which is," does no more than to emphasize Totality as the denial of being. More precisely, since nothingness is the negation of *being* (*seiend*), being is, here, for Heidegger, different from *Being* (*Sein*) as all that which is. There is more in this approach: if nothing can be without reason, Nothingness escapes reason, because only what is has a reason. The "new metaphysics" refers to Totality as falling outside of the very rationality of being, a rationality which is, to be sure, that of science.

What is important to note is that Heidegger represents a radicalization of metaphysical questioning (unthought of as such) in an era when science seemed to have rendered such a thing more impossible than ever. The question of Totality (that which is) is going to distinguish itself from the question of what is, and Totality is going to acquire a different ontological status. It is because Heidegger saw the challenge in terms of an ontological difference that what could have become a philosophy of questioning would become no more than the questioning (also unthought of as such) of philosophy. It is doubtful that the process of deconstructing metaphysics allowed the installation of a new language, not centered on beings, but able to express Being. This new language should have been born from the *question* of language, a question taken for itself, rather than being relegated, as it had been for Heidegger, to poetics or the simple historicized deconstruction of metaphysics. That is why, whether one accepts it or not, the philosophy of Heidegger cannot result in anything other than mute silence when faced with questions of the essential, as he himself recognized:

> Supremely thoughtful utterance does not consist simply in growing taciturn when it is a matter of saying what is properly to be said; it consists in saying the matter in such a way that it is named in non-saying. The *utterance* of thinking is a telling *silence*. Such utterance corresponds to the most profound essence of language, which has its origin in silence. As one in touch with telling silence, the thinker, in a way peculiar to him, rises to the rank of a poet; yet he remains eternally distinct from the poet, just as the poet in turn remains eternally distinct from the thinker.[1] (Emphasis added)

Many of the impossibilities and difficulties in Heidegger's thought are contained within these lines. The thinker should be a poet but is not. He must abandon his traditional language but cannot. Thus, we see the ultimate "solution" of silence as the essence of language, supposed to be able to express the essential as outside of speech. And in a certain sense, Being as the thinkable impossibility is already set forth as such in *Being and Time:* "Everything we talk about, everything we have in view, everything towards which we comport ourselves in any way, is being . . ."[2] The necessary result is that Being is unutterable, and, on this point at least, Heidegger never varies.

1. Martin Heidegger, *Nietzsche*, vol. 2, *The Eternal Recurrence of the Same*, trans. David Farrell Krell (New York: Harper & Row, 1984), p. 208.

2. Martin Heidegger, *Being and Time*, trans. John Macquarrie and Edward Robinson (New York: Harper & Row, 1962), p. 26.

Perhaps more than anyone else, Heidegger spoke of questioning, and people frequently have assimilated what he said into a philosophy of questioning. But he did not really think about questioning on its own terms. In *Being and Time*, he reduced it to something else, conforming thereby to the "metaphysical tradition" which he always wanted to overcome, precisely by his questioning. Passages like this one are deceptive:

> With the freely chosen level of the actual freedom of knowledge, i.e., with the inexorableness of *questioning,* a people always posits for itself the degree of its being [*Dasein*]. The Greeks saw the entire nobility of their existence in the ability to question. Their ability to question was their standard for distinguishing themselves from those who did not have it and did not want it. They called them barbarians.[3]

Heidegger defends questioning, assigning it an important but in no way fundamental role, at least in the most literal sense of the term. Or rather, it is fundamental, as even he had to recognize, provided that it refers us to something else. What does it mean, then, if not the fact that in questioning we are able to glimpse what is fundamental, which is something other than questioning itself? Are we going to question questioning, and further question that question, and so on in an indefinitive, sterile way, therefore finally to arrive at that "something else?" We could believe so, but we would still miss what directs this questioning, that is, what gives it *meaning.* The question which leads to the "something else" of questioning needs to be asked insofar as it reveals this "something else," but not insofar as it teaches us much about questioning, which is no more than accessory:

> Whenever we present the development of the guiding question "schematically," as we are now doing, we easily awaken the suspicion that here we are merely making inquiries concerning a question. To question questioning strikes sound common sense as rather unwholesome, extravagant, perhaps even nonsensical . . . and in the guiding question, this is surely the case—then the inquiry into inquiry seems an aberration. In the end, such an attitude, asking about its asking, seems nothing short of noxious or self-lacerating; we might call it "egocentric," and "nihilistic" and all the other nasty names we so easily come by. That the development of the guiding question appears to be merely inquiry piled

3. Martin Heidegger, *What Is a Thing?* trans. W. B. Barton, Jr., and Vera Deutsch (Chicago: Henry Regnery, 1967), p. 42.

on top of inquiry—this illusion persists. That an inquiry concerning inquiry ultimately looks like an aberration, a veritable walk down the garden path—this illusion too cannot be squelched. Confronting the danger that only a few or no one at all, will be able to muster the courage and the energy required to think through and examine thoroughly the development of the guiding question; and in the expectation that these few might stumble against something quite different from a question that is posed merely for its own sake or a piece of sheer extravagance, we shall here undertake to sketch briefly the articulation of the developed guiding question.[4]

This structure is clearly triadic: it is a matter of questioning the some-thing else of questioning, the thing insofar as it is questionable, that is, being (*seiend*). We question beings inasmuch as they *are* something to question (and not simply nothing). Therefore we question them about their own being, because being is that which makes it possible to ques-tion them. Since the goal of this process is to know, questioning beings (*seiend*) about what makes them questionable (that is, their very being), is an interrogation that is essential—fundamental—and therefore gives it meaning. That is the origin of the tripartition of questioning Heideg-ger presents, without any justification, in *Being and Time*. There it seems beyond question that questioning always has a *Befragte*, an *Erfragte*, and a *Gefragte:*

> Any inquiry, as an inquiry about something has *that which is asked about* [sein *Gefragtes*]. But all inquiry about something is somehow a questioning of something [Aufragen bei] . . . So in addition to what is asked about, an inquiry has *that which is interrogated* [ein *Befragtes*]. In investigative questions—that is, in questions which are specifically theoretical—what is asked about is determined and conceptualized. Furthermore, in what is asked about there lies also *that which is to be found out by the asking* [das *Erfragte*] . . .[5]

The meaning of Being is the *Erfragte*, just as being (*seiend*) is the *Befragte*, and the Being (*Sein*) the *Gefragte*. Questioning bears on beings regarding their being, but we must ask ourselves what the reasons for this questioning are, why it is raised, and what it means. This attitude implies the existence of something beyond questioning which reflects

4. Heidegger, *Nietzsche*, vol. 2, p. 193.
5. Heidegger, *Being and Time*, p. 24.

itself, a thing which grounds interrogation as much as it explains it. This is the *Dasein*, and thereafter the historical reading of philosophy as "the destiny of Being." History is a reading of Being through its secret revelations. History is what provides meaning, which makes ontological questioning possible, because asking the question of Being is always done with the imprimatur of History. History makes possible questioning about ontological questioning as a deconstruction of the withdrawal of Being. What is striking in the two cases is that the question of Being did not lead Heidegger to ask himself about the being of the question, but rather, his primary concern was to ask himself about the being through which such a question arises and which, for the same reason, is different from all other beings. The meaning of Being lies in that which makes possible questioning about Being, and what makes this possible is the being who may question Being, man. Man (*Dasein*) is thus questioned, not insofar as he questions, but to the extent that by this questioning, there can be found a privileged and *multiple* relationship to Being. The questioning of Being, I say again, is only a sign or a modality of that relationship. The possibility of the question of Being is not to be sought through its intrinsic nature as a question, but through the intrinsic nature of the one who poses the question. That shows both a retreat from and a comprehension of what must be understood, an inauthenticity and an authenticity whose very structures are plural. Hence the *Analytics of the Dasein*, which analyzes both authentic and inauthentic modalities into a great number of existential "categories" with which questioning has little to do. The proof is that the question of Being (*Sein*) is in no way different from the question of beings (*seiende*), that is, the leading question according to Heidegger, since the structure of any question is the same: *Befragte-Gefragte-Erfragte*. If the relationship to the Being of beings, based on the difference between the two, is rooted in questioning, then questioning would be able to translate this difference at the very level of interrogation. Now to question Being or beings makes no change in terms of questioning. We know the question of Being to be fundamental; we now find it present in every question, thereby making questions more unfit for differentiating what is essential and takes place elsewhere.

It is the most fundamental of questions because it is the broadest and deepest, and conversely.

In this threefold sense the question is the first in rank—first, that is, in the order of questioning within the domain which this first question opens, defining its scope and thus founding it. Our question is the *question* of all authentic questions, i.e., of all self-questioning questions, and whether consciously or not it is necessarily implicit in every question. No questioning and accordingly no single scientific "problem" can be fully intelligible if it does not include, i.e., ask, the question of all questions.[6]

Heidegger's argument is not very convincing. After all, to say that the question of Being is ontologically first,[7] since it is not so ontically,[8] is simply to say that the question of Being comes first when we ask about Being, for that is the definition of the ontological: it is that which is of the order of Being. If all questions refer to a question of what *is*, this very question is necessarily prior when one considers as prior that which *is*, and considers it as that which *is to be* questioned. As Ortega y Gasset put it:

> Heidegger's exaggeration of the concept of Being becomes obvious if one notes that his formula "man has always asked himself about Being" or "*is* a question about Being" makes sense only if by Being we understand everything about which man has asked himself; that is to say, if we make of Being the great illusion, the "bonne à tout faire" and the *omnibus* concept . . . No one therefore has seen clearly how devilish a thing the Ens is. Because he did not know this, Heidegger inflated it . . . and he extended it to *every last thing* about which man has asked himself questions, with the result that man only *is* the question about Being, if it is understood that Being is all that ultimate thing about which man asks himself, a thing which could be a mere matter of semantics, but which is not what Heidegger affirms and therefore does not have his confirmation.[9]

What Ortega y Gasset claimed in 1947 (and published in 1958) has been confirmed subsequently.

Returning to Heidegger, we may note that from the *Introduction to Metaphysics* of 1935 (published in 1952), we can identify a shift in focus: the question of the *Dasein* will give way to the questioning of the history of Being. What he says there is fairly close to what he affirmed in *Nietzsche*. The question of Being as the *meaning* of questioning compels the philosopher to ask himself about this very questioning:

6. Martin Heidegger, *An Introduction to Metaphysics*, trans. Ralph Manheim (New Haven: Yale University Press, 1959), p. 6.

7. Heidegger, *Being and Time*, ¶3.

8. Heidegger, *Introduction to Metaphysics*, p. 8. Compare the ontic priority set forth in *Being and Time*, ¶4.

9. José Ortega y Gasset, *The Idea of Principle in Leibnitz and the Evolution of Deductive Theory*, trans. Mildred Adams (New York: W. W. Norton, 1971), pp. 278, 279.

At first sight, the question "Why the why?" looks like a frivolous repetition ad infinitum of the same interrogative formulation, like an empty and unwarranted brooding over words. Yes, beyond a doubt, that is how it looks. The question is only whether we wish to be taken in by this superficial look and so regard the whole matter as settled . . . Let us be clear about this from the start: it can never be objectively determined whether anyone, whether we, really ask this question, that is whether we make the leap, or never get beyond a verbal formula. (*Introduction to Metaphysics*, pp. 5, 6)

But Heidegger adds that the leap into real questioning is historical in nature. History comes in and causes Being to emerge, a Being of which the *Dasein* will be no more than a witness to the withdrawal which is revealed. Questioning becomes listening to Being, and this silence of listening is made historical by questionings which reveal Being as an essence.

> . . . the authentic attitude of thinking is not a putting of questions—rather, it is a listening to the grant, the promise of what is to be put in question . . . The whole that now addresses us—the being of language: the language of being—is not a title, let alone an answer to a question . . . We speak and speak about language . . . Every question posed to the matter of thinking, every inquiry for its nature, is already borne up by the grant of what is to come into question. Therefore the proper bearing of the thinking which is needed now is to listen to the grant, not to ask questions . . . But since to think is before all else to listen, to let ourselves be told something and not to ask questions, we *must strike the question mark out* again when a thinking experience is at stake . . . (Emphasis added)[10]

The circle is thus complete. Questioning, at first subordinated to the questioner, then, successively, to diverse manifestations of past philosophies, must stand aside. It is the reign of silence which will henceforth await thought. And that appears to be the end of it. We cannot even think of fundamentality as such, because we cannot conceive of it in terms of questioning. Questioning is inadequately housed in a structure limited by external considerations. The result is that questioning, unable to be thought of by and in itself, has lost its fundamental character. It is derived from and articulated on the ontological triad

10. Martin Heidegger, *On the Way to Language*, trans. Peter D. Hertz (New York: Harper & Row, 1971), pp. 71, 72, 75, 76.

of being-Being-sense of Being, which only makes sense within a system where questioning *as such*, as foundational, is abolished. Being is then the unthought in every question, though the latter sends us back to it, historically or not, and, in any event, indifferently and indefinitely, without ever succeeding in grasping it.

Thus Heidegger has gone to the end of an impossible trajectory. Aware of the problematic character of philosophy, he certainly spoke about questioning, but all the while refusing to see in its fundamental nature anything more than hollow verbiage. He condemned fundamentality when he shifted it to the level of Being, throwing both of them into the unutterable and unquestionable, as the sole solution for questioning.

The precataclysmic thought of the era between the two world wars is completely characterized by this attitude. It can also be found in Wittgenstein.

3. Philosophical Problematization as Logology

What is striking in reading Wittgenstein is that his works contain omnipresent references to problematization. What is it that assures us of a correct or adequate problematization? When does it make sense? What are the problems that relate most specifically to philosophy, and how are they to be treated? What is the origin of the question of knowing, and what is the language which will allow us to succeed in obtaining an answer? Thus Wittgenstein, in the same manner as Heidegger, comes face to face with the historical situation of philosophy, but he assumes it by considering language as the means, the modality, of posing and solving a problem. Why does he set forth on this path?

We might answer with the historical argument. Wittgenstein was part of the Vienna Circle, and, with Carnap, sought to reform our conception of language by modeling it on science and the ideal language it uses, that is, logic. Logic presupposes a natural language, which it formalizes, and, conversely, logic must be referred to natural language to be understood. But what is the purpose of this formalization of language, if formalism needs to rest on that very thing, namely language, which it is seeking to overcome? Since logic is a language, to understand logic, we must understand language; but, we are also told, to understand language, we need to comprehend its logic!

Thus the twofold path. There is that of Carnap, on the one side, which consists of putting in place logical structures like those of science to the end of giving a conceptual unity to the diverse products of Reason. And then there is Wittgenstein, on the other side, who aims at understanding the relationships between logic and language before having to build a generalized logic of language, as did Carnap, who entered the movement after Frege and Russell but before Quine. This reveals the specific place of Wittgenstein in the Vienna Circle. It also allows us to understand his solution: logic is not a construct imposed on language from without, which would presuppose it in the circular kind of argument outlined above. Rather, logic is inherent in language to the extent that language is equivocal, polysemic, constantly adaptable to the inescapable diversity of its many circumstances of usage, while logic emphasizes univocity, *the* meaning which proceeds from those particular situations, the stable relationships implied by the very notion of intelligibility. Logical form gives meaning to words and to propositions, which can have many meanings because of the flexibility which natural language demands to be infinitely usable.

Logic is the deep-structure grammar of language, and it goes beyond its conceptual grammar, which is its syntax. Logic makes apparent the relationships of meaning which are not expressed in what is said, but are shown, and which each of us, as mere users of natural language, is able to comprehend. The theory of logic, then, is no more than the explicit thematization of the intelligibility naturally occurring in natural language. Logic is, of course, a language in itself, a full-fledged language, written, context-free, one in which everything is univocal and immediately meaningful because it is built to this end. Logic is, if we may say, the product of language reflecting on itself, the autonomized explicitation of the underlying structures of meaning, which we construct as we speak or reconstruct mentally as we listen to others speaking.

All of this would have serious consequences for philosophy, for the way it is to be conceived in its tasks as well as its possibilities. Before exploring that topic, let us return for a moment to what I have called the historical argument and its deficiencies.

One may always begin from the idea that one is seeing here another manner of philosophizing. This manner consists of taking language as an object and modeling it on science, as we might model philosophy in general on science, in the name of a methodological ideal (which might then be fully realized). Such an option may be challenged. If one persists in this challenge, it may be defeated just as easily as any option because of the arbitrary character of its principle. Therefore we may leave the Vienna Circle where it is, in the past. We may even reject it as antiphilosophy to return to what we can truly call philosophy.

In reality, the historical argument is a rhetorical convenience used by those who have decided, a priori, to adopt the viewpoint of externality,

one that permits ignorance. If we must consider Wittgenstein historically, and seriously, then we must understand that at stake in the debate
is the status of philosophy and its future in the contemporary intellectual universe. We must not forget that the issue of philosophical questioning results from a movement toward a general scientization which
developed in the nineteenth century at all levels of human thought and
which seemed to render philosophy more impossible than ever.[11]

Following the "historical argument" risks losing sight of the fundamental questions which Wittgenstein put before us: How can science
and its language, or simply language itself, guarantee the continued
survival or, even more basically, the intrinsic existence of philosophical problematization? Why are science and language philosophically
fundamental? What happens to philosophy when we search science
or language for the key to problems, and why is such a theoretical re-
arrangement necessary? By theoretical necessity, we mean that which
sparks thought from within, and, equally, that which historically conditioned it. Let us forget the historicity of the Vienna Circle. Let us also
forget that one can always place oneself outside, both in time and space,
and thus do without an internal reconstruction, a path which has in fact
been denied in advance by the initial taking of a position outside.

I will return to this, but we can already explain why science and language became the keys to all philosophical resolution, to all problematization. The reason for it is quite simple: in science, experience allows
us to *answer* the questions raised, just as formal language allows us to resolve all the questions it deals with. Thus there are two methods, logic
as well as experience, to give a question its univocal treatment. A language which cannot distinguish between problems and solutions allows
us neither to solve those problematics nor to overcome them, and they
are inevitably bound to arise again. Such a language is clearly illogical,
because logic is the discourse of meaning, the internal intelligibility of
language, the deep structure, sometimes obscured by the peculiarities
of *a* language (French or English, for example), the grammar of which
can disguise nonexistence or impossibility. Why do we speak here of
meaninglessness? If one asks a question, it is to answer it; a question's
meaning lies in the possibility of its resolution. A meaningless question
is an unanswerable question. If it has no meaning, it is absurd as a question; it gives us only the illusion of being a question, when, in fact, it
is a false problem. The absurdity inheres in the fact that it is asked,

---

11. As Karl Marx once said: ". . . every profound philosophical problem is resolved . . . quite simply into an empirical fact." Karl Marx and Frederick Engels, *The
German Ideology* (Moscow: Progress Publishers, 1976), p. 45.

because it does not allow the questioner to obtain what he thinks he will be allowed to obtain. And it is absurd to seek an impossible answer, that is, to ask a question which is doomed from the start to remain unanswered. It is deprived of all meaning as a question. Certainly it may always be asked in the hope that it may be answerable (otherwise it never would be asked), but such an act would be done only out of ignorance or illusion. Posing a question which has no meaning is not enough to give it the signification it lacks, as if posing it were enough to give it meaning. Belief and truth are at odds. It would not be necessary to elaborate a theory of meaning if there were no difference between the meaning of a question and the meaning which emerges from posing this question. If one asks a question, it is with the aim of obtaining its answer: this is precisely the meaning of the interrogative act. But it is entirely possible that the question is unresolvable by its very nature. The questioner, who seeks to gain an answer, thus attempts to give meaning *to his act*, but therein is mistaken, for it is his question which is devoid of meaning. It is therefore useful to show him this discrepancy, and this is the function which philosophy henceforth must be able to assume. The uselessness of posing certain questions flows from the structural impossibility of their resolution.

We read in Wittgenstein: "The meaning of a question is the method of answering it . . ."[12] and "I should like to say: for any question there is always a corresponding *method* of finding. Or you might say, a question *denotes* a method of searching."[13] The theory of meaning is subordinated to the apocritical necessity, to the demand for problem solving. It follows that the unsolvable problem is not really a problem; for lack of meaning, it cannot be so defined. It is a pseudoproblem and, by that token, cannot be posed (even though it may be posed). Alongside a linguistic grammar, which relates to *particular* languages, there is a philosophical grammar, which is concerned with language *in general*. What is apparently acceptable at the linguistic level may not be so at the logico-philosophical level. Thus we have the *Tractatus*, which tried to stipulate what logic, as "ideal" language, reveals about the deep and significant relationships in language, since it, too, is language.

Logic is what permits us to distinguish a problem from a solution, to identify the one by its differences from the other, and, as a result, to be able to say when one has a solution and when one has only succeeded in duplicating the problem. Logic, like experience, is apocritical in that it

12. Ludwig Wittgenstein, *Philosophical Remarks*, ed. Rush Rhees, trans. Raymond Hargreaves and Roger White (New York: Harper & Row, 1975), p. 66.
13. Ibid., p. 77.

provides its own means to explore, verify, and identify expressions. This is the basis of the fundamental dichotomy, vigorously reestablished by Carnap, between analytical and synthetic judgments, which constitute, respectively, the framework of logic and the structure of experience.

All this allows us to understand why philosophy, responding to the concern for problematizing problematization to meet the challenge of its own legitimacy, focused on language, through logic, and on science, through experience. This is probably how neopositivism as a philosophical movement and as a doctrine was born.

It is vital to refute, with full energy, the oft-stated opinion that neopositivism is specific in its antiphilosophical attitude. This specificity does not exist, for this same concern for purification can be found in other currents of thought, notably in France, with Bergson and Valéry. Too often the rejection of metaphysics as a constellation of impossible problems has been associated with the scientific shift, when in fact the latter is only a consequence. This association instead proceeds from ignorance of the *general* intellectual situation during that period.

4. Dissolution as Resolution of Unsolvable Problems: Wittgenstein, Schlick, and Carnap

With Wittgenstein, as with Carnap, the intention is clear. Philosophy has mixed false problems with real ones because it has lacked a language, like logic, which allows it to differentiate them. Such a differentiation could recall an even more fundamental distinction, that between problems and solutions (the problematological difference). The logic of language shows us this difference: in construing it, false problems can be revealed for what they are.

> Most propositions and questions, that have been written concerning philosophical matters, are not false, but senseless. We cannot, therefore, answer questions of this kind at all, but only state their senselessness. Most questions and propositions of the philosophers result from the fact that we do not understand the logic of our language . . . And so it is not to be wondered at that the deepest problems are really *no* problems. (*Tractatus* 4.003)

That is why "all philosophy is 'Critique of language'" (*Tractatus* 4.0031), because it is by an abuse of language that problems are posed which do not have to be posed. If their logic were to be scrutinized, it would be seen that their language in no way includes the possibility of the problematological differentiation which allows us to decide at what point we have a riddle, and at what point a solution to it. "For an answer which cannot be expressed the question too cannot be expressed. *The riddle* does not exist. If a question can be put at all, then it *can* also be answered" (*Tractatus* 6.5). Does all this reestablish that every problem is a concern of language and must be resolved through it? If that is not possible, then does the problem not exist? In reality, all that is postulated here is that if we can talk about what is problematic, we must be able to speak of what makes a solution, *for the same reason*. Which is it? If we *can* express a problem, which must be denominated a problem, we must be able to recognize what makes a question, *as raising a question*. This necessarily implies that we must be able, *a contrario*, to decide when we have no question, or no more questions. This does not mean anything more than this: either the discourse which is held does not raise a question, or else it is an answer. A question's identity permits us to identify it, to recognize it, and thus to be able to state when and how it is resolved. If a question differentiates itself from an answer, and it must be able to be so identified to be really resolvable (and not simply self-replicating), then surely, it is necessary that the expression of a question differ from that of an answer and be so identified. If there is a language for stating questions, to identify them specifically, correlatively, it is impossible not to have a language for expressing answers. It is impossible not to find this differentiation because of their indivisible complementarity, their reciprocal referral. Language must bear the problematological difference for language to be able to cope with it. I say "be able" to cope because it is essential to realize that Wittgenstein, no more than the other philosophers of his time who spoke of questioning, did not think of questioning in itself, and for itself. It was seen through something else, through something derived, beyond which one cannot go, and which serves, if you will, as a "reducer." Thus, as a matter of course, solving a problem consists of making it disappear, once resolved. Failure to do this implies that the problem doesn't exist. To say that allows us to eliminate it through a normal resolution, since showing that a problem is not a real one has the same effect as suppressing it. This explains why Bergson, Valéry, Wittgenstein, and Carnap, though having such divergent answers, had this in common, an idea which has nothing to do with "positivism" as we normally understand the term.

To focus on Wittgenstein more particularly, he says that "all philosophy is 'Critique of language'" to the extent that it is a "reducer" of questioning for him. Language makes authentic questioning possible, and what counts is to clarify this authentic questioning by distinguishing it from the fallacious kind. Questioning did not have to be theorized as such, since it must comply with a reducer, language, which gives it its scope and defines its fundamental properties. "For doubt can only exist where there is a question; a question only where there is an answer, and this only where something *can* be *said*" (*Tractatus* 6.51). Wittgenstein's reasoning is clear: faced with the problem of the impossibility of philosophy's providing itself a precise basis for resolving its problems, it is necessary to deconstruct them and see in what ways they are unsolvable. Language, through the theory of meaning and meaninglessness, is the reductionist key, for language represents the condition of possibility of the unthought problematological difference. Since Wittgenstein had no problematology, he considered as self-evident that when "there is then no question left . . . just this is the answer" (*Tractatus* 6.52). But what assures us that this indeed is an answer? Will the dissolution of questions be an adequate method of resolving them? Will this be related to what the "classical" resolution has in common with "resolution by dissolution": that both are able to make the questions they deal with disappear *eo ipso?* If this is effectively the case, would it not be essential to test the idea with the help of a theory of questions? But how to proceed along this line when one holds the idea that language and its logic are the reductionist keys to questioning? In sum, there is no way for this logology to give an account of its own "necessity" in a noncircular way, because this necessity would follow from the problematological difference, which, in turn, is itself reabsorbed into language as a means of verification. So, we can affirm the self-evidence of the proposition that it is necessary to discuss questions with a language that is sufficient for the way in which it affirms sufficiency. Does not language speak for itself and through itself, rather than through its inherent logic?[14]

This becomes a theoretical presupposition about the resolution of questions which will have consequences for the rest of Wittgenstein's thought, as we will see in regard to his concept of silence.

Before considering the very similar positions of positivists like Carnap or Schlick, I would like to provide a brief account concerning what otherwise might seem arbitrary about their position, specifically the idea that the dissolution of a question may function as an answer to it. This might seem even more paradoxical, even incomprehensible, unless accompanied by a properly articulated problematological explanation.

Let us recall what was said earlier about philosophical questions. How can they be distinguished from other kinds of questions? A ques-

14. Ludwig Wittgenstein, *Notebooks 1914–1916*, ed. G. H. von Wright and G. E. M. Anscombe, trans. G. E. M. Anscombe (New York: Harper & Brothers, 1961), p. 43e; see also Ludwig Wittgenstein, *Philosophical Grammar*, ed. Rush Rhees, trans. Anthony Kenny (Berkeley: University of California Press, 1974), p. 5.

tion is specifically philosophical when the formulation of the question constitutes its answer. It contains its own resolution within the discourse that gave rise to it as a question. By becoming conceptualized, a question reflects itself; it is reflected for and through itself. In a pantheist system, for example, *posing* the question of freedom creates real problems through the rupture which it represents for general determinism, which is equivalent to the ability to conceptualize freedom as, on some basis, possible. To answer to a question, in philosophy, is equivalent to unfolding the question in the answer(s). The problematological answer, understood as an answer, maintains the problematological difference. If we are unable to mark off questions and answers by some characteristic or determination, questions will be suppressed within some undifferentiated discursivity. This is embodied in propositionalism, which destroys the questions it cannot preserve because of its indifference to problems as such. On the other hand, if we operate on the basis of the problematological difference, *to say* that we *answer* to a *question* introduces an explicit difference by the mere use of these terms. This mark is enough to let the question be perceived through the answer which thematizes it and, at the same time, resolves it. Elsewhere, outside philosophy, the goal of the answer is not to make explicit its corresponding question but, in fact, to suppress it, to bypass it; this is the usual concept of what we mean by the term "solution."

To affirm that a question is dissolved *is* a solution, not by reason of the fact that it is a mode of suppressing the question, but because it establishes an explicit differentiation between that which is a question and that which is a resolution. By what right would the suppression of questions be the model for *all* possible solutions? This idea serves as evidence only to the extent that it feeds on common experience or science, and we know the high value attached to these two types of knowledge. It will then be an easy choice to prefer either science or experience, especially if we postulate from the start the validity of the mode of answering they both involve. This process has certain similarities to a *coup de force*, which is unavoidable. But why such a *coup de force*, such a postulate? In truth, reflection on what we need to impose as the question-answer relationship quite evidently underlies that which positivism deems adequate as a philosophical answer. But if positivism would have to make explicit the nature of the question-answer link, then it could not keep logico-experimental verification for long as *the* criterion of the problematological difference. It can only defend a *certain version* of this difference through a favored manifestation of the difference, a choice which precisely is not justified outside of this a priori idea. This means that positivism is obliged to affirm as a priori the resolutional model it advocates. Lacking any justification other than the self-affirmation of its theoretical superiority, drawing its value from its efficacy for science and common sense, positivism has no other validity than that which it accords itself. By that alone, it can be set in opposition to every other form of validity which works in the same way. No antipositivist philosophy has mistaken this.

Let us continue our analysis. When we are told that meaning is verification, we must concede the self-refutational character of such an assertion because it is unverifiable on its own grounds. I say "on its own grounds" because that criterion of verification does itself have a meaning, if we connect it with questioning as a way of establishing the problematological difference. It aims at establishing this difference by an irrefutable demarcation of questions and answers established at the level of the answer. The price paid is taking into account the problematological level as a thematic level of analysis. Taking this into account always results in an unbearable limitation for positivism, namely its own modalization of the problematological differentiation and an acknowledgment that that difference is more fundamental than all its possible derivations, including the positivistic modalization. It takes its meaning from outside itself, while within itself, it has none; thus the verificationist criterion is self-defeating. The very survival of positivism demands the suppression of the problematological quest, a quest which positivism expresses in its own ways. It must be suppressed because the integration of the problematological factum would deprive the claims of positivism of their ability to be assumed, as claims to prescribe for the apocritical (the answering) what should count as resolutional standards. It might be possible to ascribe to the criterion of signification a limited meaning, thereby escaping self-defeat, by recognizing in it a certain capacity for differentiating answers from questions. But that would have the unintended effect of emphasizing the problematological factum which positivism must defeat, because this factum is what authorizes the metaphysical discourse of the pure problematological difference. The criticisms leveled by positivism collapse on its monopolistic ambitions regarding answerhood, which it can assure nonthematically, by initially positing as the appointed reducer or displaced determining factor of answerhood, the logico-experimental.

Once we are rid of this reducer, we are left with a particular vision of what answering is, a vision inappropriate to the universalism it asserts and claims as its own, a vision which in no way can sustain itself. This is a strong assumption whose sole validity derives from that which it denies: that is, the simple internal demarcation, internal to questioning, which permits all forms of differentiation, from experimental science to the sole *logos* which limits itself in answering by merely stating what it questions. Answering about a question by affirming its unsolvability is still an answer, because there is a discourse that is related differentially and explicitly to a question. To *dissolve* is also to *resolve*, as positivism tells us, though without being able to *justify* its point, since it would thereby need to have recourse to the problematological difference. This difference, once recognized, requires an enlargement of the notion of *resolution* to the questions that positivism would like to see *dissolved* as a solution. If it were to acknowledge its foundation, positivism would destroy itself in its very requirements in regard to the metaphysics it condemns as well as the scientificity it wishes to generalize.

The positivist writer who is most explicit about what has just been said is probably Schlick. In an article entitled "Unanswerable Questions?" written in English in 1935 in the journal *The Philosopher,* he sets forth that which Wittgenstein maintains aphoristically in the *Tractatus:*

A conscientious examination shows that all the various ways of explaining what is actually meant by a question are, ultimately, nothing but various descriptions of ways in which the answer to the question must be found. Every explanation or indication of the meaning of a question consists, in some way or other, of prescriptions for finding its answer. This principle has proved to be of fundamental importance for the method of science. For example, it led Einstein, as he himself admits, to the discovery of the Theory of Relativity . . . Thus a question which is unanswerable in principle can have no meaning, it can be no question at all: it is nothing but a nonsensical series of words with a question mark after them . . . Now consider the question "What is the nature of time?" What does it mean? What do the words "the nature of" stand for? The scientist might, perhaps, invent some kind of explanation, he might suggest some statements which he would regard as possible answers to the question; but his explanation could be nothing but the description of a method of discovering which of the suggested answers is the true one. In other words, by giving a meaning to the question he has at the same time made it logically answerable, although he may not be able to make it empirically soluble. Without such an explanation, the words "What is the nature of time?" are no question at all.[15]

15. Moritz Schlick, "Unanswerable Questions?" in *Gesammelte Aufsätze* (Hildesheim: Georg Olms Verlag, 1969), pp. 369–77; quotation from pp. 373–75.

Quite naturally, Schlick pursued his reasoning toward the positivist principle that "meaning is verification" in an article bearing that title and published a year later (1936).[16] A proposition has meaning if one uses it correctly, appropriately for a given situation, and if a listener is able to confirm the appropriateness of this usage. As a result, if a question really calls for something, it has meaning; and what it requires must be discoverable, thereby verifying whether or not a proposition does respond to it.

Let us pass from Schlick to Carnap, who also defends this principle of meaning, among other things, as part of an attack on Heidegger.[17] Once again, it is necessary to understand this principle before we reject it. Its only reason for being is as an effort to avoid a language which could make us believe that one has answers when one has only questions. Any such language, where there are only questions (without answers), is a pseudolanguage, for it is impossible that there could be questions with no way to answer them, if they really *are* questions. Verification is the alignment of meaning with science. In reality, this is another case of the propositionalist criterion, because we are led once more to see the problematic in reference to the assertoric, which defines it. As a result, the criterion of meaning is powerless to support anything other than itself, and it cannot do so because the proposition "meaning is verification" is itself unverifiable and therefore meaningless. The absence of a problematological foundation has made the authors of this criterion blind to what it answered. The result of this has been an unsustainable self-justification. This is not even to mention the fact that, put this way, the criterion itself is erroneous, because it is of a justificatory, a propositionalist nature. By ignoring its own origin, which is the establishment of a valid question-answer relationship, the problematological difference, it represses all other possible modalities of this relationship. That makes sense, at least to the extent to which that relationship is not stated but is presented through one possible particularization, which is far from able to serve as a model for all others even though it appears to be more evident. It is supposed, moreover, that one has the answer, and that all that is left is to verify its "fit," its adequacy; but that grants too much regarding the reality of intellection and meaning.

In denying the necessity to confront problematization by dealing

16. Moritz Schlick, "Meaning Is Verification," in *Gesammelte Aufsätze*, pp. 337–67.

17. On this debate, see Michel Meyer, "Métaphysique et néo-positivisme," *Revue Internationale de Philosophie* (1983): 93–113, 144–45.

with it itself, positivism has been mistaken. Positivism has become nothing more than the most radical form of propositionalism to which problematology is opposed. The criterion of meaningfulness fails the phenomenon of meaning in its global sense, because it particularizes the process of meaning within the very structure of the propositional model. The criterion of meaning can only hope to be its own justification but is powerless to do so because what explains it runs counter to the justificatory paradigm. This definition of meaningfulness would thereby find itself refuted. As a result, the positivist criterion of meaning wants to set up justification as the only source of meaning possible, and as self-evidently so, through the double resolution offered by experience or logic, depending on the type of discourse adopted. By repressing the problematological raison d'être of its approach, positivism has set itself up as a reductionist logico-linguistic doctrine. It naturally put the logico-linguistic first, obliterating its problematological roots to be able to make itself an autonomous conception of science and language, with questioning merely one feature of mental activity among others. The criterion of verification becomes nothing more than a logico-epistemic guillotine, a norm and a judgmental criterion in the terrorist sense of the term. Carnap truly outlived the movement he had contributed to articulating. But even he had to take account of the impossibility of saving the logico-empiricist criterion of meaning as self-evident. He was also obliged to accept the idea that a question could be totally *external* to a frame of designation, of reference, of resolution, and still make sense. Yet he said hardly more on that subject than this: "An external question is of a problematical nature and requires for this reason an even more profound analysis." [18]

The origin of the impossibility of positivism lies in its incapacity to consider the problematological difference for its own sake. It is folded into the language and lost as a difference. It is therefore made concrete only in a second, and thus a secondary, way, by the bias of a privileged manifestation, which, denying itself as having a problematological nature, must impose itself by itself. Since it cannot be justified as privileged on the basis of that which explains it, it thereby is denied. There is an inevitable paradox: how to prove that one is answering a question by showing that one cannot answer it? We can see in this one consequence of the criterion of meaning: no proposition can be verified as an answer to a meaningless question. Unless the problematological difference is conceptualized as such, there is nothing before us but a formula

---

18. Rudolf Carnap, "Empiricism, Semantics and Ontology," *Revue Internationale de Philosophie* (1950): 11.

that is at least strange. By contrast, if one *begins* with this difference, as applied to philosophical questioning, it can be better understood that there can be an answer to a question which rejects the question as a question, even as it resolves it. But the problem is that if we ascribe meaning to that which otherwise seems to be nothing more than a para- dox or a word game, we are obliged to reach the opposite conclusion from that which positivism upholds. A philosophical question maintains itself by its very nature, through the multiplicity of *problematological answers*, variations which are dependent on History, on the succession of systems of thought.

In sum, the fact is that a philosophical question is unresolvable by positivist criteria is in the very nature of the philosophical. It is not something to ignore, but rather to be included as essential to *what* is in *question* and not simply as a result of an inadequate formulation. Such thinking would be, among other things, inadequate in regard to what philosophy is. Thus it is the general attitude of positivism toward the metaphysical which is fallacious. One nevertheless could have agreed with it in its irreducible requirement to think of questions for them- selves, but no reducer can carry out this task without destroying the very thing which is to be preserved in the theoretical. In any event, the adoption of the primary reducer, which has been the language of scien- tists, has produced the opposite effect from that which it should have had. This is because the philosophical has been completely stripped of its metaphysical foundation by positivism, to the benefit of the self- justification of the propositional model in its logico-linguistic garb.

5. *The Dissolution of Problems in Bergson and Valéry*

Contrary to a widely held notion, antimetaphysical prejudices are not confined to logical positivism. The reality is more complex. The extent of this internal dissolution of philosophy is much more widespread than generally supposed. If we limit ourselves to French thought, we can mention Bergson and Valéry.

Bergson devotes a substantial portion of the introduction to *The Crea- tive Mind* to his position on problems, and, inevitably, to the concept of "false problems" in philosophy.

> This effort will exorcise certain phantom problems which obsess the metaphysician, that is to say, each one of us. I should like to talk about those distressing and insoluble problems which have no bearing on what is, but bear rather upon what is not. Such is the problem of the origin of being . . . Such, again, is the problem

of order in general . . . I say that these problems relate to what is not rather than to what is. Never, indeed would one be astonished at the existence of something—matter, mind, God—if one did not implicitly admit the possible existence of nothing.[19]

What exactly was Bergson after, compared to one who asks himself all these questions about nothingness, or at least its possibility?

> Now, can we solve the problem this man sets himself? Obviously not, but neither do we set the problem; therein lies our superiority. At first glance I might think there is more in him than in me . . . one might just as well think that there is more in a half-consumed bottle than a full one because the latter contains only wine, while in the former there is wine and emptiness in addition. (*Creative Mind*, pp. 73–74)

The Bergsonian intuition is the guarantee of intellectual health which we must have to avoid the temptation to pose problems "which make us dizzy because they put us in the presence of nothingness."

In Bergson, we find the same preoccupation, which runs through the whole Western tradition, for getting rid of certain kinds of problems, even if its point here is to restore metaphysics in its most mystical representation, as seen in its effort to once again give a place to intuition. The process of deconstructionism and dissolution of problems has a metaphysical inspiration, at the level of the type of analysis undertaken and discourse held, even if one finds here a procedure identical in spirit to that of Wittgenstein or Carnap. Let us hear Gilles Deleuze on this subject:

> There are two types of false problems: *non-existent problems*, which may be defined as those whose own terms imply confusion between more and less; and *misformulated problems*, which may be defined as those whose terms represent mixed notions that are badly analyzed . . . One might ask, for example, if happiness can or cannot be reduced to pleasure; but perhaps the term pleasure subsumes very diverse and irreducible conditions, just as does the idea of happiness. If to those terms no natural articulations correspond, then the problem is a false one, because they are not concerned with the nature of things . . . And this is perhaps the most general fault of thought, the common fault of both science and

19. Henri Bergson, *The Creative Mind*, trans. Mabelle L. Andison (New York: Philosophical Library, 1946), p. 72.

metaphysics, to think of everything in terms of less and more, to
see only differences in degree or differences in intensity where
there are, more profoundly, differences of nature.[20]

In the case of Valéry, we lapse once more into the same concern for
going beyond philosophical problematization, considered as a sterile
approach in comparison to action and science. If one reads the *Cahiers*
and forgets who the author is, one can easily fall into the trap of labeling
the author as one of the most tenacious defenders of Anglo-Germanic
positivism! "The real fault of metaphysics is that none responds with
precision to a very precise question."[21] No one escapes: "The philosophers, Kant most prominently, are more concerned with *resolving* than
with *posing* problems. In posing problems, it is also necessary to set
forth what will resolve it" (*Cahiers*, p. 482). Thus the absurdity of metaphysics: "Who am I? You may think that is a problem, but it is only nonsense" (p. 505). Further, "metaphysical terms are promissory notes or
checks that only give the illusion of wealth. This illusion is not to be
disdained" (p. 648), because "philosophy has reached the point of re-
constituting a reservoir for traditional problems, but is not sure if they
exist other than in its own tradition" (p. 664).

Valéry thus aligns himself with the idea of "philosophy or badly
posed questions" as intrinsically identified with one another. Then
where do we get the false problem, the illusion, the enigma? "There
would not be any metaphysics if the form of an *answer* could not be
given to a *question* . . . Language owes both its virtues and its vices to
this confusion" (*Cahiers*, p. 552). Valéry is clear on this point: language
is the source of metaphysics as an intellectual illusion, because it is
allegedly impossible to establish that which we call the problematological difference. "It is enough to initiate the interrogative and self-
dubitative power, to put it on the terms of the problems, instead of
leaving it on those already given, to make us feel that problems are indeterminate and always imply other problems. Thus we have metaphysical problems" (p. 547). These are "born from the impurity of the
concepts employed" (p. 541), and they "are such that they vanish if we
enunciate them" (p. 614). "Philosophers have often considered a question as existing for the sole reason that they haven't known how to resolve it. Closer examination frequently makes it clear that these alleged
problems were in fact illegitimate" (p. 638). "A philosophical problem
is a problem that we do not know how to formulate. Any problem that

___

20. Gilles Deleuze, *Le bergsonisme*, trans. the author (Paris: Presses Universitaires
de France, 1966), pp. 6–8.
21. Paul Valéry, *Cahiers*, vol. 1, trans. the author (Paris: Gallimard, 1973), p. 492.

we succeed in formulating ceases to be philosophical" (p. 641). A question rightly formulated as a question has to include a priori the possibility of its answer, rather than its continual replication, infinitely variable. Valéry was no more willing than the positivists to concede that this replication could constitute an answer. "The form of the *question*, for philosophers, is free and is applied wrongly and mistakenly to whatever is" (*Cahiers*, p. 666). "Language is what allows this wrongful and faulty distribution of interrogation marks. The interrogative approach, taken to its extreme, frequently shows itself to be a vain enterprise" (p. 675). And how do we recognize a *true* question from the other, insoluble, kind? "One word, all by itself, must never be what creates a question. Words exist to serve as the known building blocks of questions and answers. It is essential that we never use words which by themselves pose questions" (p. 664) so that we can truly identify the differences. A false problem, on the contrary, is only a problem in the verbal sense, because language is the medium which allows, and in fact guarantees, a perpetual confusion between questions and answers. Contrary to Carnap, Valéry is absolutely convinced that language cannot offer a solution because language is the very source of the confusion. "My whole philosophy," says Valéry, "may be reduced to an effort to emphasize this precision or self-awareness which has for its effect a clear distinction between questions and answers" (p. 625). It is true that "few minds bother to think about the question before making the answer" (p. 602); to this extent there is often no question, inasmuch as there is nothing but an interrogative *form* without a corresponding *real* problem. "We must learn how to conceive of the fact that what is, is not necessarily a question. And, that not all questions necessarily have meaning" (p. 573). In fact, all that is poses a question to the extent that it is, because the tacit conformity to the given presupposes that something is enunciated (by whom?). We can readily concede that questions put about what is real continuously eliminate themselves as they are asked and re-asked according to the answers that experience suggests, preventing these questions from even being put into words. They *can* be so put, as is the case in science. We will come back to this point.

For now, let us note that once more we have a "solution" before us, one which requires the observance of the problematological difference by a privileged *modus* which displaces it, in this case by the definition of the meaning of a question through the class of its answers. This is a strange means of establishing this difference: reabsorbing it into one of its terms, the answer.

Can we pose true questions when even the type of answer is unknown to us? A question has meaning only if we can conceive of the class of things from which a response will come. We must know this class in order to state the question. Therefore, if there is none, our question creates this class, and it is not really a question but a disguised affirmative proposition. Who created the Universe? That is not a question, that is a dogma. (*Cahiers*, p. 559)

Valéry's central idea is that the arbitrary passage from the assertoric to the interrogative derives from an exclusive means, language, and that there is nothing there other than a language game.

His concept of answers rests, in the last analysis, on the problematological differentiation reduced by that which it is not. Indeed, an answer, as he sees it, is simply an affirmation which can never be problematized or made interrogatory. Only the real and its human correlate, action, allow us to resolve problems or even to pose them without ambiguity. An answer cannot become (in turn) a problem. "Any response which has meaning only in the precincts of language responds to some question which is no more than mere words" (*Cahiers*, p. 715). If we can assert that "most philosophical difficulties and problems can be reduced to errors over the true nature of language" (p. 725), we must deduce from that, "every problem whose solution is indifferent to what is practical or unsolvable pragmatically . . . is either nonexistent, purely verbal, or misstated. Thus it is always necessary to evoke the question of nonverbal verification" (p. 709). The overcoming of natural language, for Valéry, cannot be accomplished by an ideal language, as for Carnap, but by life, which poses real problems for real needs, as well as by action. Valéry rejoins the problematological concern when he says: "One might—and perhaps one should—set forth as the sole objective of philosophy to pose and to narrow problems down rather than preoccupying oneself with resolving them. It would become a science of statements and therefore a means of purification of questions" (p. 591). I say "the concern" because all that which differs from problematology can also be found in this text.

That philosophy must now concern itself with questioning is clear. To suppose, without more—that is, without *questioning* the questioning—that this preoccupation might be identified with the elimination of certain questions, in the name of an unfounded intuition about what questioning must be, cannot be accepted. Further, to consider that the problematological difference is inassumable by and through natural language is also prejudicial. Finally, that dissolution is considered as a resolution is, as I have shown, an indisputable possibility for answerhood; but it is clearly contrary to philosophy, which answers its questions in posing them. It is precisely because there is no problematological differentiation that the resolutional character of affirmations does not appear as such. Hence, due to the impossibility of making the above-stated distinction, there is a will to purify, to dissolve, to remove that which, from a problematological perspective, would pose no difficulty. From the outset, it is because one tries to think about certain *questions* without thinking about *questioning* that one is unable to think of them as questions. They no longer are distinguishable from what it takes to resolve them, and there is little difficulty in emphasizing that it becomes impossible to separate a solution from that which is its problematization.

The fact is that we operate in each instance from a preconceived idea of interrogativity that reduces it to what was chosen at the outset as a reductionist principle, as a reducer. Here, it will be intuition, there language, or its contrary, the nonverbal. This is the case with Valéry, for the nonverbal is the very place where the answer always eradicates the question, so that one could believe that there never was a question. In any event, the type of answers which emerge there do not permit confusion with questions: as a consequence, these answers will never really be answers if they duplicate the questions. Neither Valéry nor the others can imagine that an answer could state that which is problematic, while preserving the difference from *the sole fact* that it affirms it. To arrive at something that takes account of this, it is necessary to find a mode of speech centered in the question-answer pair, and not on propositions, or, as is sometimes suggested, on language itself (an undifferentiated and therefore neutral term in regard to questioning). What they seek in questioning is what they already suppose to be there. The model of science, where the answers *suppress* the questions that they resolve, where they never even let them appear, and therefore where answers are the sole tangible result, is shared by Bergson[22] and Valéry. It is seen as a relationship to Being for Bergson, and with the real, the active, for Valéry. In such a conceptual frame for interrogativity, philosophical questioning is impossible, hence the question of questioning. And this is, quite paradoxically, all the more so because interrogativity penetrates philosophy, undermining it from the outside as well as from within, thereby making even more imperative the need for questioning to reflect itself.

Contrary to Valéry's ideas and positivism in general, it is not because

22. Even Bergson, despite his metaphysical intuition, remains obsessed with science: "We come back, then, once more to our point of departure. We were saying that philosophy must be brought to a higher precision, put in a position to solve more special problems, be made an auxiliary to, and if need be, reformer of positive science . . . It is true that we shall have to bring about a perfecting of the philosophical method, symmetrical with and complementary to what positive science formerly received" (*Creative Mind*, pp. 76–77).

a question is already a response, or that an answer always signifies a problem, that the problematological distinction becomes blurred. It is necessary to conceive of it as such, from the interrogation of questioning. The fact that questions and answers are written in a definite language does not imply that the metalanguage which comprises the critique and the purification of language is the key to all the difficulties. It would still be necessary for this metadiscourse to be developed in a problematological conception of discursivity. And what Carnap has done, in the last analysis (to cite only him), is to elaborate a logic of language that is a propositional logic. There is not even a trace of questioning in such a logic.

6. Wittgenstein and the Paradox of Silence

We can find an identical viewpoint in Wittgenstein: instead of being able to express the relationship between silence and language in terms of radical questioning, this relationship appears as a paradox which undermines the whole *Tractatus*.

Silence plays an important role for Wittgenstein: it is the goal he seeks, in full agreement with his idea of philosophical resolution. Either the problem set forth is resolved, and therefore disappears once that task is completed; or else the problem cannot be resolved, and the dissolution then puts it on the same level as the other problems, making it disappear also. The consequence is that the problem, which is the object of the statement, is no more—and that discourse, which no longer occupies itself with the problem, by that fact ceases to exist. Thus silence. This is the direction taken by philosophy because its problems must receive one treatment or the other. "[This book's] whole meaning could be summed up somewhat as follows: What can be said at all can be said clearly; and whereof one cannot speak thereof one must be silent . . . I am, therefore, of the opinion that the problems have in essentials been finally solved" (*Tractatus*, preface).

All of this so far seems perfectly coherent. The contradiction emerges in the possibility and the necessity of the *Tractatus* in regard to this conception of the resolution of problems.

In fact, language speaks for itself; it is comprehensible in itself, without recourse to some language of language (or metalanguage) to provide it with a logic. Its logic is present in it. It shows itself, but does not state itself as such. Even more, it *cannot* state itself; because, if the meaning of its propositions *could* be enunciated, one *could*, in the extreme, leave

23. For more on the foregoing, see Michel Meyer, *Logique, langage et argumentation* (Paris: Hachette, 1982), pp. 66 et seq. (In English: *From Logic to Rhetoric*, Amsterdam, 1986.)

language to talk about it.[23] In enunciating the meaning of a simple sentence, we state something other than what the sentence itself states, because the sentence doesn't say, "my meaning is such and such." Therefore, one can never succeed in capturing *the* meaning of a proposition by another proposition without in some way being false to it. Are synonyms or paraphrases thus impossible? If we suppose that something is not understood at its basic level, we may restate it a second time, but what is shown must finally be able to be understood in itself. A paraphrase or a complete synonymity is thus impossible if it does not result in *seeing* what in it is unsayable, which is its ultimate meaning. This is what Wittgenstein calls the *picture*. The silence in a statement is the meaning shown.

This did not prevent Wittgenstein from saying that which can only be shown, hence the *Tractatus;* he "makes" a logic for language as if it were necessary to state what it is useless to specify. Not only *must* one *not* state what goes without saying, but even more, one *cannot* do so, to the extent to which "that which expresses *itself* in language, *we* cannot express by language" (*Tractatus*, 4.121). Is it not contradictory, in the last analysis, to say that language is logical in itself, and that one cannot depart from it, that language *shows* its structure in saying what it says, and then to write a *Tractatus* which says what can only be shown, and moreover, shown *naturally*, without an overlay of logic, which has been affirmed to be both useless and impossible? This is the origin of the suicidal self-accusation, so dear to our author: "My propositions are elucidatory in this way: he who understands me finally recognizes them as senseless, when he has climbed out through them, on them, over them" (6.54).

Silence is not merely the domain of meaning (hence, the mystic of signification for Wittgenstein), it is also the only coherent attitude when faced with the nonsense which consists of speaking about what must remain unsaid, because it is impossible to speak about it. Nevertheless, Wittgenstein speaks. Therein lies the paradox. He himself has provided the means for us to see clearly: meaninglessness is the result of the inquiry into meaning; it is the light that shines back along the path followed to show that it was useless for all those who thought the contrary. It is truly a question of philosophical problematization in the *Tractatus*. The object of the problem is this very problematization: since it is language which allows its emergence, the solution eventually winds up suppressing its necessity. And if it is said to be impossible to arrive at such a result, the process would have revealed that, as a final answer, the problem did not pertain to language, as does life or the question of the subject, for example. It is in vain, in such a circumstance, to attempt to make the problem explicit. Philosophy therefore is cognate to false problems. Philosophy is either useless, in that what we already know we no longer need to learn (showing makes speaking useless), or it is impossible, in that it says what cannot be said. It merely demonstrates, by its own impossibility and its own failure, that it is contradictory to try to make anything of it other than some sort of therapy of clarification, or one sort of nonsense which proceeds from another, leading to their mutual destruction, or, to consider it another way, to the self-destruction of all possible nonsense. The *Tractatus* is not addressed to the average person, who understands all of this (without "truly" knowing it), but to the philosopher, who thinks he knows but in fact does not. Wittgenstein thus puts himself forward as the Socrates of contemporary nihilism. Hence his own *Meno* paradox: the *Tractatus* is either impossible or it is useless, for if one knows all that cannot be said, there is no need for the *Tractatus;* and if one ignores the need to remain silent, where silence imposes itself, it will be impossible to state what is to be left unsaid. Wittgenstein demonstrates this by his affirmation of nonmeaning. Socrates, as will be shown in the following chapter, had already laid claim to an insurmountable interrogativity, which, in the answers it produced, was self-destructive. But the problem of philosophical problematization will thereby have been resolved; to that extent its usefulness will be to have permitted the useless to emerge. This is the origin of progress, of the coherence of the project, which cannot occur if one thinks of the *Tractatus* in terms of problems, which the commentators seldom do. How can we conceive a deep coherence in the *Tractatus?* The problem of philosophy is resolved at the end of the book insofar as it will have been useful to say what was ultimately useless to say—of course, as far as one had posed the problem of believing it was useful. The meaninglessness proclaimed, or at least apparent, in the book is the intentional *result* of the book, and that is not contradictory when one realizes that this meaninglessness is the answer to the question of knowing whether such and such an undertaking has any meaning *or not.* This meaninglessness is a retroactive answer, but it can only be established as an *answer* at the end of an interrogative process, and will mean for that questioning its own suppression.

When Wittgenstein tells us that he is speaking of that which always is shown and cannot be said, that is, meaning, he is playing with a paradox, and we may reproach him for this contradiction. But if we understand that there is a process of resolution in which the contradiction is the result which imposes itself on the resolution (and in so doing becomes part of the question of its own possibility), one no longer has the right to attack this initiative, as one would if one had known beforehand that a contradiction had to be the solution to it. That would come back to denying that there ever was a problem. But if that were the case, why would a question have been posed? Wittgenstein is contradictory only if we attribute to him an indifference to the distinction between problems and solutions.

That said, one can still wonder what has been preserved by establishing the coherence of Wittgenstein's approach. At its end, philosophy itself is in a bad situation. The Cartesian subject, that is, the foundation, is condemned: it is no more than the unspeakable boundary of discursivity. All of this is quite consistent with the state of philosophy at that time. The internal rupture shows up at the level of the very possibility of philosophy: the language of thought, the *logos*, as it has been labeled since the Greeks, is revealed as having become useless, because it only allows us to see the inessential as being the subject-matter of *logos*. As for the rest, only silence, whether dissolution or ultimate solution, prevails. "We *feel* that, even though all *possible* scientific questions are resolved, *our problem has not even been addressed.* To state it plainly, there are, then, no more questions, and that is precisely what constitutes our answer" (*Notebooks 1914–1916*, author's translation).

7. Question and System

Contemporary philosophy, it is useful to recall, has been battered by the death of the Cartesian subject, which has left it without foundation and therefore more problematic than ever. Silence has been its response to its despair. It is necessary to recognize clearly that alignment with the sciences, or their vehement rejection, has, in the last analysis, no other source than philosophy's awareness of its own impossible *logos*. That is the reason for the comparison with scientific problematization, which, after all, "works," and which therefore is a tempting model for imitation. There are really two choices, when all is said and done. Either philosophy will follow science in its goals and its methods and become the science of science (neopositivism), or it will respond to this crisis by realizing its own inability to state the problematical other than as a crisis. Philosophy then becomes discourse about impossible discourse, about the impossibility of even opening up any other topic than this impossible discourse. In that sense, Wittgenstein is not a "positivist," and he can be seen as standing on both sides of this philosophical break. The speech which takes its truth from the unspoken becomes essential as a *negative metaphysics*, where the metaphysical identifies itself as impossible and announces itself, therefore, as part of an ineluctable end to philosophy, a theme equally dear to Heidegger.

What remain as paths open to thought? Literature, as practiced by a Sartre or raised to the status of a model through poetry, with Heidegger, is one possibility. The shrinking of metaphysics is a confessed discursive failure that can lead, even in the best of cases, no further than to self-effacement, and which is identifiable, above all, as a renunciation. Negative metaphysics, *therefore* nihilism: such will have been the other road taken by philosophy this past century, next to that built up of positivity in imitation of the sciences. Positivism will have been the thought of a crisis, an intense crisis for philosophy, an answer for which the geographical characterization "Anglo-Saxon" is accidental. More-over, it is an answer which disguises the philosophical problem of the difficulty of philosophizing. Be that as it may, the positivization of the philosophical has been French and Germanic as well and has been the only other possibility available in response to the destruction of its foundation. Confronted with historical problematization's break-ing off what is thinkable in its positivity, in its chances of being over-come, it was necessary to realize either this failure in its modalized statement of nothingness or the displacement of positivity throughout the intellectual fields which actualize it. The two solutions were carried out as they needed to be. Today, they have given rise to the historical awareness of what they have been; this perspective even gives philo-sophical value to the impasses which inevitably result. These solutions force us, when we analyze them fully, to reconsider problematization as a question, but as a philosophical question, no longer just as a question *of* the philosophical, that is, as the historicity of nihilism.

The two answers to the internal crisis of the philosophical *logos* are rooted in the same problem: the very matter of philosophical question-ing, its object and its method. And at this level it became apparent that the problem was unsatisfactorily stated. Rather than undertaking directly to study questioning as such, contemporary philosophy has continually reconceptualized it by reducing it to something else, a "reductor" or "reducer," which has assumed the role of a first prin-ciple, but a first principle which never will admit to being what it is. If it had been necessary to state it—language, science, action, or being—as an ultimate *answer* to the *question* of principle, the latter would have destroyed itself in its own affirmation. An answer which does not refer to the questioning in which it originates cannot state itself as an answer to the problem of the first principle. The question has been veiled, a nonexistent foundation has been imposed, and therefore there was a mistake. Nothing has been offered but something oppos-able, and each position (of principle) was once again seen as put in question, perpetuating, in a way, the problematicity of the philosoph-ical in its very existence, and yet powerless even to describe itself as problematic.

We must respond to all this by considering questioning in its own origin, the philosophical beginning (or initiative). What is the result, if not making philosophizing possible? Questioning, first seen as a weakness of thought, instead becomes its very positivity. Its dissolution itself dissolves in its own assertion, a contradiction typical of those authors who, with rigorous logic, ended in intellectual mutism. What accounts for their erroneous vision of philosophy is that they could never succeed in developing a specifically philosophical resolution because their reductors are drawn from fields other than philosophy. Let us consider only the example of science. A solution there is defined by the logico-experimental suppression of the problem, whereas in philosophy, a solution cannot abolish the problem. What gives us the *right* to distinguish science from philosophy in this way? The problematological difference which should have been conceived as such can also be established by specifying that which is a question and that which is an answer, in a discourse in which we find both. That difference may be seen through the logico-experimental mechanism, for what is a solution if not the differential with respect to a question? This is the source of the necessity to demarcate them *in some manner or other.* As a result, it is impossible to affirm what has been said many times, by Valéry, in the Vienna Circle, and also by Carnap: namely that a philosophical question being its own answer, because the question is formulated in a system identical for the two items, it is impossible to differentiate the enigma from its resolution, the one being transferred into the other. But what is seen as a deficiency may be so only when seen in the light of a reductionist approach coming from outside philosophy, because all of the strength of philosophy derives from its ability to think the problematical as an answer to what is problematic within it. Seeing a problem makes me see something new. A new way of putting a question is posing the same question in other terms. To pose a problem in a field where everything seems clear is the essence of creative thought, in science as in any other domain. To raise a question is to approach reality from another angle. Questioning is constitutive of experience, both of perception and of the knowledge that results therefrom, whatever the mode of the interrogative process.

What has this first chapter on the development of contemporary philosophizing taught us? In the first place, we have learned that the pure subject, called either "transcendental" or "self-conscious," having exhausted its conceptual trajectory and as well as its ultimate resources, has left philosophy with the question of whether it can resolve its problems despite the situation. There remain only empirical sub-

jects: in the realm of ethics, it means the conflict of individual wills
(Nietzsche) and the ideologization of morality. Morality itself has
become a fiction to the extent that, after Kant, it has rooted itself in the
humanity of man, which incarnates the pure subject as a universalizing
synthesis of a norm for individual action. On the other hand, if there are
no longer any but empirical men, man as nonobjectifiable subject disappears and becomes instead possible as an object of science, just like
any other empirical reality (Foucault). The defundamentalization of
the subject means its transcendental death, and, at the same time, human existence as a transcendental *topos* for the individual is revealed as
absurd. Humanism has had its day, up to its expression in daily life. But
how can one conduct discourse based on such a reality, which is only
thinkable within the category of the absurd? Existentialism, like other
philosophies of the twentieth century, contains in itself its own way out
in its attitude, especially toward literature, and also toward historical
reflection as a discourse of transindividuality where rationality will have
found a new location. Ultimately, however, all of this will be no more
than one of the modalities of negative metaphysics, of nihilism. Among
the most important of these modalities is silence. All these solutions
flow from a nihilism that we experience, or from which we strive to escape when we abandon the philosophical. Science has played an exemplary role at this level, functioning as a model of resolution, which could
be set in opposition to the statement of impossibility.

But today all of these alternatives are exhausted, historically speaking, as soon as we think of them consciously and thematically. Our
thinking takes problematization as a philosophical concept, rather than
heading toward solutions which do not see themselves as solutions because they are conceptualized in terms of forms dictated by current
fashions, translated one way or another. Such a translation may seem to
be arbitrary, at least from a theoretical viewpoint, since it depends, beyond any specific modalization, on the unthought constituted by philosophical problematization. This is a concept which brings us back to the
request for a foundation and which does not limit itself only to a historical task. What brings positivism and nihilism together is the unreflected dilemma of problematization, unreflected in that given reflection (or consideration), their common roots would have made their
apparent opposition vanish. In reality, both are cut off from their foundation. They develop as answers which are unaware of their status as
answers, since the question which they answer falls outside of their
domain, because such a question never finds itself posed in all of its
problematical generality as a philosophical question.

Therefore, what emerges as a problem developing from the progressive defundamentalization of the pure subject is problematization itself, in its possibility for assuming itself as philosophical. Positivism and negative metaphysics see in such a problematization a crack, a flaw, in brief a *historical* state of things, without realizing that it contains a more basic requirement of the thinking process—that which History demands, to be sure, but to which it cannot completely be reduced. Thus there is a common rejection of questioning by philosophical discursivity, whether in the guise of scientism or dissolution on the one hand, or else silence or going beyond the philosophical realm to an external discursivity on the other. Whether consisting of making answers possible, therefore resolutional, like science, or of the confession of radical internal impossibility, the two answers partake of one common a priori point of view in regard to that which questioning implies, and that *they do not put into question.* However, unable to philosophize the philosophical question proceeding from the question itself, positivism and negative metaphysics both hasten to their own contradictions. In so doing they condemn themselves historically to their own problematization, which today is ours, since we are historically fated to go beyond the mere historicization of the problematical in favor of its philosophization.

Negative metaphysics, in fact, will have spoken about Being, about silence, or about the absurdity of existence as being unable to provide for a grounded discourse, or even for a conceptualization, since the adequacy to what must be stated is a priori impossible. As for positivism, it too has landed in contradiction by the nonlogico-experimental autonomization of the logico-experimental, as if the latter could impose itself out of its sheer self-evidence, whereby it can be opposed in turn to other forms of evidence which also seem "natural." If we look carefully at the matter, the worth of the logico-experimental is completely problematological, because it is a criterion of justification as a determination of answers. However, the answers are not conceived as such because they are referred to as propositions in the absence of a refundamentalized reflection of what makes possible the establishment of a logico-experimental criterion. This criterion is self-defeating, because it claims for itself the status of a universal proposition and claims to be the self-evident standard of the propositional. This criterion destroys itself by the "coup de force" of its own evident affirmation, as it evades its own norms. If it were valid, it would invalidate itself. If what it establishes could be so justified, this could only be done at the cost of accepting the problematological difference to which it is relevant. In the latter case, metaphysics as an *alternative* modalization once again becomes possible, if not necessary, because therein is located the very meaning of the logico-experimental orientation. If the latter is to find an acceptable meaning, it can only do so within a conception that undermines its universality, particularizes it as a modality, and affirms that from which it emanated, rather than letting it go by in silence because, quite absurdly, it condemns its own source.

If we can see all of this now, it is undoubtedly because the perspective of History has allowed us to travel the paths left open by the dilemma of problematization. Our own situation is no less historic than that which drove negative metaphysics and positivism down their respective blind alleys—blind for us today, because we have confirmed that the paths we have taken have not allowed us to resolve the problematization of the philosophical realm by itself, as we might have hoped at the time these paths were being explored. This is what has once again brought problematization itself into new light. Multiplied in the field of the thinkable, and before the return to a historical situation reconstructed on the basis of a philosophical refutation of this situation, problematization goes beyond its historicized reading. Thus we can uphold problematization reappropriated as an intrinsically philosophical positivity itself carried through by History. It is History that constrains us to make problematization a fundamental theoretical problem, which calls for the fundamentality of its own possibility. Historicity, as the repression of the historical, is then reconfirmed as a dimension of questioning; but this time, we may hope, it may be understood as such. Owing to this fact, all problematization is as free as any corresponding nonproblematization. Our effort here is an act of freedom in regard to History, because it constantly represses itself *as* historical, in order to be philosophical, even though, being philosophical, it necessarily imposes *itself.* We can deny the historical bypassing of the dilemma born of this defundamentalization. It can be denied as a philosophical task, despite exhausting the avenues of escape, or even in the absence of such exits. But in this way, it ends up confirming the historicity of questioning as well as its own repression, as a displaced materialization of its own questioning through derived "answers" or forms that are nonoriginary. Such a displaced questioning is here consciously recognized, that is to say, that it is at least realized as contradictory, and therefore, we may hope, unable to be assumed.

What is certain is that questioning has become, in a historical sense, the explicit positivity of the philosophical. The philosophical has no other alternative than to conceive questioning as necessary, even if historically its philosophical emergence is no more than possible. This foundational necessity can no longer be seen as a simple situation which affects—and destabilizes—the philosophical. It is no longer some piece of historicity which incarnates itself; rather, it is an inescapable necessity for a changing point of view, one which could always be avoided by the freedom which we have to refute the historical in an autonomized theoretization. But it cannot be evaded philosophically if one philosophizes about this very refutation, for the latter, *as such*, confirms questioning in its impassable radicality, even if it were dialectically so.

What has exhausted all the possibilities embodied in negative metaphysics and positivism is that we now clearly see what they respond to and what they cannot reflect without destroying themselves. To return to the initial problematization into which they insert themselves in the guise of irreducible alternatives—irreducible if we fail to see the common problem which links the one to the other, like the two sides of a coin—is to retreat, after having seen that the only outcome of the process is a set of untenable consequences. That retreat also takes us back to a previous ground of thought, the philosophical, to historicity, and not just the historical (which it represses in its autonomous theoretical position, which is the origin of the concept of validity as the very requirement of the theoretical).

Once it is realized that each of these major "solutions" responds to a problem which they could not have even posed without becoming problematology, and that, having done so, they become an impossibility themselves, then we can quite easily conclude that it is no longer possible to deny the existence of the problematological. This means, as the discussion and explication above has shown, that problematology imposes itself *practically;* hence also as a theoretical requirement to be assumed despite our having the freedom not to refuse it (such a questioning would confirm it), but rather to ignore it. The reader, having read this far, is problematologically engaged. That is why the historical reading which I have urged upon you, dear reader, is philosophical through and through in what it implies for the present. Once completed, this reading will not allow us to escape questioning in what it poses to us about itself, philosophically speaking. I think it would be contradictory to proceed to this decoding of philosophical problematization and then to negate it by practicing a philosophy that would still refuse it (though nothing prevents putting that denial into practice). Certainly, one can always *practice* such a negation, which, not being conceived as such, will not be thought of *as* negation.

All of this is to say that what all of the efforts examined up to here, beyond their various internal contradictions, have in common is an inability to understand how questioning works, especially when it is philosophical. They see questioning only through the perspective of what it is not, and thus exclude themselves from recovering it in its full possibility, something that should proceed from interrogation itself. The problematological difference, reduced to some manifestation and assimilated into a reductionist modalization, will forcibly exclude all other modalizations which are irreducible, and therefore are to be dissolved.

Is anyone to blame for this situation other than philosophers themselves? Who else is used to resolving problems without ever posing the problem of problems? But, in reality, can we truly blame them? Haven't they simply been responding, unaware of the requirements of our historical circumstances? This history has required them to take problematization into account, and it has become, since 1900, an undeniable *state of fact*. Thinking first has had to carry into effect this problematization, to absorb it, to guarantee it in its initial radicality, before being *able* to think of the radicality of the problematical in its new positivity. From then on it forces thought to turn its back on its earlier forms of evidence, which are anthropological.

Will it be necessary then to repudiate this philosophical tradition? Once again, in so doing, philosophy would be patterning itself after the conditions of progress proper to other domains. A philosophical problem is historical: that means that it is rooted in History and can be traced through a succession of philosophies. Therefore, when we speak of questioning, it is necessary to know what has been said about it and if what has been said can be helpful in our present thought. Furthermore, how has questioning been put to use in practice, especially in the philosophical field, given the fact that it could not be thought of in itself? Historically, how has questioning been rejected and displaced?

These will be our questions. For what is a philosophical problem if not a question whose answer is its own thematization? What is the rigor (and not the "method") of philosophy, if not the explication of this question-answer nexus? If philosophy is to be what it is, it will be so because, in a derived way (for us), it provides a foundation for questioning by starting from its own questioning. When philosophy has not been able to do so, then it displaced the question of questioning into something else that used to resolve the question only at the time, that is, only *for* a time. Historicity is a constitutive dimension of questioning because it makes it contemporary, renders it present each time in various forms. It is the repression of that which changes, the timeless expression of questioning, incarnated in a system self-professedly eternal in its validity, and self-structured in a certain way. For this reason, philosophy still seeks to think of itself as a system of interrogativity. Let us make sure that from now on philosophy will begin from interrogativity itself, thematically, just as the choice of freely assuming History, the constitutive act of philosophy, is inviting us to do.

Two

Dialectic and Questioning

Socrates is justly considered the father of Western philosophy because he established interrogativity as the highest value of thought. But this notion failed to survive, and its disappearance allowed ontology and the *logos* of the propositional model to take its place. Thereafter questioning was seen only as the vassal of the sovereign entity, the proposition, which was no longer called an answer. Questioning, now relegated to the ranks of mere rhetorical or psychological accessory, little by little faded from the philosophical scene, as though it had never even been a theme worthy of separate attention. With Socrates, what faded away was more of a *practice* than a reality truly understood as fundamental. In truth, questioning neither was nor could be theorized as such, which explains its disappearance and its displacement through various mediators, meant to be reducers of the problematological (what we will call here problematological reductors).

Plato, for his part, could only make obvious the problems of the Socratic *logos*, even as he was presenting it, which made it necessary that he go beyond this *logos*, and, in the end, abandon it. Aristotle followed this same path in taking up again the subject of questioning, but did so by assigning it the definitive role of rhetorical weapon, a role to which Plato, albeit in an ambiguous way, refused to reduce it, to be true to Socrates. Dialectic is really an interaction between questions and answers. This relationship, subjective as it is (to the extent that it is dialogical and intersubjective), will become the essence of the scientific method, even in such barely Socratic writings as *The Republic*. But the conflation of scientificity and interrogativity with dialectic will turn into an argument against Plato. Aristotle will see the contradictory nature of dialectic as a combination of the subjective and the objective, the interplay between questioners equated with knowledge.

Aristotle will thus be compelled to establish a clear theoretical distinction between the domain of scientificity, whose rules he will stipulate—these being logic and its syllogisms—and the field of human interaction, the dialectic. Dialectic will cease to be synonymous with science and will be split into rhetoric, poetics, and the study of topics. Aristotle will then be able to speak of questioning, since it will no longer be a scientific procedure, but questioning will now be reduced to a part of the dialectical system. Dialectic, once scientific for Plato, will become the locus of interrogativity. Nonetheless, questioning will fulfill a minor role, because it will be shared with many more important areas of thinking, where it will count for little, as in poetics. Plato, in making a science of dialectic, could not theorize questioning. Aristotle, on the other hand, in reducing dialectic to the only thing it could be, to be consistent, allowed himself to deal with the interplay of questioning and answering, but without giving it any more significance than Plato had already implicitly accorded it. Aristotle freed Platonic questioning from what made it inconceivable, although he maintained the quite secondary role it had held since Socrates.

Thus it could be written of Plato and Aristotle: "In the case of both philosophers the problem from which they start is: To what extent can intellectual advance be achieved by the method of question and answer?"[1] We know Aristotle's answer: "Now the art of examining . . . may deduce a false conclusion because of the ignorance of the answerer,"[2] which is captured in the strictly nonscientific dialectical limitation of questioning as purely refutative. How did we come to that? Why was the interrogativity of the mind as a constitutive power abandoned? These will be the two questions we will examine in this chapter, always mindful of Richard Robinson's challenge: "It is useless to look for sufficient reasons for the Platonic doctrine that the supreme method entails question-and-answer, because there are none."[3] Is that not proof that we have lost the sense of questioning which was so important to the Greeks?

1. Socrates and Dialectic: The Role of Dialectical Questioning in the Aporetic Dialogues

Socrates asks questions. He calls his interlocutors to account to show them that they do not know what they claim to know. As Socrates knows that he knows nothing, the question which begins a dialogue

---

1. J. D. G. Evans, *Aristotle's Concept of Dialectic* (Cambridge, Eng.: Cambridge University Press, 1977), p. 8.
2. *Sophistical Refutations* 8, 169b, 25, trans. W. A. Pickard-Cambridge; *The Complete Works of Aristotle,* ed. Jonathan Barnes (Princeton, N.J.: Princeton University Press, 1984), vol. 1, p. 287.
3. Richard Robinson, *Plato's Earlier Dialectic,* 2d ed. (Oxford: Oxford University Press, 1953), p. 82.

will remain unresolved at its end. It is in these aporetic dialogues that
we can most clearly see his antiestablishment attitude. His constant
target is the socially conferred authority of the so-called notables.
These people put forward opinions in the guise of knowledge and, due
to their lofty social position, are rarely challenged. Indeed, that position
seems to be the guarantee of the validity of their discourse. In Socrates'
day, the Sophists belonged to this group of leading citizens. The Athen-
ian democracy still held them in the highest esteem. Whether Sophists
or not, leading citizens like Protagoras and Hippias were admired, followed, and consulted on questions of the day.[4] Others, like Cephalus,
who pontificates upon the subject of old age at the start of *The Republic*,
were simply rich and powerful. All of these characters speak in a
peremptory fashion, with that firm confidence that characterizes those
long accustomed to being surrounded by people who play the role of
mirrors or amplifiers of the ideas of the Master. This Mastership is precisely what Socrates puts into question. The social role of dialectical
questioning invariably leads Socrates to consider ethico-political questions, such as whether excellence (*aretē*) can be taught, or whether it
takes a Master to teach it for someone to acquire it.

But virtue (*aretē*) is found in every man. No one needs another to
"reveal" it to him. Thus the famous "Know thyself" of the *Charmides*
(164d), which serves as the basis for human freedom. Wisdom is to be
sought in oneself, not from a Master who teaches it. Where would it
come from, if not from another Master, thereby making truth a merely
conventional social ideal. Virtue (*aretē*) is present in every man: it is not
a matter of technique, nor of teaching, nor is it something provided by
an individual's social rank.[5] His "Know thyself" means "Think for
thyself." This plea for freedom of thought ultimately cost Socrates his

---

4. Plato has Socrates say of the followers of Protagoras: "As I looked at the party,
I was delighted to notice what special care they took never to get in front or to be in
Protagoras' way. When he and those with him turned round, the listeners divided
this way and that in perfect order, and executing a circular movement took their
places each time in the rear." *Protagoras* 315b, trans. W. K. C. Guthrie, in *The Col-
lected Dialogues of Plato*, ed. Edith Hamilton and Huntingon Cairns (Princeton, N.J.:
Princeton University Press, 1961), p. 314.

And as to the disciples of Hippias: "Hippias of Elis [was] sitting on a seat of
honor . . . They appeared to be asking him questions on natural science, particularly
astronomy, while he gave each his explanation ex cathedra and held forth on their
problems." *Protagoras* 315c, trans. W. K. C. Guthrie, p. 314.

5. Robinson notes: "The principle that the answerer must say what he really
thinks is part of the principle that dialectic recognizes no authority . . . 'The question
is not who said it, but whether it is truly said or not.' (*Charmides* 161c)." Robinson,
Plato's Earlier Dialectic, p. 79.

life. He could not challenge mastership without drawing the ire of the Masters. When their authority was challenged, the notables, who had thought themselves ipso facto knowledgeable, suddenly discovered that they were no wiser than the lowest men of the City, and certainly less wise than Socrates. Indeed, it was the very social order of the City which Socratic questioning denounced, because social position was now called into question. The notables, under fire from Socrates' questions, must provide answers, must justify their positions. But authority, by definition, makes it difficult for those who have it to answer and to justify their answers. Dialectical questioning reveals this pretense of knowledge for just what it is: social pretense. Could Socrates, who is poor,[6] be wiser or more knowledgeable than those who are the wealthiest and the most highly reputed (the notables) for their wisdom (those who have *sophia*)?[7]

We can clearly see that questioning plays a critical role in the aporetic dialogues. The simple reciprocity of the interplay of questions and answers ascribes a definite role to each interlocutor and defines the relationship between them. This reciprocity allows us to say that each, being indifferently questioner and respondent, is the equal of the other, at least in this respect. Questioning puts the participants on the same level by conferring on each in turn the same title. Questioning ceases to be the exclusive province of he who *can* get an answer, that is, of the more powerful.

From a theoretical perspective, this kind of questioning does not lead to knowledge, but rather maintains the problematicity of what is in question. The opinions advanced by Socrates' interlocutors cease to look like the knowledge that they *seemed* to be. Questioning produces knowledge and pseudoknowledge, being and appearance, *Sein und Schein.*

Socrates and the Sophists seem to agree on one point: questioning, by itself, cannot produce knowledge of what is in question; at most it reveals that what was in question remains so. Hence the *aporetic* nature of these dialogues. Could this even be the reason why Socrates' judges mistook him for a Sophist? Like the Sophists, Socrates engaged in dialogue with youths, but unlike them, he did not lord it over them, as

6. *Socrates' Defense (Apology)* 23c, trans. Hugh Tredennick, p. 9.

7. "After this, I went on to interview a man with an even greater reputation for wisdom, and I formed the same impression again, and here too I incurred the resentment of the man himself and a number of others . . . the people with the greatest reputations were almost entirely deficient, while others who were supposed to be their inferiors were much better qualified in practical intelligence." *Apology* 21c–22a, trans. Hugh Tredennick, p. 8.

Hippias does, to give out answers. To corrupt youth implies that one
has inflated one's answers into judgments which the youth feel compelled to adopt. Is that not more a Sophistic than a Socratic approach?
The questioning power of Socrates' *logos* runs through all his conversa-
tions. The Sophist does not really like questioning, for he prefers
answers, even if they are only apparent ones. He does not state what exists, but passes off as Being what is, in fact, a sham, a deceitful duplicate.[8] If the Sophist enjoys controversy, it is not to distinguish what is
true from what is only apparently true and from what is false, but rather
to play with the shadows of truth. The controversy of the Sophists is
eristic because it aims only at victory over the interlocutor and not at
bringing truth to light. The Sophist thus can defend any cause, in exchange for money, since triumph is more important to him than truth. It
is a triumph which he can always gain over his interlocutor precisely because he can rely on the infinite variety of sensible reality; he chooses
whatever aspect of that reality which fits his argument. Yet despite his
relativism, the Sophist is dogmatic: the Sophist-Master *seems* to devote
himself to dialectical questioning, he *seems* not to have answers because
he discusses things, he *seems* not to be on the side of the notables he
happens to represent at that moment. One thing about him is real:
the Sophist is content with appearances, and, like the leading citizens,
he loves money. Even more, he needs a questioner; Cephalus needs
Socrates so much that he forces him to debate.[9] For the Sophist, the
questioner is a pupil, one who attends to a Master. This pupil's questions are not aimed at discovering an answer but at allowing the Master
to confirm his Mastership. Of course the Master answers the pupil,
since the pupil is paying to hear him, but the pupil's questioning ends
with the answer that is given (or bought). Socrates, on the contrary, tries
to keep alive the problematicity raised by the exchange, because nothing, except for the pretended competence of the Master, can justify
ending the questioning by arriving at some proposition or another. Why
would the interlocutors in an eristic discussion stop there, since, in
truth, no real answer has been given? In fact, questioning is merely a
pretext for a Master to affirm his Mastership,[10] a Mastership exercised
over every possible thing for the sake of a reputation which is itself
nothing but an appearance. The basis of competence in an eristic controversy is independent of the questioning process. The Master's competence does not rest on the fact that he produces an answer, because in

8. *Sophist* 239c–d, trans. F. M. Cornford, p. 982.
9. *Republic* I, 327b–c, trans. Paul Shorey, pp. 576–77.
10. *Phaedo* 91a, trans. Hugh Tredennick, p. 73.

reality he only produces its counterfeit.[11] He is still in the realm of the problematic when he believes he has already found the answer. Plato demonstrates this clearly in the *aporetic dialogues*, hence their name.

It is necessary to distinguish the questioning process, which occurs within a dialogue (dialectic), and controversy, in which there is only the *appearance* of questioning within what is really the Mastership of a Sophist, the supposed possessor of answers, whatever the questions (thus the independence of which I spoke earlier). The Greek city-state, trapped in appearances, failed to distinguish Socrates from the Sophists.

But how can we distinguish the kind of questioning which leads to *knowledge* from the form of conversation wherein one strives only for *victory* over another as proof of Mastership? Does Socrates not proceed by refutation (*elenchos*), like the Sophist who enters a debate only to refute and thus vanquish his adversary? How can we distinguish between dialectic and eristic, between questioning and the affirmation which results from a controversy? The problem is all the more unsolvable because questioning seems to be flawed by a paradox which precludes the use of dialectic as a means by which to acquire knowledge:

> . . . a man cannot try to discover either what he knows or what he does not know. He would not seek what he knows, for since he knows it there is no need of the inquiry, nor what he does not know, for in that case he does not even know what he is to look for.[12]

Because of this paradox, questioning does not allow us to extend knowledge, nor, therefore, to acquire it.

The paradox of the *Meno* leads us into what Sir David Ross has called the *Middle Dialogues*. The analysis of questioning, seen as identical with dialectic, is clearly centered on the ethico-political problem of excellence (*aretē*), as the *Meno*'s subtitle indicates, but is also focused on the more general theme of dialectic as a cognitive process. There is thus a shift in the concept of the dialectic. For the Socrates of the aporetic dialogues, dialectic fulfills a critical function, and, as I have already pointed out, only a minimal epistemological function. It is here that Plato seems to distinguish himself from Socrates, if we agree that the "true" Socrates is he who wrote nothing because he preferred to assert nothing, he who gave preference to question over answer. Plato, by contrast, emphasized the answer rather than the question, the solu-

---

11. *Sophist* 268c, trans. F. M. Cornford, pp. 1016–17.
12. *Meno* 80e, trans. W. K. C. Guthrie, p. 363.

tion (truth, science) rather than critical inquiry. Dialectic ceases to be interrogative, and instead becomes *the* method (*epistemē*) for arriving at *the* answer, at that which is valid in truth and reality. Socrates' interlocutors will more and more evolve into spokesmen of the "positive" theses of Plato. As Popper has shown, Plato, in ethico-political matters, manifests an authoritarianism which will be every bit as strict as that criticized by Socrates in the aporetic dialogues.

2. Dialectic and the Hypothetical Method as a Reaction to the Socratic Logos

It is in the *Meno* that the meaning of dialectic first concerns itself with the answer and how to get it rather than with the question posed. In the end, Plato will keep only the answer as essential. Plato's preoccupation will be with knowing what makes an answer an *answer*. Objective content, proof, mixing of genres, and predicative structure will be the major themes of his ontological and metaphysical approach. Because of that, I cannot agree with Richard Robinson when he writes:

> The fact is that the word 'dialectic' had a strong tendency in Plato to mean 'the ideal method, *whatever that may be.*' In so far as it was thus merely an honorific title, Plato applied it at every stage of his life to whatever seemed to him at the moment the most hopeful procedure . . . This usage, combined with the fact that Plato did at one time considerably change his conception of the best method, has the result that the meaning of the word 'dialectic' undergoes a substantial alteration in the course of the dialogues.[13]

This alteration is in no way simply the result of chance or Plato's whim. Instead, what he calls "dialectic," which he conceives of as the best method, becomes precisely that which leads to an answer, an answer presumed to be true in order to be an answer. Since truth is decided by being the *real*, we can thus see that Plato has concerned himself with ontology and metaphysics. It is true that Plato's conception of the dialectic undergoes an evolution; he differentiates himself from Socrates in refusing to make dialectic into just a questioning mode (because, in his view, if it were only that, dialectic would be limited to opinion). It would never attain truth, which depends not on what questioners know (or seek to know) or what they don't know. It would bear too close a resemblance to *eristic*, while never being identical to it. Was Socrates not mistaken for a Sophist?

Dialectic conceived of as questioning leads only to the minimal knowledge which affirms the certainty of ignorance. It does not ad-

---

13. Robinson, *Plato's Earlier Dialectic*, p. 70.

vance knowing beyond this state of not knowing. The paradox of the *Meno* is clear on this point: questioning to learn the truth is not possible. If we want to know how knowledge is acquired, we must do so in terms other than those of questioning. Plato considers this paradox a sophism, because it led him to conclude that nothing at all can be learned. But, in reality, all that it really shows is the inadequacy of Socratic questioning as a means for establishing a foundation for truth. Certainly, truth can be arrived at through dialogue; but nothing, in an a priori sense, will prove that we have found it. Nothing within the dialogue itself and nothing in the question-answer process guarantees that the answer given is adequate as an answer to the question initially posed. Obtaining truth in a dialogue requires that the interlocutors are operating in good faith. This is both a minimal condition and a subjective aspect which makes it difficult to distinguish (objectively) Socrates from a Sophist.

Acquiring truth, finding an answer to an initial question, is hardly possible if we remain in the sphere of the problematic, which is merely aporetic in regard to what is sought. Truth cannot be found through dialogue, even if carried out in good faith and without any ambition of Mastership and any show of authority. According to Plato, we learn through recollection.[14] We find *in ourselves* the truth which we didn't know. Dialogue is only an occasion to recall, as the episode of the slave in the *Meno* makes clear. Questioning, so critical to Socrates, becomes for Plato simply a means of bringing to the surface a truth buried in the depths of the soul. The theory of recollection refers to the statement "Know thyself." By remembering what one knows, one learns what one did not know, but what one learns is not taught by a Master. For from whence would the Master get his knowledge? From another Master, and so on indefinitely?

A dialectical debate among interlocutors who question and answer is not what provides a foundation for knowledge, nor what justifies answers *as* answers. At best, it is only an occasion for recollection for someone who wants to learn. Hence what is important in dialectic is what constitutes the *basis* of answers themselves. It is no longer the "answer" which matters, but it is the justificatory value of the statement which becomes necessary to study. It is thus something that no longer refers to the problematic, nor, even, to the aporetic, which it is nevertheless necessary to envision, in terms of what suppresses problematicity. What counts is to leave the hypothetical to one side during the dialectical process to reveal the apocritical (*apokrisis* = answer)

14. *Meno* 81d, trans. W. K. C. Guthrie, p. 364; *Phaedo* 72e, trans. Hugh Tredennick, p. 55.

aspect of what is said during the debate. To better understand Plato's intention at this stage, we must return to Socrates.

What is the conception of language which underlies dialectical debate for Socrates?

In contrast to his interlocutors, Socrates gives the impression of never answering and always staying at the level of questions. But in reality, Socrates both answers and refutes in the dialogues. The aporetic character of the *Early Dialogues* does not bear on the grammatical form of discourse: the affirmed contradiction, which none of his interlocutors has been able to overcome by the end of the dialogues, suffices to bring to light and put into evidence the (unsolved) problem. The problematicity of discourse does not depend on an interrogative structure—which is in no event necessary to indicate a problem—but rather on the very structure of what we call *dialogue*.

What about the *logos* in this dialogue? The participants in the debate, by posing and answering questions, gradually develop a *logos*. In so doing, they develop their understanding and are able to move the discussion forward, even to the point of posing supplementary questions if some lack of understanding becomes apparent. If each participant takes a turn as questioner, then each equally assumes (in inverse proportion) the role of respondent. In this way, dialectic—as a dialogue built of questions and answers—achieves absolute equality among its participants, unrelated to any relationship based on authority, which is eliminated from this type of discourse. Each participant occupies the role of questioner or respondent filled a moment earlier by the other participant. The *logos* which the participants share in taking part in the dialogue is the unity of difference: questions are taken as such, in distinction to answers, which are also considered as such by each of the participants.

For there to be a dialectic, a proposition—indeed discourse in general—must be able to be both answer and question, one and the other, the distinction between them appearing only in the course of the discussion. When I say "question," perhaps I should be even more precise and say "problem," since the emphasis is not on the type of sentence, that is, on whether the sentence is cast in an interrogative form.[15] Rather the emphasis is on utterances in general, which are frequently, but not necessarily, rendered in an assertoric form. We often use the expression "to treat a question" (and proceed to do so without using any interrogative sentences) when we mean simply "to treat a problem."

15. The German language draws a clear distinction between the word "Fragesatz" and the word "Frage."

Likewise, we say, "X asks if p," where "p" represents a proposition stating p, and where what X asks in asking "p" is really the question "p?" It is "p" that is in question, which implies that the assertion "p" can become a question, in the sense of being the problem put into question by X.

The *logos* is thus *apocritical*, since it is the locus of answers, and also *problematological*, since it states what it is that makes a problem, or a question (whether in interrogative form or not). An assertion which is presented during a discussion can become problematic by becoming the object of a question from one of the participants. The problematicity of such an assertion becomes apparent to the questioner, who sees it submitted for his judgment due to the fact that he is an interlocutor. But the assertion, when it is converted—from answer it becomes problem—is one and the same reality from the viewpoint of the *logos*, even if for the questioner it is a question and for his interlocutor an answer. Such a conversion presupposes a quality of *convertibility*, which is found in the *logos* itself, insofar as it can be both question (problem) and answer. Dialectical debate brings together a questioner and a respondent—which each interlocutor will, in turn, become—and thereby establishes the difference between the problematological and the apocritical. For something to qualify as an answer there must be an interlocutor who affirms it so; if this answer turns out to be a problem, it will be so only for the *other* interlocutor. The apocritical-problematological unity of the *logos* is the unity of a difference accomplished by the turns taken by the interlocutors in their dialectic relationship.

1. The conception of the *logos* which Socrates implicitly puts into play in the dialectical relationship involves the convertibility of what is in question into an answer, and vice versa. This vision of discourse, which arises explicitly with Plato through his reflection on the discursive method—the *dialectic*—makes the following fact clear: a problem can be resolved by assuming it to be so. This assumption is called a *hypothesis*. A hypothesis is a starting point for a dialectical debate; but it is also, for this very reason, a conjecture, a problematic assertion (which is the current meaning of the term, frequently, and inappropriately, contrasted with the Platonist meaning). It is so because the dialectical debate aims at putting this starting point to the test of questions and answers.

2. If the process of questioning is made identical with dialectic, the cognitive meaning of dialectic will be destroyed by the paradox of the *Meno*. Further, an answer can remain a problem. Since the goal of knowledge is to eliminate problematicity, dialectic is recollection

rather than questioning. Indeed, questioning makes recollection possible in that it is the stimulus for recalling something to mind, but it
is like a ladder giving access to the second floor of a doorless house.
The ladder is no more the house than questioning is cognition, even
if the ladder, like questioning, is necessary for gaining access.

The fact that recollection is what assures intellectual progress makes
clear, in dialogues like the *Phaedo,* in the *Republic,* or as early as in the
Meno, that Plato no longer considers questioning as *both* the ground for,
and source of, knowledge. Even if it is still, in some ways, the source of
knowledge, it is not what makes knowledge "knowledge." The foundation of knowledge has its psychological roots in recollection, while its
logical roots are in the hypothetical method, which we are going to
examine.

In the so-called *Later Dialogues,* dialectic as the ground of knowledge
no longer has anything to do with questioning.[16] The conception of the
logos which there prevails is no longer based on the question-answer
pair, but is rather focused on the objective validity of the assertion. The
emphasis will no longer be put on the presence of an interlocutor who
questions and answers to characterize the *logos.* Socrates' auditor becomes inessential, to the point of becoming simply a foil for Plato in
presenting his own conceptions.

The *logos* is no longer seen as based on the questioner-answerer relationship. The interlocutor becomes merely the passive recipient of the
discourse that is asserted. The interlocutor, made the equal of his debate opponent by dialogue, limits himself to propounding opinions
which are of no interest in themselves. "[B]ut at present," says the aged
Parmenides, "your youth makes you still pay attention to what the
world will think."[17] Such a consideration is essential to the conception
of dialectic as dialogue and is inessential to a conception based on assertion, like that developed by Plato in the *Sophist* (261d–263d). Statements are not studied as answers, but as assertions, all reference to
problematicity having been eliminated from the analysis of knowledge,
that is, from the *logos.* Judgment is studied as such, for its objective
validity as a true judgment bearing on what exists in reality.

The monopoly of judgment, and an audience whose epistemological
role has been reduced to zero, lead to a dogmatic conception of discourse and knowledge. It is through an interlocutor who both questions
and answers that equality among the participants is realized. If a listener assumes only a passive role and is content with being merely the

16. Robinson, *Plato's Earlier Dialectic,* p. 69.
17. *Parmenides* 130e, trans. F. M. Cornford, pp. 924–25.

recipient of the speaker's ideas, then we can hardly speak of a relationship between equals or of a relationship not based on authority.

In the *Middle Dialogues*, Plato still considers knowledge, dialectic, in relation to questioning, but considers the latter only as an opportunity to arouse knowledge. The Master does not inculcate knowledge in his pupil, but rather simply provides him with what he needs so that he can recollect things. If it were otherwise, the Master's knowledge would have had to come from another Master, and so on to infinity. Consequently, the Master, like the pupil, asks and answers questions about an independent reality that the dialectical relation reveals but does not create. It is the same truth that recollection seeks after, "because 'to know' means simply to retain the knowledge which one has acquired, and not to lose it."[18] Knowledge, making this reality its object, cannot be studied in terms of the question-answer relation, because such a reality is independent of that relationship. The question reveals the knowledge (the answer) which already is hidden in the mind of the questioner. What makes it knowledge depends neither on the question which, *hic et nunc*, brings it to the surface, nor on the answer, which is as circumstantial as is the question. Clearly, knowledge is not true because it suppresses someone's ignorance, an ignorance to which the question attests. Rather it is true for other, nonsubjective, reasons.

3. It is possible to establish a clear distinction between the *Middle Dialogues* and the *Later Dialogues* as far as understanding the relationship among dialectic, science, and questioning. For Plato, Socrates, however it might have appeared, undertook to study answers but without eliminating the problematic nature of the *logos*. Knowledge appears impossible to acquire through a dialectic conceived as a questioning process, as dialogue. Plato still concedes that it is necessary to question to arrive at knowledge, considered as answer. The hypothetical method makes it possible to demonstrate how the problematic nature of the *logos* may be overcome. But when knowledge is stripped of all reference to what is or was in question, then we are no longer speaking of answers. Dialectic ceases to have any relationship to the process of questioning. It becomes instead the validation of the *logos*. And when one studies answers exclusively, in their cognitive and objective aspects, they are no longer considered as answers but as judgments. This occurs in the *Later Dialogues*.

Let us now examine the hypothetical method as it is linked to the questioning process.

The hypothetical method begins from questioning and from a *logos*

---

18. *Phaedo* 75d, trans. Hugh Tredennick, p. 58.

conceived on the basis of questioning. Its goal is to guarantee the obtaining of knowledge, of a true answer. This answer cannot possibly express problematicity, so that once it is arrived at, an answer can no longer be questioned. Obtaining a true answer ends the debate which brought forth the initial question to which this answer is now *the* answer. Within the debate, there is an exchange of views: answers put forward by the interlocutors are problematized, and the debate is advanced. Putting forward an answer to a question, when that answer is going to be in its turn the object of a new question, is nothing other than the putting forward of a *hypothesis*, which is put to the test of such a debate. The objective of the dialectic in the *Middle Dialogues* is to provide a grounding for knowledge, that is, an *anhypothetical* answer. Dialectic is the method of transition from the *hypothetical* to the *anhypothetical*. The use of hypothesis was characteristic of a method used in Plato's day in mathematics: the analytical method. What does it involve?

Analysis consists of assuming that a problem initially posed has been solved, and then, by deduction, working back to a proposition known to be true. Convertibility between problem and answer is possible only because of the apocritical-problematological nature of the *logos*. This convertibility allows for considering the proposition stating the problem as a proposition-answer. The statement in question remains a hypothesis as long as it remains undemonstrated.

There is another process, also familiar to mathematicians of Plato's day, and that is *synthesis*.[19] Synthesis works in an opposite manner from that of analysis: it begins from what is known to arrive at a solution to the original problem. In this case as well, there is a convertibility from a proposition-problem into a proposition-solution. The problem is presented in assertoric form, and synthesis proceeds to turn this assertion into the conclusion of a deductive argument.

The convertibility which exists within the *logos* is what allows both analysis and synthesis to exist, since in both types of processes, the problem to be resolved is treated as an answer, one which remains hypothetical until the deduction confirms the hypothesis and makes it become an answer. Still, there is an important difference between analysis and synthesis: analysis begins from the problem itself, while synthesis begins from some other known proposition. As a result, analysis is the method best adapted to dialectical debate, when viewed as a succession of questions and answers. Synthesis is a poor method for discovery because it does not make clear how to select the original propo-

---

19. Euclid, *Elements* XIII, 1–5, in *The Thirteen Books of Euclid's Elements*, vol. 3, trans. Thomas L. Heath (New York: Dover Books, 1956), pp. 440–49.

sition, given a problem to be resolved. Analysis is more "natural" as a method for the resolution of *problems*, whereas synthesis serves to reorganize deductions so that principles—at which one *ends* in the analytical process—are presented as such right from the beginning, consistent with their nature as principles. Pappus states clearly the precedence of analysis, in mathematics as in all the sciences, and the necessity of having it followed by synthesis:

> . . . in *synthesis*, reversing the process, we take as already done that which was last arrived at in analysis, and, by arranging in their natural order as consequences what were before antecedents, we arrive finally at the construction of what was sought.[20]

Whether one proceeds by analysis or synthesis, it is necessary in each case to assume at least one proposition to be true. In analysis, we proceed from a proposition which states the problem and which we suppose to be proved: hence we arrive at a known proposition. But it is quite possible for an inference to be *valid*, even if it contains a false premise. As for synthesis, it begins from an undemonstrated premise which we assume to be true, even though it has in no sense been validated. The interlocutor must therefore agree with the one who carries out the synthesis based on the premise. Whether called hypothesis, postulate, or axiom, the premise of a synthesis avoids all demonstration and has validity only because of either a tacit or expressed agreement on the part of the interlocutors present. It is capable of being known to be true independently, but that is another problem, or rather the answer to another problem.

Plato's conception of dialectic can be reduced neither to analysis nor to synthesis: a conception of the *logos* (and therefore of knowledge) which is based on questioning permits only answers which are indefinitely transformed into statements of problems. But what Plato seeks is precisely a conception of answerhood which eliminates any possible reference to the problematicity of a statement. Neither analysis, the movement upward toward principles, nor synthesis, the downward movement from principles, can produce knowledge free from problematicity, at least where the starting point remains hypothetical in both resolutional processes:

> And this is the reason why every man should expend his chief thought and attention on the consideration of his first principles—are they or are they not rightly laid down?[21]

20. Pappus, *Collections* VII, pp. 635–36, in Heath, *Thirteen Books*, vol. 1, p. 138.
21. *Cratylus* 436c, trans. Benjamin Jowett, p. 470.

If we remain at the level of hypothesis, we believe we have found the answers by producing inferences in conformity with hypotheses, while, in reality, it is inference itself which is hypothetical because of the problematic status of the premise:

> For where the starting point is something that the reasoner does not know, and the conclusion and all that intervenes is a tissue of things not really known, what possibility is there that assent in such cases can ever be converted into true knowledge or science?[22]

What is dialectic, and how is it different from mere analysis or synthesis? In other words, how can we achieve the anhypothetical principle and eliminate all problematicity from dialectic?

3. *Dialectic, Analysis, and Synthesis*

Plato's dialectic is clearly rooted in analysis, and therefore in hypothesis. It begins from an assertion that raises a problem and looks immediately for its consequences:

> If anyone should fasten upon the hypothesis itself, you would disregard him and refuse to answer until you could consider whether its consequences were mutually consistent or not.[23]

Dialectic tries to bring the mind into the realm of the anhypothetical. Formally, for such a result to occur, the dialectical inference must proceed from a hypothesis to a conclusion in such a way that the conclusion becomes the premise of an argument which allows deduction of the first hypothesis. Synthesis, which reverses the order of analysis, must therefore be carried out *simultaneously* within dialectic reasoning. There is no longer a hypothesis in such a situation, since what serves as a premise, as a point of reference, is, in another sense, itself the final product of another chain of reasoning. This implies the complete convertibility of every term in the chain A, B, . . . Z, which is constitutive of the *logos:* this is the convertibility of a hypothesis into a solution by means of dialectic, that is, by virtue of the analytico-synthetic process.

---

22. *Republic* VII, 533c, p. 765. Compare *Republic* VI 510c–d: "For I think you are aware that students of geometry and reckoning and such subjects first postulate the odd and the even and the various figures and three kinds of angles and other things akin to these in each branch of science, regard them as known, and, treating them as absolute assumptions, do not deign to render any further account of them to themselves or others, taking it for granted that they are obvious to everybody. They take their start from these, and pursuing the inquiry form this point on consistently, conclude with that for the investigation of which they set out" (pp. 745–46).

23. *Phaedo* 101d, trans. Hugh Tredennick, pp. 82–83.

It is important to distinguish dialectic, in the way I have just characterized it formally, from analysis *and* from subsequent synthesis. Dialectic is not simply analysis *followed* by a justificatory synthesis; analysis occurs only insofar as it is also a synthesis at the same time. Clearly, one does not infer B from A, and then *verify* that A is true by deducing it from B. Rather, one infers B from A *to the extent* that B is what *justifies* A.

Dialectic is thus a synthesis that assumes an analysis, and an analysis that assumes a synthesis. It is not an analysis supported by a synthesis. Synthesis, in the second case, would be restricted to the explicit re-ordering of analysis. In the course of doing that, we fall back upon principles assumed to be true, such that these principles deductively imply the conclusion from which analysis proceeded. The goal of the analytic process is to give rise to a subsequent synthesis. Indeed, if Z is the expression of the hypothesis to be verified, and A is the proposition which is reached through analysis, it is not proper to end the analysis with A. We presume that A is true; we know A to be so for reasons external to the analytical process. If we stop our reasoning at this true proposition, it is because we can say that A being true, Z is true as well. Is this not an inversion of the analytical order?

Such an inversion is often carried out by mathematicians, who rarely limit themselves simply to analysis.[24] We may recall that Plato criticized the method used by the geometricians and distinguished it from dialectic. I believe that the reason for this is that neither analysis by itself nor analysis followed by synthesis are enough to make us leave the realm of the hypothetical. The geometrician analytically regresses to a proposition whose truth remains undemonstrated. All that synthesis does is to reverse the order of analysis to explain its results. In so doing, the geometrician has the illusion of having *validated* his hypothesis, when in fact he considered it true from start to finish. It is important to know that it is still a hypothesis and not a piece of knowledge that is scientifically established. How can it be otherwise, since analysis, like synthesis, can only work on the basis of hypotheses? The dialectician knows all of this and does not succumb to the illusion that true knowledge has been reached just because a beginning proposition has been agreed on by the participants in the discussion as a place from which they will draw all their inferences. (This is the meaning of the word "hypothesis," a word which shows quite clearly that it is a concept proceeding from dialectical concerns). The dialectician also proceeds from hypotheses but considers them as such to overcome them.

For Plato, the two dialectical devices are analysis and synthesis, as

---

24. Heath, *Thirteen Books*, vol. 1, p. 140.

indicated in the *Phaedrus* (265d). However, they are used in a manner specific to philosophy. Plato admits that one starts from hypotheses, and that one proceeds by synthesis. But to disassociate oneself from the notion of provisional knowledge, it is necessary to integrate these two movements within a single and integrated interaction, termed the ascending and descending paths to Ideas. And if we were to go from analysis to synthesis so as to account for the hypothesis without resorting to an all-embracing movement integrating analysis and synthesis, then we would mix "two things together by discussing both the principle and its consequences."[25] The dialectical approach is not an analysis which is later changed into synthesis, but an analysis which is valid to the sole extent that it *is* also synthesis. If it is necessary to prove the hypothesis to eliminate it, then "you would proceed in the same way" to account for it[26] and not have *an* analysis and *a* synthesis. The dialectic must work on the anhypothetical, and the upward movement must begin with it,[27] which is not the case with analysis, nor with synthesis, nor with analysis merely arranged in inverse synthetical order.

We must recognize that, in Plato, it is not very easy to see how dialectic differs from the combination of analysis and synthesis, or even how it could differ from them. Analysis, like synthesis, begins from something that is problematically true and can never leave this ground. Any answer, in such a conception of *logos*, can be the assertion of a problem, an assertion which is the expression of a hypothesis which serves as the basis of the dialectical relationship. Dialectic, as it was envisioned by Plato in the *Middle Dialogues*, seems to be exempt from all problematicity when it is nothing more than a composite of analysis and synthesis. But an analysis which can later be reversed into synthesis does not exclude the problematicity of the starting point. Regressing to a starting point makes no sense if that beginning, in turn, does not involve the starting point of the regression. However, the base point of synthesis remains outside the deductive process of justification. Is this not what the mathematician does and what the dialectician must not do?

The solution which remains is to imagine dialectic to be a "synthesis" of these two movements into a single one, as I have already suggested. But in this case, any reference to the hypothetical being excluded, the single upward-downward movement can only be a petition, a duplication of an analysis (and/or of a synthesis) which functions

25. *Phaedo* 101e, trans. Hugh Tredennick, p. 83.
26. *Phaedo* 101d, trans. Hugh Tredennick, p. 83.
27. *Republic* VI, 511c, trans. Paul Shorey, p. 746.

by beginning from a hypothesis. This allows us to understand why, according to Plato, one can (and must) proceed dialectically toward the idea of the Good by an upward-downward movement, without making of this anhypothetical process par excellence a reality deduced from an hypothetical deduction. The major problem is in knowing how to move from analysis (combined with synthesis) to dialectic, since this transition is what makes possible the elimination of all problematicity from the *logos*. The difficulty seems insurmountable: *either* analysis and synthesis both are apocritical, right from the start, and then we have difficulty understanding the criticism leveled against mathematics and why it is necessary to disassociate it from dialectic, *or* they are both impregnated with problematicity, and we have just as much difficulty in seeing what dialectic can add if it is nothing more than the combination of analysis and synthesis. We know what Plato's solution was: making dialectic into the justification of the *logos*. The *logos*, centered on the *epistemē*, is a priori void of any problematicity. It will no longer have anything to do with questioning or answers. It will be only an ensemble of *Ideas*. Plato, in not speaking further of hypothesis or the anhypothetical, will have expunged problematicity from the *logos*, showing de facto that it is possible to do so.

It is important to remember that at this stage in the evolution of Plato's thought, questioning simply provides the *occasion* for an answer, simply what leads to the answer's being offered. It is in no way what *grounds* it *as* an answer. This means that knowing what makes an answer valid as an answer should not be sought in its nature, its answerhood. And if by this search we mean dialectic, we must recognize that the reference to the question/answer process is inessential to the dialectical method. The ambiguity of the *Middle Dialogues* on this point stems from the fact that, on the one hand, Plato tries to elucidate the process by which we find answers, while, on the other hand, his focus on answers means that everything that is not an answer becomes inessential to knowledge. Finally, the thematization of the dialectical process leads the philosopher to focus on the validation of discursivity, independent of the questions which gave birth to the discourse as a set of answers. However, it is clear that the two processes differ, if only because, in the second, the apocritical status of the judgment is deemed incidental, while in the first it is given an essential function because it entails a reference to questions.

To prove that the dialectic enables those who dialectize to reach beyond the hypothetical, Plato will dedicate himself to showing how judgment finds its exclusive foundation in its truth as judgment. He will abandon any effort to show how dialectic provides the mind with access from the hypothetical to the anhypothetical. Dialectic will no longer be seen as a questioning method, allowing the passage from questions to answers—which it must be if we retain the concept of the *logos* as it emerged from Socrates' practice—but instead it will be a, or rather *the*, process for validating judgments. Philosophical questioning unquestionably dies with Socrates and becomes ontological, or ontological-metaphysical with Plato. Truth and reality, what really count in philosophy, will henceforth be found outside of questioning.

The question concerning the *being* of things is the Socratic question par excellence. "What is X?" is the form of the question which Socrates puts repeatedly to his interlocutors. To understand better how the transition took place from a conception of dialectic centered on questioning, to an ontological one, let us examine how being and questioning intersect, as instantiated in the Socratic question.

4. The Question of Being or the Shift from Questioning to Being

With his emphasis on questioning, Socrates brings to the fore the duality of ignorance and knowledge—ignorance which claims to be knowledge, and knowledge which knows itself to be ignorant. The ignorance present in the type of knowledge which answers nothing is, in fact, only the *appearance* of knowledge, while the knowledge which Socrates asserts of his own ignorance is *real*. Socratic questioning brings to light both the *apparent* and the *real*. It reveals a plurality of possibilities, where *the* answer is understood as just one of many alternatives. Questioning always occurs against this background of multiplicity. The goal of questioning is to find *the* answer, that is to say, *an* answer. The import of Socratic questioning is to do away with multiplicity by an answer, and to do away with appearance to reach unity. The multiple is the appearance presented by the question, and unity is reality as sought by *the* answer. It is so for every question, because it shows that it is the alternative and the multiple that must be overcome.

The Socratic question par excellence bears on the unity of the ideas debated in Socrates' dialogues. If X is the matter under scrutiny, Socrates continually asks what X *is*. Every question, of whatever kind, presumes that the X that is the subject of inquiry is *something;* otherwise the question would not be posed. Every question thus presumes, implicitly, an answer to the Socratic question ("What is X?"). Every answer to every question aims at unity, but the unity provided by an answer in no way implies that this answer itself is about unity. Because Socratic questioning explicitly tries to unmask the appearance of truth in discourse, such questioning must bear thematically on the unity of what it questions. Of course, any other question seeks unity through *the* answer that is sought, but this unity is presupposed both in the answer and in the question itself, insofar as the latter is not the Socratic question. Any other question seeks unity, because it leads the mind to *the* answer, and not because the question itself deals with what unity is.

"What is X?" is, therefore, a question whose answer is presupposed by any question about X. If we ask whether virtue is good, we are presupposing that virtue is *something*. Such radicality in questioning problematizes everything, and, for Socrates, that is the whole meaning of dialectic. Every question, like any assertion in general, presupposes that the X in question in a *logos* is something. That is the very thing that is out of the question in a discourse where the question under discussion is not the Socratic question. What X is, is presupposed in such questions ("X is blue" presupposes that X is something); the nature of X functions as the object of what will later be termed an *analytic judgment*, what the Greeks called a definition (*horos*). An analytic element remains outside of the debate and is, literally, "out of the question." It is not what the debaters explicitly have to decide on, but rather it is that on the basis of which they proffer their answers during the dialogue. This general, implicit reality remains a presupposition, a "hypo-thesis," which is susceptible of multiple interpretations. The question "What is X?" which seeks after unity, is only possible, and only posable, because of this multiplicity. The question "What is X?" can, a priori, be given an infinite number of answers, since the pronoun "what" is indefinite. This multiplicity is what leads to sophism. The Sophist plays on one or another implicit assertion to pronounce judgments on the topics he speaks about in public. The Socratic question, when posed, is aimed at establishing and making explicit a univocal answer for the entirety of the debate.

For Socrates, what X precisely is, is hypothetical in all judgments and for all questions. If there were an answer to the Socratic question, it would precisely duplicate what is in question, namely that X is something, this or that, when that is precisely what is sought. Any answer would duplicate the question without really resolving it. There is nothing a priori which allows us to distinguish between an answerer who states that virtue is *this* thing, and another answerer who claims that it is something else. It is a question of definition. The Socratic question, the supreme Socratic question, cannot but remain unanswered, hence the aporetic character of the Socratic process in Plato's *Early Dialogues*. There is agreement on the meaning of the *hypo-thesis* to the extent that it may help the debaters in a dialogue make progress, but, in the last analysis, this *hypo-thesis* remains hypothetical, which implies that it can be the object of an intersubjective *agreement* but not of a complete *verification*.

For Plato, it seems, the question of what X is can be given an answer; that is what dialectic is all about. If we ask a question about what X is, we are presupposing a thing which exists as X, for example, mud, or the sky. A prior connection to the sensible world is needed, since the question of the being of X bears first and foremost on X itself. If the question of the being of things is one whose answer is presupposed by any question about these things, it still is the last one asked when we inquire into them. When we inquire into what things are, we become conscious of them, and yet we had to be conscious of some of their properties even before asking *what* they are. Otherwise, there would be no difference between asking "What is the sky?" and "What is mud?" Both would represent only one unknown, Y, and it would no longer be mud per se, or the sky per se that we are asking about, but rather a confused and undifferentiated reality.

The question "What is X?" therefore *presupposes* a prior relationship with the sensible, with the X in question, even if that question merely *affirms* an anteriority, albeit of a different kind, the precedence of reality over appearance, of the nonsensible over the sensible, of unity over multiplicity. This "anteriority of another nature" results from the fact that any judgment, and any question on anything that is "X," presupposes that X *is* something, the very thing that the Socratic question is inquiring into. Therefore, to resolve the Socratic question, we must move in both directions, to and from the sensible, which, for man, is anterior to the nonsensible, which itself enjoys an anteriority of another nature. We do so to show how the nonsensible is the being, the essence (*ousia*) of the sensible which is in question. This double movement is analysis and synthesis. The mind uses *recollection* to carry out this process. And recollection fulfills a double role. On the one hand, it is from recollection that the dialectical movement proceeds. It reveals an "already there" back to which the mind returns. This return to anteriority occurs at the end of an analytic regression performed on the sensible. It opens up to positing a first term, which can only be first for an order other than the sensible, an order in which synthesis undertakes the explanation *in connection with the sensible* (*dianoia*). The mind frees itself from the sensible at the conclusion of this double movement by a superior kind of intellectual operation (*noēsis*) and retains only those realities discovered through *anamnesis*. *Anamnesis* is indeed the discovery of the nonsensible, but that discovery is nevertheless achieved as a result of a sensible relationship, which therefore makes it preliminary to the dialectic method as conceived by Plato. Recollection makes us aware that what we have learned and what we know are buried deep in our memories, where we ignore them. We know, therefore, that there is something anterior to the sensible which allows the discovery of the sensible as sensible. The sensible thus acts as both a starting point and an end term.

Hence, there is a new role for recollection: to shift the problem of the acquisition of knowledge from the domain of questioning to that of ontology. By connection with the sensible, one learns the thing, learns what it is, but it is not from the sensible that such knowledge originates.

Memory makes us perceive the sensible as something which was anterior. In remembering, one knows that one knew without knowing it, because one has forgotten it. The problem of the acquisition of knowledge becomes that of the relationship between the sensible and the nonsensible, called the Idea, which benefits from being anterior to the sensible. The Idea is the ground of the sensible.[28] It is discovered through recollection as being what is *in reality* anterior to the sensible. I emphasize *in reality* because for Plato the question, as I showed earlier, presupposes appearance as sensible multiplicity, and what grounds the answer as truth can only be the opposite of sham and appearance. The answer makes one learn this causality, this ontological account of what X is relative to its *nature* as a sensible object. What grounds the answer is therefore of an ontological nature, which has nothing to do with its nature *as an answer*. The question-answer relationship puts into play the sole anteriority *for us*, and not an anteriority in itself, posited by recollection as being of another nature. In general, a question always suggests the existence of a gap, which, for Plato, is between the sensible and the intelligible, whereas the goal of dialectic is to remove from the realm of knowledge the sensible, with its multiplicity and only apparent reality. How can this be done, if the answers of the *logos* always refer to questions? The *Idea* is common to both questions and answers; it is the "out-of-the-question" because it is presupposed in every question, or else repeated analytically by each one. Because it is out-of-the-question, it is a reality external to the hypotheses which are answers apt to become problems, and problems which are susceptible to being answers. If a true answer, devoid of problematicity, is only so because of the Idea embodied in it, of the intelligible put into play, then it is the intelligible which must be studied, and nothing else

28. *Phaedo* 100c–d, trans. Hugh Tredennick, p. 81.

counts. That is what Plato does in the *Later Dialogues* in putting forward a conception of language, of the *logos*, which has dominated subsequent Western thought. It will be a conception which no longer will be rooted in dialectical interaction, the operation of which was barely even studied by Plato. Instead it will become a conception of reason and language which will be based on the eradication of questioning and become centered on reference and ontology, questioning becoming then a by-product of psychology.

The field of the in-itself in its role as the ground of the sensible will become the other pole of philosophy, giving birth to theology. Aristotle, in the *Metaphysics*, attempted in vain[29] to structure theology according to an ontological conception of the *logos*, one based on the structure of judgment which originated with Plato, as just seen.

5. Dialectic and Logic

Recollection puts the acquisition of truth at the ontological level by introducing philosophical pairs such as "anteriority for us/anteriority in itself," "intelligible ideas/sensible ideas," and "cause/effect" which the latter pair implies.

But what is the connection between these pairs and dialectic, to which recollection is but the introduction?

The question of the being of X is the fundamental question of any dialectical treatment of X. What is X? Such a question, whose answer is presupposed in every question about X, produces a priori an infinity of answers. Each answer is, a priori, *equivalent* of the others. The answer "X is *a*," for example, has as much of a chance to turn out to be the answer as "X is *b*." There is nothing which allows us to know, judging only on the basis of hearing the answer, if the one proposed is the right one. It is always necessary to ask more specific questions, which allow us to narrow the problem. An answer of the type "X is *a*" to the question "What is X?" supposes that X is *something* and presupposes from that fact the existence of the sensible. Thus, it is necessary to refer to the sensible to find an answer. The question of the being of X is the last one in the sequence of questions we usually raise. Since it is based on an inquiry into the sensible, this question can only have a hypothetical answer regarding truth. Given this inevitable outcome, it matters little where the inquiry into X begins. To deal with the question of the being of things,

29. See P. Aubenque, *Le problème de l'être chez Aristote* (Paris: Presses Universitaires de France, 1962).

... everyone has long since found it a good rule to take something comparatively small and easy and practice on that, before attempting the big thing itself.[30]

If one's inquiry is about Beauty, it matters little what beautiful thing is the starting point for the questioning process. Generally speaking, one can formulate any hypothesis to answer the Socratic question par excellence if one deems that the answer to it can contribute to the resolution of the question. Thus in the *Meno*, to know what virtue is, Socrates asks if it is something teachable (86d). It is important to notice that any answer about virtue, or about any X, presupposes that virtue is *something*. If one answers a particular question about virtue, it is done to be able, *in return*, to make explicit what virtue (in general) *is*. But it is just as clear that what virtue is can only be stated hypothetically, since any statement about it presupposes the thing that is in question, and any answer about what it is also presupposes precisely what it is. It therefore can only be a duplication of the problem that is to be resolved. As Aristotle put it so well, there is no way possible to prove the essence of a thing.

But for Plato, one can nevertheless obtain a validation of an assertion about the being of X. Once a hypothesis has been formulated concerning what X is, then we return, by division, to the sensible. "[This is] the reverse of the other [process], whereby we are enabled to divide into forms, following the objective articulation . . ."[31]

Thus we find the proper nature of X addressed, what is its essence. Once successive Ideas are found, we redo what has been done in the sensible, only this time with the intelligible. It is the Same which must be stated and thus found again. Dialectic retrieves what has been analytically and synthetically learned, but keeps only the intelligible. The *logos* is governed by the requirement of *identity*. And what is said must be said as justified, as nonproblematic. This is the second *logical* requirement, one that also becomes a characteristic of the *logos*: the requirement of sufficient reason. Identity's corollary is noncontradiction. In demanding an answer, a questioner seeks one term in an alternative made up of *possible* answers, or seeks one answer from among *all* the possible answers.

The question of what X is leads the questioner away from the territory of the sensible. That requires him to make of being a domain regulated by such principles as those of intelligibility, and even of discursivity as defined in the Western tradition.

30. *Sophist* 218d, trans. F. M. Cornford, p. 960.
31. *Phaèdrus* 265e, trans. R. Hackforth, p. 511.

6. The Death of Questioning as Epistemically Constitutive and Its Consequences for Western Thought

With Plato questioning began to die, slowly but inexorably. From a position as an essential constituent of the philosophical enterprise, as it was for Socrates, it was relegated to a role of secondary importance, a psychological-rhetorical device. By doing this, did Plato commit "patricide"? Unfortunately, it is not that simple, because it was Socrates who closed himself off from the conceptualization of questioning. In his endeavor to conceptualize it through specific answer, Plato abandoned the foundational role of questioning, in spite of Socrates' new departure in philosophy, that is, the emergence of questioning *as* philosophy.

The primary reproach made to Socrates was that he was scarcely interested in answering as such. Indeed, he even denied such a possibility even though he himself answered repeatedly. Such a denial may have been the source of his refusal to write anything down. Socrates, in one sense, was at least consistent: questioning, for him, was not a matter of getting an answer but of showing that those who pretended to have answers were mistaken. The question remained intact at the end of each dialogue, but not the interlocutor. There is a positivity in the Socratic *aporias*, to the extent that it is the only possible way to distinguish Socrates from the Sophists. Socrates unmasks the false answers which the Sophists propagate, because he *knows* that he cannot answer, since he truly knows nothing. The Socratic *logos must* remain problematical; its answers must remain questions. In contrast, Sophistic questioning is pure rhetoric, in that it serves as a pretext to bring forth predetermined or convenient answers, whereas Socrates' questioning actually forbids any answer. His "answers" are there simply for the sake of expressing some question. They express it, while at the same time being impossible *as* answers.

The problematological difference, thus reduced to one of its two dimensions—in the case put here, to questions to the exclusion of answers—could not be conceptualized. The contrast between Socrates' practice, which unfolds along the two levels of questioning, and the theory which can be derived from it (though absent in the case of Socrates, a theory can be read into his thought) seems to have imposed itself on Plato's mind. What is questioning for, if not for obtaining answers?

What will Plato's response be to this objection? He will direct his full attention to the answers only. What makes *an* answer? In putting the question like that, Plato forces justification to the forefront. It could be argued that what justifies an answer will characterize it as such by refer-

ring it to questioning, despite the logico-epistemological shift embodied in the concept of justification, since the problem here is actually
about *answering*, an idea which refers us, in its very formulation, to
questioning. However, Plato did not follow this path. He thought that
an answer, by referring to a question that had been resolved, made the
question disappear. Therefore, that which justifies the answer does not
relate to the question it resolves; since the question thereby stops being
posed, reference to questioning explains nothing. Answering must be
able to provide its own justification, in a systematic way, and not just as
answering, but as a fabric of *judgments*. A judgment is the answer in
which all that makes it an answer has been drained away. If we examine
the judgment and the answer, in form the two are no different. As a
result, what makes a judgment an answer *as such* becomes inessential,
secondary, and even paradoxical if we persist in ascribing to questioning
a cognitive function, which henceforth will be assumed by the deductive interrelationship of judgments.

Dialectic, which began as dialogue, that is, interrogativity in action,
became science. This produced a major shift in Western philosophy.
The cult of science grew from nothing so much as the suppression of
interrogation to the benefit of a scientization of the thinkable. This was
truly a regressive movement, since philosophers, due to this shift in
their basic concerns, came to believe that justification (the logico-
epistemic) was the only way to deal with the interrogativity of the
mind. Indeed, this interrogativity was so displaced because they were
unable to conceptualize it as such. Socrates was unable to formulate
the problematological, and neither could Plato, for essentially the same
reason: the precedence given to only one of the two dimensions of
the problematological difference. The problematological *difference* then
vanishes, as does questioning as such, since questioning is always compelled to achieve "resolution" one way or another, but always an im-
proper resolution, since questioning is displaced into something else
and, therefore, repressed. Plato is, in his conception of the *logos*, indifferent to the problematological, perpetuating in another form the paradox of the *Meno*, which he had thought to escape or "resolve" by denying any constitutive role to questioning. Consequently, Plato was forced
to look elsewhere for this constitutive role, and the epistemological dimension ceased to be able to be characterized problematologically, as
Socrates' message would have suggested. The paradox of the *Meno*
is really nothing more than the result (if not the expression) of some
problematological "in-difference." The paradox of the *Meno* is its explicit expression. Posit this difference as such, and the paradox disappears. I know what I am looking for insofar as it is a *question*, but at the

same time I do not know it, *because* it is a question. What is in question is not the answer; it is in fact what makes an answer necessary. If we do without that distinction between question and answer, the paradox inevitably pops up again. We see this in the example of the Myth of the Cave. If one knows the truth, one will no longer think it necessary to learn it. If one does not know it, one cannot acquire it. One knows, or one does not know. Learning is impossible in these circumstances. Those who don't know, don't remember what they do know without knowing it. Therefore, no purpose is served, no door opened by telling them what the truth is. How can they seek *what* they are unaware of; and moreover, how can they even know *that* they are unaware of it?

Is the theory of recollection a good solution to this paradox? Not likely, since it merely shifts the difficulty. If I know what I must remember, then I dcn't need to call on my memory; and if I don't know what to recall, how can I recall it? Plato could only respond to this challenge by limiting questioning to a minimal role. It has always been our soul that brings this buried knowledge to the surface, and we do it by the questions we ask ourselves or by the questions that are asked of us in daily life. Thus questioning has a capacity as an occasional cause that functions to activate recollection by making it circumstantial. In such a theoretical construct, there is no need to think of a problematological difference: what is in the question is also what is in the answer. If there is any difference, it is only a transitional and unimportant one in comparison to the eternity of the known truth. We say "transitional" to underline the fact that we recall what we have forgotten and that, once a while, we need it to be present again in our mind, according to the contingent requirements of the day.

The "what" that we find in both question and answer is a foundation. It is what makes the answer be rather than not be, an opposition one grasps in the mutual exclusivity of *truth* and *falsity*, what makes X *be* this thing and nothing else (its essence). And there is more: what is at play here is answering as an ontological relationship which suppresses the problematological difference, the problematological which can no longer be assumed as such. Ontology is the product of the displacement and repression of questioning, at least insofar as ontology is the answer to the unasked question of questioning. When, for example, Socrates asked what virtue is, he expected no answer other than a contradictory one. Plato, who had a theory of answers, had by that very fact a theory of being whose aim was precisely to restrict the role of answering, rendering it occasional and rhetorical. *The very possibility of overcoming Socratic questioning in a conceptualization which includes answerhood-as-judgment necessarily implies that what can be thought is ontologized,* for to answer the question "What is X?" one must be able to assume that X *is*, and it is into the nature of this being that the interrogation is directed.

Ontology is the problematological discourse that philosophy cannot reflect as problematological without contradicting itself by being a response. Ontology originates in philosophy's inability to accept the problematological difference. Analysis and synthesis always refer to problems. Dialectic is like these in method, but without reference to problems. The ontologization of philosophical questioning reduces it to no more than an epistemological inquiry. This, of course, does not mean that epistemology should be ignored in philosophy, but it is the epistemological outlook which has shortchanged the properly philosophical by making the justification of judgments its sole and ultimate model. This is the origin of the problem of the nonhypothetical starting point, which must meet the same requirement of apodicticity as other propositions, and which must simply *be*, so that we live in a realm outside of the problematical. Hence, for Plato recollection has an intermediate place in his conception of dialectic. Did he not absorb questioning into his theory, albeit in a reduced state, thereby assuming all the criticisms directed at Socrates? For Socrates, the ineffable problematological difference manifests itself through the exchange of roles between questioner and respondent as participants in a refutational dialogue. Plato was unconcerned with this difference, which he "assumed" to exist. His preoccupation was exclusively with answers, to the ultimate point that he was interested only in the activity of judgment, the logico-ontological. He could thus effect the economy of developing a single conception of questioning, since the constitutive progress of the mind is no longer addressed in such terms. That is why Plato could speak of an *assumption;* he met the attack by changing the battleground. Implicitly, questioning haunts the work of Plato as though it were the ghost of Socrates. After all, a question represents a state of ignorance which must be overcome; what one person doesn't know may be known by another. Thus, the questions we pose have a subjective nature. If knowledge were objective, how could it be explained in terms of questioning? Is ascribing to questioning a purely psycho-rhetorical function an adequate response? Obviously not, because it is impossible to miss the fact that, for Plato, dialectic rises to the Socratic challenge by its claim to be able to *resolve* problems. Dialectic is at least partly linked to those questions of which it considers itself absolutely independent through the propositionalism it seeks to promote. But dialectic resolves problems which no longer have any right to be posed, because all is resolved, *by analysis,* into propositions. It is as though, once we set up an order which excludes them, no further questions may be posed, even though this very order was born of a need to deal with questions. This paradox will be seen again in the relationship between analysis and synthesis, as well as in the resulting status of dialectic.

Before examining this point in detail, it is important to look with care at the ontology-epistemology pair, because we often forget, especially since Heidegger, that they are *by nature* indivisible. An effort to separate the one from the other will always run aground, since they are born of the same spring. It might seem surprising to see Plato mix epistemology, in its justificatory role as illustrated in the scientific paradigm of the time, that is, geometry, with ontology. The truth, and the foundation for this truth, constitute the linkage for this interaction. Moreover, one would be justified in saying that Plato would not even have distinguished epistemology from ontology. What makes a proposition true is that it is not false; identity, in its analytical nature, is here the grounding "logical" expression of the nature of a proposition. Truth justifies a proposition in its very character as proposition.

Certainly, the epistemological search is nothing new, although, for Socrates, questioning was an ethical issue. What is new is its function as a model, and it derives this from making ontology the sole means of overcoming Plato's incapacity to conceptualize the problematological difference. Is this to suggest that such an ontological move is the cause of the lack of problematological differentiation? To the extent to which the emphasis was put on what *makes* answering autonomous, it must be said that it was rather the development of an order of judgment-as-answer (concealed as such) to the problematological challenge which simultaneously crystallized both the epistemological and the ontological. Neither is clearly preeminent over the other, but the fact is that one can take either one in its assumptions and follow through to its consequences and make the one chosen preeminent over the other. This once again shows the way in which the problematological is ignored as a motive force, ignored in the many ways in which it has effects (ways which still have not been fully assessed).

Plato's formulation has been crucial in this regard. It provided a model of the thinkable, yet one impossible to assume: (1) the ontological quest became identified with the metaphysical; (2) this quest imposed itself as inseparable from the epistemological one, in that judgment represses all interrogativity (hence its autonomy) to the benefit of an essence which justifies *what* it says as being true, that is, not false. This essence is the underlying foundation by virtue of which the justification of judgments and the ontologization of answering (it actually represses them *as* answers) are joined. If judgment is truly autonomous, it is susceptible of being truthful. It can say what it says because what it says is what accounts for it, and only that. What makes a judgment say what it says *as truth* depends on the *essence* of what is said, and thereby founds this truth according to reason. It is clear that the ontological and the epistemological are inseparable. Efforts to separate them are in vain. If their principal *concerns* are different, we must still note that they respond to the same problematological indifference, to the same demand for the repression of the problematological. Perpetuating the latter will not resuscitate a metaphysic which remains essentially concerned with the ontological. As we have seen, Kant can be read in this dual manner, but the contest between the ontological and the epistemological readings could not be resolved to the advantage of either one. To be radical, whichever one overcomes the other needs to question itself about its own necessity. To do this, it has to give up ontologizing the metaphysical, just as it renounces its epistemologizing. The question of being, cut off from its epistemological correlate, gives rise to nothing more than an illusion. It will always find itself opposed to the question of knowledge as a means of access to be questioned first. Conversely, the question of being might, in its own turn, be privileged because one only knows what is. To know what knowledge is comes back again to determining what the being of knowledge is. It is a closed circle. In the hypothesis of a break between epistemology and ontology, there cannot be a preeminence of the one over the other. It might seem surprising today to conceptualize the ontological and the epistemological as intertwined. But while they may function differently, their origin is the same. When it comes to determining what distinguishes the one from the other, we must look to functional rules, as Aristotle did when he separated them clearly into their own domains. The correlative question is whether a specific knowledge of Being (considered as a "new metaphysic") could provide ontology with a scientific status, given that the difference in their objects does not mean that there is a corresponding cleavage of the mode of access, since the epistemic is the generalized cognitive norm for all *logos*.

In any event, Plato's dialectic allows us to see the consequences of the indifference to problematology. To consider the paradox of the *Meno* as a simple sophism is to give oneself the right not to take it seriously. Failure to make interrogativity explicit displaces its paradox that results from its nonexplication in a discourse where what is problematological should be able to be differentiated and clearly identified. And we shall exclude any other solution which would explain what questioning answers as no solution at all. The problematological, unthinkable so far, is going to formalize itself another way, by means of a reductor, drawn from the abundant resources of the propositional model. This model will be unable to eliminate the problematological, which it will not even conceive as such, since this reductor has as its goal abolishing the problematological while seeming to integrate it into the system.

Ever since the Greeks, analysis and synthesis have played a determinative role as constituents of philosophical knowledge. First, Plato proposed their articulation as a *method* of philosophical resolution; unfortunately, it was a method from which all traces of problematicity were eradicated. But Socrates' questioning resurfaced time and again, though in a disguised, veiled, and even paradoxical way, up to the Platonic dialectic. Only Aristotle's view was a coherent one, but its price was too high. Analysis and synthesis, integrated as dialectic by Plato, do at least allow us to see a characteristic trait of philosophical questioning: it constitutes its own object by its very structure. By so doing, it embodies an essential and noncontradictory feature of the problematological, even when denied. That is its active presence.

7. *Analysis and Synthesis as the Primary Problematological Reductors in the Western Tradition*

Analysis and synthesis, functioning as resolutional, will determine the way philosophers think from the time of Plato onwards.

We may distinguish Socrates from the Sophists not by the practice of questioning, which they had in common, but by the nonanswer, which closes off questioning. Still, Plato falls back into the same trap of concern about answers which preoccupied the Sophists, and it is what made him exclude questioning from the theory he established. Both synthesis and analysis are methods of resolution. The latter starts from a problem solved, while the former requires an already given answer in order to arrive at a solution, which could not have been posited at the beginning. Their goal is the same, and that is why they have been considered as equivalent and not as complementary, since it is still a matter, in the two cases, of arriving at the solution to a given problem. Dialectic, for Plato, consists of analysis and synthesis combined, without any reference to the problems which need to be resolved. This is a system that pulls itself up by its own bootstraps, thanks to propositional autonomy. This is the origin of the well-known "Platonic world"—a world of Ideas which exist by themselves. Ideas become the true objects of inquiry, existing in a realm where what is asked and what is answered are based on a single *logos*, which obliterates any difference between them. Question and answer are interchangeable. That allows solving a problem by assuming its resolution, as is done in analysis. Geometry depends on this convertibility, and Socrates resorted to it to the extent that he saw the answers he was confronted with as duplicating in infinite repetition the initial question, although the problematicity of these answers was formally disguised.

Plato kept his distance from the kind of analysis so beloved in geometry, precisely because of the hypothetical nature of its results. In our terms, we would call these results problematic, but the idea is the same, since knowledge, in itself, cannot be hypothetically (problematically) true, but instead must be absolutely true, with no possibility of doubt, no propositional alternative. Hypothetical knowledge is at best a supposition of truth; that is, a discourse which can *not* be said to be true. Therefore, it is no more true than it is false. And what, then, is the meaning of a truth that is no more than a hypothesis or rooted in one? The answer, at least since Plato, is clear: such "knowledge" is a contradiction in terms. Knowledge that is only conjectural in regard to that which it purports to know is self-defeating regarding its claims to be *real* knowledge. This is because knowledge which contains no more than a possibility of truth a priori includes error as a possibility as well, right from the start. It is as if there was the possibility of a lack of fit or correspondence to reality while claiming to describe it, if not explain it. As a consequence, such a knowledge of the real could be real enough even if it does not truly describe it, that is, while eventually proving itself non-knowledge. Knowledge, because of its own inner problematicity, is knowledge of the reality it encounters only as a *possibility*, therefore not as a reality. It cannot, then, be *real* knowledge of what is. What is must be, and cannot *not* be, so long as one knows the *what* which is.

This is the status of *epistemē* since the time of the Greeks. Problematicity plays no part. Knowledge will be analyzed independently of questioning, and even questioning, as originary process, will disappear from the scene of philosophical thought.

Knowledge is then seen as the elimination of alternatives, as found in doubt or belief. One is put in mind of the famous reproof Descartes included in his letter to Regius,[32] where he drew a parallel between doubt and science, the one being defined in terms of the other by a relationship of inverse problematicity. The process of exclusion is therefore no more than an argument from absurdity. Where there is a problem expressed by an alternative, and if either term of the alternative is rejected, the other is considered *by that fact* as true and affirmed. The true nature of the problem posed doesn't matter: nothing positive

32. Letter to Regius, May 24, 1640, in *Descartes: Philosophical Letters*, trans. Anthony Kenny (Oxford: Clarendon Press, 1970), pp. 73–74.

can be known from the mere fact of problematization. On the contrary, what matters is how one deals with those opposing propositions, considered in and for themselves. Coherence through the elimination of what is contradictory becomes, as a consequence, the *only* measure of truth. Refutation, so dear to Socrates, takes on a distinctly new meaning. Dialectic becomes what it has been ever since: not a relationship grounded in dialogue, but a positivity derived from the contradiction which brings about the result by the elimination of a contrary assertion.

Plato's reproach to the geometricians on this matter is enlightening. He is not critical of their use of the hypothetical-deductive method as long as they are engaged in analysis and synthesis. There truly is no other approach to use when one begins from a hypothetical statement, from a problem which one *presumes* to be solved, that is, from a purely hypothetical, problematic solution and, as a result, which is stripped of being irrefutable truth. What Plato is emphasizing is that those who use this analytical method seem to forget this fact and instead operate as though they are proceeding from indubitable propositions. But have they ever asked themselves about their starting point, insofar as it should no longer be problematic if it is really to be an initial *truth?* This preoccupation also is the source of the idea according to which philosophy is research into ultimate principles, a concern which both Aristotle and Descartes addressed, although not as a real *question.*

Thus, when Plato speaks of geometry, he is truly recalling that "the soul is compelled to employ assumptions in the investigation of it, not proceeding to a first principle because of its inability to extricate itself from and rise above its assumptions . . ."[33] If we cannot avoid hypotheses, what can we do that we could not do simply by the use of geometry? "I mean that which the reason itself lays hold of by the power of dialectic, treating its assumptions not as absolute beginnings but literally as hypotheses, underpinnings, footings, and springboards so to speak . . ."[34] Basically, it is necessary to stay away from the hypothetical and refrain from working with it. Hence the necessity of dialectic, which seeks to combine synthesis and analysis rather than considering them as two *equal* possibilities for the deductive process. If we grant that analysis requires synthesis, due to the basic hypothetical nature of the analytical enterprise, then we have to assume this hypothetical in favor of a dialectic which allows us to operate in a way external to all problematicity. The starting point is ontologically distinct from a hypothesis; indeed, in many ways, it is its negation. Pure thought

33. *Republic* VI, 511a, trans. Paul Shorey, p. 746.
34. *Republic* VI, 511b, trans. Paul Shorey, p. 746.

functions outside of any question. Therefore, it embodies true knowledge, the stopping point in the gradual progress toward perfection.

If geometry is satisfied with hypotheses, it is because it is satisfied with analysis and synthesis, either of which it deems of equal worth for the deduction that it produces. For Plato, even if one must truly begin with a hypothesis, one cannot stay there. Analysis is not enough, because analysis *assumes* the resolution of the problem, phrased as a hypothesis.

Analysis and synthesis are not substitutable for one another. What, then, is their relationship? The answer to this question, one suspects, may allow us to understand the nature of the contradiction between the impossibility of having a knowledge that doesn't proceed from hypotheses and the necessity that knowledge have nothing to do with such alternatives. Problematicity cannot prevent errors and therefore cannot prevent the occurrence of nonknowledge.

Dialectic involves synthesis in addition to analysis. Synthesis aims at providing a *justification*—or a refutation—to one or the other of two contradictory answers assumed to be true, to one of two *propositions* where one must be certified as true against one which is not. The deduction produces consequences which also form the truth-conditions in this deduction (or rather of the principle upon which this deduction is based). This principle is verified by the fact that one has reverted to a proposition known to be true, from where the principle—but not its opposite—follows. The whole question, then, is to derive this principle from synthesis; otherwise, analysis cannot escape from the problematicity of its initial premise.

All this seems simple enough, at least theoretically, even if the application of this twofold undertaking calls for separate intuition in each specific case. Insofar as reasoning is concerned, neither analysis nor synthesis, nor their kinship, seems to give rise to any difficulty.

But can we be so sure? Let us examine things more closely. To verify, or assert as true, a proposition posed in the form of a hypothesis, it is necessary to deduce, by the process of analysis, the initial premise of the synthesis, synthesis which is the reverse of the usual order of analysis. If one cannot infer any proposition other than the one which supports the synthesis, the conclusion must be that synthesis is embedded in the analysis. It is logically inseparable from analysis, and Plato was right to raise as his objection against the geometricians that the two processes are not independent of one another.

But there is a high price to pay for this. It means, quite simply, that synthesis is, as sui generis, superfluous if not impossible. It does not exist by itself except as a mere convention or a mechanism of automatic inversion. There is in this reciprocal implication of the terminus a quo and the terminus ad quem a huge deductive circle, a petitio principii which remains in the last analysis (or synthesis) unverified, unless one sees them as equivalent propositions, since the interchangeability of A and of B amounts to a mutual implication. With synthesis impossible, it is dialectic, as Plato conceived it, which takes the full force of the blow and which cannot escape being drawn into the empire of the hypothetical. There remains, then, the mere claim of a difference: dialectic is not geometry because it *knows* it proceeds from hypotheses, while geometry, which in fact acts no differently, does not know it. How can this knowledge avoid problematicity? It can do so only by decreeing it: dialectic as such must be nonproblematical. Expressing the hypothetical character of geometrical thought as such would allow us to establish the opposition and thus to define dialectic. Achieving it, however, is another thing, and it is this which seems to have escaped Plato. Perhaps the key to the enigma is the very concept of *hypothesis*. This concept suggests a problematicity which is repressed into an answer (hypothesis as proposition), an answer which is itself not explicit as such. A hypothesis is therefore a basic concept of problematological indifferentiation, one which absorbs both question and answer into some neutral reality. Acknowledging a hypothesis as such means reflecting upon what mathematicians put into practice without confessing that they are doing so, namely that in order to know, it is important to repress questioning. This repression, if considered through the concept of hypothesis, then becomes a positive thing, for it opens up the realm of knowledge to a reflexivity which is ignored by the mathematician even as he uses it.

To be sure, there is another solution, in which synthesis is seen as independent from analysis. It is in fact imperative, if one wants to avoid circularity and make justification possible, to turn a proposition which is supposedly true into a true foundation. The synthesis which would have been part of this analysis would thus become redundant, and, if defined separately, conventional, ad hoc. This is, in effect, the reason those who have truly understood that analysis and synthesis overlap or mutually include each other have said that they are, at their base, the same thing. We are reminded of Aristotle's works, known as the *Prior* and *Posterior Analytics,* which in fact present this synthesis (that is, the syllogism). The syllogism is a way to get from the known to the unknown; we will return to this point. If Aristotle found this conflation of analysis and synthesis inevitable, Plato found it unacceptable; to admit it would amount to rooting synthesis in the problematical, when its goal was, in fact, to detach itself from any problematicity.

Let us now formulate the alternative hypothesis: analysis and synthesis are separate. What is the effect of that? We are left with a puzzle, since the ultimate consequence of analysis is *not* the principle of synthesis, that is, the reversal of the inference which has been analytically carried out. From what will synthesis thus draw its content in contrast to analysis? "If what happens in the analysis is a transition from the desired result to its *consequences* . . . , how can we subsequently invert the process and still obtain a series of valid conclusions, as Pappus' description of synthesis suggests? If *P* logically implies *Q*, it is not usually true that *Q* logically implies *P* . . ."[35] Ultimately, the supposed independence of synthesis will not allow us to claim that it is a justification for analysis, which was the original goal of synthesis. Superfluous in the first option, synthesis now becomes impossible in the sense that the paradox of questioning, as found in the *Meno*, makes it either unachievable or useless. And this is by no means the result of chance, since all the weight of the interrogative inquiry is implicitly, but intentionally, displaced onto the analytico-synthetic pair, just as Plato suggested when he called them the dialectic.

An autonomous synthesis would make very little sense if it had to support analysis to suppress the hypotheses underlying the analytical procedure. By itself, synthesis loses its own reason for being. Even more, the likelihood of verifying the conditions of analysis is very slight if this independence exists, if the starting point of synthesis is not determined analytically.

We are left with a paradox. Either synthesis is implicitly contained in analysis, or else it functions independently. If the first case obtains, hypothetical consequences are carefully selected for them to condition the synthetic decision. The whole process is circular; synthesis is not really useful as separate reasoning. Nothing different from what was admitted at the start results from this double movement. Thus, one *must* posit synthesis as differentiated from analysis, as self-sufficient, as capable of being undertaken for itself. But if one accepts this second case, it follows that one must see synthesis as having nothing to do, logically speaking, with analysis, and this raises the problem of its very possibility.

Put in other terms, the paradox states that Plato had to make synthesis and analysis independent to exclude hypotheses from analysis, and he could not do so because he could not conceive of the one without the other. If synthesis is based upon the results of analysis to confirm a

35. Jaakko Hintikka and Unto Remes, *The Method of Analysis* (Dordrecht: D. Reidel, 1974), pp. 11–12.

hypothesis, synthesis would remain just as problematic as its origin. Synthesis is useless *as synthesis*, since its very function is to let one escape from the hypothetical. Or, by contrast, synthesis is autonomous in that it is not automatically and directly the reverse of the order of analysis. Indeed, it is difficult to see how synthesis could be the proof of a hypothesis which gave rise to analysis, inasmuch as they are independent things. Plato's dialectic seems unable to go beyond the hypothetical-deductive method which it rejects in the case of mathematics. Given that fact, it is easy to see that it could not survive, since it doesn't answer the question which it assigned itself: on what grounds can the preexisting conceptual givens—termed "Ideas"—be considered valid?

It will be Aristotle who splinters Plato's dialectic. But Plato's rejection of questioning as originary or constructive will leave its mark on human thought for ever after, and neither Aristotle nor later thinkers will return to this originary conception. Even more, this fact will continue to be the basis and the driving force for the ontological metaphysics which we have inherited from the Greeks.

The fundamental mark of the philosophical lies in its indifference to problematology and the central role of questioning. To be so, reductors will have to be invented. Questions can be dealt with without being thought of as such. Beyond the criticism which can be raised against his dialectic, Plato carried out a devaluation of problematization simply by his discursive approach. He admits the hypothetical which was common in the science of his day yet at the same time rejects it on the philosophical level. He describes the hypothetical but does so in a discussion which overcomes and, in fact, kills it. The objection might be raised that Plato failed in this effort, but that was only a relative defeat, relative to a Platonic ideal of the complete elimination of the problematic. This ideal assigned his reflection an unparalleled positivity, even though it is that ideal which is the seed of its own defeat. Plato could not escape problematicity, and that produced some damage which needed to be repaired. We no longer even ask if this represents, at its heart, the essence of thought and of *epistemē*, the primary characteristics or primary quality without which they could not exist. In fact we have already noted the ambiguity of the concept of hypothesis, an ambiguity which places this concept completely outside of the sphere of thinking about questioning, that is, problematology.

Still, hypothesis is both question and answer at the same time, without any reference to these terms or to any distinction between the two. It is asexual, if we may use the term. Hypothesis thus takes part in analysis in that the latter wants to reduce through its own procedure what questioning must explain (according to Plato). Hence, it is part of the task of the analytico-synthetic to be in charge of this explanation by eliminating interrogativity in favor of pure propositionalism. For Plato, hypotheses exist to be eliminated as propositions-that-are-not-yet-propositions, propositions-in-waiting, as it were. These propositions are no longer expressed in terms of questioning in order not to have to confront the doxical—or what we would today call the subjective—and the paradoxical as one finds it in the *Meno*. The difficulty is thus completely circumscribed, and even if it were not, interrogativity has been abandoned anyway. What is left is a problematicity that is purely assertoric: a hypothesis is either true, or it is false. It can be either, so long as it has not been treated dialectically, but it still "asks" nothing. It exists outside the interrogative condition, which is completely contingent in this respect, and in the best of cases, pedagogical. We can recognize here what is to be regarded as positive in Socrates' way of proceeding. But for the rest, only truth counts: the truth a discourse has or doesn't have, about which someone *might ask* about on some occasion or another, but the answer will not affect this quality of truth that it has or doesn't have.

Beyond Plato's efforts, we may observe a successful displacement (or repression) of questioning by means of reductionist notions which are said to play the same role as questioning, but which, due to the lack of thematization of questioning, in fact end up displacing the paradox of questioning. We have seen the same thing in the case of synthesis as being impossible and/or useless in itself. Such a paradoxical displacement is inevitable insofar as its resolution would imply the explicit introduction of the problematological difference, and not its abolition in problematically unmarked theorizations that are, as such, external to questioning.

Analysis and synthesis play a key role in this regard, and not only for historical reasons, as we may imagine. They function as primary reductionist elements (or reductors) for the problematological. They were conceived of as problem-solving mechanisms well before the concept of resolution became synonymous with the analytical decomposition of a thing into its basic elements, or as synthesis in its turn became the recombination of these elements into a whole. In fact, analysis and synthesis became the reductors of the problematological difference, the one allowing us to find what the other would allow us to justify. But, by doing so, the two together conflated the quest with the question of justification. To discover something new is to be able to justify what has already been found, with little concern for the process of discovery. One may speak about the process itself, but only to reabsorb it into the whole as soon as possible. This is to say that justification and verification assign only a limited role to Reason, because they restrict it to propositions which already exist, so it matters little if such realms are called the "world of Ideas" or a "given." This enables us to recognize an identical process in a variety of different philosophies, where the same boxes must be filled to satisfy the systemic character of these thoughts, boxes which are each time labeled afresh, according to the internal features of the system.

In short, because it is necessary for propositionalism to think of resolution and the problematization of which it is the product, it is necessary to reduce the duality to something else, which will be indifferent to them, although it will need to have a similar function. This explains the gradual shift we have seen in analysis and synthesis, by which they deproblematize themselves, albeit ideally, as in Plato's dialectic.

It might be argued that geometry, which fails to recognize itself as hypothetical, and dialectic, which fully integrates this dimension, are, respectively, nonproblematological and problematological. Dialectic would thus be interrogative, not in spite of itself, but intentionally and positively, unlike mathematics. But this objection will not hold because it forgets that geometry, like dialectic, seeks to justify the assertions it puts forward. The concern is the same in both cases, but dialectic wants to eliminate problematicity by stating it and not by ignoring it. To concede hypothesis as the basis for all intellectual undertakings and proceed toward an (ontologically) primary and fundamentally nonhypothetical reality is to confirm the inessentiality and the casual nature of problematization. It is possible to be satisfied with that outcome, especially if we do not pay real attention to the role of problematization and if we fail to see that it is as unavoidable as the passage through the sensible for a soul preoccupied with the request for apodictic knowledge.

Because analysis and synthesis were the modes for both problematization and problem resolution for the Greeks, they had to be reduced problematologically. As modes of resolution, they had to be both grounds and structuring of the thinkable. Yet, they have been progressively reduced, either through de facto abandonment, as in geometry, or de jure, as in Plato's thought, and for a reason that is simple enough if we give some thought to it. From the start, analysis and synthesis have been practiced (even if not conceived of) with an underlying conception of questioning, even when they did not refer explicitly to it. Analysis presupposes a problem's solution, and that is enough to deal with the question. Convertibility and propositionalism characterize the basis of analysis. Indeed, we could even limit ourselves to speak of propositionalism alone, since the convertibility of a problem into a solution (or more precisely into a hypothesis) rests on the sovereignty of the proposition and of its reductive role. Plato did not have to reach very far to ground his dialectic in something completely outside its initial constitutive interrogativity. Still, analysis and synthesis remain ambiguous. It is equally true that Plato, at least as he expressed his intent, sought to clarify problematicity once and for all. Analysis is problematic in its starting point because it resolves a given problem and because it remains with this problem until the end (although all the while giving itself the opposite fallacious impression, due to its propositional convertibility).

We might have the impression that analysis and synthesis have served as reductors for propositionalism solely for historical reasons. After all, why them and not something else? Clearly, they do bring us back to questioning, but how do they do so essentially and not merely by accident? We may answer that if we face a problem, we can either solve it by starting from it alone or starting from something else. These alternatives are, respectively, analysis and synthesis, at least if we propositionalize them. And, as the problematological reminds us, it is essential to distinguish what is in question from its answer. If not, the result would be the fallacy of petitio principii (question-begging), where we assume what is in question as already solved, even though the answer is precisely what must be found. Inference—what Aristotle would call the syllogism, either dialectic or scientific—is no more than an embodiment of the problematological difference. A circular inference is no inference; it proves nothing about what it sets out to demonstrate. Analysis and synthesis belong to the class of inferences, or deductions. They aim to solve a question as no longer problematic, though without admitting at the outset as already solved what must be resolved. By being divorced from the problematic, analysis and synthesis, which are only differentiated by the way they embody the problematological difference, become indistinguishable. Aristotle will even call "analytic" his studies which really deal with what we would call synthesis. There will be nothing more than inference, a logic of reasoning which focuses on the propositional link as a theory of truth. After Plato's vain efforts to integrate them into a unified theory, analysis and synthesis are going to undergo an inevitable mutation. Aristotle will be the first to draw the conclusions which will be so essential for the future of philosophy. Before examining these in depth, it is worthwhile to comment briefly on what happened in this displacement expressing the historicity of questioning.

As we have seen, analysis and synthesis cannot be distinguished as inferential processes. When made strictly complementary to analysis, synthesis loses its meaning as specific. Analysis includes synthesis, that is, the verification that it is, not the invention it would like to be. Reciprocally, synthesis presupposes the existence of analysis; the two are in this way mutually equivalent. It is this which allowed Kant, in the *Transcendental Analytic*, to define the conditions of synthesis, hence of experience, in analytical terms. So understood, we can see this as a response to a question of justification, to the "*quid juris*" of the Transcendental Deduction, and that the thinking subject gains this answer in a "Copernican" manner, that is, by deducing from the reality of its own internal nature what makes this answer possible, as deduction and as deducible. There would be no possibility of considering experience by this method, which turns the subject, as such, back on itself, if the Analytic of the subject, operating on itself and by itself (that is, by the understanding) were not intrinsically synthetic. Understanding is forced to deduce itself as joined with sensibility.

In Descartes, we can observe another approach. Instead of emphasizing synthesis, the step from the known to the unknown (what Aristotle called a scientific syllogism), Descartes attacked it as sterile. He argued that it is capable only of verifying what is already known. In itself, it adds nothing and is no more than a simple expository device. It is *method* which is inventive. Not being synthetic, method is necessarily analytical. In giving new life to the analysis that Aristotle had absorbed into synthesis as related to science, Descartes established his discourse on method. The reason is that Descartes split off metaphysics from method to establish the validity of method based on some principle discovered in such a way as to put this method into play and make its autonomization possible relative to science. The method, then, will henceforth be able to use this authority.

What allows these thinkers to operate so freely and sometimes so contradictorily, as in Descartes, by putting all the emphasis on primary analysis, or, in Kant, by stressing the primary constitutive role of synthesis, is the ambiguous—even paradoxical—relationship between analysis and synthesis. Descartes wants to take Plato's side in accepting a redoubling of analysis and synthesis, which puts the emphasis on analysis and assures the redundancy of synthesis. Kant, for his part, agrees with Aristotle in assigning a synthetic character to the scientific procedure, which, with due respect to the assumptions of synthesis, must be intrinsically analytical. Might we characterize Descartes as the philosopher of invention and Kant as the thinker of justification? It might seem so at first blush. But in reality, both were working with a reductionist intention, that is, within a context of problematological in-difference. In fact, Kant spoke of the constitutive character of synthesis, exactly as Descartes did of analysis.

8. The Aristotelian Division of the Dialectic

Aristotle considered Plato's dialectic to contain two contradictory initiatives. If analysis is rooted in hypothesis, then it is essential that synthesis disassociate itself completely from analysis if synthesis is to find the kind of irrefutable justificatory value that is claimed for it. As a result, synthesis will meet the demand for scientificity, which, since Plato, is defined by placing the *logos* completely outside of, and cut off from, problematicity. This separation of analysis and synthesis entails a new understanding of what is meant by the term dialectic. Dialectic will become restricted to the field of the problematic. Since, like synthesis, analysis is an inference, in this regard they are no different; it is possible once again to call the study of synthesis the *Analytics*. A proper study of synthesis is nothing but syllogistics. Aristotle accepts the idea that analysis includes synthesis, or at least that synthesis leads back to analysis insofar as consequences are seen as inferred from positions taken for granted in both cases. What makes them different is nothing essential, because it pertains to the dealing with what is problematic insofar as it is problematic. Analysis and synthesis are redundant as ways of putting propositions in order, being undifferentiated (thus indistinguishable) on the only level that counts, and there will no longer be any form of differentiation between analysis and synthesis. The really radical distinction will be the link to the problematic, the hypothetical, which will be expelled from science. In contrast, where there is such a link, it will be dialectic, properly speaking; for Aristotle, it will be a dialectic which will capture what Plato wanted to isolate by his conception of analysis. But analysis could not be so isolated to the extent that it claimed to be scientific, and, in this respect, it could not be anything other than synthetic. Indeed, by this assessment, analysis, like synthesis, is a deduction of consequences in which only the propositional aspect is to be considered. Geometricians, so criticized by Plato, were among those who used the two techniques indifferently and who perfectly understood all of this.

Aristotle will then have to divide what Plato meant by dialectic. What was formerly analysis, because of its basic problematicity, will become what Aristotle would call dialectic. As a result, dialectic, for this very reason, could never be scientific (as Plato had claimed). Scientific analysis, on the other hand, will become identified with synthesis, that is, an inference based on necessity. Because he divided things in this way, Aristotle was compelled to construct a theory of what he called the dialectic and a theory of what he called scientific syllogistics: argumentation and science, respectively (to express them in more contemporary terms). What must be understood is that by making those domains autonomous, Aristotle took upon himself the task of becoming the theorist of what up to his time had required quite another kind of approach, in which the difference between science and rhetoric could not and had not been drawn. In summary:

> . . . the dialectic of Plato is always presented as a method leading to true knowledge, and is defined both as the art of asking well and responding well, and, on the other hand, as the art of both collecting and dividing in the realm of Ideas . . . The definition of dialectic which Aristotle puts forward puts an end to all hesitation . . . As a result, there no longer is anything in common between the search for truth and the dialectic.[36]

Let us proceed further into the examination of knowledge to which Aristotle has led us.

The syllogism is a synthesis, which means that it requires that we start from the known to determine the unknown; at least in this sense Aristotle can claim to have resolved the paradox of the *Meno* with his conception of the syllogism:

> By demonstration I mean a scientific deduction . . . If, then, understanding is as we posited, it is necessary for demonstrative understanding in particular to depend on things which are true and primitive and immediate and more familiar than and prior to and explanatory of the conclusion . . .[37]

In short,

> Before the induction, or before getting a deduction, you should perhaps be said to know it in a way—but in another way not . . . Otherwise, the puzzle in the *Meno* will result . . .[38]

Just because a conclusion follows naturally from certain premises does not mean that it is known as such. Likewise, knowing the premises which lead to a conclusion does not mean that one necessarily knows the particular conclusion which may result from them.

36. Octave Hamelin, *Le système d' Aristote* (1920), p. 230, cited in J. M. LeBlond, *Logique et méthode chez Aristote* (Paris: Vrin, 1973), p. 6 [author's translation].
37. *Posterior Analytics* I, 2, 71b18–22, trans. Jonathan Barnes; vol. 1, p. 115.
38. *Posterior Analytics* I, 1, 71a25–30, trans. Jonathan Barnes; vol. 1, p. 114 [translation modified].

For one should not argue in the way in which some people attempt to solve it. *Do you or don't you know of every pair that it is even?* And when you said Yes, they brought forward some pair of which you did not think that it was, nor therefore that it was even. For they solve it by denying that people know of every pair that is even, but only of anything of which they know that is a pair.—Yet they know it of that which they have the demonstration about and which they got their premises about; and they got them not about everything of which they know that it is a triangle or that it is a number, but of every number and triangle *simpliciter.* For no proposition of such a type is assumed (that *what you know to be a number* . . . or *what you know to be rectilineal* . . .) but they are assumed as holding of every case. But nothing, I think, prevents one from in a sense understanding and in a sense being ignorant of what one is learning . . .[39] (Emphasis added)

What is the point of Aristotle's argument? The goal of a demonstration is not knowledge or its extension. In fact, it cannot even refer to knowledge since what one individual knows is only relative and is different from what others know, while demonstration has a universal implication. Here lies the basis of a separate domain, the *ratio essendi.*

The great ambiguity of Aristotle's reasoning is that in spite of himself he pretends to describe the extension of knowledge, an extension he forbids himself even to refer to as if he were only referring to the "in-itself." The paradox is even more striking when we see the "synthetic" vocabulary of the scientific syllogism resorting to a term like "better known." In truth, we find in Aristotle a concept of scientificity which reflects the conflation of the knowing process with justification. This matter has often been commented upon:

> . . . the theory of demonstrative science was never meant to guide or formalise scientific research: it is concerned exclusively with the teaching of facts already won; it does not describe how scientists do, or ought to, *acquire* knowledge: it offers a formal model of how teachers should *present and impart* knowledge.[40]

Demonstration is an inference, a syllogism, but, as we have seen, a syllogism of a particular kind, since not all syllogisms are scientific. Dialectic also proceeds by inference. We cannot accurately say that dialectic constitutes the knowledge that demonstration develops, since there is a

39. *Posterior Analytics* I, 1, 71a31–71b8, trans. Jonathan Barnes; vol. 1, p. 115.

40. Jonathan Barnes, "Aristotle's Theory of Demonstration," in *Articles on Aristotle*, ed. Jonathan Barnes, Malcolm Schofield, and Richard Sorabji (London: Duckworth, 1975), vol. 1, p. 77.

radical gulf between dialectic and knowledge. That is because what characterizes *knowledge* is the absence of all problematicity, right from the very start, as it were. That is why everything is already known, once the premises are supplied, as is the case with scientific syllogistic. By contrast, dialectic never does rid itself of its initial problematicity, and, for that reason, never will be fully assimilated with a science: their heterogeneity is truly radical.

But the opposition no longer is, as it was for Plato, simply problematicity versus nonproblematicity. The very idea of the elimination of the former and its replacement by the latter is repressed as being out of the question. The result is a new conception of discourse, namely ontology, where plurality represents the many potential answers to a question, and where univocity reflects the unity of the true answer which will focus on *the truth*. From then on, this univocity will correspond to a reality of its own, just as movement reproduces the ontologized plurality of Being. *What is ontology if not a discourse in which the opposition between problematicity and nonproblematicity has been eradicated ab initio?* This is how ontology is marked off from science and dialectic, although it is always related to them. Indeed, Aristotle does include some reference and even some study of problematicity (in contrast to Plato). This would seem to make my position regarding the establishment of ontological discourse appear contradictory. But the fact that one can read the opposition between science and dialectic as that of the problematic and the nonproblematic compels us to go beyond such an opposition, by resorting to the ontological framework.

In science, Aristotle tells us, ". . . one cannot ask questions when demonstrating because when opposites are the case the same thing is not proved . . ."[41] Science will have nothing to do with alternatives, with problems where there is a debate between pros and cons. Rather it establishes the truth of a proposition by demonstration, precisely without any alternatives, by starting from indisputable facts. By contrast, dialectic is "a line of inquiry whereby we shall be able to reason from reputable opinions about any subject presented to us . . ."[42] Dialectical reasoning rests on questioning, and the proposition for debate is posed because it depends not on the true but on the probable, or even on opinion (*endoxon*), but surely not on knowledge: ". . . it is a dialectical deduction, if it reasons from reputable opinions."[43] Science, in fact, prohibits just the kind of inherent contradictions which charac-

41. *Posterior Analytics* I, 11, 77a33–35, trans. Jonathan Barnes; vol. 1, p. 126.
42. *Topics* I, 1, 100a20–21, trans. W. A. Pickard-Cambridge; vol. 1, p. 167.
43. *Topics* I, 1, 100a29–30, trans. W. A. Pickard-Cambridge; vol. 1, p. 167.

terize dialectic debate: ". . . if something has been demonstrated it cannot be otherwise—the deduction, therefore, must depend on necessities. For from truths one can deduce *without* demonstrating, but from necessities one cannot deduce without demonstrating; for this is precisely the mark of demonstration." [44] In science, it is impossible not to concede the conclusion of an inference. Necessity is nothing more than the propositional version of the elimination of alternatives, hence of all possible problems, and that is done at the very level of the premises.

Confronted with Aristotle's texts, we cannot escape the impression of finding there the distinction which Plato claimed to have eliminated. He failed to do so because he failed to distinguish science from dialectic by its opposition to problematicity. Reading Aristotle leaves an equally strong impression that he wanted to go beyond the distinction between problematicity and nonproblematicity through ontology, just as Plato thought himself able to do by his dialectic, which was also ontological. Is this not at least an ambivalent, if not contradictory, position for Aristotle?

Actually, by isolating within dialectic that which Plato could not, Aristotle at least gave himself the ability to address the two problematics. We could add that he had to theorize them. Thus he developed syllogistics on the one hand, rhetoric on the other, and went on to ontology to capture them both. Here a question arises: why ontology, if both interrogativity and its absence in science (although seen as positive and resolutional) have been made possible by the Aristotelian break with what Plato labeled the field of dialectics?

The answer to this question may be summarized as follows. Aristotle could not maintain the separation of science from dialectic. Problematicity will be no more than a system of answers disguised in the interrogative form, while nonproblematicity will not do without interrogation to impose itself, since the goal of science is to eliminate alternatives. The positivity of science is an ideal which was born outside of it. This total rupture proved untenable, even though necessary, since the movement from the problematic to the nonproblematic must be conceptualized in one way or another by any theorist who wants to create a valid theory of science. To accomplish this, discursivity must become central, since science as much as dialectic affirms propositions. Aristotle had no other option than to reimpose what Plato had done in regard to the anhypothetical. Plato, as will be recalled, decreed the existence of the anhypothetical by simple complementarity to the hypothetical. What it is and how one might have access to it were tricky

44. *Posterior Analytics* I, 6, 74b14–17, trans. Jonathan Barnes; vol. 1, p. 120.

questions, to be sure. But with the anhypothetical analytically embodied within the problematological in-difference as expressed by the concept of the hypothetical, Plato could play on hypothesis as resolutional, even if hypothesis never referred to questioning, and as a result could only be an answer, even though it never answers. Aristotle preferred ontology to this ambiguity, thanks to which every possible problematological duality could be expelled—a more radical stroke, to be sure, but identical in spirit to that of Plato. Ontology, primary and general, thematized as such, would be to questioning for Aristotle what dialectic had been for Plato.

The relationship between science and dialectic brings to mind again the duality of the problematic and nonproblematic. This duality disappears in the generalized ontology of propositionalism, which erases all reference to interrogativity. But in that, another difficulty emerges, none other than the reappearance of the paradox of the *Meno,* now left without a solution. All that which is *affirmed,* is, and in multiple ways. Only "multiple" is a superfluous word here because the propositional *logos,* in its origin, rests on the necessary exclusion of all possible alternative propositions. This is the origin of the idea of constraint, of necessity, conveyed by the *logos* in what it considers as assertability. With Being as pluralistic, discourse is freely able to pronounce that which simply is, that which is by accident, and that which a thing may become, merely by being other. The *logos* loses its apodictic character, because discourse is no longer limited to stating what is the case as *necessarily* being what is, thus excluding the alternative proposition as false, a proposition that must be rejected if problematicity is to remain absent from the *logos.* Problematicity, rhetorical debate, and contingency reappear as possibilities for discourse. The variety of meanings for the term "being" allows a whole range of differences to be expressed, rather than excluding one another for the sake of one *logos,* one "answer." The result is a fragmentation of both discourse and reason. A proposition which is set forth can coexist with the others that are possible on the same topic, without any need to prevail over them. By contrast, where there is a single decisional foundation, there is a unique being from which the unity of Being follows. A situation is created where, on a given subject, only one proposition is valid, and necessarily so, since no others can apply to the same entity at the same time. The unity of Being is the being-subject which underlies the process of predication. But is being truly a subject, exclusively a substance? In this regard, ontology is caught in a trap from the outset and doomed to fail; and that constitutes its original condition of impossibility.

On the one hand, Being may be multiple, scattered among various categories, including discourse. Discourse which states what *is* does so in a pluralistic way, contrary to a concern about unity, unicity, and necessity, of which propositional *logos* wants to be the embodiment. Nothing prevents one affirmation from freely opposing another, yet each of them, despite their opposition, remains propositional. Or, on the other hand, Being may be a single entity transcendent and separable from its different incarnations. This conception assures the unity of the *logos* and provides a foundation for *logos* to be what it is. This entity is the foundation, the principle, and, in this way, it provides the *logos* with apodicity. In fact, we speak here of "Being," rather than of beings. No more problematicity if the alternatives have to be decided by an eradication based on ontology. Being cannot be multiple and yet must be so; as such, it cannot be, yet it must be. Being, for propositionalism, is both necessary and impossible at the same time. It is impossible because dialectical multiplicity, problematicity, has to be propositionalized without being reduced to the *epistemē*, as in Plato. Being as such is necessary because this very multiplicity must be eradicated as well. Ontology is the answer to the question that suppresses all other questions, and whether it is asked (as in Heidegger) or not asked changes nothing as to the basic, initial contradiction within the ontological approach.

9. The Question of the Principles of Thought: Has Aristotle Succeeded in Rendering Deduction Autonomous?

The autonomization of the epistemic which Aristotle undertook necessarily reopened the question of the principles of thought. For Plato, a scientific point of departure was both necessary and merely preparatory to arriving at philosophical truth, because one must eliminate the hypothetical nature of the hypotheses by some initial awareness of this problematicity. But this development was already part of dialectic. The movement from the hypothetical to the anhypothetical is a preliminary stage for the dialectician, the one who truly knows. The search for a true starting point, rather than simply a methodological one, carries us toward a supreme, even a theological idea, which for Plato was the Good. From then on, philosophizing was always identified with a search for a true starting point, something above and beyond what science or the sensible world can reveal, something pertaining to what will be called metaphysics. But what is striking in this is that since the time of the Greeks the starting point as such has never been inquired into. Even further, it is as though the starting point was meant to avoid

questioning, to eliminate alternatives and institute apodicity. The starting point is foundational precisely to the extent that it is completely
outside the domain of questioning. Since such an eradication still refers
to questioning, it is meant to suppress it, only the anhypothetical can a
priori satisfy the query. There would be no need to go outside of the
hypothetical if the hypothetical were not the perfect manifestation of
problematicity, the knowledge with which "imperfect" sciences like
geometry are content. These sciences are characterized as imperfect
not because of their results, but because of the conception of knowledge which they implicitly reflect. Such a reflection, which pertains to
the realm of the metaphysical, has, of course, no impact on the results
themselves, since this reflection presupposes them. What is certain,
however, is that it is impossible to maintain such an attitude. The *question* of knowledge is *ontological,* not epistemic, in nature. Reasons, considered to be the reasons of things, are essences, *their* essences.

For Plato, the approach to the starting point is made through analysis. Access to the anhypothetical is only the result of the analysis which
opens up the true foundation of things as the synthetic condition. If
synthesis is separated from analysis, the question of the starting point
arises again. But here again the starting point is considered only as a
means to preclude questioning from arising, not to aid it. The beginning must be known unproblematically, and that requires a *psychology*
which teaches us the passage from the sensible particular to the universal, which is the intelligible. The principle of synthesis functions
as a principle only as it provides logical structure for this process. It is
only with synthesis that this principle is highlighted. It represents the
result of a heterogenous, sui generis, and different cognitive process,
but it is also the product of an initiative which places it ultimately in
first place by what might be called a process of reconstruction. But even
autonomous synthesis cannot derive its own principle from itself.
There is no access to it at the outset, because the principle is one
only with regard to that which follows. Thus it comes at the end,
because it is only in view of an entire series of steps that we can
know which among them was the first. The principle is first only in
regard to that which it follows. Paradoxically, it is necessary *first* to
know what follows before being able to say what comes first. A principle only justifies what follows from it but cannot justify *itself* through its
consequences. Therefore, it is less a final result than a condition of that
result.

The foregoing may appear to involve a contradiction: synthesis goes
back to the analysis upon which it depends, whether one tries to dis-

associate them or not. For Aristotle, the only way out is to see that there are two distinctly different orders, that of knowledge and that of ontology, the *ratio cognoscendi* and the *ratio essendi*. What is first in the order of essence is last in the order of knowledge. A principle can be a result, but only to the extent that it results from a different intellectual procedure. There are two types of principles[45] because the principle which underlies an inquiry that results in positing the principle of synthesis is not itself part of the synthesis. One can still wonder how, given these conditions, we can find synthesis, the *ratio essendi*, cut off from analysis, from the dialectic, which in truth it cannot do without if it is to arise at all. *Affirming* autonomy is not enough to create it. It is here we can see best how Platonism has been able to become a historical model. Plato, in fact, presupposed problematological indifference as a criterion of answerhood in that he failed to assume the interrogativity of the mind and by that failed to provide explicit access to answerhood. Aristotle, on the other hand, in decreeing synthesis to be self-supporting by virtue of a specificity that makes it autonomous, thought he was paying sufficient attention to the necessity to separate the inseparable. But it proved to be not enough, for, as will be shown, the difficulties will arise once again.

How should we think about this scission of thought, the *ratio cognoscendi* and the *ratio essendi?* Is it not well known that synthesis, which characterizes the latter, can provide knowledge, even though it is opposed to the "order of reasons?" That assessment is essentially correct, because, as Aristotle reminds us, all references to states of knowledge must necessarily be absent from the demonstrative syllogism. How then can we say that it is the role of synthesis to take us from the known to the unknown? And, if truth only exists at the level of the *ratio essendi*, are we in the realm of nontruth at the preceding level? "But in

---

45. ". . . the things that are prior in formula are different from those that are prior in perception. For in formula universals are prior, in perception individuals." Aristotle, *Metaphysics* V, 11, 1018b31–33, trans. W. D. Ross; vol. 2, p. 1609.

Moreover, "Things are prior and more familiar in two ways; for it is not the same to be prior by nature and prior in relation to us, nor to be more familiar and more familiar to us." *Posterior Analytics* I, 1, 71b34–72a2, trans. Jonathan Barnes; vol. 1, pp. 115–16.

And, "The natural way of doing this is to start from the things which are more knowable and clear to us and proceed towards those which are clearer and more knowable by nature; for the same things are not knowable relatively to us and knowable without qualification." *Physics* I, 184a16–19, trans. R. P. Hardie and R. K. Gaye; vol. 1, p. 315.

that case," Aubenque tells us, "is it not ironic to speak of a starting point that is no more for us than a barely perceptible reality, and to speak of a cognizability as such that would not be a cognizability to anyone?"[46] The dilemma is clear: either knowledge exists in both the *ratios,* or it is the exclusive province of one of them. In this latter instance, we have the *ratio essendi,* which is made up of accumulated knowledge, and the *ratio cognoscendi,* which is no more than dialectical, noncognitive, and rooted in the plausible and opinion. Or the other way around: the *ratio cognoscendi* is knowledge, and the *ratio essendi* is not. The latter case is excluded, as in the hypothesis of a *ratio cognoscendi,* which would not be conceived of as knowledge of what *is,* since knowledge could then only be demonstrative; that, Aristotle refutes as well. We are left with the first position, which states that knowledge exists as two orders, the analytic and the synthetic. We are reminded of the passage which opens the *Physics,* where knowledge is defined as the movement from what is better known *to us* to what is better known *in itself.* But here, too, there are unsolvable problems. Synthesis leads us back to analysis, from which it cannot be separated. The ambiguous role of the dialectic remains unresolved in its reliance on opinion and probability. Truth and opinion are concepts in opposition to one another, as are the problematic and the nonproblematic. Thus synthesis would have to provide a lesson in universality which, as Aubenque says, would literally be universal for no one. The *ratio essendi* cannot do without the *ratio cognoscendi,* which it postulates, but from which it must be radically cut off, since the nonproblematic cannot rest upon the problematic. Aristotle would have liked to have been able simply to decree that these two orders had nothing in common, but when examined, they proved to be tightly interwoven. The *ratio cognoscendi* is both superfluous and yet necessary to the other, and is both cognitive and noncognitive. It resolves nothing to simply say that "the universal creates knowledge by itself," since Aristotle, more than anyone, believed the universal to be separable from the particular. In short this redoubling, which seems to be the only acceptable solution, can hardly prevail since, once more, the nonproblematic fails to have the autonomy that Aristotle would accord to it.

Let us consider for a moment the ambiguous role of dialectic. What does Aristotle say of it? He says that its utility is to offer its premises to science: ". . . it is impossible to discuss them at all from the principles proper to the particular science in hand, seeing that the principles are

46. Aubenque, *Problème de l'être chez Aristote,* p. 65 [author's translation].

primitive in relation to everything else; it is through reputable opinions about them that these have to be discussed, and this task belongs properly, or most appropriately, to dialectic."[47] Logically, Aristotle could not affirm that truth proceeds from opinion, given that there is an irreducible qualitative gulf between them. Aristotle said it well: it is a difference in their very natures which separates them.[48] Given this, why argue for the contrary? The answer is simple: analysis is implicit, and implied, in synthesis, hence the necessity to divide up the *ratio*, despite the impossibility of making that happen. If we had to specify how interrogation allows us access to the premises of science, we could say that it is by the elimination of alternatives and the emergence of a correlate that is out-of-the-question. It matters little that this correlate comes from a contradictory debate or an *aporia*, based on subjective judgments, because, as we would express it today, the result is one answer that is adopted to the exclusion of all others. The difference between dialectic and philosophy, which, after all, does produce some originary knowledge, is that the latter is unopposed in this purely theoretical debate.[49] The problem is rooted in the *nature* of things and not in particular and subjective differences. The aporetic demands the diaporetic, that is, inquiry into a particular problem through the contradictory nature of its responses. This dialectical method is found as well when we come to "demonstrating" the principle of noncontradiction, the most fundamental principle of all. Such a principle cannot be demonstrated, since it would have to assume itself throughout the demonstration. This vicious circle, the *petitio principii*, or question-begging, presumes that the answer is given in the asking of the question, which would render the question superfluous because it would not really even be a question. It is significant to note that for Aristotle, this vicious circle was characteristic of the propositional realm and did not truly translate itself into terms relevant to questioning. This circle undermines syllogisms and inferences to the extent of actually making them impossible. For there to be inference, it is necessary to distinguish premises from conclusions. This is the origin of the famous definition of syllogism, a definition that seems so obvious that is problematological roots remain unseen: "A deduction is a discourse in which, certain things being stated, something other than what is stated

47. *Topics* I, 2, 101a38–101b2, trans. W. A. Pickard-Cambridge; vol. 1, p. 168.
48. For further discussion on this topic, see LeBlond, *Logique et méthode chez Aristote*, pp. 44 et seq.
49. *Topics* VIII, 1, 155b10, trans. W. A. Pickard-Cambridge; vol. 1, p. 261.

follows of necessity from their being so." [50] Syllogisms only exist because they are meant to embody (and resolve) the problematological
difference. Suppressing the latter produces question-begging, since
nothing other than the premise would result from it except itself, dupli-
cated. The additive character of synthetic knowledge is a result of the
difference between question and answer. To avoid having to ground the
synthesis in problematicity, Aristotle thematized the inference as a
propositional relationship, even in his dialectic. This leads us to question the status of dialectic as a displaced conceptualization of interrogativity.

10. Is Aristotle's Dialectic a Theory of Questioning?

If, by a theory of questioning, we mean that the author talks about interrogation, then the answer is clearly yes. Aristotle, by this definition,
would have presented a theory of questioning. But if questioning is to
be something more than disguised propositionalism, then I fear that
Aristotle merely perpetuated problematological in-difference in the
theoretization of dialectic which he presented. We might even say that
Aristotle was forced to address the topic of interrogativity, to make it assertoric, since he could not do without an analysis involved in synthesis.
By one of those great historical confusions which sometimes are part of
philosophy, we often read that Aristotle, along with Plato and Socrates,
is a "great questioner" and that Aristotle is a believer in the "motive
force" of questioning. To agree to that assessment would require that
we ignore this sentence from the *Sophistical Refutations*: "Any method
which seeks to show the nature of things does not proceed from questions." For Aristotle interrogation is purely negative and refutational;
and, since dialectic cannot be only that, it cannot be merely interrogative. Besides, what come first are not questions but opinions which
raise, or do not raise, questions. "A dialectical problem . . . must . . . be
something on which either people hold no opinion either way, or most
people hold a contrary opinion to the wise, or the wise to most people,
or each of them among themselves." [51] Questions are born from dis-
agreement; we have just been reminded of the modalities. But if all
questions presuppose a "probable thesis," as said in the *Topics*, then
theses answer nothing. The thesis must be first, or else it leads to a regression into an infinite cycle of questions. In the beginning was
the proposition, the answer which answers nothing. In short, ". . . no
one in his senses would make a proposition of what no one holds, nor

50. *Prior Analytics* I, 1, 24b19–20, trans. A. J. Jenkinson; vol. 1, p. 40.
51. *Topics* I, 11, 104b1–5, trans. W. A. Pickard-Cambridge; vol. 1, pp. 173–74.

yet make a problem of what is obvious to everybody . . ."[52] Even in the constitutive function of dialectical interrogation, we depart from a prior assertion. The questioner—because such is his role—takes on an answer which, if it resists or if its opposite collapses, will find itself accepted. Questions which are posed function as premises in regard to preestablished conclusions or, more precisely, prediscovered ones. They operate regressively, analytically, regarding those initial theses of which they are the consequents. "Opposite [to science], rhetoric and dialectic correspond to an inverse thought process: they work back from the conclusion to its premises. Indeed, in rhetorical argument or dialectic, one really knows the conclusion in advance . . . And thus it is a matter of finding . . . the premises, that is, the propositions from which can be developed the conclusion already known."[53] Such question-premises can only be reconverted propositions. Even more, the questions are only rhetorical in regard to the answers that are already at hand. We should not be surprised that problems and propositions enjoy the convertibility and interchangeability so dear to propositionalism: "The difference between a problem and a proposition is a difference in the turn of the phrase . . . Naturally, then, problems and propositions are equal in number; for out of every proposition you will make a problem if you change the turn of phrase."[54] A question, a dialectical proposition, comes down to being a true or false proposition, and the goal is to establish one or the other. Questions exist only as propositional alternatives. What is the essential nature of a question which refers it back to an alternative propositional content, where the sole purpose is to obtain a yes or no answer about this propositional content? The function can only be justificatory, or perhaps refutational (which amounts to the same thing), to the proposition contained in the question. What is asked is either a validation or an invalidation of the position; there is nothing else to be found. Knowledge is not knowledge unless it is the result of a process of validation, of justification. Therefore, only propositions (as results) are essential, and their emergence within the dialectical process is nonessential, provisional, and contingent. The dialectic, oddly, is measured by the yardstick of science—odd not for us who have seen the origins of this reductionist attitude, but odd for those who see in the dialectic an "erotetic" process, or as Aristotle says in his *Sophistical Refutations* (II, 171a18), an articulation of questioning which is interrogatively reflected in itself rather in terms of the neces-

52. *Topics* I, 10, 104a6–7, trans. W. A. Pickard-Cambridge; vol. 1, p. 173.
53. Pierre Hadot, "Philosophie, dialectique, rhétorique dans l'antiquité," *Studia Philosophica* 39 (1980): 145 [author's translation].
54. *Topics* I, 4, 101b28–35, trans. W. A. Pickard-Cambridge; vol. 1, p. 169.

sity that abolishes it. Is it necessary to express interrogativity in terms
of alternative choices, since contradiction is a propositional concept?
Aristotle has rightly said that we must either affirm or deny; it is clear
that questioning is finally no more than that, or at best preparatory to
that. What to do, then, about the difference which is unceasingly
affirmed between the propositional, where the idea of truth is central,
and the dialectical? The latter does not demonstrate anything, does not
refer back to propositions, but requests one proposition: where is it to
be found, how is dialectical reasoning different from that of synthesis,
and why does it not refer to preestablished propositions? Affirming that
". . . one cannot ask questions when demonstrating . . ." because all
recourse to *aporia,* to opposed concepts, is self-forbidden (*Posterior
Analytics* I, 11, 77a33) is to conclude rather too quickly that nothing
is asked in a scientific inference, a point which the test of circularity
refutes. The commentators agree, then, that the dialectic is only secon-
darily interrogative.[55] What really matters is propositional treatment,
the validity of the propositions contained within hypotheses. This
has no other significance than being able to define as an alternative a
proposition whose predicates might be different from what they are
now. The concept of difference here is the master-term, or what serves
the same purpose, that of *identity.* Contradictory predicates produce
contradictory propositions; but where some predicates are merely *different,* they quite simply render a proposition unnecessary. Here the difference is enough to put into question (the truth of) a proposition since it
permits the possibility of another proposition. Thus the answer is not
unique, which is to say that the question is not resolved, that it continues to be posed. An alternative arises from the only difference between
possible predicates of a given subject. That implies a duality, which the
exclusivity of truth towards that which is not truth (in this case, falsity)
will not permit. Dialectic tries to make a choice, as does science, to establish a proposition; the proposition is the *terminus a quo* and the *terminus ad quem* all at once. "Propositions should be selected in as many
ways as we drew distinctions in regard to the proposition . . ." (*Topics* I,
14, 105a33). This fact clearly bears upon the meaning, the acquiring,
and, above all, the identity and the difference which cover the whole
realm of the dialectic (*Topics* I, 13). If we think of the proposition-
problem equivalency, we find that syllogistic reasoning becomes that
which unifies them through indifferentiation. The syllogism involves
implicit analytics, with the additional differentiation between alterna-

55. Aubenque, *Problème de l'être chez Aristote,* p. 255; LeBlond, *Logique et méthode
chez Aristote,* p. 26.

tive and necessity. One does not just question, one reasons, and *therefore* questions.

> Now the materials with which arguments start are equal in number, and are identical, with the subjects on which deductions take place . . . every proposition and every problem indicates either a genus or a property or an accident—for the differentia, too, being generic, should be ranked together with the genus.[56]

These four rubrics represent variations in difference, differences of being, differences of possible attribution. Definition, and the property of a thing, are reciprocals of the subject, substitutable terms, as in "what is decent is beautiful" and "man is a being capable of learning grammar," neither of which is a definition. Other attributes might attach to the subject in a variety of degrees, like its genus, which pertains not only to this subject but to others, or the accidental, where it is the opposite thing which might pertain to the subject. Thus definition is "mostly concerned with questions of sameness and difference" (Topics I, 5, 102a8–9), and "all the points we have enumerated might in a way be called definitory" (Topics I, 6, 102b34–35). It seems clear that it was subject-predicate interaction that is, the process through which the propositional is the "erased answer" which so preoccupied Aristotle. Being is the intrapropositional link. Difference, in the modalities discussed above, reduces or reabsorbs the problematological difference. The difference is ontological. In the separation of the *ratio cognoscendi* from the *ratio essendi,* we see the uncoupling of being from knowing, disassociated but incapable of so being, paradoxically forever linked. The four modalities of apocritical differentiation will be modes only for the characterization of answers, for the treatment of questions. They will treat answering, which, since it originates in something other than questioning, eliminates itself as such, in a discourse which unifies the metatheoretical and its object in the neutrality of an indifferentiated and self-sufficient *logos.* Dialectic, like synthesis, will ontologize itself, but in fact is dialectic not synthetic in a way, just as, and just as much as dialectical analysis is, that is, without any possible disassociation?

Before we turn to ontology, we need to return again to the dialectic of principles as used in the establishment of the principle of noncontradiction. What is the significance of this dialectic for problematology? Let us recall that it is a matter of being able to show, if nothing else, that though we cannot demonstrate it, this principle is irrefutable. That can

56. *Topics* I, 4, 101b13–19, trans. W. A. Pickard-Cambridge; vol. 1, p. 169.

be shown by refuting all possible refutation. Aristotle said that in opposing the principle of contradiction, one verifies it. The important
thing, for our purposes, is not to know if Aristotle was right or wrong.
For instance, we could counter his argument by saying that what appears to be inconsistency in his opponent's argument is in fact that person's very strategy. What counts here is that the principle, which states
that one *must* either deny or affirm, has no other justification than its
own insurmountable repetition. Dialectic, therefore, has had precious
little result beyond confirming propositionalism in what can be considered as one of its most ungrounded aspects. We might have hoped that
a validation—we no longer even try to speak of a demonstration—of
the principle of noncontradiction would itself render it dialectical,
thereby showing it as related to questioning, and then establishing it as
a principle of answerhood. In fact, we must acknowledge that, if the
principle can only prevail because of its dialectic roots, it is because it is
itself dialectical in nature; it is the principle *of* the dialectic, for it marks
off the opposites in stipulating how they are to be treated. And yet no
problematological relationship has emerged, which once again proves
that dialectic is just a form of propositionalism; science is another. Thus
there is no interrogative foundation for this principle, which can only be
grounded when such a foundation exists in questioning. Nothing is left,
then, but to offer the irrefutability of its own refutability.

As to problematological indifference, we have already seen its impact on the entire field of dialectic in reducing a problem to a proposition, itself reduced, in its potential contradictariness, to variations that
are themselves signs of alternatives (and therefore questions), since
there is no longer any unique answer. Genus, definition, property, and
accident can all work to achieve that reduction. We can also see an anal-
ogous initiative at the level of *categories*. "It is characteristic," says
Aubenque, "that Aristotle designated categories by interrogatives."[57]
In fact, if we refer to the ten categories of Aristotle, we find that six of
them are expressed in interrogative form, even in the Greek, and all of
them, in the last analysis, correspond to interrogatives.[58] Action, for
example, corresponds to the question "What did X do?" Charles Kahn
reminds us that it was Ockham who first noticed this fact when he
identified it as the form of the ontological question of what the subject
is, that is, the problem of its essence. In short, categories serve to ask
questions, before they ever function to characterize the modes of pred-

57. Aubenque, *Problème de l'être chez Aristote*, p. 187.
58. Charles Kahn, "Questions and Categories," in *Questions*, ed. Henry Hiz (Dordrecht: D. Reidel, 1978), p. 227.

ication, before they ever function in any sort of assertoric manner. This is the origin of the coexistence, which we find in the *Topics*, between, on the one hand, categories, and on the other, the modalizations of identity of which we spoke earlier. The latter, which treat a variety of questions, constitute marks, origins. On the other hand, because *the* answer suppresses the plurality of answers, the differential, it is essential that we find new marks of substitutability in discourse. A category is an instantiation of such a marker: it assigns an area of univocity which is tightly circumscribed within the generally equivocal and pluralistic *logos*.[59] Given the growing role of ontology, which is going to take over the articulation of these two orders in their paradoxical interrelationship, we can observe an ontological shift of the categories, as Kahn so clearly pointed out. Both *the unity of being and the fact that being can be expressed in so many ways*, truly unsurpassable in their plurality, thereby making impossible a positive ontology (Aubenque), *cover the duality of propositional plurality and propositional identity, that is, respectively*, of the problematic and its judicative suppression. Dialectic, which has no real object of its own, and because of that can deal with any subject, will be replaced by ontology in its full generalizability. This will have the advantage of moving the irreducible opposition of the problematic and nonproblematic to a level where it will no longer matter: is being not the common element of all things, indifferently? The unity of being henceforth will carry all the weight of the apocritical decision, which will then be repressed as an answer to a specific problem. I say "which is repressed" with full intention, for the question "What is X?" will now carry with it all of the impossibility of philosophizing about philosophical questioning when something external to it is used which will not be part of an interrogation reflected as such. Propositionalism reigns supreme, both over dialectic and over science, and ontology will be essential to unify the propositional order.

The question of being, which was for Aristotle the question of the essence, will be seen in the gap in the Platonic dialectic between synthesis and analysis. This question is said to be first among all others, but how to resolve it without presupposing some sort of difference, which would allow us to say that we are speaking of X rather than Y? This distinction between essence and fact is found in the typology of questions which opens Book II of the *Posterior Analytics*: the *that*, the *whether*, the *why*, and the *what*. These are the four possible alternatives: the *that* (*oti*) which originates in an initially given propositional fact that the *why* (*dioti*) justifies through a proposition; the *if* (*ei esti*) establishes the

59. Ibid., p. 229.

proposition which the *what* (*ti esti*) determines. In other words, the "what" answers what is asked, always, but it is possible, even if more indirectly, to confront the propositional choice (the "if") and to do it (the "that") by establishing one proposition rather than any other proposition (the "why").

It is not the essence of X which comes first; there is a lot to know about X before we can even try to say what its essential nature is. The Socratic question, the being of X, is primordial only with regard to a movement of inversion. That explains why it is a presupposition in that second (or derived) order. Meta-physics is *prima philosophia* only within an intellectual universe that separates *being* from *knowing*. This is a separation that is difficult to assume, for how can we posit being without relating it to an order where affirmation and knowing occur at the same time? And on the other hand, how can we imagine that one *knows* something that *is* not? Thus the debate, eternal and absurd—because completely ill-stated—about the priority of being over knowing (there is a being of knowledge) and the reverse (being does not exist in itself); once one attempts to affirm this, one refutes oneself.

Let us go a step further. What is being asked when the question "What is X?" is put? Nothing requires that what must be, or can be, provided is what Aristotle (and others) called the essence. To generalize, being is no more than this absolute movement of presupposition, which is empty and which corresponds to nothing but this movement itself. In that event, questions about the being of things, or about "Being," must be understood as requiring the suppression of the problematological, a displacement which certainly reveals it, though purely formally, and only as an absence. As to questioning itself, it was already no more than a mere part of the Aristotelian dialectic.

11. From the Question of Being to the Being of the Question

We conclude this chapter on the dialecticization of interrogation, which, in the last analysis, was no more than the first step in its repression as and for ontology. We have already seen that Aristotle isolated the question of being by placing it within a movement of synthesis, where it is effectively but artificially first. We have also noted that analysis and synthesis have distributed themselves thoroughly in science and philosophy. We might have thought that ontology, in its general sweep, would capture all in its global approach. What we have instead, with the *ratio essendi*, is an autonomization of the realm of the ontological. And that is knowledge. What can the *ratio cognoscendi* make us know? What it must do, it cannot.

The famous distinction between "beings" and "Being" is far from contemporary. It is nothing other than the product of the division of the two *ratios*. It is because they cannot coincide that "being" for the *ratio essendi* can never be completely identified with the factual knowledge provided by the *ratio cognoscendi*. There would be no ontological difference if Being were but the product of some *a posteriori*. Then to affirm that Being lies at the core of all affirmation is to ignore the movement which led to synthesis, to reversal, where the last becomes first. If we overlook ontology's occupation of the terrain of synthesis, ontology being itself a victim of the answering-as-a-norm imposed on dialectization (perforce analytical in the geometricians' sense of the word), we risk committing the same type of error as did Plato and Heidegger. Their analysis was this: to diagnose an illness in someone, it would be necessary that I have prior knowledge of the illness, or to orient myself in the present, past, or future, I would have to know what time is. But, as St. Augustine clearly told us, it is in fact the opposite which occurs. We could continue this line of reasoning: do we have to know questioning to ask questions? Clearly, that is absurd. Common sense quite rightly prevails over philosophical pretensions reduced to ontology, saying that one does not need these so-called prior elements of knowledge about what X and Y are to deal with them. Prior knowledge of this sort is prior only to philosophers who are detached from reality by their preoccupation with ontological concerns. An atheist can be a good geometrician, just as a carpenter can be extremely knowledgeable about wood, whether or not he has thought deeply about wood's essence. How can we hope to persuade our carpenter that the opposite is true when facts run counter to the ontology that seems to have been identified with philosophy by our contemporaries? It is at this point, I think, that thought about philosophical fundamentality loses its credibility, becoming instead an intellectual artifice, and a sterile one at that. This is because, for many years, we have been mistaken about what is fundamental.

Let us look more closely at the question "What is X?" Nothing in it stipulates that it is a question about essence rather than anything else, for example, about a particular but identifying characteristic of X. What are we asking when we ask the question "What is X or Y?"? Let us consider an example before embarking on an investigation into the formal structure of this question. What is literature? In truth, that is quite a good question. However, it does not specify the type of answer needed to answer it. The proof is that with such a question, one can be asking a variety of things, for example: What renders language literary? What conditions must be met to make a particular work literary? What is the effect produced by what we call literature? And so on. Clearly none of these questions exhausts the literary field, but each might represent what the questioner wanted to know when she first asked the question. Whether the question is about a certain type of language, or an effect, or a corpus of literature is of little importance. Perhaps even the very essence of language can be found embedded in this or that answer. But there is no a priori assumption of what *the* answer should be when we confront the formulation "What is literature?" let alone a request for an "essence." This question does not say that such an essence exists, or if it did exist, that it is what is being asked about. One can certainly think it, but then the presupposition would be that Being or essence is the object of the question "What is X?" Such a presupposition would be something out-of-the-question, that which renders it rhetorical. This is truly the function of ontology. Questioning is closed by and upon the essence; it has been that way since Aristotle. But let us recall that essence cannot be demonstrated. For, as we have seen, to demonstrate it is to confirm the problematological difference, although in a propositional manner. This will be the conception of inference, where nothing of the problematological can be found, a conception which Aristotle will codify and which will prevail for two thousand years. Noncircularity requires the "other thing" which is found at play in the syllogism, but why, in a deduction, is some "other thing" required rather than the same thing? No one has answered that question, even though many authors, from Descartes to John Stuart Mill, have endlessly repeated that there can be nothing else in the inference of a conclusion than what is posited in its premises. So be it. What we want to emphasize here is that a propositionally reduced inference gives a false conception of inference. Inference cannot be explained as a mere propositional link which would be purely assertoric.

Essence is undemonstrated because it is the subject of the inference, which is out of the question in the questioning to which every syllogism refers us. If not, we would have to fall back on a *petitio principii*, or some question-begging process. That is why essence, thus subject-matter, is out of the question. But it is also that which permits a question, or in this case, a syllogism. The circle is closed: essence both conditions and determines what a question will be. What is a matter of debate, even if contradictorily so, is attribution. Thereby we have the famous codification of propositionalism: a judgment is made up of a subject and a predicate which identifies it (its being), and *logos* will no more, as in Plato, be made of a mixture of ideas. The unity of Being, which is expressed in so many ways, will be reduced to its essence, as Aristotle pointed out in the *Metaphysics*.

Inference will become the key connection because of the general propositionalization of the problematological difference. Dialectic, like ontology, will be under the rule of the syllogism, making more enigmatic than ever the schism between the analytical and the synthetic. Plato was unable to distinguish clearly between analysis and synthesis. The former includes the latter, even though the two must separate for synthesis to verify analysis; hence the unifying role of dialectic. Nor could Aristotle do much better. Certainly, he was able to codify dialectic rules and syllogistic forms, but that proved insufficient to render valid his problematological reduction, indeed, his indifference to the problematological. This in-difference to problematology was decreed in and through an "elsewhere," where it never was mentioned. There is inference in argumentation, just as there is learning in science. Both the best and least known are dialectical concepts which the syllogistic must employ to work synthetically.

If there is truly a neutral universal question with regard to its possible answer, it would be the Socratic question. Any other question comes with limiting presuppositions, implied by their possible answers, whereas the question "What is X?" can make its answer coincide with its presupposition, namely that X is this or that, which is precisely what we are really asking. This suggests that such a question presupposes nothing, so that any answer will work, or else that the question points to every possible presupposition analytically, as Kant maintained. We can affirm that one question is primary with respect to all others, including the one where the presupposition is the answer, just as we may be entitled to say that this questioning is empty, literally *indifferent* to what resolves it. It is thus primary, but synthetically so; it is logically primary, even if ontology ends up occupying the whole synthetical scene from Plato, or at least from Aristotle, onward. Being and knowing are going to be very difficult to separate despite efforts in that direction, including some current ones which seek to isolate ontology in a more radical way.

What must be remembered is that the radicalization of ontology was already initiated by Aristotle. For Plato, analysis included synthesis. It is hard to see what would allow synthesis to prove the analytical approach, unless analysis could a priori interact with its inversion, that is, with synthesis. Otherwise, synthesis would be miraculously able to verify something which was affirmed as independent. But synthesis cannot function by itself, which Plato understood when he tried, admittedly without success, to group both analysis and synthesis under one heading, dialectic. Aristotle could not find an escape through reseparating them, although he quite justifiably assimilated synthesis to its analytical counterpart. The separation of analysis and synthesis is what allows us to avoid the contradiction inherent in the two points of departure. But this separation does not help us much in understanding the distribution of knowledge in two forms, which never do appear to be distributed. Aristotle made synthesis strictly ontological, and, in so doing, enclosed analysis therein. Being is everywhere. Therefore, the unity of Being will be enigmatic, because it is expressed in so many ways: in plurality, hence the analytic dialectization, and in unity, thus synthesis, which makes possible the constraining inference of the demonstrative syllogism. The opposition between the problematic and the nonproblematic is thereby displaced, reduced, or to put it more accurately, ontologized. The *ratio cognoscendi* is no longer correlative to *Being,* but rather, in preparation for its connection to truth, will be in contact with *beings.* At least that is the appearance, or the appearing, if we want to be generous in speaking of these phenomena. The major ontological dualisms were established by Aristotle. Synthesis and analysis will multiply and create thereby endless dichotomies. They can be found in science as well as in reasoning in general. Ontology, starting from the Socratic question "What is X?" will become synthetic above all, subordinating to itself an implicit analytics, which it deploys according to its needs. This conforms perfectly to the evolution of ontology: the question of Being quite exhausts the being of the question; every question comes down to this eventually. Ontology must lay the foundation for synthesis, for otherwise synthesis would have an irresolvable problem of finding a starting point. Besides, synthesis is incapable of making itself autonomous. It can only hark back to its alter ego, which it wants to be externalized. Once again we are confronted with the inability to undo the analyticization of synthesis, unless we do so by means of a decree. Ontology was the ultimate effort of the Greeks to achieve the impossible.

The analysis of the question of being impels us toward essence as ultimate meaning. The price for this once more is a form of problematological indifference. When we identify a specific difference, it is, by purely internal critical processes, evidence of an obstacle to overcome. The multiple aspects of Being, its *polysemya,* must result in unity, but Aristotle, as we have seen, could not conceptualize that unity. Recourse to ontological transcendence remained the only path open, but in following it we have shifted the difficulty to God.

The question of Being does not refer to *ousia* except by some preestablished imposed reading of the question, the origin of which we have discussed. The only valid reading for a question like "What is X?" is that Being denotes the plurality within answerhood as composed of possibilities of answers, a priori inscribed in the fact that there is a question. Being defines the unity of the question by the plurality of its answers, expressing the difference between question and answer as the problematological difference. Ontology is a transformation of this reading, which sticks closer to the question as such without assigning it, from outside, a role *which it does not have.* Being is the operator of the questioning of the problematological difference. It does not force us to reach essence, for no one answer more than any other is *required* by the Socratic question, now become ontological because of the impossibility of reflecting questioning as such.

As for Being itself, it cannot be questioned in isolation without, as a question, being referred to questioning, which, by so doing, it would cease to abolish. That implies a reversal of ontology, a reversal we have called "problematology."

Three

From Propositional Rationality to Interrogative Rationality

1. The Crisis of Reason

Western reason is in crisis. It can account for everything except that it must account for everything. Rationality is a value, the very standard of all values, the "categorical imperative" par excellence. However, rationality, as a sort of moral requirement, is not supported by any kind of necessity, since it has become the foundation of all necessity. But this foundation is now once again put into question, since the evidence of what is rational, which is our heritage from Descartes, has lost its foundational fecundity. In fact, we now speak of the death of the subject, and that subject is, precisely, the "Cartesian subject," the *Cogito*, whose function had been to be the out-of-the-question of *all* possible questions, serving as the absolute, radical, and universal key to resolution. The ethical field arrives at its full completion with Kant; Cartesian prudence remained external to it.

Once the Cartesian subject is put into question, rationality is attacked at its very heart. Because it lacks the roots to enable us to think of resolution (and of questioning) as such, rationality is problematized in its entirety. It becomes a deductive, propositional rationality that rests the assertoric role of reason on some fundamental assertion, such as the *Cogito*, that verifies the content of its assertion through its own assertability. The result is that we are immediately plunged into the realm of the propositional, which reflects its own closed nature by the irrefutable evidence it provides itself.

Descartes is truly the thinker whose analysis lies at the core of our rationality and its fate, including the final break with the model of reason which we now face. If the crisis of the foundational has destabilized our heritage of rationality and steered it toward certain ends and the use of sui generis modalities, it has not altered the fundamental assumptions of the traditional idea of reason, even if it has deconstructed it. Clearly this type of thought, as it is now defined, is simply marked by a minus sign, instead of being truly overridden by an awareness of its own deficiency.

The example provided by science and its technique illustrates the point. The crisis of reason is nothing other than the crisis of the subject. That we have no foundation to unify our conception of the world does not destroy this conception, but it does fragment it. Science without a subject, like the dehumanized ethical norm, is going to be able to triumph unopposed and without having to account for anything except its own assurance. Internal rationality, now fragmented and autonomous, still will be legitimated through efficiency, because it will no longer have to rely on anything other than itself. Just as in the *Cogito*, it imposes its own norm of resolution without having to relate that norm to any external totality, where an internal, but global, norm is lacking. The new rationality will be analytical in the sense that it will concern itself with the deconstruction of problems without any concern for their reintegration into something larger which can give them meaning.

What does such a tendency toward general fragmentation mean? First, it gives the illusion of unity to reason because it suggests that *all* reason can be characterized this way. The image is a paradox; its internal content contradicts the intended vision. If everything pulls apart, breaks itself into distinct and autonomous pieces, into rules that have only selective application, then we can no longer speak of a normative *model*, except in the very assertion of this breakup. "It is necessary to go all the way, to ask whether the ultimate outcome of all this is not a new step in the Reversal of the rational into its opposite. A new step, to be sure, but of the same kind? Or new, because of its irreversible nature?"[1]

And there is a second observation: the crisis of reason necessarily leads to overrationalization in every field. The fragmentation of the thinkable corresponds directly to the abandonment of a single norm of resolution. Thus we have flexible and adjustable resolutionary models that emerge from close adaptation to their objects. Thought becomes manipulative: trial and error becomes necessary, linked to the reality of objects, because thought fails to have a unique, preestablished standard of rationality, which could always be false because it cannot adapt itself a priori to the particular requirements of each situation. In this way, thought becomes *technique* regarding its object, while it *theorizes* itself as *science*. Indeed, by being unable to go beyond verificational behavior, rationality strips itself of any propositionality which is not reduced to

---

1. Dominique Janicaud, *La puissance du rationnel* (Paris: Gallimard, 1985), p. 41 [author's translation].

tested scientificity as embodied in the atomized and analytical relationships which so typify science. The problematization of the thinkable, experienced as a negative feature of thought, impels us toward a scientific overcompensation, based on assumed technique, since science guarantees each new result one by one, but without any concern for, or any necessity of, a global reflection. Therefore, science becomes the implicit norm of rationality and of the thinkable at the same time, because science is the perfect embodiment of the analytical nature of the mind, and because science, in the last analysis, does achieve a sort of unity by default, creating a limited model of resolution which functions satisfactorily because components are isolated and analyzed into parts. Scientificity is really the substitute for, and the displacement of, thought that lacks a first principle, and for which it becomes the implicit principle, the norm which imposes itself without being able to justify itself, but also, and above all, without *having* to do so.

The dilemma we face is this. On the one hand, we may reject science and open the door to irrationalities of many kinds: religious, political, or even purely theoretical ones. Or we may accept as fact a generalized scientificity and the necessity of the technical and the operational, and thereby close the door to all reasonable rationality (in the proper sense of the term), knowing that the rationality in such an enterprise cannot provide a foundation for itself and therefore is self-defeating. As a consequence, whichever path is chosen, whether partial overrationality or irrationality plain and simple, reason is no longer foundational of anything, not even of itself. Technical performance, the fact that something "works," is raised to the same philosophical level as, for example, religious dogma.

The ambiguity of the position of those who reject science today, even where they do so to cover up a cultivated ignorance, arises from the fact that in trying to find an originary rationality, they condemn its most fully developed form. That suggests the question of whether this rejection leads to obscurantism or, quite the contrary, compels one to fight against it. The choice between these two solutions walks a fine line. The criticism of science often is joined with a celebration of "something beyond" which is thinkable but must be left unsaid, often restored on behalf of values purely and simply asserted to be valid in terms of a tradition historically experienced as prerational (and therefore as antirational). All of this follows because of the inability to devise a new space for rationality within which a proposition, even a scientific one, would have its place and its legitimacy, at a specific and different foundational level, one that would be nonpropositional and nonassertive. For the assertoric cannot ground itself, and even if it were thought that it could (with and since Descartes), it could succeed in so doing only in a hidden way, through some problematological inference, as will be seen hereafter. Reason will become problematological, or will not be; only such a conception establishes the assertoric on a foundation by its integration into interrogativity, consecrating the assertoric as apocritical, which refers to the problematological, resolving it through differentiality. Propositionalism results in the impossibility of any overcoming, and in so doing leaves no way out other than the implicit or, worse, the irrational, though it claims to be its inverted norm and to embody universalism. And that is the problem: if Western Reason seems to have run out of options, it is because it has always functioned based on its own assertive character, of which, as Descartes argued, it reflects its own internal evidence.

In truth, we assert only to answer, and no assertion of any sort can emerge by its own assertability, as though it answered nothing but its own necessity of existence. Every assertion answers a question within which it originated. The mind progresses only by asking itself questions, and not by deductively rationalizing results which result from nothing, since they "resulted" only from themselves. Indeed, where would the beginning point be, if every result had to be derived from another one, and it from another? Reason would receive no other support than from some self-imposed starting point. God being "dead," we are left with nothing more than an irrational chain of reasons, where we can account for everything *within* the chain, but not for the chain itself, that is, the *initial* necessity of the structure itself. Thereby the whole edifice is undermined.

Reason, when conceptualized as a justificatory propositional chain, cannot ground itself, and that explains the crisis which inevitably occurs when critical attention is brought to bear on the originary, the foundation, for the historical reasons which we have traced. The weak point of Western rationality is its starting point, since what grounds it has to remain ungrounded or "grounded" only in itself. The crisis of reason which we observe today is nothing more than the crisis of *one kind* of reason, that is, assertoric reason, the assertoric as the exclusive model of rationality, an assertoricity that had to impose itself. The assertoric homogeneity which has characterized the thinkable since the rise of Greek philosophy was bound to be in crisis from the moment that the basis of the assertoric, which reflects its asserted universality, was revealed to be problematic. As a result, the problematic is the ineffable of the assertoric order.

Reason has closed itself off through its generalized propositionalism, condemning as irrational any solution which tries to respond to this radical, and inevitable, internal crisis. When Western rationality was unable to integrate the problematicity that was its fundamental determinant in a positive way, it could only break apart when confronted with problematization as a historical fact. Problematology, on the other hand, brings to light the rationality of the rational. It illuminates its very structure, even when rationality finds itself cut off from its roots and replaced by a superstructure built upon itself, qualified as autonomous. The explanation of nonassertoric fundamentality is the only answer to this crisis of the subject, because this crisis breaks the equation between the rational and the propositional, emptying a rationality reduced to assertoricity pure and simple. It shows that the Cartesian question, as a question about foundations, must be reasked, for its own sake, and as such, that is, as a *question*, to adequately position reason and thought with respect to the assertoric schemes of which they are only one part. Descartes is not only the originator of a model now in crisis, but he is also the one who first provided the example of radical questioning, though expressed in the terms of the initial assertoricity which he had always bestowed upon reason. It was a kind of questioning which, though repressed, is nonetheless present. The Cartesian approach certainly responded to a foundational crisis of his time, and it still shows what must be understood by the term "a philosophical foundation," and thus has impact beyond its obsolete conclusions.

2. The Cartesian Crisis and Its Contemporary Heritage

The crisis of reason is above all a crisis of the consciousness as the locus of absolute and originary reflexivity, which has finally absorbed the whole *logos*. We could have believed, or at least hoped, that the opposition between negative metaphysics and neopositivism had been overcome and that we were on the path to a new contemporary philosophy emerging from the resolution of their antithetical perspectives. In fact, despite the vocabulary employed, we have seen nothing of the sort. Certainly a lot of things have happened since the positivists faced off with the nihilists, the latter believing that all solutions—including science—were impossible, the former convinced that science was the only hope. What remains from this double flight, and what has implanted itself into contemporary thought, is a crisis of principle, of the status of humanity, of the subject as such, indeed a crisis in Western rationality and its possibility of progress. The assumed view of rationality (assumed because it was unable to describe itself as a conception) which has prevailed is an incomplete model which nevertheless has been universalized into every level of everyday life, as well as into the sciences. It appears global, but only because it is affirmed as the *only* model possible. As a parochial and pragmatic rationality, technically adapted to the mastery of a *given* end, it can only be an ideology. It can never claim to be *the* rationality, even though it effectively functions as though it were. Therefore, the false impression persists that a certain kind of positivism is still alive, when in fact, from a philosophical point of view, it is dead. Positivism's specificity was precisely its expressed wish to pass for an explicit codification of *the* global rationality, as it claimed it should be.

In sum, it is the assertability of reason which appears to be impossible to globalize. However, contemporary thought has felt compelled to turn a negative into a positive, to build from this historical handicap a constitutive characteristic; the absence of principle somehow became a position of principle, diversity became a treasure, the originary subject nothing but a trace. Fuzzy and metaphorical language became the essence of the *logos*. It seemed to follow the saying, "If you can't avoid it, at least make the best of it."

It is clear, however, that this enterprise cannot hide the shaky foundation of pure contingency on which it is built. It seeks to pass off accidental traits as necessary ones, to put forward what results from an outdated and now negated state of affairs and to present this negation as though it were the constitutive part of our very being. Thus the fact that the ancient source of thought, Man, is dead, means neither that the quest for a first principle is vain or impossible, nor that Man is but a trace, the affirmation of emptiness, a void. These terms, as an ahistorical expression of a certain stage in our history, do not express what we are in reality.

Concepts such as these have emerged from the death of Cartesianism. These concepts use an apparent positivity to cover up the impossibility of going beyond that which is already past, of filling what has become empty reality, solely by turning that emptiness into the very positivity that is to be recovered. The emptiness is, in turn, due to the lack of principle. But it is paradoxical to continue to work with categories which we know to have become inadequate by trying to turn a lack of relevance into a substitutive relevant feature. It is paradoxical to say that a certain conceptual reality no longer functions and then to perpetuate the lack of reality by claiming that the lack *is* the reality. How can we both claim that the foundational subject cannot be addressed any longer, and then make of this feature the very essence of anthropological discourse, if not of human reality itself? Do we not persist in thinking in the same terms as before, but inverted?

The *trace* of the originary, for Derrida, works just as well as the originary itself: it produces itself by obscuring itself and becomes its own effect; displacement becomes creation. The inadequacy of the originary to itself, as measured by the *logos* of the originary, is another old idea of propositionalism which can be found as early as Descartes, since the *ratio cognoscendi* cannot establish as first what is *really* first. Hence the analytical regression either to the innate or to an a priori originary which can never be conceptualized without gaps as well as an everlasting inadequacy. Is it not quite simply an insurmountable contradiction to want to declare the death of Cartesianism, while in the same breath overcoming that death by stating that the subject is a trace of itself? Is this not justifying what has been avowed to be unjustifiable, namely that the foundation *is* anthropological? Derrida himself recognized this problem, although he rejected the criticism because it would rest upon a requirement of identity and coherence:

> For example, the value of the transcendental arche [*archie*] must make its necessity felt before letting itself be erased. The concept of arche-trace must comply with both that necessity and that erasure. It is in fact contradictory and not acceptable within the logic of identity. The trace is not only the disappearance of origin . . . it means that the origin did not even disappear . . . From then on, to wrench the concept of the trace from the classical scheme, which would derive it from a presence or from an originary nontrace and which would make of it an empirical mark, one must indeed speak of an originary trace or arche-trace.[2]

Without concepts such as *trace* or *différance*, what translates is the subject's distancing from its own statements, from discourse itself, so that it becomes impossible to conceive of the subject as if it were still the master of (its own) discourse as an expression of itself. The *différance* is this shift, this vain effort by the subject to recover the subject, endlessly postponed and different in the movement of discourse regarding this originary. The subject will be uttered and referred to in an endless chain of literal signifiers, in a network that displays it and, at the same time, distances it from itself.

Lacan says it this way: "The signifier is what the subject represents for another signifier," an expression famous for capturing the sense of the gulf between the subject and itself, of alteration by exchange, of which the stage of reflection is the true beginning. How can the subject insert itself between the "I" of discourse and *itself?* Perhaps as it does in Barthes, where the subject no longer adheres to the text, where it is only the mouthpiece and not really the author in the theological sense. Lacan makes of the subject this empty presence, a rupture which

2. Jacques Derrida, *Of Grammatology*, trans. G. C. Spivak (Baltimore: Johns Hopkins University Press, 1974), p. 61.

makes man no more than a symbol, whose signifier is cut loose from any fixed relationships to the signified, and replaces it. Hermeneutics, therefore, must come into play. The subject, set apart from itself, has to wear a mask, establishing its identity through repression of the other that it is as well. Identity is gained at this price, and the condition, if not the result, is the unconscious. The rhetorical difference with oneself is thereby repressed; it is rhetorical because its identity is only figurative and not literal. The logic of the "I" regains control by this trick of self-deceit, which an individual plays on himself, creating a logic of identity which is the logic of *its* own identity. The lack is nonidentity, the mark or the sign of the dethroned subject. But are we really just little Cartesians, afflicted with an Oedipal complex toward a Cartesian father figure? Are we not rather a problematicity which no answer of any sort can completely absorb?

Cartesian reasoning was only able to survive by exclusion, by guaranteeing itself a monopoly in its field (if one believes Michel Foucault). For this sort of reasoning to be dominant, it was necessary to exclude madness, which is the out-of-reason par excellence, and also to exclude all those who reject the rationality of the social order, of all who fail to adhere to the moral norms which proceed from Reason. If we admit the existence of the insane person or the sociopath, we admit that there is abnormality. Human sexuality illustrates the arbitrariness of such a conception of normality, while at the same time showing it to exist.

Certainly the philosophical movement that made human subjectivity nonfoundational is larger than Derrida, Lacan, or Foucault. It is seen in destruction of the ancient harmonies, for example in music or painting, which have become more abstract than ever.[3] It is the death of form in poetry, as with Mallarmé, Eliot, or Pound. It is problematization of prose, which decenters narration, depriving it of any privileged position

3. "Paul Klee himself makes the link between painting and music. He calls his dispersed attention that can attend to the entire picture plane 'multi-dimensional' . . . and also 'polyphonic.' This too is a good name . . . The musician like the painter has to train himself to scatter his attention over the entire musical structure so that he can grasp the polyphonic fabric hidden in the accompaniment." Anton Ehrenzweig, *The Hidden Order of Art* (Berkeley: University of California Press, 1967), p. 25.

The fragmentation of totalities breaks the gestalts and the relationships between form and content, the unity of the point of view, and the unity of the "subject": "The claim of melody to represent the conscious gestalt of music is seriously challenged in favour of a more profound reasoning. Serialization discards every remnant of an identical sequence . . . The identity of temporal sequence as the principle of an acoustic gestalt is paralleled in vision by the identity of spatial distribution. It is difficult to recognize an object if it is shown upside down, almost impossible if the spatial relationships between its elements are scrambled up. But this is precisely what happens in Picasso's portraits and in his arbitrary conglomerations of the human figure." Ehrenzweig, *Hidden Order*, p. 34.

capable of delineating a precise beginning or end, presupposing a total-
izing subject (as the "nouveau roman" illustrates). Enigmaticity becomes the very object of fiction, as in Kafka. Consider the story *The Test,*
where a servant is finally hired for *not* having answered his employer's
questions, indeed, for not even having understood them. This lack of
comprehension is precisely what gets him the job. This is an interesting
allegory of the affirmation of problematicity as a new positivity, an allegory of Kafkaesque absurdity, if we still follow a scheme of thought
which cannot deal with problematicity without falling into a contradiction, resulting from problematological indifference.[4] This is the origin
of so-called absurdism which arises within propositionalism as the impossibility of conceptualizing the problematic in its positivity, because
the latter is irreducible to an assertoric order.

What is certain is that *logos* seen as generalized propositional assertability is going to find itself under fire because of this crisis of reason.
The answering process will increasingly become a problem, though un-
recognized as a problem. The object of fiction is not thought of as such,
even if it brings something into play. Answering, when it becomes its
own object, gives rise to the question of language and, to put it in a nut-
shell, begins the twentieth century. If neopositivism is an epistemology
without a subject because it is purely logicist in spirit, it is structur-
alism which favors linguistics by inserting the subject within a tight network of differences, of signifieds and signifiers. Myths no longer have
any individuality or any authorship whose identification would provide
the meaning. Meaning comes instead from the relationships between
myths, each a signifier of all the others. The subject is not the origin of
symbolism but exists within symbolism, where everything in its structure refers to everything else in an interplay of differences. The subject
is structured as part of a network which defines the subject as having a
meaning; in itself, it means nothing. Subject, in its own nonidentity,
becomes just one difference among others in a generalized system of
possible differences.

Heidegger had already abandoned the idea of subject with his *Dasein.* But it is important to note that Being, as I have shown, is a problematological operator. It opens a question to a multiplicity of answers
and to the identification of *the* answer. Ontology obscures the problematological and does so precisely because it finds "difference" where no
difference exists. The question *on* the question of being, seen from the
perspective of human possibilities or through the history of so-called

---

4. For more on this point, see Michel Meyer, "Kafka: dilemme et littérature," in
Annales de l'Institut de Philosophie de l'Université Libre de Bruxelles, 1985.

conceptualizations about this question, is nothing more than what we have called the question of problematization. This question itself is negated because it is Being which links questions (in their multiplicity and possibility) to answers (in their real unity and identity). Heidegger's thought arose in an era of intense problematization, of the defundamentalization of subject as a way of defining a new thought that went beyond both humanism and the primacy of the subject. With the growth of problematization, it was natural that answering would give rise to the question of what answering is, in this case to the question of being (before truly tackling language, the very *Sprache*), to try to preserve the Aristotelian ontology which puts an end to all interrogativity with a neutral and a neutralizing displacement. Ontology so considered, but no longer positively practiced, is the expression of a problematization which grows but which does not reach the point of being thematized in and for itself. This is because to question being is indirectly to repress the question of the problematic itself, by using the traditional means of reducing it to the order of answerhood and language without having to inquire into in its underlying interrogativity.

Answering will also become, for Heidegger, an inquiry into language. Answering will become more and more its own object in all traditions of thought, including both the Continental and the Anglo-American. Discourse becomes its own referent in literature as well, where we see it in the fictionalization of the fictional, the appearance of the "book within a book" (Borgès), of the reader within the book who alters the text by becoming a part of it (Calvino). Answering which thematizes itself does not do so as such, since questioning continues to be subjected to the Platonic condemnation. This is why this thematization of answering arises at the very heart of the propositional order which it disrupts. Ontology will be seen as the expression of something beyond Cartesian subjectivism in being the thought *about* ontology which cannot be carried out by ontology itself. We may see in this ontology-as-rupture the Heideggerian response to the crisis represented by the German defeat of 1914–18. But answering which reflects itself is language which becomes its own object as an activity. Is such activity reducible to the propositional? Will it still be possible to limit the utterance of discourse to its mere results? The propositional is falling apart: from the spoken, one moves to speaking, to the act of speaking, and so to the *fact* of putting forward a proposition. In evolving from the statement to its utterance, we have unquestionably abandoned the simple realm of the propositional, though without coming to grips with answering itself, that is, by referring it to the foundational moment of questioning. In so doing, however, we introduce the distinction between reason and proof:

the reason (or motive) for speaking is distinct from the proof of what is said; "*what* is said" refers us back to an order of causes which are grounded in the object, in contrast to the reasons (or motives) found in the subject. Here it is important to see clearly the essential connections which exist, in spite of what appears to be autonomy. This displacement refers to the subject who makes the statement; it thus focuses on the notion of intentionality. Discourse is now seen as an act, an action, an activity. The names of Searle and Austin are usually associated with this new conception. But the mere fact that the main focus is put on the motives for speech, on the question of "who is speaking?" to explain the meaning and the validity of what is said, will call to mind a certain Marxist attitude, which evokes the name of Althusser. Furthermore, the simple fact of considering motives rather than proof will also trigger the renewal of rhetoric in the twentieth century, first with Perelman, and later with Ducrot. It would be a mistake, in the name of opposition and differences of various kinds, to refuse to see what all these approaches, however distinct, have in common, and that is an identical base, a response to the same fracture in the foundational identity (Fichtean, to be precise) of modern subjectivity.

The death of the subject means that man is reborn as something else, gaining, so to speak, a new identity. The fact is that the subject became something other than itself, as seen concretely in rhetoric, in semiotics, in the rupture of causality as experienced in the emergence of nonconstraining reasons; the result is that we now see the subject *as* rhetorical, as a source for enunciation, as the locus of reasons in contrast with a chain of irrefutable proofs. The subject will become rhetoricized, in the larger sense of the word "rhetoric." It will become what it *is* by each time being *something other,* and therefore what it is not, a consciousness directed upon its objects rather than itself, a sort of self-unconsciousness, always running itself against its own presence in an order of language referring to something other than the subject itself. The subject ceases to be foundational, and one can speak of it more easily, beginning precisely from the fact of speaking. Reflexivity loses its primacy, to the benefit of the operational. Its ability to be something else, to be temporalized in its opposition to itself, and change as such (A becomes non-B after having been B)—all of this suggests a basic idea, the problematic, the alternative (B or not B), the fact of being able to respond to what one is through the assertion of one's constitutive problematicity. Thus, we can have an A which is B *and* non-B, insofar as it is revealed to itself through the alternative embodied in the problematic.

The question of what we are to ourselves includes all alternatives, all the possibilities of being something other than what we are now. Is this, therefore, the way to understand the rhetoricization of the human, as an answering process which expressly imposes itself? This subject which is itself while not being itself cannot be taken literally for what it is; one can simply figure it out. It is the very trope, the source of all tropism. It is located by relating it to the propositional order itself as *being* the fracture of that order. It *is* just that. Ontology, the destruction of ontology as a historical reading of its eternal impossibility, the *Dasein*, the relentless inadequacy to itself, discrepancy with itself equated with inauthenticity, an otherness which is basically defined by reference to a *tradition*, to a propositional order which prescribed for the subject the requirement of having to be its foundation. The two go together; if the subject *is* the other, by what prior ontological and temporal identity can we differentiate them? And as for the opposition between the literal and figurative, can it even be conceived of outside of a rupture of the propositional? With the death of Man, what has disappeared is Man as foundation, giving rise to a vacant anthropology, for which the "past" becomes preeminent. What is destroyed is the equation between the identity, the subject, the foundational, and the human. Humanism, foundationalism, and the very role of the subject will only be criticized through an amalgamation because of a shift which can only be thought of as radical, since it cannot be understood through an evolution of answerhood which accounts for such primordial changes. The very questioning which directs answering towards its own self-consciousness, so that it becomes expressly problematological, leads the conceptualization of the subject to be A and non-A, an alternative, a possible which propositionalism condemns us to perceive in terms of opposites. It would be more useful to see the larger problem of which A and non-A are only the indications. Rhetoricization, which asks us to see what man *is* by examining what he is *not*, suggests that this is only a manner of speaking, namely a figurative one. By adopting such language, we have not abandoned the old territory; we have simply adjusted ourselves to its requirements as though they were still valid, since we are still accepting this new contradiction as a perfectly legitimate propositional mode, as long as it is no longer taken literally. Propositionality becomes tropological, not problematological. All this becomes nothing more than a way of not saying what one means to be able to continue to say it. This is close to the torture of language, by which one can put forward any idea at all, using the most abstruse verbal constructions. Such a way of proceeding amounts to using a discursivity which we would have liked to be able to overcome, although we recognize that it is impossible to do so.

One might even be tempted to see in the death of the subject a sign

of a radical break, as the very word "death" would suggest. Discontinuity becomes the essence of the historical. But this would be a fallacious
view. Man arises as a central character only to disappear as no longer
fundamental two centuries later due to an underlying logic of continuity. It would be anachronistic to isolate this phenomenon and project
this discontinuity as a generality of history so truncated in terms of that
oppositional appearance-disappearance (of Man).

When we speak of ground, we speak of a foundation. Such a relation
defines itself problematologically as a differential transition, so what is
in question demands an answer that does not simply duplicate the
question. And if the goal of answers is to express questioning, the difference must still be made at the reflexive level of interrogative thematization. Such is the nature of inference, from which man cannot escape. Because questioning could not be reflected as itself, inference
could only be a propositional process. And inference will undergo an
evolution in its conception, creating a conception in which the causal
and mechanistic interpretation is exemplary inasmuch as it puts human
reality in the forefront. Causal inference and anthropological primacy
will be intrinsically linked. Indeed, causality is defined by the regularity of the inference AB so that from A, we can deduce B. If there is no
unique subject "A" underlying any "subjects" of possible judgments,
then necessarily there could never be a causal AB relationship, wherein
A cannot go with non-B, any more than non-A could go with B. This
means that A implies B just as the same cause produces the same result.
If A, man, ceases to be foundational, it is man himself who may be in
question, who may be thought of as one alternative, A or non-A, with
which B may be associated. This produces the collapse of a causal inference into a semiotic one (A is merely the sign that there is a B),
considered to be a preproblematological inference. What change will
inference have to undergo to become causal, with the result of the
grounding of causality in mankind? And a subsidiary question: why will
the deductive model of reason collapse, or more precisely, give rise to a
new conception of inference in which man is more subjected than sub-
jecting, as had previously been the case?

We begin with the latter question.

The more problematization affects thought, the more the subject
is questioned. And the more the subject is the object of questioning,
the less it commands answering as the operator giving rise to answers.
That means, in what is only seemingly a paradox, we may speak further
of the subject, of its role and its place, situating it by its relationship
to something other than itself, since it has ceased to function as a
principle. With an answering that becomes problematic through the

questioning of the subject, the latter is problematized through the question of *logos*. The subject of discourse, which asserts itself and thus conditions access to answers, is going to be put into question in that very role; that is, it will be subjected to the inference of which it thought it was the master. Unmasked, disarmed, the subject is going to see itself subordinated to *logos*, a *logos* whose rules will strangely (and falsely) establish themselves as autonomous. Causality, which once determined the conception of inference itself, with man as its support, will reappear as closer to the problematological relationship of "question implies answer," a relationship which, in a given problem, allows us to pass, directly or not, to the answer. Given that A is no longer in question, we can make answers about B and therefore about "B?" to the extent that B is in question, with only a minimal possibility of having a non-B. Inference, through answers, aims at excluding one or the other term of the alternatives: we have thus moved, through A, to the answer about B. We could also say that B, rather than its opposite, is *associated* with A; one could say that the presence or the occurrence of A *means* that of B, and not the contrary. Formulating the passage in terms of *meaning* corresponds to a *logos* defined in terms of causal relationships which are dereified, and as a consequence bear upon the structure of the *logos* and no longer upon the constitutive and transcendental freedom of mankind. By this dereification, which destroys the constitutive role of the subject with respect to reality, a role imparted to that subject since Kant and Descartes, inference is seen as structure of utterance and is cut off from a referentiality which is posed as the different, the external, and conditioned by that structure. But if we now speak of reference, it is to demarcate through signs what does or does not denote it. Adherence to the referent is broken: language will speak about itself to the extent it speaks of other. Meaning and reference: by the mention of the fact that such a thing as reference exists, we are postulating a difference from a pure extralinguistic reality, which one would like to see abolished by the idea of language-based referentiality itself. It is so in Frege, but it is also in Saussure, Derrida, and Lacan where the chain of signifiers is seen as independent from its relation to what is signified. Thus we have the arbitrariness of signs. Man-as-foundation guarantees the necessity of a referential link: it is a matter so evident that it is not even mentioned as long as it remains so. If there is a split in the signifier-signified relationship, ipso facto that underlines that the former guarantee of adequacy has ceased to exist and that the a priori foundation of this adequacy has vanished. Inscribed within the semiotic order, the speaker has ceased to be foundational. What finally needs to be kept in mind is the progressive movement which governs the very conditions of inferentiality, that is, its signification *as* a process of meaning. There is a rhetorization of the subject which comes into play, with, as a consequence, the emergence of psychoanalysis and the renewal of textual analysis. The subject, far from being the answer which is the source of all answers, the constraint which excludes all alternatives, shows itself to be rhetorical, an a priori closure of answering, an impossibility of questioning, which forces the questioner back upon himself. This calling into question allows him to see himself as always other. Sartre, for example, will continue to speak of Cartesian consciousness, but he will add to this consciousness both alterity (by definition) and bad faith (otherness, therefore the unconscious). If he was the last philosopher to resort to the illusion of the Cartesian primacy of consciousness, he was still unable to avoid its trap.

What do we mean when we speak of the paradox of consciousness?

A. All consciousness is self-consciousness.

The contrary is impossible. "[I]f my consciousness were not consciousness of being consciousness of the table, it would then be consciousness of that table without consciousness of being so. In other words, it would be a consciousness ignorant of itself, an unconscious—which is absurd." [5] Sartre's is surely the ultimate attempt made by the philosophy of consciousness to extricate itself from its own difficulties. The philosophical importance of Freudianism is primarily justified by an effort to respond to the difficulties imposed by the philosophy of consciousness as the philosophy of the Absolute.

B. Consciousness is not necessarily consciousness of itself.

In reality, if, following Sartre, we hold A (above) to be a true proposition, we can no longer deny that B may be one also. "Usually, when we are conscious of an object, we are simultaneously not conscious of our consciousness. Focusing attention on our act of consciousness would in fact make less precise and less effective the action we would exert upon those objects." [6] Thus, when I do something, I am not directing my consciousness upon myself while I do it. I do it, and that is all. That does not mean that I am unconscious of what I do:

> The more knowledge there is, the less there is knowledge about
> knowledge. That is what confirms one of the most apparently

5. Jean-Paul Sartre, *Being and Nothingness*, trans. Hazel E. Barnes (New York: Citadel Press, 1971), p. 1ii.

6. P. D'Arcy, *La réflexion* (Paris: Presses Universitaires de France, 1972), p. 5 [author's translation].

insignificant experiences. We perceive not only without knowing what perception is, but even without knowing that we are perceiving . . . The most sophisticated, the most complex man, in the great majority of his innumerable actions . . . does not know that he knows, is not conscious of his consciousness . . . If I see a color, a shape, if I remember an incident from my past, if I associate or dissociate such and such ideas, if I pursue a pattern of reasoning, I am not *necessarily* conscious of what I am doing . . . It is not easy for me to view this picture, to resolve this problem, by taking the viewing of the picture or the resolution of this problem as objects of examination, meditation, or knowledge. I cannot know something and at the same time know that knowledge.[7]

Therefore, "when the subject pays more attention to the object which is presented to him by the act which he experiences, he becomes more absorbed in dealing with this object, and the more the subject forgets himself . . ."[8] For example, if one is counting, one is completely absorbed in the accomplishment of this action, which is no doubt desirable to avoid errors.

Ever since Descartes, for historical reasons, irreflexive thought has been identified with consciousness. What happens if we admit that consciousness is always conscious of itself and that the unreflective activity of the mind is not conscious activity? What we usually call "consciousness" would then be the consciousness of unconscious thought. But in that event, it would no longer be self-consciousness, which is contrary to one of the hypotheses (A). To be able to become conscious of this second consciousness, a third would be necessary, for which the second would be unreflexive, which is false *ex hypothesi*. So Sartre is correct in affirming that (1) if consciousness characterizes the life of the mind, and (2) if all consciousness is self-consciousness, then (3) the irreflexive life of the mind is consciousness, just as is its reflexive life. But what must be established is exactly the validity of point (1), and we are going to show that to be impossible. And as to point (2), we have already seen that it is unacceptable.

If reflexive consciousness has irreflexive consciousness as its object, the latter in order to be consciousness, and thus self-consciousness, would require that it be consciousness for a third consciousness, which . . . etc. It is this infinite regression which formed the basis of

7. S. Lupasco, *Logique et contradiction*, pp. 76 et seq., cited in D'Arcy, *Réflexion* [author's translation].

8. Aron Gurvitsch, "A Non-Egological Conception of Consciousness," *Philosophy and Phenomenological Research* 1 (1940–41): 325.

Sartre's reproach to Husserl. "Then, each time the observed consciousnesses are given as unreflected, one superimposes on them a structure, belonging to reflection, which one doggedly alleges to be unconscious." [9] Section 15 of Husserl's *Cartesian Meditations* is specifically referred to:

> If the Ego, as naturally immersed in the world, experiencingly and otherwise, is called *"interested" in the world,* then the phenomenologically altered—and, as so altered, continually maintained—attitude consists in a *splitting of the Ego:* in that the phenomenological Ego establishes himself as "disinterested onlooker," above the naively interested ego. (Edmund Husserl, *Cartesian Meditations,* trans. Dorion Cairns [The Hague: Martinus Nijhoff, 1960], p. 35)

Sartre, to avoid this regression, refuses to make consciousness an intentional object of itself.[10] Thus, self-consciousness cannot be expressed by the relationship knower-known and cannot have an epistemological relationship with itself. One might wonder how Sartre could even *know* what consciousness is like, since consciousness can come to my attention only through consciousness. If it does, it must escape knowledge. Although Sartre speaks of a *unique* consciousness, we must not mistake the matter, for we have two kinds of consciousness, or two modes of being within *one* consciousness. Irreflexive consciousness, being intentional, has an object. Reflexive consciousness, by contrast, thematizes irreflexive consciousness, its content, without being its object. Thus, if consciousness is unitary, *it must be what it is not, and cannot be what it is;* that is to say, it is dual, at the same time directed intentionally toward an object and yet not capable of being so directed. Through synthesis, the two consciousnesses may perhaps be made to constitute just one, but only by means of postulating a third which synthesizes them. And if it is the second which synthesizes, then the first, not being the synthesizer, reveals they are still two different consciousnesses.

The paradox of consciousness may be stated thus: either consciousness is self-consciousness, or else it is not. (1) If consciousness is not self-consciousness, then it is unconscious. That is absurd. (2) If consciousness is self-consciousness, either irreflexive thought is consciousness or it is not. If it is not, we fall into a contradiction (since consciousness is consciousness of an unconscious thought, then consciousness is conscious of being unconscious of itself). On the other hand, if un-

9. Jean-Paul Sartre, *The Transcendence of the Ego,* trans. Forrest Williams and Robert Kirkpatrick (New York: Farrar, Straus, and Giroux, 1957), pp. 55–56.
10. Sartre, *Being and Nothingness,* p. 19.

reflected thought is conscious, then we wind up with another contradiction (since a conscious thought is always a reflexive one according to
hypothesis (2), it cannot be irreflexive).

Put still another way, the paradoxical question comes down to this: is
irreflexive thought consciousness? Suppose that to be so. Either consciousness is self-consciousness or it is not. Since irreflexive thought
is possible only if it is not *eo ipso* reflexive, conscious of itself, the first
hypothesis must be rejected, as shown previously (B). We have shown
(B) that this is false. In the second case, we would have an unconscious
consciousness.

Is it nonetheless possible that irreflexive thought may not be consciousness? Let us suppose that for a moment. Consciousness being
consciousness of the objects that intentional consciousness aimed at
through irreflexive thought, consciousness would thus be consciousness
of an unconscious thought, which is contradictory.

What will result from the rhetoric about the subject is a schism between its identity and this alterity. The contradiction will be resolved
by the introduction of the postulate of the unconscious. The unconscious is what will embody the rhetoric of the subject. The determining primacy of the unconscious will make subjectivity "something" always displacing itself, a fictive identity, something globally referring to
the other. It will tropologize itself; the "New Rhetoric" is then anthropological by destination. The explosion of discourse into metaphors, as
in Lacan, will be supposed to be adequate to its object, which is the
subject, even if the fact of saying anything at all completely destroys
this supposed adequacy and (what comes down to the same thing) also
verifies that adequacy, whatever is said. The subject remains no less an
alterity, an alternative, because it is both problematic and problematized. In fact, it is a problematicity which continues to be unable to ut-
ter itself, but which is stated as signifying, to the extent that the
signifier refers to something other than itself and *is* only because it is referring to otherness. It is a referentialization which, taken literally, in
turning back upon itself, can renounce its own identity by bringing to
light the discrepancy with itself (*la différance*) as a rupture of the referent and the literal. The subject, rhetoricized in this opposition, in this
nonbeing which it *is* also, will *eo ipso* become an object of debate and
questioning, even though the subject still is unthinkable *as a question*.

This rhetorization is nothing more than the nonconstraining nature
of the operator "subject," due to the otherness it embodies, which is
due as much to its unconscious as its consciousness (of which Sartre correctly said that it is what it is not and that it is not what it is). The fact of
being able to be something other means for subjectivity that it is no

longer the identity underlying all temporalization, all predicative structures. It is itself in becoming. The dialectic which places the subject
under its laws learns, as a consequence, that the discovered facticity, or
detranscendentalization, puts the subject, like inference, in a more flexible position. Rhetoric, dialectic, semiotic—it hardly matters what term
is used. They all refer to the same state of affairs, namely that inference
is going to be weakened in some way or another by taking account of
nonidentity. What does the idea of questioning refer to, if not the plurality of answers which a question a priori implies? Would there even be
questioning otherwise? Subject and inference will remain linked, but
the evolution of this relationship makes it impossible to maintain any
anthropological priority. The concept of meaning, of referral, comes to
the forefront because it enables an inference not to imply a necessary
conclusion; therefore, it reveals alterity in the inferential process. Absent the interrogative conception of inference, we are left with a nonconstraining conception of signs, as if this concept summed up all by itself the problematization of the causal link, when, in fact, it actually
obscures it. It is really important to take note of the following fact:
causality, like deduction in general, constitutes *a* method for solving
problems. As such, causality and the other types of inference are not
considered as bringing about a problematological difference. Thus,
analogy, causality, and semiotic relationship, where from an A one
passes to a B, are presented as if they were autonomous entities without
being perceived as historical stages in the evolution of thought. Questioning, in considering itself alone and not as derived from something
else, makes clear the distance which separates, and thus unifies, these
different moments that cannot be isolated when inference is conceptualized and made resolutional. The negation of questioning is the negation of this historicity, a negation which autonomizes into distinct
moments (or even into linkages that are purely extrinsic) the process of
resolution of problems. These moments are all the more distinguishable when they bear distinct names.

The inference which is problematized as a causal link is going to become an argumentative one, but it will be a wholly propositional argumentation, since it deals only with opposing theses and not with questions, on the basis of which a questioner would have to choose to reach
an answer. That is why we cannot be satisfied with a simple reapplica-
tion of the classical theory of rhetoric into a new one (as in Perelman),
even if it seems explicable from a historical point of view, as we have
set forth above. An inference which describes a course from A to B
without excluding non-B will necessarily present a problematological
conclusion, about which one would say simply that B is indicated

through A. Contemporary theorists speak of "implicature" and "semiotic implication" based on the relationship between consecutive signs, without seeing in this a new form of inference. If A's function is to indicate B, then this is a semiotic function linked to the general rhetoric of inference whereby a question B is resolved by dependence on A. Why can one speak of B? It is because one has spoken of A: the link between A and B does not depend on either A or B as such, or to what one or the other refers to (causality), but to the fact that if someone *says* A, he or she would or could then proffer B. It is in the "saying" and not in the "said" that one finds the truth of this latter statement. A and B form a double alternative (A? B?), and an inference is an answer to a question where the *other* question is given as solved. A sentence like "John has arrived" would no longer be able to justify itself by the simple fact that it is true, since that evidence would impose it independently from any other consideration. Rather, we draw our attention to the reason which justifies the fact that it is said, beyond taking its truth into account. The reasons for what is said will thus be found in the utterance itself rather than in its content. This raises the current and very important question of the relationship between the two. Let us note clearly that even if we had begun on the road toward problematization, the latter still remains nonthematized. For, no more than causality, which is a process for the resolution of questions, the rhetoric of inference has been understood as being linked to a conception of the problematological.

Let us take up our question again about the anthropological shift. Many have found there a radical break initiating the whole era of fragmentation. What is true in this view is that thought at large has been chopped up into pieces because of the lack of a foundational principle: morals, like ideologies, that is, values in the largest sense, have lost not only their justifications but their ability to be justified. All cultural forms have taken active part in this disintegration at the same time that they themselves were split into many fragments. This is the origin of intellectual fashions.

Even more essentially, it can be argued that the concept of man-as-foundation rested on a hierarchy that has now been dismantled by the social movement toward egalitarianism. In place of the "Grand Bourgeois," whom Marx justly denounced as oppressors, have come the "petite bourgeoisie," as if a claimed equalization of conditions had affected only those concerned about rising socially within the system (we have socialism when the petite bourgeoisie rises and fascism when it falls). For the petite bourgeoisie, everyone is equal to everyone else; this would be the mimetic hell described by René Girard, where content, or the signified, will be the Other as signifying. This completely empties the subject of what still remained of its true content and self-confidence. Each person wants what the other wants because the other wants it, and not because of intrinsic reasons, which are now lacking. Man becomes a being without qualities, an empty vessel of exhausting narcissism, where each person is the frustrated accountant of his neighbor's actions, the shopkeeper of his own arrogant stupidity, totally immersed in his own well-being and the promise of being "like everybody else": in short, somebody who counts. This is at the expense of someone else, who does the same because he is the same. How to be different, to be oneself, when one is no more than a decimal within a mass number, and what is more, when one wants to be so? The death of man as pure subject allows for mere empirical subjects to appear as referring to one another. It is a play of mirrors, where each one aims at *the* universality of one's own ego by imitating someone else's, and vice versa.

If man is problematized as the pure, foundational subject at the end of an evolution which finally has put him in question in this regard, it is no less true that this claim to "purity" is a modern one. Before the humanism of the Renaissance and its Cartesian philosophical conceptualization, man had no truly privileged place in the order of things. It took a reinforcement of Platonism, along with the emergence of a subject beyond the scientific and the mathematical as its counterpart, to see the reestablishment of analytical link. This was in contrast to Aristotle's position, which had reduced that link to a syllogistic relationship. The perverse effect of this attitude had been scholasticism passing for apodictic, mixing indistinctly with the scientific, when in fact it was no more than low-grade rhetoric. Constrained reasoning as practiced by the geometers was lost at the same time. Here again, history progressed little by little because history is made that way. We do not truly realize at the moment when things happen that they are important, because the course of history is continuous, and significant situations rarely occur all of a sudden. The emergence of causal inference occurred with resemblance as a background, a resemblance which would give rise to the deductive order for Descartes, and the principle of association for Hume. It is not, as Foucault argued, that deductive knowledge is cut off from the entire universe of resemblances because it would deny their validity, while previously, resemblance made knowledge.[11] There is,

11. "Similitude is no longer the form of knowledge but rather the occasion of error, the danger to which one exposes oneself when one does not examine the obscure region of confusions." Michel Foucault, *The Order of Things* (New York: Pantheon Books, 1970), p. 51. Resemblance and deduction are terms which consecrate their own irreducibility. But they are concepts of a certain historicity, of a problematic of which they are examples.

more profoundly, a hazy identity which must be reaffirmed by criteria which would permit us to identify clearly what is different and, therefore, to analyze those things that are distinct.

The concept of identity underlies resemblance as it does deduction, which, it must be repeated, proceeds from the problematological difference. In the absence of that difference, resemblance and deduction will clearly appear to be heterogenous. Resemblance establishes identity when deduction refuses to do so. But deduction, just like resemblance, operates on identity, and, as a result, on difference as well. To establish a (deductive) order between A and B so that B proceeds from A is to declare them different. To seek order is to assure that nonidentity will be known as such and, on the contrary, that equivalencies can be established. On the other hand, deduction is also a kind of comparison. It is a relationship between two items, a process dear to Descartes, as his *Rules* and his *Geometry* confirm. The association of an A with a B will remain the act of a subject, inasmuch as A and B are both submitted by the subject to some deduction or, beginning with the following century, to experience. The Cartesian break, if there is such a thing in propositionalism, was the result of a shift in how inference is understood, where everything was the sign of everything else, where questions could be answered in many ways. This led to a veritable impossibility of answering. This is explained by the fact that every question, in a way, allows for alternative (and opposed) propositions, which, far from eliminating the question, maintain it *as* a question, that is, rhetorically, by asserting irreducible points of opposition which will translate it. The real subject will be Man, who will be the key to propositional resolution, by which a subject (matter) of an utterance will be the projection, the image of the (human) subject, beyond all possible opposition. Predication becomes possible through the stable identity of the subject with the proposition which accompanies it. It is because *I am* a subject that I can form the idea of a subject, thus of a predication, thus of a judgment. A subject identified by what is said of it by a predicate can just as well take an opposite predicate: its identity as a subject is not stripped from it, and rhetorical contradiction is excluded. It is impossible to say something and its contrary as well. The substantiation which reifies ideas guarantees a new status to their relationship: causality gives content to the ideas we form of them. Descartes says:

> For example, I think that a stone is a substance, or is a thing capable of existing independently, and I also think that I am a substance. Admittedly I conceive of myself as a thing that thinks and is not extended, whereas I conceive of the stone as a thing that is extended and does not think, so that the two conceptions

differ enormously; but they seem to agree with respect to the classification "substance." Again, I perceive that I now exist, and remember that I have existed for some time; moreover, I have various thoughts which I can count; it is in these ways that I acquire the ideas of duration and number which I can then transfer to other things. (*Third Meditation,* in *The Philosophical Writings of Descartes,* trans. John Cottingham, Robert Stoothoff, and Dugald Murdoch [Cambridge, Eng.: Cambridge University Press, 1984], vol. 2, pp. 30–31)

But what is the nature of this transfer? It is the philosophical itself, in the strictest sense of the term: if I can conceive of diversity and apply it to a substance, in this case myself, a multiplicity of predicates will be how we characterize substances, or substance *in general.* Reflexivity will then function as a principle and even will be the principle of causality, because it is through reflexivity that thought provides a substantiality to itself, and thereby an objective or objectifiable correlate to deduction as rooted in the thinking subject.

Before Descartes, man did not appear as the foundation because, quite simply, inference was not causal: any proposition could answer any question. Let us put it even more clearly: the process of answering was unaware of itself as inferential. It requires causality for inference to be able to more adequately conceive of itself. It is only when the analogical mode of answerhood is put in question that the constraints on answerhood appear through the agency of something out-of-the-question, something that would be the first answer, the model for all others, the *Cogito,* as an affirmation of anthropological primacy. All the same, it is through questioning what is out-of-the-question that inferences free themselves from this primacy, "decausalize" themselves, and take on other, larger forms. A new deducibility emerges, defined from a *logos* which reflects itself through locating this problematization outside of all possible problematization of itself.

Roughly speaking, contemporary thought thus has conceptualized the *logos,* integrating therein the crisis of the subject, thereby forbidding itself to overcome it except by denial. It is a *petitio principii* (begging the question) to refuse to attempt this philosophical recentering, since one gives to oneself, as an answer, a question one refuses to ask, precisely because one already has the answer to it.

There is scarcely any doubt that philosophical thought is not to be found in the many fragments which have resulted from the lack of a first principle. Each of these fragments expresses a point of view, but nothing more. And, as with partial rationality, it will be said that there is *the* philosophy of this or that point of view. Ethical nihilism, the loss of values, the arbitrariness and opposability of theses, existentialist absurdism, sophistics in content as well as in form—the delirious verbal gymnastics of the 1960s and 1970s amply illustrate my point—are the most obvious manifestations of the flight from the originary, which still could not be conceived *as* other than subject. Reflection could muster itself to overcome its own crisis only by giving itself a new foundation rather than by denying a priori the validity of such a problematic. What has been shown here is that the defundamentalization of the subject has followed the same development of problematization which had seen the subject become fundamental after the Renaissance. Mechanism lives on, but its effects vary. The problematization of discourse has required, against the backdrop of rhetoric, a subject that is more out-of-the-question than the subject (matter) of judgments could ever be. With a problematization which grows and then affects the pure subject, in turn, we are no longer assured that we can draw B from A rather than the contrary; the subject A itself includes an alternative. Man becomes a question and thus becomes empiricized like everything else. Subjective experience becomes its own variation: A goes with B as it would with anything else. Thus A does not support B more than any other alternative. What changes is the status of the subject; what is perpetuated is questioning in its historicity.

Philosophy has forever been the most radical quest that there could be. Herein lies its specificity, notably in regard to the sciences. Philosophy undoubtedly has known a crisis of foundations, as was the case for other disciplines at the end of the nineteenth century. Let us not take the easy path of perpetuating scattered philosophical reflections on many subjects, which are without results because they are without principle. If we did this, philosophy would renounce itself, both in its historicity and in its traditional calling.

3. Historicity and Questioning

The question we now face is the meaning of this return to Descartes. Basically, it involves establishing a relationship between a historical reading and the creation of a philosophical beginning. The paradox is that while Cartesian thought apparently exhausted all of its resources, we cannot avoid drawing on them once again. Indeed, is that not the very paradox inherent in all philosophizing? If we think of philosophy as an ensemble of propositions whose validity is in question, then it is clear that we are going to run into a web of contradictions, even of errors, and, in any event, into doctrines which leave the questions it deals with unresolved. The contrast with science is striking. Philosophy makes no progress, if by progress we mean an accumulation of results built one on another. Such an approach is completely consistent with at least one model of reasoning, one which knows no answers and, therefore, no questions. It ensues from a context of in-difference to this key duality, and thus finds it easy to devalue a type of thought where answers are entirely oriented toward questioning and its expression. If we truly understand that philosophical *answers* are problematological, even when, ignoring the problematological difference, they pass themselves off as "results," (which may end in self-destruction), then we will have understood that philosophy perpetuates itself by the opening up of its questioning. Answers serve to put things into question and to stimulate the philosopher, who then cannot but consider the history of philosophy as his most contemporary interlocutor. Thought is constantly called upon to question itself, through the succession of answers, all of which originally expressed questioning, or even questions about questioning, because they are philosophical. The question has been repressed and displaced through a derivation (*elle dérivait*), like the implicit of a constant necessity, and paradoxically affirmed in a discursivity which presupposed the question of questioning without ever being able to express it.

The idea of *derivation* is critical at this stage. What do we understand by derivation and "derived?" Let us consider a simple example. If someone says, "Napoleon was the victor at Austerlitz, as well as at Jena and Auerstadt," he is speaking indirectly, in a derivative manner, of Napoleon's military genius. It is not expressly stated, but it is stated just the same, almost in spite of itself. Therefore what is (indirectly) in *question* is his military genius, even if the *question* is not explicit at the beginning. Or, we could just as easily say that the question is more about Napoleon's military successes than his genius, or that this is an answer to an implicit question about his greatest victories, and so forth. Since no question is made explicit, we *derive* its possible existence. It is the product of an inference; and, by the same token, a *plurality of questions* is implied by the very idea of a reading of what can be derived from the explicit. In short, the question of the emperor's genius is here a *derived* question, derived from an answer and not from an originary question, since, at the origin, no question had been explicitly posed before this answer was made.

It is exactly the same with the question of questioning in relation to philosophical answers: such a question is derived from the answers which displace it or, in a certain way, deny it, even as they put the questioning process into action. This perpetuates the paradox of the *Meno*.

The process of derivation is thus a reading of the past in light of the present which allows us to decode *it*, but it also creates the possibility of *other readings* according to the type of problem posed. If it is a derivation, then, certainly, it is a nonoriginary formalization of what is deemed to be first, or anterior, in this case questioning. But it also suggests that something is adrift, as connoted by the very concept of derivation. Indeed, by means of the passage to the present which allows us a reading of the past, we have access to the *history* of the *process*. Philosophy has been adrift for as long as it has been unable to perceive itself as the question of *questioning*. It has been adrift because it first separated from its originary reality without recognizing that it was originary and also because of its later historical development.

Philosophy has always been radical interrogativity. In this sense, there is an articulation with the historical and the variable at large, decipherable from what is constant, from which the variable and its forms can be identified. I call this relationship *historicity*, and I call its evolving part the *historical*, with which it is necessary to contrast it. The historical, for philosophy, is the succession of doctrines in all their diversity and mutual opposition, or simply in their heterogeneity. Historicity, by contrast, is defined by the problematological nature of these philosophical doctrines as they pose questions, as they *are* questions, and insofar as the question is about radical questioning through answers which express it differently, therefore derivatively. The interrogativity of philosophy lies in its very history, and in that is truly the secret of the "living Plato."

What is important is to understand the true difference between historicity and history. History, traditionally, knows only interruptions, individual events which follow one another, each of which constitutes a more or less radical break from the one which preceded it. These events are discrete moments which, because they are disruptive, make things change: there is movement from A to B, as from a cause to an effect. Historicity, however, is different. It views the past in the light of the present. It sees in the past, a present which is going to develop progressively and occur differently from the past. There is no hidden finalism nor any anachronism in this view. Historicity is an articulatory concept in the sense that what is posed from the outset is the relationship of the present to the past. It is the past-for-the-present, and not the necessity of Becoming as contained in an original and unknowable, yet overdetermined point of departure. Furthermore, the reproach that this is an anachronistic projection cannot be maintained, since there is in the concept of historicity a search in the past for present elements only inasmuch as they have played a role in that past at some originary stage;

in fact they cannot be seen as independent. Further, it is quite clear that the impact of the present permits a variety of readings, to the extent that the past finds itself clarified through the derivation of certain present factors chosen from among possible alternatives. The past does not exist in itself; it exists only through the process of derivation.

The reading of History which must be discarded is that which ignores historicity. That reading considers historical events as facts, in the manner of, say, physics. Events appear as chunks of the past—the historical will be the memorable—and their succession is a process which places them only in an external relationship to one another, each being autonomous, but each giving rise to the other. Historical facts exist by themselves. The historical relationship is that which links two autonomous facts, A and B, whose succession is perceived causally, as embedded in the facts themselves. Historicity, on the other hand, sees the relationship between A and B as the inclusion of B within A before a gradual differentiation separates B from A. The B/A relationship evolves differentially, by correlation, and it winds up in making A the explanatory cause of B once the difference between them becomes apparent. Let us consider an example: the French Revolution. At one time it was seen as a whole, a fact unto itself which would have to be studied as a national event. In this interpretation, it represents a rupture with the Ancien Régime, although ensuing from it: A causes B, and in this case B is the rupture, hence the revolution. But as François Furet has ably demonstrated in *Penser la révolution française* (and in this he follows Tocqueville), the relationship between the Revolution and the Ancien Régime instead resembles a continuous progression, where the key concept is the centralization of the State, with the renewal of national structures that such a centralization implies at any given time, when the relatively closed nature of the State in regard to its upwardly mobile forces impeded the strengthening of the State. It is unimportant here whether the explanation is correct or not; what counts is to understand the approach which conceives the Ancien Régime as including the centralization, thus the Revolution, whose radically ruptive nature becomes much more relative.

Historicity understands historical causation as a relational difference, a correlation in action, as shown earlier. In the case which is of greatest interest to us, namely questioning, the contrast between a reading of the historical, a reading rooted in historicity, and the one which takes the historical as an objective and external given, is striking. One could say that there is a time when questioning is thematic for itself, and an earlier time which ignores questioning as such. This bifurcation is quite clearly not a false one but somewhat incomplete because of question marks which subsist behind those which are directly indicated. The impression conveyed is that there is a sort of break, an "epistemological scission" between an erroneous beforehand and a truthful afterwards. How can change be explained if there is such a radical break? And above all, how to explain the awakening, the revelatory leap, since the anterior is irreducible, in terms of explanation, to that which follows? Such a view, as I have said, has as its only virtue the ability to raise a problem. In this case, it raises the question of the historical nature of questioning through the question addressed to questioning itself. We will return to this point. For the moment, it is important to contrast such a reading with that which can be made if one relies on historicity.

It might be objected that no one questioned questioning before problematology and that therefore there *is* such a rupture. To speak of questioning *as such* would mean no more than the fact that questioning has never been questioned, that there has been no questioning which is directed upon itself, not even in a derived way. This is the source of the criticism that there is an anachronism in such a remark. We have refuted it. But what is problematic in an objection that reduces historicity to the analysis of "gross historical facts" is that it presupposes a conception of the past wherein everything is implied to be in a latent condition. But this presupposition is curious in that the past cannot exist in itself in any event, regardless of any questions of the present. When answers are referred to some past, it is always as an articulation upon the present. Our position is that it is just the same thing to say that questioning has not been questioned as to say that it has been questioned but not *as such*. For if questioning has not been questioned as such, then necessarily questioning has been questioned through something else which displaces it, and which symbolizes the requirement of the radical interrogativity by which the need to philosophize has always been expressed. The questioning which is absent from reflexive philosophizing is present in another way. It is therefore manifest in something different from what it really is, though quite real in its effects. A reading which denies historicity and one which involves it both arrive at the same result, in that it is unclear how one could relate to one's past outside of one's own present, even if such a position is denied. Human thought has indeed questioned questioning "before," but not thematically. This has implied other forms of questioning as well as having perpetuated the paradox of the *Meno*.

In a parallel manner, the reflexive thematization of questioning achieves its full and adequate expression at the moment when everything which has been said to represent a difficulty becomes identified as problematic and, therefore, surpassed as a possible expression or derivation of the problem that radical interrogativity poses to itself (since it is radical). It is *historically* surpassed. Moreover, the reflexive nature of questioning is differentially inscribed as the process by which the problematological difference posits itself, the source of all possible difference, inscribed in a past which denies questioning as such to express it in another way (for *us*, only, it is paradoxical). Questioning which is questioned as such and for itself is a modalization contained in the radical interrogativity of philosophy. A question is derivatively present in all the answers which deny it and which deny themselves *as answers* for us who today have the possibility of such a reading of the past, a reading which is derived *from* the emergence of problematology. The question of questioning as totally transparent in itself is implicitly included in what preceded its identification and what made it possible. This question, in its problematological form, is no better than any other, since all the others also respond to History. But underlying the other "answers," the explicit question which is posed today is immanent for them, although, or rather because, it is derived from them as a presupposition which ends up being fully explicit. The *before* and the *after* become, respectively, an unperceived internal presence and a presence made autonomous. The one flows from the other according to the differential relationship "*the more . . . the more . . .* ," that is, the more the pressure to state the interrogative mounts because of a generalized problematization of the culture, the more interrogativity will tend to make itself explicit. Therefore, questioning has always been in question, but in various ways. It is no anachronism to question Plato, Aristotle, or any other thinker about a relationship to problematicity because, in a derivative way, the same problematic can be found at the base of all their problematics, since this is the problematic of the foundation itself. The question of questioning will not be understood as such, if one begins only from its mere asking as a starting point. What causes it to occur will not be understood if one refuses to see in it a characteristic of the thought which existed before it was born, so to speak. It would not be understood what causes it to be so, if one is unable to overcome what prevented it from assuming its appropriate form. It will not be understood if we fail to recognize that we have not passed miraculously from an absence to a presence, but only that we have progressively and ever so slightly moved to the perceived facticity of that presence so that it has become possible to single it out and identify it as distinct.

One could hold the same discussion in regard to anthropology and humanism. The latter was born de facto with the Renaissance, de jure with Cartesianism, only to disappear later, at the end of the nineteenth century; this is Foucault's familiar thesis. But rather than speak of a double switch, of a before and an after, it is more accurate to say that philosophy spoke of Man before humanism did and that it continued to do so after its defundamentalization. What really changed between these two moments was the role of Man, which was to assume a unique preeminence. But not much can be known about what appeared and disappeared, that is, about what has evolved, if our thinking is limited to cutting history into two periods, one before and one after making Man foundational. To integrate this significant event into our understanding, it is important to see that Man "existed" well before his philosophical primacy, and that this primacy resulted from a gradual development which occurred during the Age of the Renaissance. This movement belongs to an evolution marked at one time by humanism, and, later, by the defundamentalization of the subject. The central place of Man is consistent with the particular role he played in this development. But this role cannot be separated from the larger historical process, which Man did not create. If one starts from Man-as-fundamental as evidence of his *fundamental* role, established as an epistemological break from what went before, then one is constrained to *accept* what should rather be *explained;* such a view of things makes the "point of departure" inexplicable. No theory based on the idea of a cutting off of the past *can* satisfactorily explain the threshold events which proceed from these breaks. Man, to take up our example again, has not always been a subject, but his occupying that role can nonetheless be read, among other similar essential features, from philosophies which did not include (and could not have included) him as the first principle.

As has just been seen, the notion of historicity is crucial in more than one respect. It offers us a nonpositivist view of History insofar as it sees events not as disjointed occurrences, but rather as overlapping and evolving gradually one into and with the other, correlatively and differentially. Causality is a relationship of meaning and pertinence, not an external force; this suggests a monism that is inconsistent with the complex interplay of the elements of reality. While "epistemological breaks" pave the way for the irrational, or at least for the inexplicable, historicity allows us to see the new as at once a (weakly) differentiated function of the (far distant) past, and still as an autonomized effect. Furthermore, this is what one "knows" of, for example, the emergence of Man as foundation or the upheaval known as the French Revolution. This is not to say that there are no breaks in History, but simply that they are not total, that they appear against a background of variously correlated and evolving factors, interactions which bring about breaks at other levels. A "break" in History represents the primacy of one factor at a particular moment, which alters that factor into a fact, different from that which preceded it. It might also be said that such a "rupture," in the sense one usually understands the term, is a single moment in a differential relationship, a relationship which is denied as historicity. The historical will no longer be anything more than facts external to, and broken off from, one another. This is the sole vision that will prevail if one loses sight of the role of historicity in the reading of the past *as* reading of the past.

What lesson may we draw in regard to questioning? How does historicity concern us beyond the mere relationship between the history of philosophy and the pertinent questioning that is relevant to it?

It is undeniable that the question of questioning determines historicity and does so from the moment that we realize we cannot approach this matter without asking why the question hasn't been posed up to now. Putting the question of questioning to oneself inevitably raises the question of why it was never before questioned. Why pose or not pose this question? What seems to be a historical fact becomes instead a simple formal alternative. The historicity of nonquestioning, or of questioning, represses the historical beneath reality to reduce it to a nonhistorical matter. Indeed, one could put the problem another way and make it a more historical question: why has this nonquestioning (of questioning) been perpetuated up to the time of problematology? But there again the result will be the same. Reference to the historical simply puts on the latter the responsibility for that nonquestioning. Historicity will find itself associated with the suppression of questioning insofar as it is unable to thematize itself. Because this nonthematization is historical, historicity becomes the denegation of the historical and, as a result, of itself. But with the emergence of problematology, historicity becomes explicit as an internal repression within questioning, one which represses the historical while, and by, answering it. Historicity is thus a self-repressed questioning. It represses itself as historical, displacing itself through successive expressions which appear, not just relatively, but absolutely. In place of the characteristic problematicity of philosophy will be substituted a pretension to truth, a truth that is purely assertoric, even if not autonomous and scientific. Historicity turns questioning from itself and directs it to something other than itself, in this case, the answering process; not so much as it *states itself*, but in *what* it speaks about. Historicity thus allows the real to be seen through an interrogative prism without the prism's being perceived. Further, it gives to the real an ontological and ahistorical status. It is a present and a presence, because the real will always be the real. Historicity, because it engenders answering within questioning itself, is truly the dynamic of the problematological difference. Historicity makes apparent the externality of the interrogative act by the suppression of that act. It is the "phenomenonalizer" of the world. Questioning will be historical only in detaching itself from it, only by making itself autonomous. It is a relative autonomy, although theoretically absolute. In fact, we are present here at the raising of the theoretical into an autonomous domain. Historicity, if reflected upon, will not repress this repression but *will* make it understandable.

If historicity is the repression of interrogativity, then how is problematology historically possible? A negative answer would, in fact, seem to be untenable; it would be self-defeating. By expressing itself, questioning represses the problematological difference as the object of that repression, but it does not abolish it, for it thereby still affirms it. It shifts the difference as a thematic requirement of reflexive discourse into something else; because it is a constant and a "natural" requirement of questioning, beyond the event which actualizes this expression, the problematological difference places itself outside of historicity, which dynamizes it as a constant. The questioning which *asserts* itself is none other than the repression of historicity in *its* role of repression, which is abolished. What becomes known is the role of historicity that allows thought, subjected to History, not to have to take History into account each time to consider the real as present and unalterable, a form of necessity which imposes its presence outside the vicissitudes of time. Questioning, therefore, excludes historicity as an external condition, once the two are able to be set forth. Questioning which reaches the level of theoretical autonomy through the problematological moment is revealed as outside of History. Historicity continues to separate itself from the historical according to laws that are sui generis.

Historicity which expresses itself, asserts itself as different from questioning. It affirms itself as *not* being questioning and, it might be added, as being its variant. Historicity speaks *of* questioning; it is, in fact, the discourse *of* questioning, its reflexivity as a problematological difference, its own historical differential. The identity is actually broken in the process by which questioning is put into discourse, a process born of its own assertability. In this sense, historicity assumes the role that the transcendental played for Kant; the transcendental, in the last analysis, is no more than a particular example of historicity. The possible, which defines the transcendental, has above all been a logical notion, a *mode* of answering which today must be conceived of as a mode of *answering*. What is the possible if not an alternative, offered by answering, in response to a question? If it is possible that John may come, he also might not come. The question is still there. On the other hand, if it is impossible that he won't come, then he must come, and that is, indeed, the only (possible) answer.

All this is to say that historicity is the possibility of questioning as being the problematological differentiation which represses the question to give rise to answers. Historicity, in its reflexive stage, makes possible an answer which sets forth questioning while at the same time maintaining this very difference.

Historicity appears to us as the denegation of the historical. It *actualizes* it, in the true sense of the term. Historicity allows the historical to be conceived of as reality, which suggests an ahistorical permanence. Historicity is the articulating concept between the present and the past. It conditions any reading of History, which we will write in lower case, "history," to distinguish this reading from its real object. Historicity, being the repression of the interrogative relationship in regard to *what* is asked, to what is the object of the questioning, is at the same time the condition of its objectivity, and even of its objectivation. The past is brought up by forgetting the present which it makes possible. This does not mean that we are returning to the hypostasis of the past as a bloc of gross facts, to be considered only in their external heterogeneity. What is implied in the objectivation of the past is, quite simply, history, the phenomenonalization of the historical, the depresentification of the factors constituting the real, that is, their evolution in regard to a present from which they are absent or, on the contrary, for which they are determining. Historicity thus having become "conscious," the objectivation of the past is carried out according to a certain factualization of the differences of History, with, even more, an awareness of the process by which this factualization occurs. It prohibits the positivization of the past as self-sufficient in the manner of physical facts or of a particular (hi)story. Thus, it is not a matter of renouncing history as it has been written since the time of Herodotus, but instead of taking up "facts" in the light of the implicit questions which determine the factuality of these facts, their being present, so to speak. Doesn't the word *history* denote *inquiry?*

As for philosophy, it is completely within the hold of historicity. The constant interrogativity of philosophical answers which follow one from the other is the present which it experiences. Philosophy, as a victim of the propositional model, has been immersed in the ambiguity of a concern for answers (but not as such), while only caring about *what* they problematize, therefore knowing quite well that they were not necessarily true.

There is a historical continuity in the philosophical realm which underlies this progression of answers, to the extent that they are answers. Each philosopher, implicitly contesting them, once again takes up the question of philosophy and poses anew the question of the originary without seeing that, in so doing, he is furthering the movement which makes philosophy evolve. On the other hand, even when he starts again from zero, he still perpetuates the philosophical tradition, as paradoxical as that might seem. If we have the opposite impression, it is because we are under the sway of the propositionalism of answers. The validity of past answers is denied to rethink the originary and create something new. And it is done that way every time; it is this very radicality which will guarantee philosophical permanence.

Thus Descartes. He seeks a radically new foundation, but this foundation will turn out to be nothing more than that which propositional reasoning was after. In fact, he reproduces the rationality which he set out to ground.

4. Historicity and the History of Philosophy: A Derived and Deriving Presupposition

Philosophy's characteristic lies in the fact that it solves its problems by formulating them. The reason is that philosophy, as radical questioning, can only question itself about itself, precisely *to the extent that it questions.* From that, and that alone, flows the idea that to question in philosophy does not produce anything other than the answering itself. The articulating phrasing of questions retains that problematological difference, rather than posing that difference thematically, as we have done here. But philosophy, never having thought of this difference, never having been *able* to think of it, has been no less able to make it work as a constant presupposition in the precise sense that has just been stated. Aristotle deduced the validity of the principle of noncontradiction from the contradictory questioning which he adopted, just as Descartes would later deduce the undeniable necessity of the *Cogito* from doubt itself.

Doubt will indeed be a disguised affirmation, just as the absolute requirement of noncontradiction and the hypothesis of its own contradiction had already been for Aristotle. The propositionalist *coup de force* which made reason assertoric by postulating it where and when it comes to be asserted through some mode of questioning, but negatively so, rested, in the last analysis, on an interrogative deduction. It was an interrogativity which was repressed, since it could not be thought of as such, since it could only be thought of through assertions, assertability becoming the model and the unifier of reason.

From the moment that philosophy ignored its role as an interrogative dynamic, it could only displace the radical requirement of problematological differentiation, which, nevertheless, it practices. Aristotle and Descartes, to cite only those two, proceeded to an interrogative deduction. However, they could not conceive it as such because of their

subjection to propositionalism, even though they were aware of the
specificity of their reasoning. Aristotle set its reasoning apart by calling
it dialectic. As for Descartes, he set the power of his reasoning over
against syllogistic sterility, all the while not knowing clearly himself
whether it was a matter of a deduction or intuition. The philosophical
specificity of his reasoning remained unreflected in his philosophy, for
he, like Aristotle, failed to make room for any inference other than that
offered by the resources of propositionalism. The difference shown by
their approaches to reasoning is therefore smothered by a single norm,
the propositional deduction. However, there is for them a particular, irreducible type of inference, which links a proposition to that which it
answers and which is only *differentially assertable*, or problematologically
so, if one adopts our terminology.

Despite its contrary *practice* of radical reasoning (although untheoriz-
able in specific terms), philosophy has displayed a real problematological in-difference, and thought has continued to question in spite of
its affirming, an affirming of something other than questioning. In so
doing, it has displaced questioning as a fundamental implicit assumption, as a hidden requirement, to be translated (even if indirectly) as a
problem determining an entire matrix of specific *questions*. In this way,
beyond any idea of "method," questioning has imposed on philosophy
its content, the *meaning* of its questions. What can disguise this fact is
the plurality of philosophies and their (entirely or partially) contrasting
views. But these are only propositions and structures built of propositions, arranged in comparison to one another, defining themselves
within relationships of greater and lesser difference, all the way to
being radically different. The history of the thinkable is therefore abolished in an ahistoric reality which suggests an unchanging philosophical
reality. However, questioning is the basis of every possible difference
because it defines, intrinsically, answering itself, which is thereby established differentially. If there is an answer, and therefore a question,
then there is a difference. A difference does not exist in itself but as an
articulation, as a problematological concept. In itself, the plurality of
philosophies bears witness to this relationship to questioning while, at
the same time, repressing it. The historicity of these philosophies is the
repression of their history, producing the illusion that they draw their
validity from and upon themselves, independent of *what* they originate
in. What is nevertheless true of questioning is that it represses itself
within that which it generates. What is false from the viewpoint
of historicity is true of structure, which is why nonproblematological
philosophies are important for problematology. But historicity being
part of questioning, the perpetuation of this repression, as constitutive

of questioning, nevertheless cannot be part of the present endeavor, since it is essential that the repression be expressly taken up and *not* ignored. The philosophies address more or less the same questions, each one granting itself an absolute pretense to truth, absolute because it represses any historical determination, almost as if each was a translation of the "Absolute." This evolution being erased for each of the philosophies, the scope of any philosophy so conceived is reduced considerably, because philosophy then offers nothing more than a juxtaposition of different theses all the way up to mere propositional opposition, the true *or* the false.

There remains the relativism which puts these doctrines in their historical context, despite their explicit claims of anhistorical truth, of a philosophy that has to be rendered adequately in its sole content. Relativism is historicism when it fails to understand History, because it fails to see in what it studies that which runs through History, makes of it a continuous thread, and ties it together. It isolates philosophies analytically, and in an effort to save each, destroys the whole. It links them differentially through a historicity which then represses the common link, the historical, and which places them *all* outside of History in a universe of absolute validity. Relativism truly undermines this claim, reducing it to what it is, but at the price of failure to comprehend the constant repression of what is philosophically originary. In short, "relativizing" philosophy amounts to no more than relating it to something other than itself, making it an answer to an unasked question, which is external to it, thereby abolishing its radicality, which nevertheless expresses the specificity of philosophy, if not its meaning. Finally, it fails to perceive the very interrogativity which recurrently animates it and ends up in a historicized duplication of its problems, which nevertheless persist. Relativizing amounts to reducing thought to mere points of view that want to cancel every (other) point of view and in so doing cancels itself. Through relativism, the *historicity* of philosophy is lost, that is, the *dynamic* which consists of locating in a nonhistorical way a historical relationship to questioning. Relativism studies philosophies one by one, in their context, so to speak, but loses *the* philosophy which is found in each of them. That is, it loses the interrogativity which, though historically determined, is modulated in a constant way, by successive and continuous differences.

Relativism and anhistorical juxtaposition suffer from the same flaw: they are *unable* to comprehend the problematological difference as historicity, as a constant which is continuously repressed and differently translated in the course of the evolution of thought. An articulation of the Same and the Other, the problematological difference is historicity as the modality of historicized repression of the interrogative constant, as the differentiating modality of what is *constantly* integrated as *new*. If we deny this difference, nothing will remain but the succession of the Same, which in fact abolishes the succession; or we will only take into account succession as a continual alterity, in which case philosophical continuity disappears. In both cases, where articulation is absent, philosophy is betrayed to the gain of one of these two terms of the repressed difference. If questions find answers in their own affirmation, and if there is nothing but affirmation, then we run straight into the double consequence of not having any question in the field of the thinkable, while having *in fact* only an opposable and contestable problematic, once it is reduced to the assertoric level which monopolizes thought, because there is no "solution" in such a project of theoretization. The Same is this constant, the Other is its destruction, which constantly verifies constancy. By that, it allows the only relatively stable thing to be the destructibility of "solutions," which shows quite clearly the paradoxical character of a failure to take into account the problematological difference. Philosophies are answers which are unaware of this very feature of theirs, whether in being only "historical," or in being absolute knowledge itself, negating all other philosophies. Historicity repositions the ahistorical historically and, in so doing, allows the integration of philosophical differences as variations of the same fundamental preoccupation. The historicity of philosophical questioning compels us to inquire into philosophy along these two lines.

What questioning qualifies as problematic, even if displaced into this or that which *is* problematic, expresses a vision of the fundamental, of the relation to the real, of the human involvement therein (followed through all the ramifications of being human), even if understood as subject. Answers can be criticized. In fact, they will *have* to be criticized upon the ground of their philosophical rigor, given that the activating principle of the philosophical must not remain outside of the explicitly philosophical. Therefore, it need not produce further difficulties. But the problematic, on the other hand, arises from the problematological difference which is its conditioning force, not of the undefined variety of answers, but rather of the underlying constancy of questions which make up the philosophical itself.

5. Aristotle and Descartes

Aristotle exemplifies the paradigm of philosophical "demonstration" when he considers the principle of noncontradiction. He did not adequately prove it, but he did put forward what might be characterized as a problematological inference, which consists of deducing an answer from the sole fact of posing a question. But if the difference is denied, we have a deduction which is not truly a deduction, which science may well deny, because it is only when results are proven logically, in the strictest sense of the term, that science is considered truly to have been attained.

If we reflect on this irrefutability of noncontradiction, we see clearly that there is a problematization from which an answer is inferred. This is the specific characteristic of philosophical reasoning. Why is that the case? Because philosophy is not just questioning, but radical questioning, which implies that questioning cannot escape from itself. Reflexivity is the master term of the philosophical. By questioning questioning, philosophy establishes itself philosophically but not historically. Historically, philosophical questioning was born from the collapse of nonphilosophical answers, those from mythology, for example. Such a birth only produces a qualitative advance if it gives rise to a constitutive process that is thematized on the basis of self-generated necessity. This process actually took place, but then shifted ground, and questioning from that time no longer was conceptualized from itself.

It might be thought that philosophical rigor—which consists of answering by thematizing the questions themselves—allows for complete variability in philosophical content, or it lacks its own justification which can be opposed to other ways of understanding philosophy. Philosophy has never questioned questioning despite a long succession of philosophical approaches. Yet it has always been determined by a radical questioning whose properties are no less present in their effects. Philosophy instead spun off a series of presuppositions regarding its affirmed radicality. This is the paradoxical shift which is amply illustrated in the *Meno*.

Let us speak now of the present. If philosophy posits itself as radical questioning, it can only reflect this interrogative radicality in its very questioning, whatever may be the *affirmed* object of some particular philosophy or other. What has been termed *philosophical rigor*, to avoid making it a copy of the scientific method, flows from such a content, that is, questioning, from which it is in no way detachable, to be, for example, just one possibility among others. Therefore, there are questions which have no meaning, in philosophy as elsewhere; and there are questions which even are totally absurd, but quite clearly not for the narrow reasons put forward by the positivists. A question which has no meaning is a question which fails to comply with the problematological difference; it does not take account of the difference between the known and what is to be known. The known functions here as what has already been answered. A problematological answer, in identifying this difference, creates meaning. Certain answers, therefore, derive meaning from the systems of thought in which they are found; others, by contrast, define the system of reference. Such is the characteristic of the foundational questions of philosophy which later will engender more "classical" questions, to use the terminology of another system of questions and answers such as science.

If we look to the argumentation of Aristotle to justify the absolute primacy of the principle of noncontradiction, we will observe that there is a "deduction" which starts from questioning itself. The simple fact of putting this principle into question would be sufficient, if we adhere to the propositional theory of questioning, to verify that which is under questioning. Translation: to submit to an alternative. If we contest the principle which affirms the alternative as submitted to internal exclusivity, we pose an alternative with exclusion as an end. The questioner becomes a being who refutes. That is why, in spite of the approach which is effectively consistent with what we said earlier about philosophical reasoning, problematology does not reach full fruition in what Aristotle proposes.

Descartes, as we shall see, did no better with the celebrated *Cogito*. But where the linkage between these two thinkers is most striking is perhaps in the role that they assign, for the one, to the principle of noncontradiction, and for the other, to evidence. The two are supposed to proceed from themselves: the criterion of evidence is self-foundational to the extent that it is self-evident. If we dispute that, we are disputing our internal light, which enables us to understand anything. As to what might properly be termed philosophical demonstration, it will be exemplified by the Aristotelian questioner-objector and the Cartesian questioner-doubter.

Why reject ontology? As "undiscoverable science," it does not allow anyone to discover anything. Everything is mixed with everything else, since everything "is." Internal distinctions can only arise from an elsewhere that ontology cannot account for, at least without some *coup de force*. How can one give oneself conditions of access to what exists, when one has, as a sole basis, only an indifferent and neutral perception in regard to these conditions? To speak of *being* can even be said to be impossible, since such a discourse provides no guarantee whatsoever of any truth: it is just as opposable as anything else. In short, ontology destroys itself when it pretends to be capable of treating something beyond itself as discourse, where it cannot go, but which is supposed to validate ontology. But one cannot say both that we start from knowledge to reach the knowledge of beings and at the same time root knowledge *in* being and condition the process of knowing in Being as the only path of access. It is a question of method. Once he reversed an order of priority into an order of reasons, Descartes, it is true, paid little attention to ontology. How could he talk about being, if he did not have a theory of true discourse?

There will be a unity of method and metaphysics in Descartes. This method will also apply to science, thereby guaranteeing the unity of human thought in its relationship to everything that exists.

Descartes shifts the unity which Aristotle wanted ontology to assume to the level of method. Ontology had as its role providing criteria for answers while abolishing questioning and therefore answerhood as such. Descartes will assign an identical role to method. Such an approach can be explained by the rejection of syllogistic, but, if we look more closely, we see that it is synthesis which, in fact, is rejected. Along with synthesis, Descartes gets rid of ontology (whose role is that of synthesis) and demonstration, in the sense Aristotle meant the term. Demonstration requires that premises be better known than the conclusion, but premises can be so characterized only if they precede the conclusion they imply, only where the conclusion is already known. This postulates a prior knowledge of this conclusion. Hence its circularity, which led Descartes to say that syllogisms, and ontology too, are sterile in that they make nothing known:

> . . . we should realize that . . . dialecticians are unable to formulate a syllogism with a true conclusion unless they are already in possession of the substance of the conclusion, i.e., unless they have previous knowledge of the very truth deduced in the syllogism. It is obvious therefore that they themselves can learn nothing new from such forms . . . (*Rule Ten*, Cottingham et al., vol. 1, pp. 36–37)

Recentering on analysis is going to give geometry and mathematics a privileged role. The Aristotelian synthesis is circular because it is analytic. Consequently, it is necessary to begin from this very analysis to distinguish it from synthesis, which "sometimes enables us to explain to others arguments which are already known. It should therefore be transferred from philosophy to rhetoric" (ibid., p. 37). It is understood that it is now synthesis which is going to define dialectic.

Certainly, geometers use synthesis, "not because they were utterly ignorant of analysis, but because they had such a high regard for it that they kept it to themselves like a sacred mystery" (*Second Set of Replies*, Cottingham et al., vol. 2, p. 111). So be it. What matters is not that analysis invents what synthesis merely presents, but that it is necessary to reinvent invention and, as a result, to isolate analysis as an approach *sui generis*.

The idea which animated Descartes was neither so simple nor so obvious as he claimed it to be. If method needs a metaphysic to justify it, in return, an approach to metaphysics is tributary to method. Thus, there is a unity to method and metaphysics, and it is at the heart of a unifying conception of human reason. This runs counter to the Aristotelian concept of science, divided according to genres (*Rule One*). And there is equally a circularity between metaphysics and method. Descartes needed to disengage himself from ontology, from synthesis, and from the syllogism. He sought to reestablish the virtues of analysis at the most fundamental level. Criticism leveled against the ontological tradition and its sterile syllogistic are consequences of this initiative, which finds its strongest echo in the sciences. Because of the circular syllogistics which characterize it, ontology is poorly adapted to advance knowledge through its differentiation into scientific disciplines. An analytic must itself be a theory of knowledge, a *ratio cognoscendi*, where order, that is, noncircularity, will be respected. It will be an order of reasons in which what *comes* first really *is* first, and is not first inside a split Reason which is divided with itself in order to avoid contradiction.

6. Analysis and Doubt in Descartes

We have seen clearly that we must at the same time unify metaphysics with method, and then separate them to overcome traditional ontology. This proved to be an impossible task for Descartes. His answer was to establish an analytical inference to arrive at the first metaphysical certainty, the *Cogito*. Such an inference is necessarily rooted in a foundation free from doubt, since it is a radically *first* foundation, first even as to method. Once method is *validated* by this first principle, it must reestablish itself at the general level of the *ratio cognoscendi:* it provides the whole structure of that *ratio*. Analysis will have universal value in any possible science. How does it differ, then, from deduction in the Aristotelian, and therefore classical, sense of the term? The analytical *order* is above all an order, and, what is more, an order of knowing. Knowledge of A will precede that of B, if the first is necessary to the second, even though the relationship between A and B can be reversed. But what is essential must be sought at an even more fundamental level.

The critique of synthesis, in the scholastic sense of the term, is going to turn synthesis into an object of doubt; and, even more, synthesis contains doubt within itself to the extent that anything can be affirmed or rejected within it. Therefore, according to Descartes, it is rhetorical. Doubt thus is the inability to distinguish the true from the false, that is, to say that synthesis is the opposite of knowledge, which is (in turn) the suppression of all doubt. Doubt is methodological but also metaphysical, because it undermines the ontology whose supremacy could only be synthetic. The doubting of synthesis, in and against itself, propels doubt elsewhere and transforms it into a constituent in regard to what is constituted, if we want to be so generous as to consider synthesis to be constituted knowledge. Doubt is therefore complementary to synthesis. It grounds the specificity of analysis and consecrates it as well. Doubt, indeed, is not a manifestation of skepticism but has a constitutive role insofar as it enables one, by its suppression, to reach the true rather than the false and hence to arrive at knowledge. It puts itself at the very foundation of method; it is the "*other*" of the already known, which it constitutes through and as the eradication of any alternative. Doubt is to knowledge as the alternative (of the true and the false) is to truth; in this case, the two ideas indispensably refer to one another. If Descartes starts from doubt to establish what should come before synthesis, that is, analysis, and makes it the basis for knowledge, it is not for autobiographical reasons, as suggested in the beginning of the *Discourse on Method,* or even in the *First Meditation.* Doubt is universal by the simple fact that it must refer to all possible knowledge, even possibly including sensibility as much as mathematics. Many Anglo-Saxon commentators have failed to understand that; for them, the reasons for doubt are rejected as excessive or else simply judged to be unacceptable, because these writers, as good empiricists, accept the cognitive value of the senses. Beginning from doubt is considered to be unreasonable. The same criticism, although with other arguments, can be found in Austin or Kenny. This misunderstanding of the Cartesian argument is due to the fact that these authors overlook Descartes' constant concern for opposing the value of synthesis. Descartes does this by the expedient of putting into question the scholastic-ontological tradition and all of the knowledge for which there is no demonstrative path to truth. This opens a path to eliminate the false, the alternative, in short, the *doubt* which would let us oscillate between the true and the false.

If Descartes found it necessary to begin from doubt, still it was not doubt which constituted the necessary foundation of the *ratio cognoscendi.*

7. *The* Cogito Ergo Sum *as Problematological Deduction*

The foundation of the *ratio cognoscendi,* the first answer, is the *Cogito.* Doubt simply expresses the problem. Posing it gives the answer: I doubt, and *at the moment*[12] that I doubt, I think, and, as a result, I am. This is not only not out of the question but, on the contrary, creates an undeniable result.

The *Cogito Ergo Sum* poses serious problems. Recalling these difficulties is not an end in itself. What is important to show is that these difficulties are born from the inability to conceive of questioning as such. For Descartes begins from doubt, which is truly a mode of questioning, but never does he consider his way of thinking as a questioning process, though his reasoning aims to be the foundation for any possible reasoning. Still, Descartes undertakes an inquiry into radicality as no other philosopher has. That is why today he retains a prominent place, beyond the customary cliché in all the texts, which designates him as the "father" of modern philosophy.

What Descartes put first, in the sense of being prior to *all evidence*, is also first from the viewpoint of absolute justification. It goes without saying; that is, one does not ask oneself if what is absolutely first must have this precise characteristic of evidence as a justification, rather than another. That would imply a particular conception of what counts as a principle, a principle which should be first. "Just two reasons are enough to prove the point," wrote Descartes in a letter to the translator of his *Principles of Philosophy*. "[T]he first is that the principles are very clear, and the second is that they enable all other things to be deduced from them. These are the only two conditions that such principles must meet" (Cottingham et al., vol. 1, p. 183). But is it evident that the absolutely first principle, which is the *Cogito*—God will be identified as more truly first later on—must be *evident*? But is evidence evident as a principle? Insofar as it is a neutral notion in regard to interrogativity as expressed by doubt, but exhausting every other alternative, evidence defines answerhood (but not problematologically, because it is neutral). Such answerhood is not perceived, since Descartes' problem is not put in those questioning terms. Still, the idea is factually there: the suppression of all alternativity, which implies a self-sustained necessity, and thus no more useless doubt, because it escapes from the order of assertions.

Evidence is what asserts itself as coming from itself: it is evident that evidence itself is evident. All this is circular, but evidence has the advantage of saving us from raising the question of what needs to be established as a principle. The function of evidence is to eliminate prob-

---

12. "I am, I exist, *is necessarily true whenever it is put forward by me or conceived in my mind*." Descartes, *Second Meditation*, in Cottingham et al., *Philosophical Writings*, vol. 2, p. 17 (emphasis added).

lematicity; it is itself nonproblematological. It asserts as nonproblematic the imperative of the nonproblematic; this will not be questioned. Even more, the nonproblematic will not be thought of as the resolution of the problematic, but as its absence, due to the repressive indifference to any reference to this forbidden couple. Evidence thus clearly defines the foundational requirement of such a view by putting that necessity forward as *external* to all interrogativity. It does so by presenting itself as something which neither can nor should be put into question, since evidence proceeds from itself alone, establishing the reflexivity whose thinking subject will soon be conceived of as the first expression. In short, we do not pose a question which does not pose itself, and that is the status of the principle, of the *Cogito*, the first unquestioned affirmation, if we *decide* to doubt everything. Thus, the starting point is asserted but does not provide a place for any of the sort of questioning which should characterize it. And with that, the circle is closed.

What are the consequences of all this? First, we have still not truly *inquired* into the philosophical starting point. This does not mean that what is absolutely first has not been addressed; rather, on the contrary, because it *has* been addressed, it is literally in *question*, but only in a second and secondary, derivative sense, because we can find in the question of the apodicity of all affirmation the resolution of the problematic of the true starting point (the *Cogito*). But it is understood, or rather admitted, to be the primary affirmation only in a particular and unquestioned sense. What is first is so in an assertoric order of discourse. Doubt is put forward only to be dispelled.

We return to Plato, the first opponent of Aristotle, if we can make use of the historical *a contrario*. Plato also thought that interrogativity is secondary to knowledge, and even that it hides its true nature and the sources of its validity, which must therefore be found somewhere other than in reference to the problematic order and its suppressive correlate, answering. If we think of doubt as an interrogative modality, one result necessarily will be that questioning will not know how to support an answer in its very value *as answer*. Its value can only arise from doubt.

So at the starting point, there must be the *cogito* rather than the *dubito*, both amalgamated into modes of thought (*cogitatio*), thought or thinking being defined by affirming rather than asking. Thought comes down to propositions, and questioning is seen as inessential due to the idea of truth as eliminative of that doubt. Questioning is now seen as belonging to the assertoric field of *cogitatio*. I doubt, therefore I affirm that I doubt from that very moment, and I cannot doubt that I doubt when I doubt. The *cogito* is assertoric; it affirms its own certainty, its own validity that is beyond doubt, for if one doubts, one still thinks. In short, it is *assertive thought* which provides a foundation to the order of reasons; it is not *questioning* which, because of the modality of doubt, is rather the weakness to be eradicated. It is important to affirm with certainty, because the uncertainty of doubt contains within it no judgment, no possible positivity. The proof of that is that it is enough to doubt, thus to *affirm* one's doubt, to be sure of something, to know that one is thinking by means of such an affirmation. It is evident that Descartes did not in any way disassociate thought from its affirmation, from metathought, and that the two come together in a perfect intuition. This intuition consists of saying that each time one doubts, one is *certain* that one is thinking, because to say that one doubts is to doubt no more, but rather to assert something in the most positive way possible. In Cartesian doubt (which is more than an intuition because Descartes makes doubt identical with its expression) there is the natural reflexivity that accompanies every act of the intellect. Consciousness, as this immanent and natural reflexivity will be called, will inevitably be intuitional. It is not *doubt* that brings about its own suppression in and through a first answer, because doubt is radical, but rather it is the *expression* of doubt, the *fact* of doubting which avoids doubt and which, as a consequence, is doubtless. Descartes says it well in his *Second Meditation:* the *cogito ergo sum* "is necessarily true whenever it is put forward by me or conceived in my mind" (Cottingham et al., vol. 2, p. 17).[13]

Doubt bears within itself the reflexivity of thought. By doubting, we *express* a doubt, but that assertion is itself in no doubt. Hence the absolutely (justified) first affirmation, the *Cogito.* Its validation rests on the idea that one makes of its validity, thus of knowledge: this is the elimination of the problematic. This cannot be said without presupposing a reference, which is excluded, to the dialectic of questioning, which consecrates answering as the suppression of the question or, at least, as its overcoming through problematological differentiation. Once such a reference to questioning has been excluded, one must presuppose justification as evident, but justification will have to be self-justified as the ideal of knowledge, an ideal embodied within the criterion of evidence. Moreover, doubt, if it cannot be the starting point, will nonetheless embody the first certainty, the *Cogito,* for doubt implies its own suppression, or rather, the expression of that doubt suppresses it. This paradoxical result is explained by the fact that doubt is a disguised assertion, a positive thought and *not* a question. This is a demand from analysis: doubt resolves itself in its supposed solution; or, more pre-

13. This is why Descartes needed to introduce God to establish a nonproblematic validity.

cisely, it converts itself into its own answer. But for Descartes, there has
been no real question about doubt: to doubt is already to think, and to
think is already to know that one thinks.[14] We are faced with an answering process which is such only because there has never been a question,
as such, posed. And, at the same time, because doubt plunges us into
problematicity, we cannot emerge from it with only the *Cogito*. Hence
Descartes' recourse to God, as being analytically deduced from the *Cogito;* such a recourse to God only receives its validity rather than conferring that validity. This produced the famous "Cartesian circle," born of
this double imperative: "If the Cogito is used to prove God and God is
used to prove the Cogito, we are no longer confronted with a *nexus ra-
tionum,* but with a paralogism, a characteristic violation of the basic principle of the order . . ."[15] God has the problematic validity of equations
developed from doubt, and at the same time he suppresses their problematicity by his role as absolute guarantor. There is no escape from the
circle, because the *dubito* is at once real doubt and its opposite, that is,
an affirmation, positive knowledge. If the *Cogito* is truly the absolutely
first and certain principle, then there is no need for God. And if God is
needed, then the *Cogito* which allows us to deduce him is not an absolute truth. How can God play the role which Descartes assigned him,
if God emerges from the *Cogito* which he is supposed to validate, all the
while being as problematic it is? Plato, analysis, synthesis, and their impossible relationship—all of that arises again, but now displaced.

Descartes thus carries out a double *coup de force:* on the one hand, he
makes of doubt an assertion of thought because he defines thought as
"everything which we are aware of as happening within us, in so far as
we have awareness of it,"[16] presupposing the *Cogito* as self-consciousness from the start. On the other hand, he allows doubt to serve as disguised positivity and not as a manifestation of interrogativity. The proof
is that if one doubts that one thinks when one doubts, then one is mistaken, since one cannot doubt that one thinks when one doubts. When
I doubt that I think, I still think, which shows that when I doubt, I
think that I think. Doubt is therefore recast into positivity. Thought
affirms itself, by itself, through doubt addressed to itself.

The *Cogito* therefore is implicit in doubt, because (a) doubt has been

14. Descartes, *Principles of Philosophy* I, 9, in Cottingham et al., *Philosophical Writings,* vol. 1, p. 195.
15. Martial Guéroult, *Descartes' Philosophy Interpreted According to the Order of Reasons,* vol. 1, *The Soul and God,* trans. Roger Ariew (Minneapolis: University of Min-
nesota Press, 1984), p. 167.
16. Descartes, *Principles of Philosophy* I, 9, in Cottingham et al., *Philosophical Writings,* vol. 1, p. 195.

defined as thought, and (b) thought has been defined as an immediate, absolute, and indubitable reflexivity. But is doubt not the opposite of the indubitable? And yet it is necessary that the one engender the other; I doubt *everything*, therefore *nothing* can bring me out of this doubt. So what does Descartes do, since he desperately needs God? In the name of the reflexivity of those mental operations already discussed, he first identifies doubt with its reflexive expression, since both are a *cogitatio*. For from (universal) doubt, nothing could emerge which is not doubtful, since it destroys beforehand every possible affirmation, including that which would allow doubt to be resolved. It is therefore essential, while waiting for God, to extricate oneself from this in one way or another. The *Cogito*, presupposed as *the reflexivity associated with positive thought* distilled into the expression of doubt, allows us to draw the positivity of thinking from that very doubt, self-identified by its expression. It is the *fact* of doubting which is indubitable; and, if one assimilates doubt into the fact that one doubts, something positive is accomplished by doubting everything, something that cannot be doubted. What does doubt consist of, precisely, if not the fact of saying it or conceiving it, in short, of reflecting it? But has one not reflected any *thing* at all, if everything is found only in reflection? Is reflection merely its own object, self-imposed as an empty movement, simply turning upon and around itself?

We can say without hesitation that the confusion between the interrogative order and the assertive or assertoric order is at the base of the major difficulties which we experience in reading Descartes. We can think especially of the circle and the inferential nature (intuitive or not) of the *Cogito*. We will return to this point later, but for the moment I would like to stress how the lack of differentiation between the interrogative and the assertoric results in the impossibility of developing an adequate problematological language, producing the most serious difficulties which Descartes' thought finally will encounter.

Doubt escapes its own grip; its fecundity lies in this ability. We can doubt everything except the affirmation which has just been made of it; that affirmation necessarily escapes doubt. Doubt, being universal, nonetheless bears on *every* affirmation and affects the objective value of the affirmativity of the mind in general. So that the validity of the affirmation which emerges from Cartesian doubt might not fall within its scope, there should exist a language which would not itself be problematic and which, being literally problemato-logical, since it expresses doubt, would escape it. The affirmation of doubt, free from all suspicion, implies a language *of* doubt different from that which is *in* doubt. If it is preferable not to speak of language here, then let us say, rather (although it will come around to the same thing), that we are imposing an assertoric dimension which affirms doubt beyond the simple fact of putting into doubt every affirmation. But Descartes allowed no place for a problematological difference like this one because, for him, doubting is not asking but already means thinking, and thought has a non-problematic positivity which renders it apocritical. Why does he adopt a unitary position in this regard? He cultivates the idea of projecting the process to validate the *Cogito* onto all the other sciences which need a method that conforms to human nature. This, in turn, implies the unity of the human mind, of demonstrative reason at large. They cannot be separated. Therefore, in discovering the metaphysical principle of the *Cogito*, Descartes put its precepts into action: first, doubt all, to accept as true only what is justified. Then analyze complex elements into their constituent simple parts, because the *Cogito*, analytically, contains the knowledge of my existence and that of God. Third, reconstruct the whole into a single chain of reasons. Finally, see that you do have everything: to arrive at a totality presupposes that we have an absolute and global term. These become the well-known four rules of the *Discourse on Method* whose justification flows from the validity of the *Cogito* which utilizes them to verify itself and, thereby, to establish them.

In summary, Descartes knew only one order: that of proof which validates any discourse. Inference, the *search* which leads to absolute certainty, must immediately be identified as absolute certainty, as indubitable truth. It must assert itself as evidence at the same time that it must be demonstrative. This leads to one well-known paradox of the *Cogito:* is it an intuition or a deduction?[17] Descartes holds to both terms of the alternative; he cannot do otherwise. But that is not all. The method that allows discovery of the truth is a fact of consciousness, buried within a consciousness which can find only what it already knows. Descartes is really on Plato's side and in opposition to Aristotle in bringing back the theory of reminiscence:

> As to the fact that there can be nothing in the mind, in so far as it is a thinking thing, of which it is not aware, this seems to me to be self-evident. For there is nothing that we can understand to be in the mind, regarded in this way, that is not a thought . . . we cannot have any thought of which we are not aware at the very moment when it is in us. (*Fourth Set of Replies*, Cottingham et al., vol. 2, p. 171)

17. Jaakko Hintikka, "Cogito, Ergo Sum: Inference or Performance?" *The Philosophical Review* 71 (Jan. 1962): 3–32.

Looking for truth by the process of analysis is thus only recovering what has already been put into our consciousness, something that has been forgotten but which the mind has the power to retrieve. Descartes continues:

> In view of this I do not doubt that the mind begins to think as soon as it is implanted in the body of an infant, and that it is immediately aware of its thoughts, even though it does not remember this afterwards because the impressions of these thoughts do not remain in the memory. (Ibid., pp. 171–72)

Analysis is reminiscence at the same time that it is deduction. That is why Descartes, in the *Second Set of Replies*, upholds the idea that analysis is invention. At the same time, it is quite clear that demonstrative justification, and analysis as well, are limited to operating on what is already invented, on a given. "As for the method of *demonstration*, this divides into two varieties: the first proceeds by analysis and . . . shows the true way by means of which the thing in question was discovered methodically" (Cottingham et al., vol. 2, p. 110; emphasis added).

It is contradictory to identify research with justification insofar as research discovers or invents the given which justification takes hold of. The only exception is if one adopts Plato's solution of progress in knowledge as a demonstrative or "mathematical" process, resorting to what, before this operation, had no right to epistemic existence. Such a solution, we must recall, merely shifts but still repeats the paradox of the *Meno*, and does not resolve it. But at least on this point, Descartes is consistent: imagine that the decision to doubt, its affirmation, did not have the positive reflexivity of consciousness, whose certainty of itself is indisputable truth. We would then be obliged to concede that a search for truth, when it precedes its acquisition, puts us in the realm of nontruth. How can the true emerge from the nontrue, even if it is said to be only problematic, as is doubt? It is necessary to be already within the truth when one searches after truth, and that proposition is not contradictory, or at least does not appear so, if by a search we mean a demonstration of what is already known, but ignored until analytically proved. That is why Descartes, in the last analysis, knew only one language, that of justification: as to that which should express what comes before and leads us to the objects of justification (and which Descartes himself moved toward in the *Cogito*), it just didn't count. He reminds us of this in the tenth paragraph of Part 1 of his *Principles:*

> I shall not here explain many of the other terms which I have already used or will use in what follows, because they seem to me to

be sufficiently self-evident . . . And when I said that the proposition *I am thinking, therefore I exist* is the first and the most certain of all to occur in anyone who philosophizes in an orderly way, I did not in saying that deny that one must first know what thought, existence and certainty are and that it is impossible that that which thinks should not exist . . . But because these are very simple notions . . . I did not think they needed to be listed. (Cottingham et al., vol. 1, pp. 195–96)

It is not only a matter of language, but one of *logos* in the sense that there is an area of truth sui generis which corresponds to a particular type of language. An argument which consists of rejecting questions like "What is X?" which are ontologico-synthetic, and which Descartes refutes with his preference for the analytic, becomes irrelevant. By using the cover of this rejection, he changes the question of what paved the way for the *Cogito* into a scholastic exercise. In reality, he wants to avoid dealing with the question of the status of truth in a type of discourse that searches for truth before having found it. Or else he is obliged to say that truth is always found and that there is no need to search for it other than by justifying what one knows without knowing it, because it is only known "virtually," as he says. And when we try to learn what the *Cogito* and the *sum* mean, it is not some kind of scholastic or ontology that we set forth, but rather counter-problematology. If science existed only at the level of conclusions, and thus only from the moment that God's existence had been demonstrated because, recalls Descartes, "[W]hen I said that we can know nothing for certain until we are aware that God exists, I expressly declared that I was speaking only of knowledge of those conclusions . . ." (*Second Set of Replies*, Cottingham et al., vol. 2, p. 100), then what can be known before knowing that? That is indeed the question; and it is not a scholastic one, even if Descartes ignores it under that pretext. If no knowledge can be invoked which does not follow the order of truths, does the principle which affirms that it must follow this order itself belong to this order, or, on the contrary, is it applied to this order as a result of an external will? This principle is then doubtful, and the whole order of reasons succumbs to doubt, when it really should be overcoming it. That is what we really mean when we say that the Cartesian idea of knowledge is rooted in evidence, that is, that it is self-foundational or, in subjective terms, based on what we call "intuition."

Although the reasoning which *leads* to the first principle of order may be an intuition, it is also inferential, for even if the indubitable validity of intuition may be as self-dependent as it is, we can only arrive at such a principle if we begin by doubting everything. These so-called "two languages," intuition versus deduction, can make us forget that there is really only one possible language because of the unity of reason as self-foundational evidence that is distributed in the conclusions of deductions. Although Descartes did not doubt the value of logic—or reasoning, as Nietzsche claimed—Descartes *did* retain this dual language of intuition and deduction. This allows for a double reading of the *Cogito* because, for Descartes, deduction prevails where intuition, when faced with trying to take in all at once the greatest of complexities, cannot function and must be relayed by inferential decomposition of order to avoid confusion. As Roger Lefèvre reminds us: "As deductive certainty depends on ideas and their linkages, it follows that a simple deduction is an intuition of relationship; a complex deduction, a relationship of intuitions." [18] Double language, once again, is to be understood as an equivalence.

Be that as it may, the difficulty in which the discourse *of* doubt put us, in its being identical to the discourse we doubt, results once more in the mixing of the problem with the solution, which is the essence of the vicious circle. It is the necessary outcome of analysis when it claims to attain truth. It (pre)supposes truth, and then erases the supposition. The famous Cartesian circle, which always takes us back from the *Cogito* to God, lies in the necessity of using valid discourse to validate discourse; that is, in this case, to demonstrate that God exists. It is essential that we move immediately into the realm of the discourse of truth, since there is really no other discourse, even when the problem is to *arrive* at truth, and not to *presuppose* it, in which case the quest is pointless. One could certainly oppose the order of things to the order of reasons, as Gueroult suggested in referring to the dissociation of analysis and synthesis. "But if we situate ourselves according to the point of view of the *ratio cognoscendi*, the Cogito is the only first principle, while if we situate ourselves according to the point of view of the *ratio essendi*, God alone is the first principle, since being the author of all things, he is both the principle of the Cogito as simple consciousness, and of the objective realities . . ." [19] However, the principle of knowing, to be objective, must be a principle of knowing *things*, thus an objective principle. Besides, is it possible to imagine that an order of reasons would operate without a corresponding order of contents? And, symmetrically, we can note that the order of objective necessity is not an order of which one

18. Roger Lefèvre, "La structure du cartésianisme," *Publications de l' Université de Lille* 3 (1980): 17 [author's translation].

19. Guéroult, *Descartes' Philosophy*, vol. 1, p. 165.

can speak, nor which one can *think of* without postulating that there is a discourse and a thought which allows access to it. A discourse about an order of things considered as independent from all possible discourse autonomizes this order within a discourse that becomes impossible to sustain. How can one gain access to an order of *things in themselves,* an order which is different from the order of discourse and analysis, when, to speak about it, it is necessary to arrive there in a certain way, and when, as a consequence, this order cannot be absolutely autonomized? What can one say about something one cannot speak about? What would a *ratio essendi* be if it fell outside the order of knowledge? We *literally* cannot know. That is why Descartes says in his *Sixth Set of Replies:* ". . . for we must begin with knowledge of God, and our *knowledge* of all other things must then be subordinated to this single initial piece of knowledge . . ." (Cottingham et al., vol. 2, p. 290; (emphasis added).

There is something artificial about the dissociation of analysis and synthesis. The two overlap, as Descartes admits, when in his *Second Set of Replies* he redemonstrates synthetically the results obtained earlier through analysis: ". . . the method of demonstration, this divides into two varieties: the first proceeds by analysis and the second by synthesis" (ibid., vol. 2, p. 110). Some might prefer the one to the other, depending on the objective sought, but they lead inevitably to identical results. The idea of God is analytically contained in the *Cogito,* which signifies nothing more than this: synthesis is immanent to analysis. Once more we encounter Plato's idea concerning dialectic and its twofold movement.

In short, the opposition between analysis and synthesis is as untenable in Descartes as it was in Plato. The conclusion is worth what the principle is worth: everything is in doubt, therefore *nothing* is certain, and if we are truly certain of this, then we are clearly in a contradiction. This is the basis of our thesis of the schism between the problematological and the apocritical, which suggests that one can answer about questions and still respect the problematological difference. The kind of synthesis which duplicates the results of analysis too often makes those who defend the point forget that analysis cannot emerge from its initial problematicity other than by the waving of a magic wand, thereby making of doubt an affirmative thought that it is not and consecrating the emptiness of reflexive immanence, a reflection which seems to have no object other than itself. For when I doubt I do not think of myself in the process of doubting; I refer myself to something else. Otherwise, it would not be just the unconscious which would be impossible, but many other elementary activities of consciousness: when I look at this inkwell on the table, I do not see myself looking at it, nor

do I think of myself looking at it. I am totally absorbed in my visual preoccupation.

In reality, if I doubt, I question; and should I doubt this too, I would
question again. That is really the sole and single answer which imposes
itself and resists further questioning by confirming itself. This duality
is impossible for Descartes, since he denies the problematological difference, but there is no escape from it: if I think, then I question. Descartes, under the influence and requirements of propositionalism, sac-
rifices his thought to the assertoric: I doubt, therefore I affirm that I
doubt, and I affirm *myself* in so doing. The fact is that there cannot be a
regression of the type "I affirm that I affirm . . ." because when I doubt,
and in doubting that I doubt, all I do is reaffirm it, keeping intact this
primacy of affirmation, which prevents the process from going on to
infinity. However, and in spite of himself, what Descartes draws is nothing but a problematological inference, since he goes from doubt to its
resolution on the basis of doubt itself. Such is truly the essence of philosophical reasoning. As a philosopher, Descartes nonetheless proceeds
by questioning, although he moves away from any reflexivity of questioning itself by excluding all reference to interrogativity, falling back
on the classical version of deduction, which, even when not in the service of ontology, is justification. The *Cogito* does not exemplify the standard form of deduction, but a problematological inference. It is no
longer easy to know if it should be labeled a deduction or not. This
is the origin of Hintikka's famous question ("Inference or Performance?"), although we could say that the problem was already being
posed by Descartes' contemporaries. Descartes, quite embarrassed by
his analytical model, clearly sees that the *Cogito* is an inference, but a
very special one, an *immediate* one as it were, in that it does not resort to
external premises. Is it then a matter of intuition, the mysterious operation which will later become a faculty, whose role seems to be defined
residually or negatively (as that which must enable us to know, though
not deductively) to comply with the necessity for evidence to be evident by itself? Intuition is the irrational within absolute reason, and
thus it reveals the impossibility of such an absolute in the sense that a
principle cannot be itself *principled*, as Descartes puts it.

Intuition puts us in contact with "clear and distinct ideas," which
have no properties other than those truly imposed by themselves.
"Thus everyone can mentally intuit that he exists, that he is thinking,"
says Descartes in *Rule Three* (Cottingham et al., vol. 1, p. 14). This poses
the well known problem of the nature of the *Cogito*, set forth by Gueroult and reprised by Hintikka: "Descartes refuses to consider the
Cogito as reasoning. He has, indeed, effectuated a philosophical revo-

lution directed against Scholasticism, and therefore could get himself enslaved to its methods. Why then did he persist on at least three occasions (the *Search for Truth, Discourse, Principles*) in presenting the *Cogito* in the form which he himself denied?"[20] Descartes himself denies the deductive character of his reasoning:

> And when we become aware that we are thinking things, this is a primary notion which is not derived by means of any syllogism. When someone says, "I am thinking, therefore I am, or I exist," he does not deduce existence from thought by means of a syllogism, but recognizes it as something self-evident by a simple intuition of the mind. This is clear from the fact that if he were deducing it by means of a syllogism, he would have to have had previous knowledge of the major premiss "Everything which thinks is, or exists"; yet in fact he learns it from experiencing in his own case that it is impossible that he should think without existing. It is in the nature of our mind to construct general propositions on the basis of our knowledge of particular ones. (*Second Set of Replies*, Cottingham et al., vol. 2, p. 100)

Descartes, by putting himself in the context of the order of reasons, which is exclusively justificatory and deductive, could not recognize the problematological inference which is embodied in the *Cogito*. On the other hand, he saw clearly that "I think, therefore I am" is unlike a propositional deduction in the traditional sense of the term. Hence his embarrassment: he denies that the *Cogito* is a deduction but presents his reasoning in deductive terms because he does not know any other type of inference. The necessity of the *Cogito* rests on the impossibility of any answer other than that which is given, once we have opted for doubt and its assertoric reading. This necessity resembles intuition— since there are no external premises—as much as an act of understanding able to accredit the "performative" thesis that Hintikka spoke about. The truth of the saying is revealed in the fact of saying, and this truth results from a certain type of linguistic usage, linked to verbs like "I promise," for example, in which the promise lies only in the act of uttering it. The promise is entirely in the act of utterance, in the fact of saying "I promise." Even if such an analysis of the *Cogito* should prove plausible, it would do no more than support our fundamental idea, that there is a language which captures the sense of interrogative reality and, in so doing, opens a realm that is out-of-the-question. That there is inference, a passage from one realm to another, and that it is a form

20. Guéroult, *Descartes' Philosophy*, vol. 2, Appendix.

of deduction where a conclusion imposes itself as being out-of-the-question, is one of the most important outcomes of our philosophy centered on problematological difference. The "I think" will be performative only if there is associated with it, as presupposition, the reflexive act of making an conflation between thinking and the fact of thinking, where thinking is nothing but its own utterance. Such an amalgam results from generalized propositionalism and its epistemic counterpart: an ideal of reason that is justification.

Performativity, as a theoretical view implied by propositionalism to enlarge itself, is thus too narrow to apply truly to Descartes. Even if the sentence "I ask . . ." does coincide with the act of asking, even if the request does not in any way exceed the act of formulating the question, that is only true for the first person in verbal usage. The individual who says "He is asking for bread" is not *himself* asking for bread. Descartes, on the other hand, believed that he was bringing to light universal subjective properties and not a linguistic fact "in the first person." Therefore, if I can say of someone else that he thinks—and Descartes sometimes explicitly involves his readers, with the help of the word "us" (see the *Principles*)—then do I have to conclude that he *is* (for how could he think and not be)? In what way is there still performativity, if not metaphorically? Besides, performative interpretation does not always work. Descartes shows clearly (*Principles* I, 9) that his conclusion remains valid for any feeling, to this extent: if I feel a thing, I know what I am feeling, I think of it, and as a consequence I must truly *be* to experience it in this way. But "I feel" is not performative of "I am" unless what I have said heretofore about the immanent reflexive character of thought is supposed. This property may condition performativity, but in a different sense from that practiced by the linguists who today hold this theory. Performativity, and what Grice calls "implicature," are at best only consequences borrowed from the terminology of linguistics, unfortunately stretched to usages quite alien to performativity as one usually conceives it *stricto sensu*.

Why is doubt the sole foundation of the *Cogito*, although Descartes claims that there is no other foundation than the *Cogito* itself? Answer: one can doubt that one thinks, walks, eats, or anything else, but one cannot doubt that one doubts. In short, it is because any other "conclusion is not absolutely certain. This is because . . . it is possible for me to think I am seeing or walking . . ." (*Principles* I, 9, Cottingham vol. 1, p. 195), but then I think, and therefore the only point on which I cannot be mistaken is that I am, says Descartes.

To sum up, after having discarded the "gadget" of performativity, we are once again faced with the tension created by the inferential nature of the *Cogito*, an inference denied but practiced. To tell the truth, doubt will carry its solution within itself only if it is radical, philosophical. If I doubt that I am walking, I well know that I doubt, but I still do not know for sure whether I walk or not. On the other hand, if I doubt *everything*, I go beyond this universal doubt by affirming my thought and myself. The contradiction between *universal* doubt and its implicit resolution, which prevents it once and for all from being truly total doubt, is solved if we admit that there is progress in knowledge, a progress which unfolds through time, a progress confirmed by the idea of God. The knowledge of God makes it unnecessary for us to have to follow the same path over and over again because he enables us to retain the conclusions we obtain. All this, as we can easily realize, is the result Descartes was aiming at in his *Meditations*. Nevertheless, consciousness initially is self-transparent in some innate way, and the idea of my existence and that of God, too, initially reside together in me. As a consequence, universal doubt and its resolution coexist in my mind, and doubt itself prevents full resolution. Virtually, and actually, because the power to doubt everything necessarily impedes the power to resolve (although they represent the same power), and because it is impossible to doubt *everything* (unless this should already be the solution), one no longer doubts everything, etc.

Let us conclude. For Descartes "I think, therefore I am" is true because if I think, I must truly be, not the "I" of the speaker but a universal "I," symbolized by thought. I am not just *some* thing, I am a *thinking* thing. By an extension, inherited from the tradition that he denies, Descartes assimilates the "I am" to the "I am a thinking *substance*"; for what am I when I think if not precisely this? Clearly, one cannot jump from "I think" to "I am," but only to "I am thinking." Even Hobbes, as a true Englishman who distrusts words which *seem* to refer to things without actually doing so, remarks (*Third Objections*) that the *Cogito*, as an inference, is a curious one. What is Descartes' answer? "When I said 'that is, I am a mind, or intelligence, or intellect or reason,' what I meant by these terms was not mere faculties, but things endowed with the faculty of thought" (*Principles* I, 9, Cottingham vol. 2, p. 123). Why does he proceed from the property to the thing itself? Because "[w]e cannot conceive of thought without a thinking thing, since that which thinks is not nothing . . . It may be that the subject of any act can be understood only in terms of a *substance* . . ." (ibid., vol. 2, pp. 123–24; emphasis added). That is why I am if I think; that is, I am a thinking *being*.

But the question of thinking has to be posed, in one way or another, to reach the stage where the Cartesian premise is established, though it contains, propositionally speaking, its diverse conclusions in a circular

way, because the problematological inference presupposes what the answer is all about and does so by necessity.

8. *From Analytical Inference to Problematological Inference*

We find in Descartes the same ambiguity in regard to analysis as that
which was brought to light in Greek philosophy. Analysis is both equivalent to synthesis and different from it. Analysis contains synthesis as
an inverse movement, but for synthesis to work effectively and resolve
the paradox of the *Meno*, it is necessary that it be conducted independently, as external to analysis. But that renders synthesis simply impossible. It is hard to see the interest in an independent synthesis. Indeed,
it cannot truly be "independent" in that it functions only as an inverse
response to analysis and does not exist outside of it. We could truly say
that synthesis expounds what analysis invents to be able to distinguish
them. But the Greek geometers used the one in place of the other, and
not one after the other, which Plato had recommended as a way of verifying the results of analysis and for the sake of establishing philosophy's
own requirement for departing from the hypothetico-deductive to establish a domain for absolute truth. The geometers proceeded as they
did not because of any so-called weakness in their reasoning, but because they perhaps understood better than Plato had that synthesis and
analysis were redundant, and that having one meant that one could dis-
pense with the other. Hence the indiscriminate recourse to either one
and the lack of necessity to supplement the one with the other. Yet synthesis necessarily presupposes the existence of analysis, whose results it
expounds and reorganizes.

But Plato would not have wanted an approach still tainted by an
initial problematicity: deduction must not be rooted in the hypothetical. Synthesis does not simply develop the results of analysis, it is foundational to them, because it is different from analysis. We can see the
differentiation, if not scission, as the ancestor of another split, equally
untenable, between discovery and justification in science; discovery
will become purely rhetorical, as dialectic is for Aristotle. To arrive at
his goal, Plato proclaimed synthesis as autonomous, but he was not able
to prove it so. This is an autonomy which, by definition, means that one
begins right away in the realm of truth, of the nonproblematic. Analysis
by itself can only produce the hypothetico-deductive. Plato's dialectic
attempted to accomplish the impossible by reintegrating analysis with
synthesis in a unique combination. Something of this kind would have
been required to escape the terrible paradox presented by a synthesis
that is both independent of *and* dependent on analysis. Aristotle will re-

ject this Platonic effort, because analysis so dialecticized will nevertheless retain all of its initial problematicity. We continue to begin from a
problem that is already resolved, or at least supposedly so. So long as we
have not cut the umbilical cord of synthesis, synthesis will have to displace the initial problematicity. Synthesis will be ontological to be fully
demonstrative. It will begin from what is known, *known* as being precisely that which is said *to be* such. Since philosophy needs a starting
point that is without doubt, it will not be completely and authentically
doubtless except by becoming ontology (the science of Being). The
synthetic knowledge which will be developed within the framework of
the ontological view of philosophy will be the source of all knowledge
in virtue of the syllogistic method which will be utilized by all the other
sciences other than the science of "Being as being."

It is essential to understand that philosophy, from the beginning, has
obscured all reference to resolution and questioning by singling out
analysis and synthesis, and that both have operated in tandem with a
propositionalization of inference. There are problems which can be resolved by themselves, as in philosophy, where their thematic expression is already their solution. In that regard, the analytic method does
fit. Descartes confusedly recognized it: he defended the idea that
analysis and synthesis are equivalent, yet still he extolled analysis as
first for philosophical research. But he continued to believe in their
equivalence, for he was the heir of the idea of the impossibility of addressing the question of questioning itself, and of the propositional displacement of the reflexivity of such a question. If the method of proof is
twofold, then we must prefer analysis, because it "is the best and truest
method of instruction" (*Second Set of Replies*, Cottingham vol. 2, p. 111).
As for synthesis, to which Descartes will also turn in his *Second Set of
Replies*, it "is a method which it may be very suitable to deploy in geometry as a follow-up to analysis, but it cannot so conveniently be applied
to these metaphysical subjects . . . In metaphysics . . . there is nothing
which causes so much effort as making our perception of the primary
notions clear and distinct" (ibid.).

Let us be clear about this: by analysis, one enters the realm of certainty and evidence of truth; nothing hypothetical can interfere, which
is a great difference from what happens in analysis, according to Plato.
"This is why I wrote 'Meditations' rather than 'Disputations,' as the
philosophers have done, or 'Theorems and Problems,' as the geometers
would have done" (ibid., p. 112). Analysis, as Descartes clearly states in
his *Second Set of Replies*, is demonstrative.

Then where does this difference between analysis and synthesis
come from, a difference which is evidently not limited to directing the

propositional movement? It is necessary to return to the problematizing and the resolutional origins which establish the features of and the differences between analysis and synthesis. Either questions can be resolved from themselves only, or else external elements are needed to find a solution. In this second case, we are faced with a synthesis, which operates from some *middle term*. We return to the famous syllogism with its structure built of three components, all of which, however, are completely propositionalized. Nowhere does it appear that questions are raised nor that inference is aimed at translating and resolving them. When Aristotle defined the syllogism as "a discourse in which, certain things being stated, something other than what is stated follows of necessity from their being so" (*Prior Analytics* I, 24b19–20), he did not give a clear account of the relationship to otherness, or the existence of difference which is the fundamental characteristic of the syllogism. Now, let us suppose that this difference does not obtain, which, of course, remains unperceived as an expression of problematological difference, then, what one has is a vicious circle, a process of question-begging. This latter term is apt in that it captures what goes on at the level of circularity: what is problematic is supposedly resolved, and, in that way, we fall into problematological *indifference*. As for propositionalism, it conceptualizes circularity at the only level where it can work, and affirms that a conclusion is contained in its premises, and that such a fact renders the inference invalid. However, the reason for that cannot be conceived by or through propositionalism, since it concerns a respect for the problematological difference, the necessity of not answering by simply duplicating a question. This is true except for philosophy, where, clearly, the goal of answering *is* questioning, but where the difference is nonetheless established because of the *formulation* of that difference.

The syllogistic inference is born of synthesis as a propositional movement, and the analytic inference is necessarily devalued because it is rooted in the unknown. The propositional ideal will be actualized in synthesis, which operates directly with truth. Analysis is more appropriate to its discovery, as Descartes said, and to the philosophy which begins from problems, but because problems are propositionalized, analysis is left in an ambiguous status. For analysis is actually demonstrative. Truth proceeds from itself, as it were, through the agency of the *ratio cognoscendi*. The analytical order, in the last analysis, must coincide with the results of synthesis, hence their equivalent value in producing truth, even if synthesis is simultaneously affirmed as purely reproductive.

But the problem is even more complex. Order plays an essential role for Descartes. It is even constitutive of science, as it is of philosophy. It immerses us into truth, which proves that the order is not ontologically neutral. Yet, it is different from the order of subject-matter and things: what is the first according to the order of reasons is not first according to the order of things. This is a contradiction. Where could one find the identity of truth? For what is thought of separately is also separate in reality (*Letter to Mersenne*, Dec. 24, 1640). Rational priority is therefore likely to be an ontological priority. What is posed first must coincide with what *is* first, if thought lies in the realm of truth. But we know that for Descartes it is nothing of the kind: since the *Cogito* is not ontologically first, but it is God who is, it is also God who is the synthesizing principle which is included analytically in the development expressed by the *Meditations*. The order of the *ratio cognoscendi* engenders knowledge as to things, for to invent (in this context) is to justify, to demonstrate, to "pro-pose" what is true. The confusion, the conflation between the two *ratios*, arises at the very moment when it is critical to keep them distinct, and yet when it is impossible to do so. The search for truth is phony research, since everything has already been found, and since we are able to find by reflexive analysis truths for which we require only evidence or intuition. Propositional reflexivity is self-imposed reflexivity as a criterion of this evidence; by generalized reflexivity, the analytical method of metaphysics becomes the model of all possible methods, and of scientificity at large. The *Meditations* are the true foundation for any "discourse on method." It is clear that here we have a foundation for propositionalism, constantly in play, and used by Descartes. It is foundational in that the basic principle of its functioning is guaranteed, and even renewed, by its being rooted in the subject at a time when many features of discourse were validated by their being rooted in the understanding.

The Cartesian inference is only possible through the initial propositionalization of the *Cogito*. "I am" does not follow from "I think," but from the *enunciation* of my thought. Thus from its reflection can be inferred the *enunciation* of my existence, since it is not because I think that I exist. There is here an analytical regression from effect back to cause, but the inference is only justified as a chain proceeding from the *Cogito* to the *sum*. The principle of inference, whose foundation is at stake, is presumed to go beyond saying, establishing thereby the criterion of evidence. The idea that the *sum* is contained in the *Cogito* can be defended, in the sense that affirming *that* I think means nothing more than affirming *that* I am. Stating B is substitutable for stating A, but B is the cause of A: if one can state A, it is because of B. What Descartes was considering was the inversion of this order, since there had been a passage from analysis to synthesis and the possibility of passing from the one to the other. What is more important to see is the chain of problematization which allows inferring the answer from the question, a chain which I shall term the *problematological inference.*

It is useful to remind ourselves of the problems encountered by the analytico-synthetic pair. Descartes needs to divide Reason into analysis and synthesis to avoid the circle which consists of presupposing that very rational order which is in question. It does not prevent him from actually presupposing the existence of that order, by using it, beyond the simply repeated affirmation of the unity of Reason. Descartes knew only the propositional order, and it is precisely that order which must be established, due to all the doubts that scholasticism had generated concerning the possibilities of establishing such an order. In fact, these doubts confirm the order of necessity by the assertoric reflexivity that they express. This assertivity of doubt proceeds from itself and deserves no justification. It belongs to the "clear and distinct ideas," like wanting, feeling, or thinking. Descartes must split Reason into analysis and synthesis, criticizing the one to the benefit of the other to be able to affirm them later as equivalent, if only from the pedagogical point of view, and therefore to be able to proclaim Reason as the unity of the propositional field. Will analysis then be the inventive mode of Reason, and synthesis the fulfillment of the requirement for a justification? Some texts might lead us to that conclusion. But analysis is also a demonstrative inference. It does not place us prior to truth. At the moment that we search for the truth without having it, analysis plunges us into the world of truth and the chain of propositions justified as indubitable. Descartes could only accomplish this by establishing the unity of Reason, of analysis and synthesis, of what we search for and what we justify. When we decide to search for truth without having it yet, then we would already have it; radical doubt always destroys itself, if it is truly radical. This shows clearly that searching for truth, in the way one usually means it, is impossible. The period of time which could separate the moment of radical doubt from its self-suppression adds nothing: it is reversible time, in the most literal meaning of the word. Because there is a split, and because, simultaneously, analysis finds itself *opposed* to synthesis, Descartes will speak rather contradictorily of the order by which Reason progresses, invents, finds truth. As a consequence, we face the paradox that the mind does not have the answer at a time it has got it; and this because there *is* no answer since there has never been a question. Such a paradox is countered by the autonomization of analysis and, as a corollary, by the redundancy of synthesis. What we are bound to accept is an inevitable circularity. Doubt is a rhetoric of affirmation, a rhetoric which denies itself as such to reveal nothing but its mere ancillary surrogate and occasional aspect regarding propositional truth.

The circularity we observe in Descartes' reasoning results from his failure to distinguish the language of validation from the language to be validated, the problematological from the apocritical. Circularity is a process whereby one gives as an answer what is yet to be established as an answer. As a consequence, problematological in-difference becomes synonymous with circularity; there is a complete assimilation of the problematic with the resolutional. On the other hand, if we admit that Descartes proceeds to a problematological deduction which allows the passage from a question to an answer, then the accusation of a vicious circle fails, because this notion only applies within the propositional realm. Descartes presupposes what is in question in the demonstration of the existence of God as well as in the *Cogito*, which already contains the *I am*. Even more, the *Cogito* poses as already in existence that which is deduced a priori (when that very existence is precisely the question), even if existence is, by all evidence, linked to the predicate of the thought of which it is the substance, the support. There indeed must be a subject which *is*, which exists, in order that it be given these attributes.

The kind of circularity which would discredit the problematological inference would be one that would presuppose an answer at the very stage of the question, it being admitted, moreover, that the answer to that question does not consist of simply an articulation and expression of the question. In philosophy, as we have seen, the goal of answering is questioning itself: propositional circularity thus is structurally inevitable. The passage from question to answer is here an inference, and Aristotle's propositionalist conception of inference has made us forget what really underlies it. But the truth about the reasoning process is that it is a movement from questioning to answering, and the peculiarity of philosophy is that is makes the inference circular from a propositionalist point of view. That is why philosophy needs to focus again on the originary as problematological, and why it needs to be able to conceive of itself according to the problematological difference to avoid becoming circular. One could also add, along with John Stuart Mill, that *all* logic is circular, since nothing more can be found in a conclusion than that which is already implicitly contained in its premises. This could be said in behalf of problematological in-difference, where questions and answers are conflated. On the other hand, logic is not actually sterile, if by this required difference between premises and conclusions, that is, by answering the question by not simply repeating it, the mind can progress de facto, even if, de jure, Mill's criticism may still be true.

Descartes expressed the same reservation about logic and rejected synthesis without being able to identify the distinguishing characteristic of his own philosophical inference. It goes without saying that by staying within the basic tenets of the propositionalist sphere of thought, Descartes could only move in a circle. As we have noted, an answer which arises from questioning itself can only be circular with respect to propositionalism if the difference between the two is not made explicit through the problematological discourse which precisely establishes that difference. Descartes circularized his inference, and the inevitable circle became a vicious one because of the propositional conformity which it supported. Here it becomes clear that Cartesianism no longer can be saved. Even if it illustrates the problematological inference and the philosophy of its embodiment, always actualized in a specific way, Cartesianism is nonetheless entirely beholden to the propositionalism which it helps to establish. Descartes can only deal with doubt by reducing it to a mode of affirmation. Propositionalism's validity is never challenged. It serves to resolve every question, since that is what Descartes wanted to provide a foundation for, while he is using propositionalism as *evidence*, an evidence for which it would be necessary to find the originary *intuition* that verifies it. Descartes thus uses the problematological inference in spite of himself, as Kant will do after him in the Transcendental Deduction of Categories. Because of the results of Cartesianism on what is originary, the method and primacy of consciousness once again spring from a negation of the problematological, are able to be produced by it and are supported only by a practice which is the problematological deduction. If problematological deduction had been able to be thought of in light of the difficulties arising from the *Cogito*, from its circularity and the autonomization of the analytical order, the result would have been in conformity with the goal of radical questioning. It would have been completely different, and one would have had to concede to the reality of a *logos* made up of questions and answers, capable of reflecting itself through the problematological difference as found in differentiated answers, that is, apocritical ones and problematological ones.

Beyond this shortcoming, or this impossibility, it is important to see what changes when Descartes is compared with Aristotle. The principle of noncontradiction was the foundation of the Aristotelian *logos*, as the *Cogito* would be for Descartes. Was the Aristotelian foundation of the propositionalist *logos* so deficient that Descartes would have to displace it, or even to find another point of foundation, if there is to be one?

Aristotle accorded a positive role to dialectical refutation, to the extent that contradictory theses could be solved, and in so doing allowed truth to emerge, through an argument *ad absurdum*, so to speak. But the mechanism is purely propositional; it works on theses taken as such and presupposes the principle of noncontradiction. As a result, the principle of noncontradiction is going to become the keystone of propositionalism. How can such a principle be validated, since its validation presupposes its existence? Aristotle is going to imagine an opposing principle to this one which will give it all its credibility, through the impossibility of opposing it without at the same time verifying it. And yet nothing prevents anyone who denies the principle of noncontradiction from accepting contradiction, and thereby the inconsistency of his position. The latter consists of putting contradiction into practice while denying it at the same time. He would confirm this incoherence much more than he would express some underlying will toward consistency. If the proposition "A is B and non-B at the same time and within the same relationship" cannot be maintained without applying the very noncontradiction which it denies, this will disturb no one but the one who *already* adheres to the principle. We are left again with evidence as the ultimate criterion of propositionalism. It is this evidence which Descartes wants to include thematically. For Aristotle, noncontradiction means the identity of the subject submitted to predication. We can say B and non-B, but only for a subject which maintains its identity as subject. What changes is the predicate; from B one passes to non-B. Young Socrates becomes old, and the old Socrates is the same as the young one. With Descartes, it is not a matter of producing a propositional theory of answering, but rather being able to distinguish between answering and nonanswering, between the apodictic and the rhetorical.

In short, Descartes wants to find the true subject beyond *judgment*, with a view to regulating opposition, that is, *rhetoric*, which syllogistic logic has not been able to demarcate clearly and distinctly. The identity of the subject underlying its predicates still could not prevent contradiction. Eventually, what is this sensible appearance which Descartes so strongly criticized if not otherness, the power to be something else, therefore, the inability to really be a subject, if by subject we understand that which remains an identical substrate of change and not a phenomenalization thereof? If the subject were susceptible of being something other than what it is, it would only be the illusion (an appearance of) that object. This implies that one speaks falsely, mistakenly, about that object by calling it a substance. As such, it cannot serve as the subject of a judgment if a contrary judgment regarding it is also admitted. The sensible is of the same nature as rhetorics which pertain to the order of the opposable and the appearance of truth, whereas what is required is the wise identity of the impossible contradictory. The true subject, then, is the *Cogito*, and what can be projected from it, including the general idea of subject, including propositional subject, as the basis of the necessity of true judgment, in which it alone reaffirms itself through its own negation and sustains itself through all possible appearances, and even through all imaginable, sensible illusions. The subject as a principle, and, above all, as a principle of an anthropological nature, located in the very utterance of its own reality as subject, was born with Descartes. But what we can see perhaps a little better today is the rhetorical closure operating with the shift which makes man foundational, a place man had shared with God, at least at the first stage of Modern Philosophy. Through this closure the propositional order rhetorically excludes rhetoric. To say that is not to express one of those facile paradoxes to which modern thought is so partial. We need to grasp this formulation for what it affirms. The *Cogito* is a rhetorical reality which closes the propositional order on itself, doing it so that no matter what question is put, including one about the *Cogito* itself (which thus is also put once more into question), we revert to the *Cogito*, undeniable in its self-confirmation, its self-sufficiency (as substance). This is what counters any contradictory affirmation, in that such an affirmation always presupposes an "I" who affirms. Whatever question can be posed can only lead to the *Cogito*. Is that to say that no answer has any solution other than the *Cogito*, and that no really new question is possible? It is undeniable that the *Cogito* is the agent of answering, and that it is hard to see an answer which is not sustained by the consciousness that I have of answering. But to infer from this that self-consciousness makes the whole of answerhood, up to its very content, there is a step which even the doctrine of Cartesian innateness does not allow us to cross.

With Kant, things are clearer, because the "I think," which must accompany any representation, is only the *form* of the answer, not its content. There is no answering that does not perpetuate the model of answerhood represented by the *Cogito* as the absolutely first answer. But what animates Kant's thinking as well as Descartes' is a particular practice implicit in problematization, which was ended by rhetorization, by the automatic and *a priori* falling back on the affirmation of the subject as the model of any conceivable affirmation, hence of Reason itself. No problematization, nor problematology, would be able to emerge for themselves, despite the initial *dubito*, because questions receive in advance their ultimate answerhood from the subject's self-affirmation, as if they had been resolved in advance, or, at least, as if the answer had been predetermined a priori in what characterized it as an answer. A question thus is necessarily rhetorical, for it is no more than the *form* that has been derived from foundational asserting, which then makes it vain and redundant. The *Cogito* rhetorizes every possible question by leading the question back to some judgment whose form a priori derives from the utterance of its own nature as principle. The *Cogito* eliminates all opposition, in the guise of a response, answering by an automatic reduction to a doubt-free anthropological substratum. But if the *Cogito* is the rhetorical agency that closes the order of judgment on evidence, then it can *only* rest on its "own" evidence, and with the goal of freeing this order from that very rhetoric, as symbolized by the endless debates of medieval scholasticism. The paradox of thought that emanates from Descartes consists of allowing consciousness to play the role of rhetorical barrier, preventing any emergence of rhetoric. This presupposes some unconscious in consciousness, that is, a monopolistic, imperial necessity, accompanied by a repression of the motivations that directed this invasion of the field of the mind and intellect, motivations which are opposed to this monopoly, if they could be expressed. In reality, the propositional order has a merely rhetorical foundation: that is to say, it is not really grounded, properly speaking. To avoid all rhetorics as well as any real problematization, consciousness reduces the latter to a disguised affirmation by means of the self-affirmation of its a priori power of universal resolution. This power is quite illusory and rests on the transformation of every true question to some prior affirmation. Such an affirmation is modeled on, and supported by, a self-consciousness which unifies the diverse and conflicting theses into an unchanging repetition of reflexive consciousness, whatever these theses may be. Consciousness, in being repressed in its rhetorical role, only allows us to see a propositional order, one which responds to the demands of the apodicity which serves as the criterion of truth and science. And at the same time it represses its own repression considered as the rhetorization of all rhetoric, an operation which consists of bringing every real question back to the kind of evidence for which there is a unicity of answer which must preexist the question for that question to make sense. But can we honestly surrender to the position that every question is decided a priori on the basis of the postulate of generalized consciousness? Is this not a rhetorical function, an automatic closure which the imposition of the primacy of consciousness aims at eliminating from the order which it defines? Rhetorization carried out by consciousness functions like answering, that is, only through the a priori suppression of all actual questioning. As a result, consciousness answers by making all actual questions impossible, and that necessarily places it outside of questioning or, in its own opinion, although it cannot think of

them as such, within the realm of solutions. If questions cannot be understood as questions, then answering is equally impossible, and no
coup de force can change that, even if the *form* of answering is quite often
cast in the discourse of assertion.

Since Descartes, consciousness has become the rhetorical agency
through which every question can be reduced to answers which no
longer pose problems. It is the very principle of deduction, which contains its conclusions within its premises. Make *everything* deductive: is
that not the ambition of the mechanistic view which so characterized
the classical age? Rhetoricization proceeds by the self-denial of answering, of the referral to questioning (which the concept of answering, by
definition, contains within itself). It is thus clearly the a priori mode of
the resolutional which transforms every question into something else.
That implies that a question is never really itself: problematological inference is therefore and thereby done at little cost. We will come back
to that later. In any case, consciousness progresses through a problematization bound to remain unreflected as such. Fixation on the result
and obsession with deduction allow us to see them as products of that
propositional obsession which leads to negating what falls outside itself,
though, at the same time, it is this outside that makes propositionality
possible.

The subject, now identified with consciousness, is going to repress
the rhetorical function of consciousness. It will even repress the very
fact that there is repression for consciousness to play the totalitarian role
of being the a priori criterion, both necessary and universal, of the resolutional process. If it is going to be able to resolve all possible questions,
it is necessary not only that consciousness make them rhetorical, assur-
ing at least the form of every possible resolution (independent of the
content of the question that has arisen), but also that this function be
hidden for the subject, so that it assumes it unconsciously and denies
this unconsciousness, if the subject is to be able in good conscience to
reject rhetoricization and, as a result, all ideology. Perhaps, to make this
clearer, it would be useful to recall here what we understood by rhetorization. When we say that we are faced with a rhetorical question (of the
type "Don't you find this man dishonest?"), we mean that we already
have the answer in the question that is posed; that the question, which
seems to refer back to the will to know, and to suggest the possibility of
an alternative as a solution, in fact leads only to a single proposition
which we hold implicitly from the start. As a result, we can see that
making every possible question rhetorical consists of giving oneself the
identity of the answer, of reducing every new question to a problem
that is already resolved, or of getting rid of any alternative in regard to

the old question as being a prolongation of preexisting answers. We can ask in all honesty, what harm can there be in proceeding that way? Is this not the secret of propositional deduction? But in fact, it is paradoxical to treat a new problem by reducing it to what has been previously solved, because what went before cannot have resolved *everything;* it is this anterior resolution which engenders the very problematic that arises. Novelty would be impossible; one could only move in a circle. Once again, we have the traditional criticism leveled against propositional deduction. Rhetorization gives the illusion of having an a priori power of resolution. Whatever the question posed, whatever its content, a solution is provided formally (Kant) by the unity of the pure subject, of the "I think," which is the out-of-the-question that governs all answers. This means, basically, that answering is possible in that the *Cogito* is the answer-criterion of any answer other than the very first of them. So be it. Where the illusion arises is precisely in this purely formal overcoming of problematicity. Is the new and innovative solution to be pursued a synthesis of pure form, or is it rather a matter of content?

What is certain is that the process of rhetorization has the effect of reducing what arises though it is itself irreducible. It solves in advance what has ceased to be out-of-the-question; in short, it transforms what is in question into an answer without *truly* establishing a solution for what remains an open alternative. In sum, a question which opens up the field of constituted knowledge cannot, because of the alternatives it poses, allow itself to come down to an identical answer, and always the same one, which would be the source of non-A just as well as of A. It is important to remember here that the deduction only adds knowledge to one or the other alternative but cannot be considered as globally innovational. It only organizes knowledge already constituted. Its purely formal progression is pedagogical or justificatory as to what must have been found. It resolves nothing that has not already been resolved, except for individuals who ask about *results* not already known to them. Deduction allows an individual to assimilate results which he can then make his own. If there is synthesis in deduction, it must be understood in the narrow sense of an individual apprenticeship to be conceived in terms of questions whose answers already exist because they have already been produced elsewhere. Deduction orients the new in regard to the old by turning every question which is asked into an anticipated answer; this circularity has been well stated by John Stuart Mill. In the end, nothing new has been created by such a proof. Deductive reasoning consists of resolving in an a priori, formal way, only those questions contained in answers accepted at the start. Deduction, perhaps paradoxically, is a perfect rhetorical device, unsuspected in this respect by all those who see in it only the rigorous process of science. Deductive reasoning truly eliminates all problematicity, and therefore all debate, but it does so only by concealing from itself its circularity which *immediately* excludes any interrogativity that surfaces. It can only serve as the locus of already established answers, and that is always the case when questions disappear. This has produced the temptation of claiming as resolved those questions which arise through deduction, which gives the illusion of a result, obviously a purely formal one. As Aristotle said, deduction reduces the questions it poses and those it resolves to those previously resolved, that is, the unknown to the known.

The challenge which Descartes had to confront is thus quite clear. It was to establish as foundational the propositional order, which works deductively (and also by intuition), and at the same time to attack its deductive sterility. That explains why he was unable to give his inference any other status than a deductive one, why he was unable to rightly distinguish the *Cogito ergo sum* from traditional reasoning. Above all, Descartes denied problematization, since the only link he recognized was assertoric, as being the very object of his foundational approach. He was thus unable accurately to conceive of the problematological inference which nonetheless marked his way of reasoning, however implicitly.

An inference, as we have seen, is the passage from a question to an answer. It is a problematological idea which propositionalism could only make assertoric at the cost of making it circular. I have termed "problematological deduction" a more specific type of reasoning, which puts in play a particular question-answer relationship. The problematological deduction consists of passing from question to answer *from the question itself;* the formulation of the question provides its very answer. This would be "analysis," if analysis had not abolished the problematological difference in the assertorization of the problem which it assumes to be the sole point of departure. Analysis is envisaged as the mere deductive link between judgments. For, quite clearly, Descartes himself developed a problematological inference when he pronounced the equivalence *Cogito ergo sum.* This "deduction" is not syllogistic, and if it ever turns out to be an intuition, it is so only at the very end of the process.

In a question which is expressed through doubt, there is a statement which escapes doubt and which is that "I think." In putting into question that I think, symbolized by the fiction of the Evil Genius, there is a reaffirmation of this statement, which has for its subject (and all judgments have a subject) the "I am" of the "I am thinking" which the *Cogito* presents to us. There had to be a subject if there was a judgment, if the monopoly of judging had to be established anew. As Leibniz says:

". . . to say 'I think, therefore I am,' does not truly prove existence through thought, since thinking and being thought are the same thing; to say 'I am thinking,' is already to say 'I am.'" (*New Essays*, chap. VII, no. 7). The question of knowing whether I am is already decided by that of knowing whether I think, when the first one is supposed to be established by the other. From a strictly deductive perspective, the procedure is circular, therefore vicious. In reality, we once again face a problematological inference. The answer "I am" emerges from its own questioning, which is nothing other than thinking. How could I doubt that I am, if I am doubting? The answer already is in the question, which itself is no other than the rhetorical form of the statement "I think."

With rhetorization, as we have seen, what is affirmed is the impossibility of questioning, except in the form of rhetorical questions. All problematization is immediately resolved—through the form of the answering alone, as Kant will say later—which, at any rate, renders questioning, as such, impossible.

We can thus understand how the collapse of the primacy of consciousness is identified with the unveiling of the rhetorization of the subject, to the unveiling of its own repression, to the emergence of the unconscious. The subject thereby becomes rhetorical and ceases to be foundational. The rhetoric which reveals itself in its faculty for rationalization and closing off of subjects is still a propositional rhetoric, a rescuer of old ideas, and not the coming of a new interrogativity sui generis. What is revealed is the closing of the subject and not its possible opening into the problematic, the problematic would finally cease to be repressed. For it is important to see that revealing the role of rhetoric as a process of closure does not modify rhetoric—that remains propositional—but simply attempts to show how this obscuration and closure occur. Rhetoric will be revealed for what it allows within the propositional order without bringing about any change in the nature of either. Unmasked, it will no longer be the resolutional a priori that it was.

Today, it is unthinkable to try to ground rationality in the subject and self-consciousness. Sartre was probably the last to try it, but Heidegger had already renounced it, despite the ambiguity of the *Existential Analytic* in this regard.

To be consistent, it is necessary that the new rationality of the *logos* root itself in interrogativity in an originary way. If I doubt everything, it must be concluded that I question; and if I question, I must be able to express that fact otherwise, differently, even though this is already an answer. The problematological difference imposed at the level of the *logos* allows me to say that I am a being who questions. But we could just as well doubt that it is necessary to begin from the fact that I doubt. Interrogativity is thus the only reality at our command. And with it, the question of *logos*, as the proper working out of this interrogativity, becomes thematizable.

What follows are the *meditations on the logos* which result from our inquiry.

F_{our}

Meditations on the *Logos*

First Meditation: On the Question of the Logos

Our first task in considering the *logos* is to rethink what the term means. Such an enterprise might seem unnecessary in an age which has seen so much research on language. But the *logos* is something else: it is the language of reason in its full extent, and not just in one or another particular aspect. The studies heretofore devoted to language show, more often than not, a complete lack of unity. What may be richness for the sciences, which multiply levels of analysis and fragment the objects of their study, may be impoverishment for philosophy, which seeks after basic principles and global analyses. And, of course, the question of the *logos* may be falsely labeled "philosophical" and might better be analyzed in a scientific and dispersed way. Nevertheless, even science can scarcely consider such an analysis to be satisfactory for all cases. The infinite diversity of linguistic phenomena has produced many limited studies which have obscured what *logos* really is, in spite of their intention to illuminate its nature. This multiplicity of approaches and points of view—usually labeled syntax or grammar (generative or nongenerative) and with a semantic, pragmatic, or logical dimension—still has not been able to answer the question of knowing what recourse to language means.

Paying attention to one type of linguistic phenomenon, chosen more or less randomly but consistent with a researcher's purposes, is certainly not a vain enterprise; it is merely an arbitrary choice. But to justify the choice, our researcher must fall back on a theory of language, a theory which is precisely the one he pretends to discover or validate by relying on the particular phenomena which he puts forward. A scientific theory certainly can accord a privileged status to any facts that it wants to, without thereby excluding any other choices. But having done so, it should not pretend that it had captured *all* of the reality of language. Its results will be limited, in proportion to its choices. Any conception based on a scientific approach delivers only the results it is attempting to use as a model of prevailing theory. As a result, the language of those results becomes, in a fashion, the very result of the question of language. Such a science-based method tries to regroup partial elements to make them something general, to add up specific facts to assimilate the *logos* into a huge field of linguistic facts. This, of course, presumes a conception of the *logos*, of reason, which reflects both its expression and its structure, a presumption nonetheless denied by scientists as being too philosophical. The scientist, in avowing a preference for facts over philosophy, nonetheless expresses a certain philosophy, a philosophy of language which is itself left unfounded, but which pretends to show the proper behavior we should adopt regarding language. It specifies what is to be understood and what is to be neglected—in sum, what defines reason in speech.

Should language be considered according to the model of science, if not itself seen as a science? Should science be *the* language par excellence, in spite of its inescapable analytical rationality and fragmentation? This very question itself should be considered as impossible, due to the synthetic, unscientific presuppositions involved in it. Propositions asserting that language is a static result, or perhaps a justificatory rationality like that of science, escape such a definition or, rather, such an a priori statement, because they are themselves unscientific. The latter statement would be self-destructive if put forward. This clearly proves that language cannot be reduced to what positivists affirm it to be; that is a self-defeating view, even though language *can* express scientific results as well. We may, then, safely leave to science its concern for identifying and explaining particular facts of language. This will allow us to raise the question of language in general to undertake the quest for language in its problematical unity of *logos*.

The question of *logos*, of language in its general sense *as* language, is posed here without any sort of a priori assumption. The question is important. Thought about language implies the possibility of a language of thought. This formula might seem merely rhetorical, but in fact it expresses a fundamental and essential requirement imposed by contemporary thought. To think of language means opening up thought to its own language, the language of thought. Herein lies the fundamental question of our meditation on *logos*. Without such an approach, how can we hope to create an appropriate place for thought, one which will not be built on worn-out forms of language? The term *forms used* implies usage of forms. It is those very forms which we must take account of and which contemporary analysis assumes to exist by affirming them, defending them, and arguing about them. But is there another way to proceed? We shall come to that later. We can say here that if we do not elaborate our thoughts about language, the language of thought will disappear, de facto, if not de jure, into forms and usages which alienate thought to other preoccupations than itself. This alienation which swallows up thought relies on a use of language which is not its own.

The question of *logos*, then, is posed as the fundamental question of thought. It is fundamental because it rests on no prior answer, hence on no question that is more primary. It is fundamental too, because it presents itself as naturally being the source of the first answer to the first question. Fundamental, and therefore philosophical, such a question is exempt from presuppositions and from any extrinsic assertions which do not derive from questioning about *logos*. Such external assertions might be discovered at best after or within a questioning process, but a questioning which by definition would not be our own. This identification of the question of *logos* as a philosophical one is not a product of whim, nor even less the result of an arbitrary definition of philosophy. A philosophical question goes to the very root of things and, in so doing, frees itself from all presuppositions. This is the way in which the "return to things" (that is, what is in question) ought to be understood. When a question is presented, the possession of wisdom on that question is not given, but must be sought. We "love" the answer, desire it, seek after it: *eros* animates *erotesis*.

The question of the *logos* is a philosophical question because of its very nature. The way we deal with that question is not the result of a choice as to the elaboration or the resolution of the question, as if there were other ways to address it. To see this point more clearly, and to begin on the path toward a solution, let us return to the *question* itself. If one asks question X and does not derive the answer from the question itself, one must necessarily admit other propositions to obtain the answer. Propositions like these, when they are used to resolve question X, play the role of answers, at least partial ones. But such answers are going to be answers to specific questions which have not explicitly been posed during this questioning process. The status of these propositions is therefore controversial, as are the propositions themselves. They are *answers* to the extent that they appear during some questioning process, but they are also not answers, to the extent that the succession of questions which are presumed to have been posed in fact never have been (at least during *this* questioning process). What are they in reality if not judgments which have simply been admitted without justification? We have presupposed without proof that they really *are* answers. The ultimate "answer" closing the inquiry opened by the initial question X would therefore not answer it, since it would rest on "answers" which cannot fully be considered or accepted as such. The closing answer will have solutional value only in the exact measure that the judgments in which this ultimate answer originated present a solution to the initial problem.

Certainly the initial question might require that a series of successive questions be posed, questions which are easier to answer or whose solutions are already known. Still, the answers which are obtained in this way must be accepted as answers to claim that name, that is, each of the successive questions should rely on facts which are themselves out-of-the-question. Clearly this brings us back to our initial problem: how to obtain an answer to a given question without using at the outset answers which are not answers with respect to the initial question? In sum, once a question X is posed, one must either find an answer directly from within the question, or else invoke external elements to find it. Either these elements are themselves the answers, or they are not. If they are not, then they are not answers at all; and it is hard to see how they could pretend to be the source for the *final* answer. And if they *are* answers, they, in turn, result from questions. In order not to descend into an endless regression, let us admit for now that these results are obtained directly. Inevitably, the fundamental problem recurs: how to move directly from question to answer without any intermediary; how to arrive at a judgment that will serve as an adequate answer to the initial question? This is quite a serious problem, because it involves considering the individual questions seriously, by posing them as questions.

This discussion confirms that when it comes to the *logos*, there is no linguistic fact which can be invoked in an a priori manner. Choosing one from among others equally deserving would allow for an answer which would not really be the answer, as long as there are other answers which are equally responsive. But by what criterion would we choose, if not under the implicit aegis of a particular view of language for which we cannot finally fully account since it would be presupposed by any answer we would formulate on the nature of language?

How can we inquire into the *logos* without presupposing at the same time the form of the answers which we would accept to our inquiry? What is the precise question which we must address concerning language? How can we even *formulate* this question without already having arbitrarily oriented our research in a particular direction which could be leading us to error? Would the unity of language not escape us because of the particularization to which we would have surrendered? How can we correctly identify *the* particular question we should ask without falling into the trap of anticipating an answer to it? Such an answer would inevitably be as particularized as the question which would have given rise to it. Further, such an answer would only be "valid" as an answer to the extent that we would have implicitly given it to ourselves at the beginning of the questioning process. It would be difficult to support the proposition that it is still a real question, since question and answer would have been amalgamated from the beginning.

Thus, for the question of the *logos* to be taken *as a question,* one must not presuppose *anything* other than the question itself. Even more, one cannot formulate the question as asking this or that, or this rather than that. In language, the only Archimedean point left to us is the question itself; that is, the fact is that it is posed as a question. This is not much, even if we are reassured about the radical and philosophical nature of the question, since there is nothing else but the question to nurture the inquiry. Is that enough? The question of language taken for itself, that is, short of any formulation or individualized determination, must be able to lead us to the answer. It is from that question, and only from it, that we may proceed, for it is language itself which is in question, and not any of its privileged aspects. What can we derive from this question itself which would unlock its self-contained answer?

A question, once posed, is itself a linguistic fact, literally a *speech act.* Herein lies the obvious, basic fact of language from which to start. A question immediately places the questioner within the *logos,* which makes it possible to overcome the apparently insoluble difficulty raised earlier, that is, knowing how to approach the *logos.* The only fact of language on which the *philosophical* question of *logos* can and must rely is the fact that we have here a question. This does not imply that the question presupposes the answer. By itself, the question of the *logos* remains indeterminate because no particular formulation is chosen. Therefore, it cannot presuppose anything. That we might be able to infer the answer from a bare question does not mean that the answer is presupposed by a question, nor that we have put it there. To say that a question allows us to obtain the answer because it is language is not the same thing as saying that the question already *contains* the answer, let alone affirms it. We can reach the answer only by questioning the question, but the question, by itself, asserts no answer at all. It says nothing, since its only reality is its being a question, with no further specification. Thus, it is in a very precise sense that we must understand the idea that the answer is "in" the question. The question itself does not presuppose an answer, even if *posing* it implies the possibility of obtaining one.

Agreeing to regard a question as a question clearly obliges us to recognize the presence of a difference: that of question and answer, of an answer which lets itself be drawn out of the question but which does not allow itself to be reduced simply to that question, if there is, indeed, a question.

In affirming all that has just been said about the question of the *logos*, including the fact that only this question can and must complete our initial research, we are finally past the level of the initial question. We now put into play a discursivity which is not the question but which speaks of it. Speaking this way about the question goes beyond simply raising the question. Having done so, we have acknowledged that there is, in the speech act which consists of posing and elaborating a question, a requirement we have to take account of, namely the distinction between question and answer. An answer arises from the question of *logos:* the *logos* itself is made up of questions and answers. Such a difference is essential to the *logos* and is a requirement born from the necessity to take questions seriously.

To affirm that language reveals itself in the question whose theme is language itself asserts something about the ultimate nature of language. This is tantamount to answering the initially-posed question. But here, answering does not close the inquiry. Closing the inquiry would require that the question disappear and only results remain. To say that we answer about language is certainly not enough to conclude that the question is closed.

We answer about language. As a result, we have confirmation that it is language that enables us to question. In affirming this, we are not just questioning, but we are already answering, and even saying that we can proceed to questioning through asserting. An affirmation which claims that language serves *only* to question would be self-defeating.

Thus, the purpose of language is to express problems and what we believe to be their answers. This is certainly the primary truth about *logos*. Such answers result from our questioning about language. An assertion is therefore an answer, and, to the extent that we are answering about language, our very assertion implies that to affirm is to answer.

Let us clearly note that the *difference* between question and answer, which we have identified as the fundamental answer to the fundamental question of the *logos*, is not simply a matter of form. A question need not be rendered in an interrogative form any more than an answer must have an assertoric phrasing. Any effort to force them into such forms is the result of unfounded presuppositions, devoid of the authority generated by philosophical questioning as it is pursued here. Nothing so far in this meditation on the *logos* would permit the inference that a question could only be, or must be, in an interrogative form, nor that an answer must be an affirmative or a negative statement. In fact, the only requirement is the *problematological difference*, which *is* the difference between question and answer. The sole fact of posing the one and the other *as such* suffices to mark such a difference. The existence of the problematological difference is the fundamental and primary answer generated by the question of the *logos*. Any other answer would, as an answer, assume that the *logos* is made up of answers while at the same time refusing to assert it. According to our hypothesis, this answer would refer to something else. And this other answer could not claim to be fundamental. The objection that the question of the *logos* is just as arbitrary as any fact of language cannot usefully be maintained. It is true that there is no necessity to pose such a question. It could, in fact, never be posed. It would still be true that this question, in itself, would represent a fact of language as particular as any other. But we can discard this objection. For either the answer to the question of the *logos* is in effect the affirmation of the problematological difference, or it is not. If it is, as has just been shown, it provides an effective characterization of the fundamental reality of language, regardless of the fact that the question could have not been raised, and no matter how arbitrary was the decision to ask it. Such an answer is nevertheless the true answer to this question; whether or not the question is actually posed would not change a thing. To be valid, the objection must challenge the answer, not the question. Even if the question is no more than one particular speech act among many, still the answer is nothing but that which was sought. What is more natural, for that purpose, than actually to pose the question?

We answer by affirming, by asserting that to answer *is* to affirm. We have been producing assertions from the very start. We have spoken of the question of the *logos*, and in so doing we have answered where there was a question, without having stirred up any confusion. This confusion—itself problematological in the sense that it wants to abolish the difference through indifference to questioning—arises when we take a question as an answer, and vice versa. The reason for this is that we who consider questions through discourse also put into play the problematological difference. To make that clearer, we could say that an answer is apocritical when it deals with an answer, and problematological when it refers to a question. We can, therefore, speak of questions and answers, and even refer to our own discourse by explicitly recalling that difference to ourselves. Thereby we maintain it as the fundamental structure of the *logos*.

In answering the question of the *logos*, we have discovered that it is composed of both questions and answers. We have also learned that this difference is not simply one of syntax. By the term "question," we mean "problem," and not "interrogative sentence." Thus we can interchangeably say "treat a question" and "treat a problem," or we can speak of "what is in question" to allude to a problem we have to face. In such expressions, there is no precise mention of any specially privileged linguistic form. Moreover, the use of any particular form is something which needs to be explained. Any *logos* is question or answer, and the difference has to be marked in one way or another. For there to be *logos*, it is necessary that what is a question be capable of being distinguished from what is an answer. What is more obvious than the form of the sentence to show this difference? But the correlation between question, problem, and interrogative sentence is far from an automatic or a constraining one. There are interrogative sentences that are affirmations and even orders: "Is he not a dishonest man?" "Would you pass me the salt?" On the other hand, if the *logos* is either question or answer, it is not at all necessary that linguistic forms be reduced to interrogative or declarative sentences. Affirming that the *logos* can be a question *or* an answer finally comes down to the fact that all discursive activity is a questioning process.

At this point in our inquiry, we should have in mind that questions and answers can be problematological answers and apocritical answers, as if questions were answers. That only appears to go against the problematological difference. In fact, the *logos* reveals itself as an answer from the very moment that it is questioned. But what question does it answer? In any case, the *logos* is a questioning *process*. In explicating, in responding, it has to put into practice the very problematological difference of which it is an effect, as answer.

Let us look more closely at the last point. Discursive activity, being question and answer, manifests itself as a questioning process at two levels: that at which the speaker or author *wants* to say something, and that at which he *does* say something and makes explicit what he has to say. Explication is tantamount to responding; we use language *in response to* certain concerns. Answering occurs at the level at which what needs to be said is said, a passage from the implicit realm, a development of the mind, to the explicit world of language. The *logos* covers both the explicit and the implicit, and is a "language" of problems where the unconscious mixes with the historical. The *logos* is not limited to linguistic manifestations but also includes "reason" and "mind." Those who use explicit language do not elaborate on their questions, as does an attorney during cross-examination. If we believed that, we would be bound to fall prey to the fallacy that questions should be identified with interrogative sentences. The questions which puzzle or move a speaker or author most often remain unspoken, and only the answer is uttered. This is due to the problematological difference: what pertains to problems must differ from what pertains to answers, and the opposition between the explicit and the implicit which stems from that problematological requirement is the most natural opposition. If the *logos* is made up of questions and answers, and if both can accurately be characterized as answers (problematological and apocritical, respectively), what do they answer? The *logos* answers what we are, namely a problematicity embodied in history and formed by implicit questions, which are articulated in the unconscious. There is language because we, as questioners, here questioning the *logos*, are subject to the problematological difference. This very difference, which constitutes the *logos*, also creates its very texture, for what the *logos* answers cannot vanish in the answer, lest the *logos* lose its own reason for being.

Second Meditation: From the Explication of Problems to the Appearing of the World

The explicit is in fact an answer. Many studies of language have shown that assertability is the primary feature of language, that is, the basic form from which all other functions could be derived. This doesn't seem to be in question for scientists, who, finally, have to feel justified in being solely interested in what they can observe. The observable does not have to be justified, since it functions to justify and to explain. But if we really want to understand what communication means, if we really want to transcend those partial analyses that isolate small points of observation, then we cannot be satisfied with such an a priori assumption. The question of the *logos* is the *logos* as a question. By "*logos*," we do not mean a particular language, nor even speech, but the whole *concept* of language. This is where the inquiry of the linguist diverges from that of the philosopher. The linguist must always study *a* language, and this will always be a particularized study. A language has a specific syntax and semantic structure. Because of that, the usual process is to focus attention on sentences, sentence structure, and isolated examples of usage. A philosopher is interested instead in looking into universality rather than any particular phenomenon, that is, into what makes such things as semantics or pragmatics possible. This is something that no particularist analysis, no matter how thorough, can do. In questioning the *logos*, we are responding to the point that to think *is* to question. Further, because using language relies on the interrogativity of the mind, it is itself a thinking act. Nietzsche said, "Speaking is basically raising a question that I put to someone to find out if his soul is like mine." Thus the question of the *logos* leads us to consider the interrogative function of language. This is surely a meeting ground for linguists and philosophers. What must be noted at this stage of our inquiry is that when we make answers about questioning, we actualize the problematological difference; we even reflect it at some metalevel. We can, therefore, draw some conclusions about the linear consistency between language and metalanguage, a linearity which allows a sentence like "I am telling you to close the door" to be interpreted as (saying the same thing as) "Close the door!"

If speech is most apparent through answers, it is because, prior to all answers, there were questions which quite literally *animated* the speaker, even though it is only the answers that are heard or seen; the questions, as a consequence, do not appear. Ordinarily we mean by the word "question" an interrogative phrase, but such a phrase already belongs in the realm of the explicit. For a better idea of what needs to be understood when we hear the word "question," we need to think of expressions like a *question of life or death*, or a *question of money*, or even *to weigh a question*. All of these expressions have the advantage of breaking the too obvious and unquestioned linkage between a question and a language fact such as the interrogative form. An interrogative sentence is already an answer, though a problematological one, which shows that problems can also be stated if, for example, it is necessary to make them known to obtain a solution. The problematological difference, apparent in the opposition between the explicit and the implicit, operates at the explicit level through formal marks. These are the materials on which linguists work. If everything that is explicit is an answer, nothing prevents us from answering *on* a question, and not simply *to* it. Our own process in these "Meditations" shows this clearly. To the extent that we preserve the problematological difference in our answering, we explicitly introduce questions in it, either in a peculiar form or by specifying that the issue under discussion is a matter of problems and not solutions. A sentence like "Would you pass me the salt?" has an interrogative form because it is necessary to communicate to someone else a specific request for cooperation. A solution need be no more discursive than a question must be. A sentence like that above illustrates the part played by the problematological answer: it is a partial resolution, a preliminary stage leading to the final result, an apocritical answer. A problematological answer is therefore a preparatory answer leading toward a solution, without which the solution never would be reached, since, to be reached, it must first be marked off *as* the solution-to-be-reached, that is, as different.

Together with the opposition between the implicit and the explicit, there is even a differentiation between the problematological and the apocritical within the explicit itself. And this differentiation, as we have seen in our examination of the *logos,* can be reduced to the mere statement that there *is* a differentiation in the explicit statement of a mere difference. There is here a necessary and sufficient condition which governs the *logos* through and through. Answering, to be both apocritical and problematological, must refer to two types of questions. An answer must not be problematological in regard to the question it resolves (the apocritical dimension); if it were, the answer would be circular, that is, one would have to conclude that to state a question would automatically be tantamount to offering its answer. This trap is avoided by making explicit the problematological difference, which allows us to recognize that there is answering in the thematization of the questioning process, and that questions and answers differ due to the very fact that we assert them as different.

An answer, because it is an answer, is both apocritical and problematological. It is an answer to a question, but it can also express a *distinct* question. Is it not within the very nature of the *logos* to perform *both* these functions?

We may also consider this from another viewpoint. With respect to *one* given question, a problematological answer cannot be at the same time apocritical, and vice versa. By contrast, if we consider another answer, it can be both. If we wish to be even more specific, we could say that a problematological answer is *necessarily* apocritical, since it is an answer. We could say further that an apocritical answer, which suppresses the question it resolves on the ground that it is no longer a question, also suppresses its own appearance as answer; and, by doing so, it becomes autonomous in regard to the question it meant to solve. It does not assert itself as an answer, nor does it stipulate the question it answers. It merely says what it says, without saying that it says it, and without proclaiming itself as an answer. Consequently, we use the term "reference" to mean the "what" which is in question. An answer which denies itself as being an answer to make apparent what it says will appear only as a judgment, even though it is rather the *something* which it deals with that will draw attention. An answer which represses its interrogativity will seem to be neither apocritical nor problematological. Nevertheless, an answer puts the question of what is in question within what is said, of the reference as question. An answer poses the question of its own question, which it resolves, and that latter question disappears because of the solution. The question of which question it is apocritical *for* is raised by its absence from the explicit, since this very question is left unsaid within *what* is said. We can deduce from this fact that the problematological character of what is explicit will allow it to be phrased in terms of an answer. The explicit both raises and expresses the question of which question it answers. The problemato*logical* character of the (apocritical) answer has to do with the question it raises for us, which refers to the question it resolves. Generally speaking, the problemato*logical* is therefore the very link which associates questions with answers. And this is the way to conceive of problematology. To sum up: an apocritical answer, repressing its answerhood, also reveals the problematological link to a question as a question whose answer consists of finding that to which what is said is an answer.

An answer is apocritical in regard to the question which gave birth to it, and problematological in regard to another one. The problematological difference is therefore implemented, since question and answer are not within the same process—are not, for the same basic problem, rendered indistinct. Further, an answer which distinguishes itself from a question as apocritical expresses another question. Thus it is problematological for the question to which it is *not* an answer. The fact that answers are both apocritical and problematological, because it is the nature of the *logos* to be so as its constitutive difference, accounts for what can be called the *independence* of the answer. From this follows the *autonomy* or the *objectivity* of language, two concepts we must approach carefully. The concept of autonomy suggests that discourse is in itself some autonomous reality: this is a conception of Reason which has to be rejected. The concept of objectivity seems to suggest that there is another realm of language, a subjective one, which would elude us if we were not able to postulate some sort of *transcendental subjectivity* present in each of us, itself identical to the *objectivity* of things, and different from each empirical individuality. How can we conceive of this subjectivity in a coherent manner, since it is all at the same time unique, empirically based, and beyond the reach of others' objective vision, though it is, from the moment *we* speak about it, the opposite of all that? This is an unsolvable problem which stems from the division between objectivity and subjectivity, and it can be left at that. Answers are independent. This reflects the idea of reference, since answers must be independent *of* something. But this referral is conceived precisely as the affirmation of an X (a question) which has now become inessential. Answers are thus able to be freed from the questions which gave birth to them and, in turn, can themselves serve as questions, or else count as firm results in the eyes of those who accept the relevance of those questions and the resolution which ensues from them. An answer to a question, once found, suppresses the question. The question is resolved; it is posed no more. The answer has a validity of its own, and that makes it easy to forget that it is something more than just a judgment, that it had been *an answer,* and thus that there had previously been a question.

Answers become independent and repress the relationship to the question they come from. They become liable to being related to other questions by answering and/or expressing them. These are the only possibilities available to a *logos* which is both question and answer. Answerhood is not simply the result of some particular process but is also marked by the fact that answers become independent of the very process from which they originate. Even if it is a result in regard to some originating problem, it can as well be a result for other questions. This is the basis of what is called the "objectivation of subjective results" and what has allowed idealism to pretend to reach reality from some particular point of view. The *logos* at work in this doctrine suggests the independence of results, however concealed it may be, that is, without an explicit thematization of the *logos* as a questioning process, a thematization which sets Reason apart from any idealist, realist, or nominalist perspective.

The language of reflection is possible insofar as it is marked by the problematological difference. Answers can deal with questions insofar as this *meta*level embodies the difference between, respectively, the apocritical and the problematological type of answerhood. Each of these second-level answers, to the extent they are explicit, are also respectively apocritical and problematological. Often, problematological answers are unspoken. When they are expressed, because they are distinct from apocritical answers, the difference between the two must be identifiable in some way. They are presented as different on the level of the secondary process, because they are not answers for the questioning process within which they are problematological, and because of this, they are not even asserted. Propositions, by their very nature, are propositions of answers, and problematological answers are not what we are looking for.

The word "answer," when associated with the concept "problematological," indicates the existence of an implicit language, capable of becoming explicit. Problematological answers thus become real answers and turn out to be apocritical as well. But as such they answer a different question, one where the goal is precisely that of making a problem explicit. For the latter, problematological answers are, and will remain, despite all explication, a language which is left unexpressed, because it is not through speaking, nor by the very fact of asserting one's questions, that one gets an answer. What has to be obtained eventually through the questioning process is nothing but this answer. Undoubtedly, this is the origin of the problematological difference. Questioning

is *useful* on the sole condition that it differs from answering, and that is
only possible if we know what is considered to be an answer and how it
is different from what is considered to be a question. This difference is
the solution to the paradox of Plato's *Meno*. Form alone cannot provide
the distinction between questions and answers in most cases; the explication of the answer and the repression of the question will materialize
their difference. As long as answers are the *goal* of our linguistic and rational activity, questions are not made explicit, except where absolutely
necessary. Why express what goes without saying, what presents no
problem, especially when it is not what is sought after? One *could* do
it; one could answer by making explicit what was in question by asking a second question about the first, and on and on, I would imagine.
In virtue of the problematological difference, questions do not permit themselves to be assimilated into the answers which convey them.
One could deduce from this, a little facilely no doubt, that answering
and questioning are perpetually missing one another, constantly falling
short when trying to reach one another, trapped in an endless cycle
wherein the signified somehow evades its own significance. There
would be a choice between (1) having an unspeakable questioning
process (due to the principle of difference) and (2) reducing questioning to answers, making questioning itself into something other than
what it is, transforming a question into an answer, and abolishing the
very specificity of questioning. If we look more closely, it is precisely
the problematological difference that spares us from being caught in
this old dilemma. Answering contains the problematological difference
within itself, including the repression of its own apocritical character
left unreflected. We have emphasized this earlier in our discussion.
When answering bears on questioning, it does so by virtue of the problematological difference which is kept between them, as answering, as
questioning. Far from absorbing or waiving the question away, the answering process makes questioning what it is; it adequately captures
the notion of questioning. The verb "to be" relates us precisely to what
is in question as ceasing to raise a question. The answer *is* an answer
even while abolishing itself as an answer and creating instead a duality
which has been called in propositionalism a subject and a predicate.
In reality, what is in question in a proposition is treated as out-of-the-
question, and this answer rests on the inscription of the problematical
into the answer. By the suppression of the problematical, the answer
suppresses any reference to its own answerhood. The answer says what
it says without stipulating that it has such a goal. An answer articulates
the difference which it presents in other ways, displacing the focus onto
what is said, rather than on the fact of saying it, letting itself be forgot-

ten in the appearance of its object, which is not reflected as an object itself, which results in this phenomenalization being carried out as *logos*.
If there is a subject and a predicate—a complementarity which has
been a mystery ever since the birth of propositionalism—it is due to the
taking up of the problematical which is transcended and maintained at
the same time, an *Aufhebung* which allows us to locate what is in question in what is said, if not in the saying itself. The notions of subject and
predicate are thus problematological realities. They are denied that status in the theory of propositionalism, which really can neither do without them nor explain them fully.

An answer which is apocritical and problematological necessarily
deals with a question since it is an answer. However, it does not stipulate which question it is, since it is disguised as an answer. As a result, it
conceals its difference. What it is in question is left unsaid, just as the
answer is not stated as an answer. As a consequence, the answer neither
refers to itself nor to the question it repressed, but instead refers to
something else, to what is in question as being out-of-the-question,
since it is the answer. Reference emerges in the appearance of what was
in question by way of the dynamics of resolution which externally posi-
tivizes the *what* of questioning. The appearance of the referential arises
in the process of answering. Reference is not a *given* from reality; it is
what arises in the temporalization of the interrogative repression. What
is in question becomes that which has been answered and is no longer
in question. Language can reach the truth, just as it can give the illusion
of truth by a referentiality which lacks a real object, is without a real reference. This truth is determined by the simple fact that the *what* which
is in question is designated referentially by the answer, even where
the interrogative "*what*" doesn't correspond to anything. Presented as
something that no longer poses a question, what is in question in
the answer is made referential at the same time. The appearance which
emerges from the interrogative process reveals itself to be a mere
appearance. Syntactically, a proposition like "Napoleon won the battle
of Austerlitz" can be made explicit by the equivalent sentence, "Napoleon is the one *who* won the battle of Austerlitz," where the meaning
of the word "Napoleon" is made more precise by an interrogative term
which designates it apocritically, assertorically, at the same time that it
allows us to designate it as the referent. Interrogativity thus brings up
the "world," which finds its constancy in the out-of-the-question as
constituted by the answer. This constancy, this identity, which is a result of the repression into the answer of all that which was in question
within it, evokes a question which is referred to as ceasing to be the
source of any further question. Such self-repressing answers direct our

attention to their externality, and their signifying nature here lies in their referring to something else. A theory of static reference is one where language is related to *what* is meant, as if these two terms existed independently of one another. Such a theory will root its analysis of knowledge at the level at which the game is already over, that is, strictly at the point when results are present, without truly understanding that reference only exists for the *logos* which understands it as independent. This formula is only paradoxical if one ignores the dynamic aspect of referentialization, as it has been described earlier, as a questioning and answering process.

Judgment, as it has been conceived of for the last two thousand years, can no longer be conceptualized in the same terms. If we simply see a proposition as a combination of a subject and a predicate, we lose its specificity, its being an answer, an answer which is what it is only in regard to what is in question (even though the question ceases to be problematic). Interrogatives disappear, and Napoleon simply becomes the victor at Austerlitz. In fact, the terms of judgment correspond to questions which are treated as no longer questionable. They solidify in regard to the interrogativity they express even as they repress it by answering it, and even as they avoid affirming any correspondence to it in any way. What is in question at least finds its place through a descriptive term, the subject of the proposition (of the answer, in this case), a term which requires precisely the deletion of the interrogative. "Do you know *who* Napoleon is? He is the one *who* . . ." If one leaves the question aside and assumes it to be well-known, fully resolved, nothing is left but Napoleon as the victor at Austerlitz (among several possible answers). The "victor at Austerlitz" responds to what is in question and remains what the answer is all about, namely Napoleon.

An answer is problematological to the extent that there truly is *something in question* in it. It is apocritical when it judges that something is no longer a problem, no longer a question. Answers autonomize themselves into judgments and free themselves from questions, so that there is no longer anything more than a relationship of complementarity between two terms. The *logos*, settling within judgment, conflates and displaces the problematological difference. That is, it articulates its referentiality to a deleted interrogativity. A predicative category refers back to the subject in question, although the question can bear on the category itself (after all, *what is* Austerlitz?), and we shall fall back on the same judicative structure as when the subject was the object of questioning.

The independence of answers gives them a validity of their own, beyond the circumstances which gave rise to them. The *logos* is able to refer us to what is beyond language (the "reference") because this *perceived* externality actually falls within it. Reason, recently conceived of as identical to the *logos*, since it emerges from the question of the *logos*, suggests the independence of its own results. The "objective world" inevitably ensues from such a reason, and the *logos* is guaranteed to have access to it. Still, it is necessary to approach this concept of an "objective world" with the greatest of caution. It harks back to an outdated, if not fallacious, tradition, because nothing is more problematical than the existence of "the World." It is supposed to be the fixed referent, but it is nothing but the constituted matter of the interrogative relationship, an interrogativity which is negated as if it were self-evident for all to see. In fact, the totality of things refers us to an external point of view that enables us to speak about it as a totality.

And beyond everything, what is there if not nothing? The solution which proposes turning the world into an attribute proper to human reality, rather than an impossible totality, is no solution, because there is nothing which can prove that the world as so defined coincides, or even is capable of coinciding, with the "real world" outside. If we say that the latter is the objective realm, we imply thereby that human reality is subjective. Such an ontological limitation is impossible to support; in fact, it has posed unsolvable difficulties. How can we have (objective) access to the subjective realm if what is subjective is no more than that? How can we speak of it except in objective terms? Why should we accept such a dichotomization as unquestioned, though clearly understandable from a historical perspective?

What is outside the *logos* is accessible to it. The validity of "logical" results is in itself a fact of the *logos*, one that allows it to refer to a reality other than itself. This vision of what constitutes reality for human beings, prisoners of the *logos* as questioners, differs from any form of empiricism or idealism. The empiricist bias starts from facts and things whose independence is set forth at the very start of the philosophical quest. The possibility of such an inquiry becomes a mystery, since the very reason for its necessity is left unaccounted for as being nonempirical. As for idealism, it makes the product of thinking an outgrowth, an effect of subjectivity, and it postulates the independence of these results without any basis for so doing. In the last analysis, is it not a matter of proving that a result is, by nature—by virtue of its being a result—independent of that from which it results? But such a proof is missing in idealism, even in its most elaborated version, that which resulted from the "Copernican revolution." An object only exists as object in regard to a particular subject, and what the object is in itself remains unknowable. The solidity and consistency of objects cannot simply be a result of some subjective projection. Proving the independence of phenomena requires discovering corresponding elements in reality which exist in themselves, the noumena, which correspond to these objects. Positing the existence of such referents is possible only by abandoning the Copernican viewpoint, by the philosopher's putting himself outside of and above everything, because for a subject there is no object which can be other than a phenomenon. But a thing which exists in itself, as postulated by the philosopher, destroys itself when that philosopher posits from the beginning that there is no knowledge possible which does not emanate from the subject. Sirius's point of view is untenable and its validity impossible to demonstrate. This viewpoint is not "Copernican," since it presents a reality which is inaccessible to the subject, while at the same time maintaining that there is no possible knowledge except for that of the subject. Objectivity, that is, the objective independence of the subjective products of the mind, is acquired at the cost of abandoning the subject's viewpoint. This is undoubtedly a tautology, but it reveals an unavoidable process. If we base our thinking on the subject, the "I," we will never have access to any independent realities unless we abandon, sooner or later, the "Copernican" approach.

The problematological approach is *radically* different. The philosophy of questioning, which we are offering here, aims to show that reflexivity is immanent in any process of questioning and that it is embodied in the problematological difference. An interlocutor, or a reader who is focusing on some answer, does so starting from the base of his own questioning process, which is, to a degree, secondary. It is therefore possible to answer, from an external perspective, to or about a primary questioning process, to reflect the boundaries and progression within a secondary process, without violating the general "laws" of questioning. Quite simply, the problematological difference must be respected. Who is this "I," if not the questioner himself? There is an "I," in fact, only because there is questioning: man is the only being who can pose the question of man, and having done so, the only one who can answer "I . . ." It is this which will always distinguish man from even the most sophisticated computer. What is this "I" if not the problem that man poses for himself? It is because doubt is a modality of questioning that the affirmation "Ego sum" can result from the statement "Dubito." But Descartes is hardly justified in posing the "I" as the primary reality rather than the questioning process which produced that result. Cartesian questioning is not nearly as radical as its author pretended it to be, because his analysis of reasoning, from which the "I" results, derives its validity from a process and a quest which are never questioned but rather presupposed.

If we follow the problematological approach, the "I" can "go out-side of itself," at least to the extent that the "I" is the questioner. A questioner has access to independent realities, since such an access inheres in a questioning process, that is, a process where results are independent if they are results at all. The "I" thus becomes the "he" condemned by Copernican idealism. It is because he is a questioner that the "I" can become *other* and thereby assume an externality which is impossible for an idealism centered on the "I." An adequate and con-sistent conception of human reality suggests the decentering of the subject.

Finally, let us carefully note that the "I" is none other than he who questions *himself* in each of his actions, each of his gestures, each of his thoughts. To speak, act, or think one must on each occasion have a question in mind. We are perpetually put into question by all those questions which impel us to resolve this or that. Who are we if not the very question which underlies all questions and constitutes our own self?

Third Meditation: Dialectic and Rhetoric, or the Presence of the Other

Our questions about the *logos* have put its role squarely before us and revealed clearly its fundamental nature. But what have we learned from such discursive questioning about discourse in general? Above all, we have learned that the double role of questioning and of discourse about questioning reveals what we have called the problematological differ-ence, sustained through the answers which deal with questions and questioning. The dualism of the apocritical and the problematological corresponds to this required continuity at the level of answers. Every answer, even if we know to what question it responds, evokes the ques-tion (the problematological effect) to which it is an answer, the question for which it is apocritical. It is an answer even when it does not state it-self as an answer, and even when it does not refer itself to a definite question (even if that question is known right from the start). An an-swer conforms to its apocritical nature when it no longer refers to a par-ticular question. Still, it would be erroneous to conceive of it as a judg-ment. While it may be loose from its origins, its nature as *logos* cannot cut it off from the interrogativity it embodies. As an apocritical-prob-lematological reality, answers seem autonomous. The self-sufficiency of answers has always been associated with the idea of truth. But truth cannot be its own result, produced as if by magic, or as the fruit of some revelation, of what might be called an "unveiling." In reality, truth can-not come from anything other than some prior inquiry and only has meaning if there is some question from which it originated or another that put it into a new context.

An answer is both apocritical *and* problematological. Whenever we say that an answer by its own interrogativity calls forth the question to which it is the solution, we implicitly introduce a questioner, one who either already knows the question or, on the contrary, is seeking it. If the questioner knows the question, the answer reveals itself as an answer and is not, in this sense, problematological. Such knowledge recalls an earlier raising of the question, and the answer as knowledge is the result. The participation of a questioner is the implicit assumption which is involved in the apocritical-problematological reality of the answer. Indeed, an answer would not be both apocritical and problematological with regard to the same questions, given the imperative represented by the problematological difference. As a consequence, it is clear that a different questioning process must be involved; that suggests either another questioner or else another problem, to which the answer would serve as a solution or a stage in the reaching of one. It would invoke either another problem or another questioner.

Thus, an answer's essential function is not only to respond to a certain concern, but in so doing also to be dialectical. Either the existence of two questioners or the existence of a new problematization of an answer means that dialogue takes place. It is the nature of the *logos* to be addressed to someone, even if that one is passive, and therefore to have a respondent (even if the respondent is the questioner himself). A questioner can easily assume this double role, which calls to mind a well-known passage from Plato's *Theaetetus* where Plato defines thought as the soul's dialogue with itself about a question (189E). Answers, within a single process, become in their turn the objects of questioning for our questioner. In this way a new line of questioning can enrich an earlier one, which can thus be brought to completion, weakened, or used for other purposes. Cognitive and epistemological advancement is made possible in this way. I think this must have been what Plato had in mind when he identified dialectic with the attainment of knowledge. This process, however, is not affected by the presence of two participants rather than one. If there is an effective dialogue among questioners, each will in turn be the respondent as well as the questioner, confirming the materialization of the problematological difference by the contextualization of the roles of questioner and answerer.

To this point, we have been able to meditate from our own questioning, from the very fact that we have undertaken it and that we have been questioning our own questioning as *logos* or, if you prefer, about *logos* as questioning. Will this allow us to characterize further how dialogue works? No doubt it will, for in order for there to be effective dialogue between two interlocutors, there must be a question upon which discussion takes place. What is likely to occur in this situation, and what can we infer from it? First, we may note that if the answer of the one meets with the agreement of the other, that is, answers his questions, there will be no debate. That presupposes that the addressee asks himself the question which is raised, either prior to the answer or because of it. The addressee questions the answer which is submitted to him. He treats it problematologically. What answer might be given to the question of the addressee which is raised by the speaker, if not the discovery of the problem which underlies the speaker's discourse? The speaker's intention is somehow reconstructed in the dialogue, as required by the very fact that there is a dialogue. This is the origin of the hypothesis of sincerity and other conversational maxims. An addressee addresses the speaker's answer, because it is problematological for the addressee. The latter is committed to judge the answer or, if taken from the viewpoint of the addressee, to answer the question itself. He tests the adequacy of that answer or, more simply, its truth, since it is a matter of verifying the specific property of the answer in regard to the question evoked for the audience. When a speaker proposes an answer to a question that he asks himself, the audience answers this same question by asking if the answer given is truly an answer to the question raised; this is a reciprocal relationship. We could also suppose that a speaker puts the question explicitly to his listener rather than simply supplying him with the answer, or else that he proposes an answer, but in question form. Such a question could be said to be rhetorical because of its form alone. But if we think about it carefully, this dialectical procedure is globally rhetorical in that a speaker is presenting to someone else's questioning ability that which he believes, a priori, to be a solution. The rhetorical dimension of the *logos* proceeds from a concern for taking into account the other's questions and answering them. We shall have convinced someone if our answers are solutions to their questions. Might one say that dialogue is the reverse of argumentation in that the one assumes some initial divergence, whereas the other ceases when agreement is reached? But is it not also the goal of dialogue to persuade another?

Whichever might be the case, for the moment it is important to understand how the problematological difference is marked in the structures of dialogue and to see how it eventually determines it. Taking turns in dialogue actualizes the differentiation between what poses a question and what forms an answer. One could deduce that what is an answer for a speaker is a question for the listener, even if one has to refer back to the same answer through the "discovery" of the initial question. Inasmuch as the problematological difference becomes apparent through the alternative roles taken in a speech situation, form becomes more freely used in terms of the imperative of problematological differentiation. The simple fact of speaking to another puts him in question, above and beyond any possible matter of form. This may well be the origin of the relatively universal observance of the forms of politeness. In a relationship built on dialogue, an answer for one is a question for another because any answer, by its very nature, is capable of being transformed into a question, and vice versa. An assertion which is the subject of a dialogue, the matter in question, is itself indifferently question and answer; it is the dialogue's protagonists who make the difference.

Context is the relationship between effective questioners, a relationship that transforms what is *problematological* in the answer into something which is *problematic* for someone. Context is the problematological differentiator; it embodies the participants' knowledge and their knowledge of the other's knowledge (or their own knowledge) as to what is still in question and what is already resolved. This includes various presuppositions and sociocultural variables. It informs the questioners about their relative distance. It is the link in the problematological difference. In this regard, form and content vary inversely. An impoverished or hazy context, a more undifferentiated one, means a weakened dialogical or dialectical reality, and an increased formalization of what is said with respect to the problem treated, a clearer recognition and stipulation of what is out-of-the-question. Form constitutes the information which the context fails to provide, because the social and psychological distance between speaker and listener is wide, and because an audience is undifferentiated, numerous, and anonymous. As a result, a speaker can never know precisely what an audience knows or doesn't know about a question the speaker wants to address.

The double nature of an answer, apocritical and problematological, allows us to understand the contextualization through dialogue of the problematological difference. The presence of others makes apparent another dimension of language, its rhetorico-argumentative aspect. In dialogue, each person takes the other's place in turn. Each one *is* the other, standing for himself and for the other; therefore, each one must know at least a little bit of what the other knows. This is the basis of *common* sense, the commonplaces that people share. Moreover, each must know that the other knows them. Each knows, and knows that the other knows (or at least thinks he knows), which allows them to address the other in a relevant way. Relevance consists of relating oneself to the other's questions by one's own questions, without questioning his answers. Hence there is the link between irrelevance (im-pertinence) and impertinence (non-pertinence). Being able to assume the listener's point of view to answer him allows a speaker to anticipate and plan his adaptations to the audience and develop a number of persuasive techniques. So does tactfulness, insofar as one always questions others simply by calling on them. Form represses interrogativity in the act of answering, which therefore does not present itself as an answer. This allows the audience not to answer, since the latter is not explicitly put into question. When one does put a question to someone, the other must become aware that he is in question, that he must justify himself by adopting a definite standpoint on the very question as he justifies his answer. A speaker is all the more convincing when he leaves the conclusion to the other to draw, rather than immediately supplying him with the answer and leaving him with little choice in the matter. Fuzziness in ideas has the same effect, and the more vague answers are (for example, when they use popular terms like "liberty" or "justice"), the more personalized are the answers requested from the audience.

Fourth Meditation: The Question of Meaning, or Meaning as Question

A listener is potentially an explicit questioner, as is a reader, although rarely will a reader be able to question an author directly. Whether he agrees or not with an answer to a question, a listener will make his own assessments about the adequacy of that answer. This process is called *comprehension*, or, if we want to refine the expression, it can be called the *hermeneutic process*. An answer does not state its *meaning*, since it doesn't say, "This is the question which I am resolving," nor does it identify itself *as* an answer. It refers to what it says without saying that it does; it suggests its meaning without stating it. Meaning here remains implicit; it corresponds to the implicit character of understanding. The meaning of a discourse is provided by the problematicity it deals with. When someone speaks of the meaning of a sentence, for example, he is referring to *what is in question* in the sentence. To see better how this process of comprehension works, let us suppose that a discourse is difficult to interpret. The answer thus is a question for the listener regarding what makes it an answer. It is for him a problematological answer, as it is an apocritical one for its author. It is *because* the answer is both problematological and apocritical that it has meaning. In the listener's search for meaning, a listener whom we have supposed to be in "semantic rupture," there is, therefore, the question of the question to which an answer is an answer. The latter question will be an apocritical answer for the hermeneutic process. If the question had been immediately made explicit by the speaker, it would have been *from his point of view* a problematological answer. If we now leave these points of view aside, it would no longer be possible, in the process of comprehension, to see anything but the passage from one problematological answer to another. This substitution, then, ends up with a purely apocritical result. Giving or acquiring meaning consists of substituting for an assertion which poses a problem an answer which states what is in question in the assertion, and which shows in what way it is an answer. Thus, there is an equivalence between an initial assertion and the answer to the semantic inquiry. The two must say the same thing. Their identity is based on the fact that the question which is discovered or received by the addressee is that of the speaker-author. This is the idea of empathy, which has for so long served to illustrate the phenomenon of understanding, even if it is only a particular instance of problematological reconstruction. If an author cannot answer our questions about his discourse, and if the discourse is unclear, a reconstruction of meaning originating in the text will be unendingly multiple and definitively problematic, if there ever can be definitiveness in this. In reality, if one considers answering in a general sense, comprehension consists of bringing it back to what it solves, not necessarily through a *literal* equivalence but through a *problematological* equivalence.

Five

From Theory to Practice: Argumentation and the Problematological Conception of Language

Our discussion of the interrogativity of the *logos* has permitted us to infer its triple articulation: hermeneutical and semantical, rhetorical and argumentative, dialectical and dialogical. We have traveled far from the classical model based on the trichotomy of semantics, syntax, and pragmatics, a model that embodied the propositionalist view. The old trichotomy represents propositionalism in the process of discovery of the other linguistic dimensions, which somehow had to be reduced and unified through propositionalism's basic assumptions. This is the operational base for such important linguists as Chomsky and Ducrot, or logicians like Frege. Frege, for example, roots his analysis in the proposition, the isolated sentence, to develop a conception of meaning in language which he presents as general. As we have seen, this conception does not stand up to analysis.[1] For *the* sentence does not exist in real language use, where there is always a context of utterance which situates the sentence in a given perspective. Rather, we might speak of *sentences*, since to isolate any one sentence is already a particular kind of usage. We might add that linguistic understanding is not reducible to a sentence-by-sentence parsing of individual truth-conditions. Understanding *Don Quixote* is not accomplished through an analytical process of the deconstruction of its individual sentences.

Ducrot also is quite aware of the breakup of the old tripartite model and of the effects of context on meaning (pragmatics and semantics becoming indissociable). But still he holds on to the theoretical presuppositions of propositionalism. Thus we find within the whole of his work a constantly restated opposition between *sentences* (*phrases*) and *statements* (*énoncés*):

1. This point will come up again. The reader should consult Meyer, *From Logic to Rhetoric;* see also Michel Meyer, *Meaning and Reading* (Amsterdam: Benjamins, 1983), chap. 1.

I have just said that the thesis which I will defend here bears on *sentences*, not on *statements*. This renders our task easier but it also implies a limitation. First, the limitation. A description ought to be applicable to any utterance of interrogative sentences, without any hope that exceptions will prove the rule. The fact that a sentence embodies an instruction to find, through its utterance, such and such a type of argumentative use does not imply that all possible utterances of such sentences must be developed in conformity with that argumentative use.[2]

It appears that the goal of drawing this distinction is to clarify the contextual nature of meaning, its variability according to statement-situation, termed its "argumentative value." Why are we then told that these statements are not necessarily argumentative, since that is the very basis of the distinction between sentences and statements? In fact, Ducrot subscribed to the propositionalist position that separates meaning into *a* meaning, derived from its sentence (its semantic description, if we may so call it), and *the* meaning, which is linked to a particular utterance of that sentence in a given context. And about propositionalism? We read further: "We will say that a statement expresses one or several propositions, meaning by that term not a grammatical proposition . . . but a purely semantic entity."[3] Meaning is grounded in the grammar of the sentence and is presented:

> . . . as a complex of instructions, provided to the person who must interpret the statements the sentence expresses, instructions which make precise certain manipulations which must be carried out to associate meaning for these statements . . . The instructional nature of meaning appears directly here, when we introduce argumentative variables within it, as Anscombre and I have systematically done.[4]

This idea relies on the distinction between meaning and significance, between statement (or utterance) and sentence (or phrase). A sentence is the propositional entity par excellence, an "abstract linguistic entity, purely theoretical, specifically a group of words combined according to the rules of syntax, considered completely outside of any discursive

2. O. Ducrot, "La valeur argumentative de la phrase interrogative," in *Logique, argumentation, conversation*, ed. A. Berrendonner (Bern: Peter Lang, 1983), p. 81 [author's translation].

3. O. Ducrot et al., *Les mots du discours* (Paris: Editions de Minuit, 1984), p. 7 [author's translation].

4. O. Ducrot, *Le dire et le dit* (Paris: Editions de Minuit, 1985), p. 181 [author's translation].

context."[5] Do we really have the right to give ourselves over to a language that is never stated or uttered, knowing that sentences-in-themselves do not exist? "The concept of meaning on which I have founded my work is not, properly speaking, a hypothesis susceptible of being verified or proved false, but rather is a result of a decision, justified by the work it makes possible."[6] So be it, but why uncritically assert an ad hoc conception of language? Why refuse the theoretical systematization that these fruitful individual analyses presuppose? And why surreptitiously introduce one which is itself unfounded? Hence the question of what links the various case studies admirably carried out by Ducrot and of discovering what they reveal about the nature of language. Do these questions themselves not verify a theory, which is none other than the problematological conception of language?

We can now move from the theoretical to study the practical consequences of all this. As we have seen, to speak is to raise, or at least evoke, a question, even if that question presents itself in the form of an answer. This is quite removed from our preconceived notions about the communicative nature of language. It calls to mind Ducrot's old caution that:

> . . . anything that can be said can be contradicted. The result is that we cannot put forward opinions or wishes without at the same time setting them up for others' eventual objections. As has often been noted, the forming of an idea is the first—and the decisive—step in its becoming a subject for debate.[7]

Because there is potential questioning, there is debate, hence argumentation; this implicit relationship to some originary question is contained within the utterance as its meaning. And let us not forget that what is in question in speech is truly what we mean by the sense or meaning of that discourse. Argumentation and meaning are thus linked, and this linkage suggests how Ducrot can imply that the instructions which he posits as determinative of meaning are really a request addressed to an audience, an interrogative "asking that the listener find within discourse such and such a type of information and use that information in such and such a manner to reconstruct the meaning intended by the speaker."[8]

If one does not subscribe to problematological theory, it might seem

5. Ducrot, *Les mots du discours*, p. 7.
6. Ducrot, *Le dire et le dit*, p. 182.
7. O. Ducrot, *Dire et ne pas dire*, 2d ed. (Paris: Hermann, 1980), p. 6 [author's translation].
8. Ducrot, *Les mots du discours*, p. 12.

surprising to maintain that any statement, though presented as an answer, could actually raise a question. Let us consider some examples:

1. There are some good policemen in this town.

This is certainly a banal statement. Upon reflection, we find that it suggests that there may be other police officers who aren't so good. How does such an alternative suggestion arise? Simply by presenting itself as an answer to a question, whose alternative answers are thereby evoked as implicit possibilities—just as implicit as the question itself.

2. A father to his son: "Your mother is right. You should eat before you go to school."

The statement "Your mother is right" clearly evokes the possibility of the opposite answer, an opposition which in this case is probably brought to light by a refusal or protest of some kind by the son. In any event, a question is raised which the son probably has not raised directly, but which weakens the mother's position by suggesting that it might have been asked.

3. I attended the lectures given by your predecessor. He was very good.

Having once made this remark to one of my old professors (now a colleague), I was quickly put in my place by the following answer: "Thank you. But do you mean I'm not such a good teacher myself?" Was that really what I meant to say? Certainly not, as I quickly protested. But when looked at more closely, my professor's reaction was quite logical. For in addressing him in particular, I suggested a concern which prompted my question: "Who is the better teacher?" When I mentioned the one and not the other, my professor, who was the "other," himself answered the question which was suggested by my assertion and to which I had already given an answer which excluded him.

4. He will certainly come tomorrow. He will come tomorrow.

The adverb "certainly," like the construction "without doubt," in fact introduces uncertainty and doubt. Their use raises a question which otherwise would not even have been suggested by the very denial which they present. An expression like "He will certainly come tomorrow" denotes a greater degree of problematicity than the other expression. "He certainly is intelligent" tells us that he probably is not, in contrast to the statement, "He is intelligent," which squarely says so without raising any question about its own content, at least by means of language.

5. Is he not dishonest?

The very posing of the question suggests that the person in question is indeed dishonest. This question suggests an alternative through the use of a negative term. Nothing is left of the alternatives but the term, which has not been eliminated. By choosing this strategy, the speaker refuses to take responsibility for an assertion which could be defamatory. It is left to the one addressed to draw the conclusion, to answer for himself a question which the speaker does not choose to present as an explicit assertion. The speaker does not work from a prior statement that he puts in question; rather he makes, he creates, this assertion by expressing his question. Would the speaker ask if X is *not* dishonest if there were no question of his honesty, if there were nothing to indicate that X is not honest? Even if our speaker did not use the negative form, he would nonetheless put into question something which for X should probably not be questioned, namely X's honesty. But here the speaker does so without taking a *formal* position on the answer. Perhaps it is a matter of degree. We might think of the American political candidate who said, "I assure you that my challenger is honest." If he said it, it was because the question was posed, and his challenger might be discredited. Thus the act of asking someone, "Are you honest?" is scarcely less harmful than asking him, "Are you dishonest?" since, if the question were not relevant, then why raise it?

Thus a speaker can more or less formally call another into question, as he can put himself strategically in the other's place (polyphony).

6. Freudian Denial

This mechanism of denial follows from the same principle used in the other examples listed above. Suppose that someone says, "I have nothing against you," or "You know very well that I wish you no harm," or some other formulation of this kind. Hearing it, one would have every reason to have grave doubts about the sincerity of the speaker. Why is this so?

In saying "I have nothing against you," for example, I am answering a question which seeks to know whether or not I *do* have something against you. The negative term in the answer has the effect of negating any question on the topic by canceling that which could have suggested it. The speaker could even claim that the question is out of place: this speaker raises a question by his answer to indicate that the question has no meaning. Such an answer is truly contradictory, because it is hard to see how one could answer a question and at the same time suggest that the question did not arise. As a consequence, the answer suggests a question wherein coherence would require us to think that what we have is not the answer. The question remains, but with it the other answer as the solution; that is, that I do have something against you.

7. Today, who supports the existence of the ether?

Answer: no one. The question isn't about knowing whether there is someone who defends this idea, but, on the contrary, to indicate that

nobody does, and that by this raising of the question we are emphasizing this impossibility. The conditional serves to render hypothetical
even the very statement of the question: "Who would even dare to raise
such a question?" The question, its very possibility questioned, is rendered impossible as a question. All that is left as an answer is the impossibility of asking it, which implies the nonexistence of a potential
questioner asking it.

8. *P but Q*

We could also include the famous example of *p but q*: "The weather
is beautiful, but a little cold," where there is a debate over the question
R/non-R, such as, "Are we going to take a walk?" with *p*, which argues in
favor of *R*, and *but q*, which leads to the opposite answer and even, since
it is stated, which eliminates *R*, which is implied by *p*.

The point here is not to repeat Ducrot's acute analyses, but to place
them in the philosophical context of a general conception of language
and illustrate it with the help of independent examples, drawn for other
purposes, such as that of linguistic analysis.

9. *Emphasis and Phrasing*

It is well known that apparently identical sentences will have different meanings if the emphasis is put on one clause rather than another.
In reality, the difference depends on the question which underlies the
statement. I might say, "Pierre arrived by car *yesterday*," and "*Pierre* arrived by car yesterday," which would indicate two different things, and
therefore have two different meanings, depending entirely on what is
in question.

In the first case, the question which the statement proposes to answer is a *when* question; in the second case, it is a *who* question. Because
the questions differ, the same semantic translation does not apply interchangeably to both: "Pierre (not John) arrived by car yesterday," and
"Pierre arrived by car yesterday (not another day)." By clearly stating
the opposition, the contrary response is excluded; as a consequence, the
initial problematicity dealt with by the statement disappears. The apocritical character of the judgment is established simultaneously with
the communication of its (implicit) meaning. "It was Pierre *who* came
yesterday" clearly has a different sense from "It was *yesterday* that Pierre
came."

The same problematological analysis can be found in Donellan's
contrast between the attributive and the referential use of predicates.[9]
If, for example, I say, "John's murderer is insane," I might be intending

9. Keith S. Donnellan, "Reference and Definite Descriptions," *Philosophical Review* 75 (July 1966): 281–304.

to say two things: (1) to kill John is to commit an insane act, or (2) the person who is accused of the murder is insane. In the latter case, even if found not guilty under the law, this person could still be deemed insane, for I can evaluate the individual as what *I* think he is, independent of his legal culpability. In the first case, we have attributive use of the predicate, in the sense that I qualify the act and, only as a consequence, the one who has committed it. In the second reading, John's murderer can be just as insane in my eyes regardless of his legal culpability, while in the first reading it is *because* he is culpable for this act that he is insane. If we look closely at this matter, there are, once again, two implicit questions: *who* and *what*. It is these two questions which make possible the two readings, thus the two interpretations.

This analysis works equally well for the concept of presupposition. Negation and interrogation maintain the truth-value of the presupposition of the affirmation, while other implications cannot withstand this double test, such as the *subtext* ["sous-entendu"] and the *cotext*, or what is explicitly posed in a statement (*le posé*, to use Ducrot's term). A statement like "John has stopped beating his wife" presupposes that he had been beating her. If one either asks the question or answers it by denying it (Has John stopped beating his wife? John hasn't stopped beating his wife), one still presupposes, in both cases, that he had been beating her. The validity of that test comes simply from the fact, in this case, that the statement of this question doesn't really seek to know whether John beats his wife or not; the problem is posed as already resolved. As a consequence, the interrogative operation (the posing of alternatives or the negation of one alternative) applied to the initial statement will have no effect on the predetermined answer contained in the statement itself. We might even say that presupposition is the very condition of questioning, and, *a fortiori*, of answering, whether positive or negative. This accounts for the possibility of such a test as the one for presuppositionality. But Frege, who explored the matter, did not stress that interrelationship, because mathematical propositionalism, with its emphasis on truth-values and "objective thoughts," prevented him from relating these phenomena to interrogativity. In fact, in any question, insofar as there is a problematological answer, we can locate the problematological difference which is marked by the old opposition between the known and the unknown, which Descartes addressed in his *Rules*. To be able to ask anything, as well as to answer, it is necessary that one *know* what it is *to know*. If the notion of a priori has any validity, it might be justified in this manner.

There are quite clearly other types of implications, contextual ones, for example, which are presupposed (in a certain way) and which do not comply with the test of presuppositionality, and for a simple enough reason. If I say, "James is not very clever," what is implied, or "implicated," is that James is stupid. This is what the answer is all about, and if I put it into question, I immediately put in question the implicit question which was considered solved. If I ask, "Is James not very clever?" far from presupposing that he is stupid, I suggest the very opposite by putting into question the affirmation that he is possibly not very clever. The test of presupposition depends on the dissociation of questions. In the case where it applies, there are two different questions, one resolved, the other to be resolved.

10. John is not as tall as Mary.

In making that statement, the question of whether John is taller or shorter than Mary is raised. This alternative is implicitly solved by the answer (since the question is implicit, we may call the solution an *argument*) that John is shorter. Still, one could just as well have concluded that, since he is not *as* tall, he could be *taller;* equal height is the only alternative that is excluded in the statement.

In fact, to understand the argumentative mechanism, to understand that it is the problematological one, it is helpful to contrast this example with its opposite: "John is not as short as Mary." In the first case, what is at issue is whether John is equal in *height*, which implies through its solution that what is in question is equality as measured by tallness; it is in respect to tallness that John's physical stature is unequal to Mary's. The only thing left is to infer that it is by *shortness* that inequality appears. No other law but a simple problematological analysis is applied. On the other hand, if I say, "John is not as short as Mary," I put the question in terms of shortness, and the solution implies that John is *taller.* The adjective *short*, as its opposite just above, indicates the point of the question, that which is in doubt and which determines by exclusion of alternatives the only remaining possibility.

11. Even John is taller than Mary.

The word "even" reinforces the status, the nature of the question which is set forth: it indicates that a question which could have been present in the listener's mind has no reason to persist, if indeed it ever occurred. The opposite might have been believed, that the little John is shorter than Mary; the question could have been to know if Mary is really as short as people think. But that question cannot be asked any more. The word "even" suggests a question that should not be raised any longer. If I say, "He is intelligent, and *even* kind," I emphasize by this word "even" that any question about his positive character must be considered to have been resolved once and for all, thanks to this supplementary argument in favor of the initial (or supposed initial) answer.

Let us note that predication has argumentative value because it distinctively refers to something which is in question, even if only implicitly so, something about which we are making a judgment when we affirm that "X is Y." We exclude the possibility that X could be anything else in answering that it is Y; and for this reason it is no longer in question, if X had been the matter in question at the outset. If we think of "X is Y" as answer A, we can imagine that A is a problem as much as it is an answer to another question. Thus one would have a new structure of "A is B" as an inferential, interpretational link, where to say A is really to say B, and to say "X is Y" means something else, namely that it is B. If A, then B. We could also have imagined a controversy over X in A.

The examples presented in this chapter have clearly illustrated the problematological conception of language and confirmed that language includes both argumentative and pragmatic elements. We should not surrender to the positivist illusion which reduced the philosophical to the merely linguistic, a shift which reflected the lack of a systematic philosophical theory, as is illustrated when language games and case studies multiply. The *integration* of a supposed rhetoric, originating in individual facts which are supposed to exist in themselves, amounts to developing an implicit conceptual frame which does not *have* to justify itself, precisely because it depends on facts. Such a methodological empiricism would allow us, under the guise of observations about language, to believe that we can do without a fully articulated conception of language, and by that, without a theory of argument. Such a received view of science relies on a very sketchy vision of what science is; science cannot be limited simply to storing up examples, however theoretically generative these are presented to be.

What was important here was to bring together the realm of experience and the articulation of the *logos*, established independently from experience. In each case we have seen that to argue is to debate a question through the use of statements that, even as they deal with the question at issue, do not pretend to close it off forever. To argue is to confront an interlocutor with a question, often through an inference (frequently an implicit one), which he must answer because he himself is a questioner when confronted with that question. Because the answer can be one of several things, it is only possibly true. The implicit allows the speaker to escape responsibility for presenting *the* answer; he must propose it but is not in a position to impose it.

The relationship between the explicit and the implicit is what defines the *argumentative* nature of language and thereby defines the inference which it brings about. In dialogue, where the movement from question to answer occurs through the use of turn-taking, inference assumes a different character. Dialectical (or dialogical) inference relates the question to the answer through the context, which, as we recall, includes commonplaces, indirect presuppositions appropriate to the particular situation, and the role of subjectivity which literally is implied in the alternating of roles. *Context* is an essential problematological concept, since it is what guarantees the effective implementation of the problematological difference. Is dialogue, therefore, itself an inference? That would explain, and even be the source of, the conversational "rules" defined by Grice. According to Grice, certain principles of discussion are always presupposed. For example, when participating in conversation, it is necessary to provide the information asked for, neither more nor less; it is necessary that the exchanges in conversation be truthful, pertinent, and easily understood. All that is quite well known, but if we look at the matter a little more closely, we will find that the above-mentioned requirements are conditions of a dialogical answering process. An answer must answer a particular question (therefore it has to be relevant) and make sense as an answer to *that* question, without implicating other questions. We could pursue this generalization in adopting a theory of speech acts, which is only a partial theory of language use as a questioning and answering process. Quite obviously, those acts always refer to particular questions which preoccupy the speaker and which make those problems understandable to a listener, for example, to prompt him to act. If one asks a locutor the meaning of his act, that meaning remains though the performative structure has disappeared into the explication of what this speech act is; for example, when the statement "Close the door!" really means "I order you to close the door." The latter statement can be rendered by a preformulation with "I say" to maintain the problematic strength of the act. It is an order here but could be a promise, a request, or whatever.

All of this has led us to develop a problematological conception of meaning.

S_{ix}

Toward a Concept of Meaning:
From the Literal to the Literary

1. Meaning and Truth-Conditions

If we accept the traditional approach to philosophy, with its primary focus on propositions, we note that the meaning of a proposition is provided by its truth-conditions, which give rise to equivalent formulations of the proposition. Let us use an example which will allow us to explore the traditional propositionalist notion of meaning in language. If someone says "It's raining," I understand this assertion *if* I know exactly what occurs if the proposition is true, that is, when it really is raining. The word *if* brings us back to the problem treated as already resolved and even as nonexistent. In this case, one could say that the *meaning* of this statement is provided to us by its truth-conditions. I envision an event, a fact which is described, and in so doing I am assured of having grasped the meaning of the sentence. Even more, if someone asks me what I mean when I say, "It's raining," I can then produce a new statement bearing directly on the matter of what happens when it rains, thus conveying its truth-conditions. *If* "It's raining" is true, then "Such and such a phenomenon is occurring" is also a true statement. A description of rain, if rain occurs, will define the meaning of the word "rain." Frege expresses this identity in stipulating meaning by the use of the *sense-reference* pair. A proposition which has the same *meaning* as another, which specifies the meaning of another sentence, *refers* to the same thing, *says* the same thing, but differently. Only the *expression* changes, because it embodies the mode of presentation of the thing, of the *reference*. Frege calls this expression of reference its *sense*. Thus "the pupil of Socrates" and "the master of Aristotle" have the same meaning in that both refer to the same person. However, the meaning is *presented* differently, since Plato is presented in different lights in the two phrases. If the emphasis is put on the relationship to Socrates, Plato is not identified in the same way as he would be if the primary interest is his relationship to Aristotle. If A is what gives meaning to B, it is because both refer to the same reality, but seen in two ways: Plato *is* Aristotle's teacher, and Aristotle's teacher *is* Socrates' pupil. One could say the same thing as well in another way: one can give meaning to B *through* A. The *sense* clarifies the *reference*, and the correlation of the one with the other is what provides *meaning*.

All this seems clear, and even empirically grounded. We all know that if someone asks us the meaning of a statement we have just made, we repeat it in another form. And we know just as well that if a professor, in a large classroom, says "John, come to the board," the request will only be understandable if we know accurately to which "John" the speaker is referring when there are several people in the room with this name. The sentence makes or has sense, as is clear to everyone, but it lacks *specific* meaning until *one* person named John is designated as the one to whom the speaker refers.

2. Limitations and Criticisms of the Propositional Theory of Meaning

It was immediately apparent to Frege that two propositions cannot be substituted for one another simply because both refer to the same reality. For, according to Frege, all propositions, whatever the specific content of each, are meant to refer to truth, and truth is what, in the last analysis, they all can be reduced to. Two propositions which would express the True would, by that *sole* fact, mean the same. They would have two different senses because they would say what they have to say differently; they would, however, have an identical meaning. As a result, the meaning of "John is tall" could be "This table is rectangular," if we assume that both *refer* to what *is* (the case); therefore they are true by the same token.

What did Frege do when confronted with this difficulty? He introduced the *principle of composition*, which says that the meaning of a proposition depends on the meaning of its *constituent terms*. For two propositions to have the same meaning and, as a result, be substitutable, it is necessary that each subject and predicate be *respectively* substitutable, that each has the same reference, although expressed differently. Thus, "John is not married" has the same meaning as "John is a bachelor," because "John = John" and "bachelor = not married." The word "John" refers to the same individual; the sense, therefore, is also identical. The concept of "bachelor" *refers* to the same state of being as "not married," which makes all those individuals designated by the term "bachelor" fall into the same category as "not married." A different sense results here from the fact that the expressions are not the same. As a consequence, from a purely semantic viewpoint, the sentence "John is tall" is distinguishable from "This table is rectangular," since neither of the subjects or predicates is substitutable because they do not have the same references. The propositions included in these sentences are both true, but their substitutability does not depend on any kind of global reference (saying what is true). Rather, it rests exclusively on the respective references of the constituent parts; as a function, it depends on the value of its arguments.

In thus avoiding the worst difficulty, Frege chose an escape route which considerably limited his concept of meaning. It is purely analytical; one seeks meaning entirely within the elements of a sentence to understand it. That would imply that to understand the meaning of discourse, we have to deconstruct it sentence by sentence, and then deconstruct, in turn, each sentence into individual subjects and predicates.

This is not even to mention the difficulty encountered in literary works of fiction which have no objective referents, no truth-conditions; nor are we discussing nondeclarative sentences which also (but for different reasons) do not have truth-conditions, since they are not assertive. In short, when there is no fixed literal meaning established in everyday speech or in scientific language, meaning loses all meaning. If we look at this more closely, such a limitation implies just this: propositions, as the only truth-bearers, are the only significant units.

3. The Principles of a Unified Theory of Meaning

Even if we can agree with Frege and say that understanding the words of everyday language consists of knowing the reality they designate, and in so doing, arriving at a variety of possible surrogate terms, we still need not agree with his claim that we have here a general conception of meaning. His view pretends to be able to deconstruct language by breaking it up into various units, namely, into *sense, reference,* and *meaning.* The subject of a proposition might have a reference, but where do we find that of the predicate? Must we agree with the idea that *concepts* exist as predicate references, to the same degree that the truth-values could exist, as Platonist correlates of propositions? If one does follow Frege on this point, the inevitable result is the quarrel, medieval in all respects, between nominalism and realism, which not only Frege, but also Quine and Putnam reawakened.

We limit ourselves here to the basic task of explaining referentiality as a criterion of meaning at the level of words and propositions, the latter considered as autonomous entities. But we might note at the same time that propositions exist only within discourse, within contexts, and that the act of isolating them is already a result, a practice, and not a given. However, in linguistics textbooks propositions are studied as entities that are logically autonomous, and as though they were evidently so. Autonomy, as we have seen, is completely a relative matter, itself the product of a dynamic. Starting from that point, it is impossible to approach the question of meaning outside of the idea of discourse, even without accounting for the reality of fictional discourse. What better test is there for any language theory that wants to be comprehensive than literature? Might we therefore be able to find in literary theory the generalizable concept of meaning which we seek? Unfortunately, the answer is no, and for an obvious reason. It is because those who preoccupy themselves with literature quite often proceed analytically—in the name of science, that is, out of respect for empiricity—as did the linguists we met in the preceding chapter. They study works and authors in isolation. One doesn't need a philosophical view of language to operate this way. There is a presupposition of a philosophy of language which one need not make explicit or even justify. Do literary works not speak for themselves? Things have undoubtedly changed a little, and properly so, due to the self-referentiality of literature, which we addressed earlier. Literature, tending more and more to pose itself as its own object, has placed its own language into the foreground of literary criticism. And another pitfall appears: that of theorizing language as modeled on the language of fiction. Just as Frege had in mind the univocity and objectivity of mathematico-experimental language when he spoke of the *logos,* Derrida, for example, presented a more literary conception of the *logos,* founded on the *non*referentiality of language, on its rhetorical, tropological, and nonunivocal nature: a figurative conception. But this is a nonargumentative rhetoric: signs refer to one another indefinitely, without denoting any reference as privileged or literal. The lack of meaning would not result from a debate, an implicit conflict between opposite and irreducible functions, but from an inability to express its true object, except in a derivative, or arbitrary (after Saussure), almost conventional manner. There seems to be no inference in this rhetoric, so often opposed to the "other" rhetoric of Aristotle (as revived by Perelman) and distinct from that of Barthes, for instance, who envisioned a "new rhetoric" stemming from the *logos* of fiction.

Thus we arrive at the other question, a hermeneutic and not a semantic one, that of the meaning of texts, including literary ones.

4. Meaning in Literary Theory

We have now seen how Fregeian logicism can be rejected on the grounds of his answer to the question of meaning. We can reject it because discourse cannot logically be seen strictly as an analytical assemblage of added-up sentences, and above all because the referential relationship to external reality postulates that discourse itself must refer to something other than itself. Unlike the literal and referential, the literary and fictional are deviations from the norm as defined by everyday language. Rhetoric will be figurative, secondary, derivative, additive. "Since ancient times, rhetoric defined figures as modes of speech which are far from natural and ordinary, that is to say, as linguistic deviations," as Jean Cohen reminds us.[1] He adds: "The poetic begins from the very moment that the sea is called 'the roof' or ships 'doves.' There is in this a violation of the linguistic code, a linguistic deviation, which the old rhetoric called a 'figure,' and which is for poesy its sole object."[2] The word "deviation" implies that it is the literal which is primary, and the figurative which derives from it. Present-day *literary* rhetoric, stemming from Nietzsche, contests this order of priority because, according to him, it is the metaphoric which is primary and the referential function which is arbitrary and which inserts itself into this hazy picture to eliminate its vagueness. Man is an artist and a poet before he is a tradesman: "What, then, is truth? A movable host of metaphors, metonymies, and anthropomorphisms . . . which have been poetically and rhetorically intensified, transferred, and embellished, and which, after long usage, seem to a people to be fixed, canonical, and binding. Truths are illusions which we have forgotten are illusions . . ."[3] Further on we read: "Logic is merely slavery within the fetters of language. But language includes within itself an illogical element: metaphor. The initial power produces an equation between things that are unequal and is thus an operation of the imagination. The existence of concepts, forms, etc. is based upon this."[4] Truth and reference are therefore secondary and imposed only by an act of will: "We speak of a 'snake': this designation touches only upon its ability to twist itself and could therefore also fit a worm. What arbitrary differentiations!"[5] In summary: "Only by forgetting this primitive world of metaphor can one live with any repose, security and consistency: only by means of the petrification and coagulation of a mass of images which originally streamed from the primal faculty of human imagination like a fiery liquid, only in the

1. J. Cohen, *Structure du langage poétique* (Paris: Flammarion, 1966), p. 13 [author's translation].

2. Ibid.

3. Friedrich Nietzsche, "On Truth and Lies in a Non-Moral Sense," in Nietzsche, *Philosophy and Truth: Selections from Nietzsche's Notebooks of the Early 1870s*, trans. and ed. Daniel Breazeale (Atlantic Highlands, N.J.: Humanities Press, 1979), p. 84.

4. Nietzsche, "Drafts [Entwurfe], #177," trans. Daniel Breazeale, in *Philosophy and Truth* (Atlantic Highlands, N.J.: Humanities Press, 1979), p. 94.

5. Nietzsche, "On Truth and Lies," p. 82.

invincible faith that *this* sun, *this* window, *this* table is a truth itself, only by forgetting that he himself is an *artistically creating* subject, does man live with any repose, security, and consistency." [6]

This idea of the *logos* aims at showing that comprehension, because it makes plurivocal discourse literal, is in fact obsessed by the regulating norm of truth, the concern for a correct interpretation set forth as a principle. But deconstructionism, in seeking to return to the metaphoric mark, rejects this referentialist *coup de force*.

The most striking characteristic of this modern perspective is the crumbling away of the possibility of comprehension, of the possibility that the meaning of texts exists. Language denies any such possibility by its fictionality, its nonreferentiality, if one follows the philosophy of deconstruction. What more is there to say of this theory, which claims to be meaningful, except that the textuality of a work deconstructs its message, and therefore *all* meaning. But a *literary* text cannot be a *literal* one: the fact that it has several readings is its only reading; the unity of its meaning becomes the breaking up of meaning. Its figurative nature reflects itself as the impossibility of saying whether what is stated means *this* rather than *that*. There are multiple interpretations, and it is this multiplicity which, through deconstruction, is identified as *the* text. This helps to explain why a number of literary texts—the "nouveau roman," for example, or the works of Joyce, or Kafka, break up poetical unity by repeated splittings which, by gradual stages as the reader proceeds, destroy any idea of *one* exclusive meaning.

Even if contemporary literature lends itself more than anything else to the loss of meaning and to the opening up of multiple interpretations of its content (linguistically rooted in the figurative nature of discourse), nevertheless, figural language cannot be the model of *logos*. We can call into doubt the validity of the antireferentialist approach to meaning, since we continue to interpret works and assign meaning to their content, even as we admit that many different competing readings of the same texts are possible. In fact, antireferentialism gives too much credit to its opponent. Indeed, it assumes that opponent is correct. In identifying meaning with reference, and, correlatively, the absence of meaning with the lack of reference, fiction seems to fall outside of the whole question of meaning. The result is that the language of fiction is deemed to be no longer able to say any *thing* in particular. Given that hypothesis, it becomes obvious that we cannot understand literature any longer, since we can only misunderstand it. But who said that meaning was either referential or nothing at all?

6. Ibid., p. 86.

Clearly, we face two theses about language, each with its own prejudices and unquestioned preconceptions. One is that of referentialism, which relies only on everyday or on scientific language. Referentialism sees sentence-propositions as autonomous, and as understandable in themselves, through some internal analysis. The other is antireferentialism, which, far from contesting this approach to meaning, rather takes discourse, and even fiction, as its point of departure to see the figurative rather than the literal as the primary nature of language. But no matter how we deny meaning, it comes up again and again in readings, which then can only be misreadings of the text, resulting in miscomprehension. This is due to the fact that according to this view any meaning in particular, however imposing itself naturally, is fundamentally impossible. The opposition between the literal and the figurative is here reversed: antireferentialism considers language above all as figurative, with literal meaning as a sort of *deviation* from its basic metaphorical process. It becomes a deviation in that it derives from a need to assign some arbitrary meaning to language to allow it to function in everyday uses, precisely as science proceeds when it ascribes conventional meanings to its symbols.

5. Literal and Figurative Meaning

We might wonder which came first: the literal or the figurative. Propositionalism is not able to answer, because, in truth, there is no first element, thus no linguistic deviation from whichever is chosen, the literal or the figurative. When there is a case of split meaning, there is an appeal or a question, produced by the statement itself, often within the text of the statement (or statements). If I say "It's one o'clock" to tell someone that it's time to sit down to lunch, then it is clear that I wanted to say something other than what I *factually* did say. It is a little like someone saying, "It's a pleasant day, *but* a little warm," not as an answer to a question about the weather, but to a question about taking a walk. In these two examples, figurativeness emerges as *the other answer* in that the explicit response shows itself to be a problematological answer.

In the example of "It is one o'clock," the answer raises the problem that the question it literally answers is not the one which in the immediate instance it resolves. Why announce the time if no one has asked what time it is? Why raise a question which is not posed? Here, it is not the question of time which is at issue in this answer, but another to which this is an indirect answer without saying what it is, without announcing what really is its question. The question within this question is put to an addressee who places it in context and infers an answer which will make clear what "It is one o'clock" really responds to. And it can be, among other possible meanings, a question of taking lunch. Context, clearly, is what allows us to proceed to a valid inference. What is important to note is that it is quite difficult to say if "It is one o'clock" is the figurative expression for "It is time to eat," which is the literal sense of the original phrase or, on the contrary, if "Let's eat" is the figurative sense of "It is one o'clock." Which is the literal and which the figurative here?

Clearly, the literal and the figurative function as propositionalized categories of the problematological difference, repressed by that propositionalization by the way, because one is led to *search* for something other than what is said *in* what is said, a search whose outcome can only emerge *through* what is said. Deciphering meaning, as we saw earlier in the *Fourth Meditation*, consists of questioning an answer as such to specify what the discourse answers, which brings us back to the question to which it *is* an answer. There is a substitution insofar as a statement is replaced by an answer which is both a response to the question of meaning and an explanation of the statement as answer (of its answerhood). The questioner-interpreter inquires into the statement and finds the question to which it responds. In short, he presents the statement as an answer, reproducing its content, but this time in relation to what it solves, so the interpreter answers his own hermeneutic question. In summary, the reader-interpreter retraces, in reverse, the steps of the speaker-author. Interpretation only makes explicit an implicit question. While the speaker proceeds from a question to move toward an answer, interpretation moves away from the answer and back toward the question, which allows the addressee to see in what respect a response is an answer.

In this regard, an answer which expresses its own intelligibility does not distinguish itself from one which is relatively opaque as to its own meaning and which therefore *demands* of its readers an effort at reconstruction, because it does not state its meaning. In both cases there is a substitutional reading which puts the discourse in question in terms of a solution. In such cases, we pass from one discourse to another, which states the apocritical nature of the first discourse. Having said all that, there remains one essential distinction to note. In a literal reading, what is in question in the answer is made known *by* the answer. Literality means there are no surprises: we have here an answer which poses no question and which expresses what was in question as ceasing to be questionable. It is, to put it in classical terms, a purely propositional answer. We would search in vain for any interrogativity, since it has been suppressed. Everything is there, so to speak, hence the notion of "semantic autonomy," on which Frege's principle of composition is based.

In contrast, where there is a duality of meaning, the answer raises the question without thereby suggesting to what question it is a solution. In fact, because of its problematological character, it invites another answer. It activates the questioner-interpreter who has a constitutive role to play, being involved in the very textuality, because of the division of meaning into literal and figurative. This pair functions as a reciprocal duality, an appeal which is unavoidable and a reminder of what happens when we fail to understand a proposition. The result is that the duality of meaning works just like a call for understanding, like a resistance of the meaning, like some intelligibility to be recovered. If interpretation always involves substituting one answer for another, nevertheless there is still a difference. Sheer literality preserves a given content, while the redoubling we have spoken of has the effect of directing us back to a problematicity which obliges us to rephrase our answer. A figurative substitution is therefore the fruit of a construction developed from a perspective placed outside of the statement, though evolving from it. This kind of statement leads to its own problematization, not becoming a answer except through reconstruction. By contrast, a literal meaning is purely duplicative, even if the questioner-interpreter himself puts the answer into question.

Given the problematological nature of discursivity in general, dual meaning is an intrinsic possibility of language. Thus, a questioner-hearer (or reader) can always find a double sense to anything said to him, to the point of perpetually imagining an added intention to a statement (an intention which then expresses another problematic). This can lead to an existential sickness, a maladjustment, a split personality, or to paranoia. In a dialogue, meaning can always be made explicit by interrogation. Suppressing interrogation puts one back into strict literal statements where everything is already understood and admitted. Discourse is always elucidated by means of direct interrogation. If one answers directly a speaker's question, there is no inference; that is, in fact, the goal of this type of dialogue. When a speaker seeks to make an inference through rhetoric embedded in what he says, his listener will find a resolution, even in the worst-case situation, thanks to the explicit requirement for specification. This cannot be said about texts and other writings that leave such interrogations unanswered, because their authors are not really engaged in a dialogue with their readers, contrary to a frequently stated analogy.

In concluding this section on the literal and the figurative, we can say that it is useless to see their relationship as hierarchical, or to claim that one is a deviation from the other. There is a rhetorical structure in this pair, a request and therefore an answer beyond the answer which does not need to be reproduced, but rather to be realized in another form, an irreducible answer, although it can be discovered through substitution. But the *products* themselves cannot be substituted. Rather, we depend on a problematic which takes account not of what is spoken, but of the *act of speaking,* an implied and implicit meaning. Figurativeness is an inferential appeal; textuality, that which is written, does not allow for the eradication of the questions emerging from deliteralization. Certain texts clearly are more figurative, thus more problematic, than others. The problematological nature of the *logos* is the basis for the splitting of meaning into literal and figurative. By a certain placement (or implementation) of interrogativity, what is said leads us to the act of saying it as answering that interrogativity, thereby posing the question of *its* own question. In other words, the nonliterally said is incomprehensible without some reference to the act of saying, understood as a response. What is said appears to be put in question, thereby revealing discourse as indirectly related to questioning, and the act of speaking, to the expression of problems. The duality of meaning moves the focus of our attention from what is uttered to the utterance itself, to the fact of speaking as revealing an interrogativity bearing on the initial content. The act of uttering will be correlatively understood as an answer, one which responds to the question raised by the very content of the utterance.

No doubt we should ask ourselves if the duality of meaning can be marked off from the simple process of comprehension, both finally being based on the problematization of what is problematological. In the case of usual and everyday comprehension, literalized if we may say so, what is in question in the answer is going to become explicit in the answer which stipulates the meaning of this first answer. We will see shortly what the concrete effects of that are. By contrast, in the deliteralized sense, what happens is more specific: what is in question is revealed as not being *the* question ("It is one o'clock" does not really answer the question, "What time is it?" in the earlier example). This raises the issue of knowing to what other question such an affirmation responds. There will be another question and therefore another answer, still substitutable *as* an answer but *not* as an assertion ("I think" is not identical to "I am," unless they are identical answers to an initial problematic). In the splitting of meaning, the gap between the answer and what was in question within it reopens the issue of their adequacy, since one does not have the question which provides meaning from the moment when one has a figurative answer. The problem which this answer embodies must lead to another answer, inferred through the agency of some question to which both answers can be considered as solutions.

"It is one o'clock" and "It is time to eat" (as "It's a pleasant day but a little warm" and "Let's not take a walk") are equivalent answers because both answer the question "Isn't it time to get to the dinner-table?" (or, in the other example, whether or not to take a walk). If taken literally as assertions, that is, independent of a particular question which the context identifies, the two statements mentioned above are not mutually substitutable. But as *answers,* they are. A nonliteral reading does not raise only the issue of meaning, but addresses it to the discourse as a way of doing, as a speech-act. It creates the question of its own meaning through what it says by not saying it and through what it doesn't say while still saying it. Such a nonliteral reading makes it impossible to find solely within itself the question which it resolves, that is, *what* is in question. It puts a sort of pressure on the reader, who cannot now passively receive an answer and its question as some given intelligibility, almost automatic, as something which does not pose a problem, or if it poses one, as solving it through some semantic substitutionality for what is already literally there.

The literal-figurative connection is an inference, suppressed, it is true, by a dialogue of exploration with the author of the inference pursued by the addressee. That is what explains, to my mind, the argumentative and rhetorical aspect of all figurativeness, ranging from speech-acts to the uses of symbols, from metaphors to literary allegories. There is no longer any opposition between the classical inference and the interpretive derivation, a process of interpretation that "simply" reveals meaning. As a result, there is no more need to oppose literary rhetoric to argumentation in everyday language.

6. The Problematological Conception of the Meaning of Sentence and Text

As we have previously emphasized, the meaning of propositions and the meaning of discourse, fictional or not, arise from a unique process, from a single intellectual activity: the hermeneutic process, which can lead to a variety of interpretations or to a single one. However, all our tradition tries to make us think the contrary: namely, that sentences have meaning, either based on truth-conditions, as in Frege, or on more contextual and hazier variables, as in Wittgenstein, Austin, and Searle. Also, our tradition argues that there is a different sense for discourse, distinct from the one we find in sentences. Such a view has even degenerated into a conception of meaning and textuality in which meaning has become a question without meaning. The concurrence among interpretations is more of an indication of the inevitable plurality of meanings, revealing the never-ending hermeneutic *coup de force* that cuts short and misleads, but cannot really provide an understanding of *what* is meant. In short, the only option remaining is to proceed to an analysis of symbols, without trying to grasp some univocal meaning in them, since there is no such thing as *the* univocal meaning. Comprehension then becomes comprehending that we no longer comprehend, and what passes for criticism concentrates on tropes, on the insurpassable rhetoric of the text. Barthes says: "Interpreting a text does not consist of giving it a meaning (more or less founded in the text or free from it); on the contrary, it consists of appreciating what plurality the text is made of" (*S/Z*, p. 11). Must we truly resign ourselves to the abandonment of meaning, because of such a hermeneutical plurality?

The presupposition here is the traditional equation according to which reference = meaning. The question which we must face is to know when and why referentiality produces meaning. As soon as we provide the meaning of any term within a sentence, we are making reference to what that term designates, and in doing that we develop an equivalent sentence. If I ask, "Who is Napoleon?" because, for instance, I don't understand the sentence "Napoleon won the battle of Austerlitz," the answer consists of saying *who* Napoleon is, of providing a specific reference for the name: Napoleon is the *one who* did this or that. One could continue to explain *what* he did, *who* he had been, until the one who asked the question is presented with some designation which is familiar to him, which poses no further problem by allowing him to focus on *that which* has been set forth as identifying the Napoleon *who* was *in question* in the initial sentence. One would, further, be able to proceed with a similar analysis of another term in the question: for example, Austerlitz, *which* is the region *where*, etc. In short, as the reader will have noticed, each time a reference is specified, we use an interrogative, one which designates, denotes, and introduces the reference, at the same time that *what is in question* is also specified by that interrogative.

Thus a sentence like, "Napoleon won the battle of Austerlitz" is equivalent to "Napoleon is the one *who* won the battle of Austerlitz." If one is able to presume that such a statement is clearly understood by the listener, then one can do without the interrogatives, which can always reappear if the speaker is mistaken about the level of understanding of the listener. The point is that the absence of interrogatives in a sentence relates to the belief that speaker and listener share an entirely equal level of understanding. The speaker treats the problem as resolved and therefore, in his words, presents only his solution to it. The literal meaning of some discourse is like the semantic autonomy of a sentence which is understood by itself, which no longer questions what is in question in it. The result is an answer not stated as such, because there is no longer a problem to refer to. The absence of interrogatives in a sentence suggests a level of completely shared intelligibility. But that does not imply that the syntactic structure of assertions derives from interrogativity in general (though to speak is always in some way to make an answer to some problem). Such a conclusion would in fact suggest that we think of the interrogativity of the mind as though it were a grammatical category, which it is not. Failing to use interrogative words or clauses simply means that one is treating questions as already resolved, and, as a result, treating them as though they should never occur except on the off chance that something expressly raises them and brings them into the discussion. Moreover, a statement can anticipate certain requests for precision without even waiting to learn if in fact they will be made; the maker of a statement then resorts to interrogative clauses to detail exactly what he means when he uses the words he uses. The more the speaker uses explicit interrogatives, the more he has judged his *statement* to be problematical; he takes on as his own task the posing of questions which his listener could or would have posed. Meaning is not altered by such a process, it is merely made more explicit.

An answer does not state itself as such; consequently, it does not stipulate its meaning. It affirms what it says without stating that it is doing so. Meaning, therefore, in the ordinary case, is implicit. It is made explicit when what is in question needs to be specified in the answer, which becomes all at once an answer *and* a restatement of the problem posed at the start. Nothing changes in regard to the question under debate, which explains why "Napoleon won the battle of Austerlitz" is the equivalent of "Napoleon is the one *who* . . ." Meaning is what relates the statement to its own initial interrogativity. Giving or making explicit this meaning consists simply of *stating* this interrogativity, explaining how a statement constitutes an answer and how it *refers* to a particular question. Through this referral process, we hark back to what Frege called *the reference*, for even if *what* is in question is not stated as a question, and even if neither the answer nor the question are stated as such when meaning is provided, reference will nonetheless surface as *what had been* the question. This is made perfectly apparent by the interrogative-referential usage of relative clauses.

It is clear that speakers who want to make themselves understood don't say: "the meaning is . . ." Instead, they say whatever they have to say. In brief, the question-answer relationship, even if it is immanent, remains implicit. An answer says something else, something other than itself, since the goal of the questioning process is not to state itself as questioning but to say something else, to state the *what* of the question. The answer, which is the result of the process, does not have as its goal simply a referral back to the questions which made that answer possible, nor to state it as an answer, that is, as this referring process; rather, its goal is the stating of that "something else." The answering aspect of the statement, its answerhood, is repressed by the answer itself. It has an internal relationship with the originating question, an ability to deal with that question, that is, with the *what* of a question. Thus it has an effective referential function beyond itself, directed toward what is external to itself. An answer says *what* it says without saying that it said so, without referring to itself. The nature of an answer is not to state itself (as an answer), but to say *something*—more precisely, something-which-is-in-question—and because we here face an answer, to state that something as being solved, as ceasing to be in question. This question appears as what is necessarily absent for discourse to render *something* present. For example, if my problem is that I want to know what you are going to do tomorrow, your statement "I'm going to town" answers it. I am *not* asking whether you are saying to me, "My assertion that I am going to town answers your question," because the fact that this assertion is presented as an answer and preserves the meaning of the original answer does not imply at all that you are going to town. I ask you to answer me about an action, *not* about an assertion.

Because the goal of answers is not to state themselves as such, language signs essentially refer to something beyond them. This is the traditional definition of sign. We know that there are paradoxes which are bound to arise as one attempts to apply self-referential properties in a systematic manner to a group of propositions, directing referentiality to itself, as it were. Nonetheless, one answer can refer to another answer, just as it can also express a question. Therefore, we can see that there are apocritical answers and problematological answers. I have emphasized the fact that this distinction keeps intact the problematological difference to the extent that the two kinds of answers integrate that problematological difference in their quality as answers. To make it more concrete, in using language one knows what is in question; therefore, one does not have to mention it. The answer does not state itself. The discovery of its meaning proceeds from the context and from the information it contains for the audience. The hearer of the question functions like an implicit questioner: he considers what is said or written as an answer. The question found therein appeals to him for this or that reason—if only to let him show a certain lack of interest, for example. He becomes a questioner because an answer is proposed to him. But an answer to what, for what, about what?

The meaning of an answer is its link with an identifiable question. If its meaning is unclear to the person to whom the answer is addressed, it would still be necessary to resolve this problem by offering an answer which duplicates the initial answer because that would make clear the latter's character *as answer.* This referral to a speaker's question is explicit where there is a specific question about meaning. The answer that ascribes the meaning is obviously equivalent to the signified answer because both answer the same question. For example, "John is a bachelor" = "John is not married." If the first statement responds to question Q in context C, we can assume that the second one answers in the same way. Clearly, this is not an automatic equivalency, for if the question is "Will you provide a sentence which includes just two nouns?" the two statements cease to be mutually substitutable. The first is no longer the same as the second, because now it is a question of producing a whole with two nouns. In short, the meaning of a statement does not depend on itself alone, but on the question which it must be made to address.

Thus, the meaning of a statement depends on its nature as an answer, and that presupposes a precise question on which the statement's meaning depends. An answer claiming to be equivalent assumes its equivalency based on its relationship to that same question. So, it could well be true that "John is a bachelor," has the same meaning as "Albert is a short man," if the question had been to construct a two-noun sentence. An answer which gives a meaning differs, however, from one which has a meaning that the former stipulates, due to the fact that they emerge from different problems. Indeed, an answer has a meaning because of its link to a question which it repressed and left unexpressed in its very content, which is *other* than the stipulation of that link, of the question as treated. The answer resolves it, and the question which is no longer posed can at best only be derived from the answer as having been resolved by the answer. Often, such an answer is not identified as such, which would once again be an indication of the presence of a question even where it appears to be absent. The answer does not simply state itself, but rather states something other than itself, its object. Nevertheless, we may fairly say that it treats a specific question in what it says, without really saying "This is the question presented" and "I am its answer." The presence of a question as implicit to any statement, confirmed by the fact that it is an answer, shows us that any statement *has* meaning. The meaning may pass unnoticed by the questioner. The answer that the questioner seeks is bound to duplicate the answer he didn't understand; but, if he didn't understand it, it is because he didn't see what question it answered. The question has escaped him, and, as a consequence, the goal of the answer generated by his hermeneutic interrogation is the discovery of this question, which he failed to see in the explicit. Because meaning is found in the question-answer complex, there is no linguistic transaction which is devoid of meaning. The meaning may be immanent as being what is in question in what is said, even though it may be problematic for the nonparticipants or simply, for the interlocutor, in the discussion in question. The meaning of terms is referential only to the extent that the explanation of their meaning, or even the assumption that such a meaning exists, can be found through interrogative terms which provide the very objects of questioning. Something must respond to names, and to predicates as well, and it is this response which provides meaning. Clearly, answering can arise from a question that does not bear on the terms of the answer—not all interrogation has that as a goal—but there would be no judgment at all if a certain need had not existed. It is necessary to get rid of the *what* which gave rise to the question as a question, and to answer to *what* was in question by treating it as no longer at issue.

All this points to the conclusion that the formula *reference* = *meaning* is, in the last analysis, a truncated equation, one which depends on questioning for its validity. Even where discourse is not referential, there still is meaning, because meaning is provided by the relationship to the questioning process that the discourse supports. Quite clearly, propositionalism, by definition, will find it impossible to unify all these universes of discourse: referential, textual, and fictional. Since it cannot conceive of questioning as such, it sees only partial effects but interprets them each time as the whole of meaning. That is why, as the foregoing discussion has shown, meaning, where it is embodied in a literal statement, if not in a logical relationship, is associated with reference, and by this association is linked to truth-conditions (if truth exists). Propositionalism, however, cannot understand meaning (or significance—when it distinguishes the two) in terms of reference, without explaining it, for it is incapable of considering questioning as such, without forcing it into its own categorization. Those propositionalist characterizations (that is, its categories) can survive only by limiting the analysis strictly to propositions considered in themselves, by themselves, and for themselves. When we shift to another approach to language, either we must renounce the concept of meaning, or we have to change the meaning of meaning. This is a double setback, and an inevitable one if we cling to this thousand-year-old conception of how human thought works.

In a general sense, to understand discourse is to see it as answer, that is, as an answer to a question of knowing what it answers or what is the question within what is said. One can certainly adopt the method of antireferentialism and give up all hope of ever discovering the meaning of texts, taken as texts. A good example, which will allow us to contrast this doctrine with problematology, can be found in Kafka's famous story, "The Test," which was mentioned in chapter 3. A deconstructionist analysis would certainly point up the absurdity of the story, as though that were the ultimate *meaning* of Kafka's work. By contrast, problematology remains open to the coherence of meaning, but in a newly conceived way, untranslatable into those outdated and inadequate categories, requiring a new mode of thinking, which is all the more necessary since the crisis of values seen in Kafka's work has continued to worsen.

To recall the story, it is about a servant who despairs of ever finding work. One day, in a café, he finds himself sharing a table with someone. The other asks the servant a series of questions, but the servant can answer none of them; indeed, he finds that he cannot even understand the questions. The servant is apologetic and starts to leave, but his new acquaintance tells him to stop, saying, "That was only a test. He who does not answer the questions has passed the test."[7]

We can readily acknowledge this as a great example of Kafkaesque absurdity. In reading this short story, we are struck by its paradoxical anticlimax. How can you possibly pass an exam by not answering the examiner's questions, or worse yet, by claiming that you do not even understand what the questions are asking? In fact the servant symbolizes the servant of literature. The latter is in the same situation regarding a text he has just read as is the servant regarding a mansion where he wants to work.

The reader is thereby confronted with his own role as reader, with his relationship to texts in general, because of his identification with the servant in the story. That implies that the question of meaning can no longer even be posed, and in fact that the only answer is the rejection of such a question. The answer to the question of meaning is that this question itself has no meaning, or no longer has meaning. The reader passes his reader's test, becoming a servant of the text, if, like the servant in "The Test," he recognizes that he never will be able to grasp the meaning of the question of meaning.

This point illustrates a larger issue which characterizes modernity:

7. "The Test," in Franz Kafka, *Shorter Works*, vol. 1, trans. Malcolm Pasley (London: Secker & Warburg, 1973), pp. 137–38; for a more complete analysis, see the *Annales de l'Institut de Philosophie de l'Université Libre de Bruxelles*, 1985.

the lack of any unifying sense. This is true in painting, in music, or, as here, in literature. "The Test" can thus best be understood as an allegory of "contemporary" literature which deconstructs any univocal meaning. In discovering that there is nothing left to understand, we understand everything; we have passed the test of the text. But is that affirmation not itself contradictory? Can we truly say that the meaning of a text consists precisely in the utterance of its own lack of meaning, and if nonsense is not the object of the text, is there still a remaining Kafkaesque absurdity? Such a viewpoint is well within the purview of a conceptual scheme that provides no place at all for questioning as such. For if the answer to the question of meaning is without a solution, it is preferable to understand that question as devoid of *any other* solution than the affirmation of this very question, that is, of meaning as questioning, since the question *of* meaning does indeed have a solution: the question *as* meaning. The problematicity of a text, the enigma which it expresses, might be the only answer which we are allowed to derive from the text, but it *is* a response, all the same. If we cannot answer on the problematical and express it, then problematicity becomes paradoxical to express, and the secondary and nonproblematical discourse whose object is problematicity destroys itself and leads to its own impossibility. This is the origin of the absurdity. And yet the only answer to the interrogativity of a text is the acceptance of that interrogativity, of its real problematological makeup. An answer which is a question, without the awareness of their intrinsic difference, becomes paradoxical, absurd, and self-defeating, especially in a conceptual universe in decline, such as Kafka's.

The problem Kafka puts before us, quite literally, is the fact of the literary, and of discourse in general, according to a variable and determined proportion of problematicity. Kafka made problematicity the reference of his own problematic, so to speak. As a result, literature became the only place where problematicity *could* reveal itself, more or less indirectly, since in truth, the problematical, even if experienced, could not be thought of *as itself.* It had to be fictionalized.

If we limit our thinking to referentiality, which leads to a view of meaning as propositional equivalence, we will be in the same circumstance as Pierre Menard, the character created by Jorge Luis Borges. Menard rewrote *Don Quixote* right down to the last comma in order not to lose any of the original.[8] If the meaning of a sentence is indeed to be found in an equivalent sentence, then can we not say that the meaning of a work is in the ability to rewrite it? I have elsewhere called this *The*

---

8. J. L. Borges, "Pierre Menard, Author of the Quixote," in *Borges, a Reader,* ed. E. R. Monegal and Alistar Reid (New York: E. P. Dutton, 1981), pp. 96–103.

Paradox of Don Xerox.[9] Such a gap between proposition and discourse is artificial, just as referentiality has turned out to have a (denied) relationship to questioning. Making questioning explicit, in the case of texts, has nothing to do with literality. To understand a text is to root it in what it resolves, in what it deals with. Nothing in all of this suggests that what is in question is included (and literally so) in the answer, as a component of that answer. The relationship between text and interrogativity is necessarily more general, because a text is a unitary whole, not simply a collection of independent propositions (liable to be analyzed as such) which have been strung together.

Thus, there is a distinction to be drawn between what is in question in an answer and the question it deals with, what it *talks about*, the question it *talks over* and which may differ from the question that is *resolved in* the answer in a *derived* way. The reader will already have identified in this characterization the opposition between the literal and the figurative. Let us go back to our old example, "It is one o'clock." There is a question of time, but time is not what this statement is about. Rather, it deals with another thing: whether it is appropriate to interrupt a conversation at a certain point to eat lunch. When it comes to the analysis of texts, we have the same dichotomization at work. On the one hand, there is what each sentence says, but beyond that there is the whole, which is more than the simple accumulation of questions taken one by one. Textuality, or discursivity if we prefer, has the effect of making figurative the language it involves. Indeed, the meaning of a text is determined by its components but is not rooted in them; each of the sentences in a text refers back to the text itself as the locus of its deeper meaning. This is to say that it is impossible to interpret these sentences independently from the cotext. Even more clearly, this is to say that the text functions as the problematological differentiator, since sentences are problematological answers. The textual meaning is the apocritical one, that which resolves the problematicity of the text (its textuality, if you will). Once known, such an apocritical answer provides the general coherence for the overall meaning, what the whole "means." Understanding a text consists of relating its component parts to the problematicity which they implicate. This kind of research purports to analyze *what* is resolved, and *how* it is resolved, in relation to what resolution is made. To be able to see better what is going on in the poetics of a work, or in its interpretive reconstruction, we have to resort to the *law of complementarity*, which was presented in our "Meditations on the *Logos*" (chapter 4).

Before studying the specificity of fictional meaning, let us conclude

---

9. See Meyer, *Meaning and Reading* (Amsterdam: Benjamins, 1983).

with the question of the unity of meaning. Giving meaning always comes back to stating what is in question, relating the discourse under consideration to that to which it responds. This amounts to considering discourse as an answer, a concept which suggests a problematological articulation. Literal meaning is the answer which does not leave (or no longer leaves) any further question to be dealt with, whose meaning should be specified through interrogative clauses. A text must be taken as a whole. Understanding a text requires that the reader bring out a problematic at the end of an *interactive* process where the reader once more raises the issue of what questions are asked in the text. This process consists of taking these questions as the literal expressions of a figurativity embedded within discourse. This kind of figurativity will be all the more problematic because the text itself will be *literally* enigmatic.

7. The Law of Complementarity as the Basic Principle of Literary Rhetoric

This principle is a matter of the articulation of form with context. Context, in the case of dialogues, for instance, allows the demarcation of the problems *to be resolved* from the solutions. In the absence of such a context, defined by the interlocutory relationship and the *topoi* which it presumes, it is form which must assume for itself the problematological difference.

What is intrinsic to literature is that it incorporates as cotexts what the other forms of language leave implicit by virtue of the context. The problematological difference must be established in the text itself, but in a deliteralized way, which is the effect of textuality as it has been previously defined. Obviously, texts can be found that are very close to reality, which imitate it, and which therefore create an impression of verisimilitude. We might think, for example, of romances or crime novels. A problem is posed at the start and resolved at the end. The story incarnates the problematological difference, a difference which means that the narrative is an intrigue in every sense of that term. If we think of it in terms of its relationship to reality, it is truly *mimetic* to the extent that extensive literality produces a certain realism.

Literality, in its turn, is the product of a problematological difference made explicit in the text itself. The text problematizes reality, which it describes as "resolved," as making obvious that things are what they are and nothing else. Extensive literality is in fact extensive referentiality. A reality common to reader and speaker is present, even if not apparent. Nothing problematic emerges except for the problem itself, which defines the intrigue and leads it to a conclusion through the unfolding of the narrative. But even in the case of the maximal literality of literature, there is still figurativity, certainly to a minimal degree, which is defined by the unity of a text as such. It is, in fact, the problematological difference itself which is left implicit but which is, literally, "at work" here. Because the text does not *say*, "This is the problem" or "This is the solution," it fictionalizes both and makes their differentiation implicit, without any appeal to context but only to cotext. To unify a text by reading is to find in it a problematic to which it is the solution, a problematic which the text more or less literally suggests.

Conversely, the less a problem is literally identified as such, the more the function of form will be to indicate it. By form, I mean textual arrangement as much as style. For it is necessary that a text carry out the problematological difference one way or another, as the *logos* it is. The less a problem is stated literally, the more it will be stated figuratively, and the more that problematicity will be the text itself as discursive form. The more the text is deliteralized, the more its relationship with reality is problematical, and problematicity, which is formalized, will present itself in an answer that is all the more problematological. The more a problem is formalized, the wider the gulf between the literal and the figurative, the less the text is resolutional or apocritical. It is certainly an answer, but a problematological one, demanding much more from the reader (that is, a dialectical determination of meaning) as a highly enigmatic text which less directly states its meaning. This increasingly esoteric textuality, along with formal discontinuities, means that smooth progress toward the achievement of resolution is interrupted. Time itself becomes problematized in that it is the dimension which brings the reader from the problem to its solution. The increased role and function for the reader, the breaks in temporal linearity, and the death of the subject as giving a unifying perspective and overview for fiction all go together with the increased problematization achieved by form. The reader must retrace his steps to respond to a textuality which asks more and more from him; the text will not terminate with its physical ending, but must be completed with a second reading, delving into the very enigmaticity which the reader gradually discovers. The role of the reader, as Wolfgang Iser has pointed out so well in *The Act of Reading*, is the greater as the text means less per se, and demands so much more. When the narrative unity has been destroyed by the lack of a narrative *viewpoint*, given through a single narrator, the reader inevitably finds himself problematologically involved in the apocritical nature of the text because of the text's very form.

As a purely problematological solution, a text makes a literal appeal to figurativity, to the reader's imagination. This is even truer where the degree of problematization is greater, when the common reality is more problematic, and when there is less common referentiality for reader and narrator to refer to. The text is less mimetic, the imaginary element greater. Formalized problematicity works together with dereferential-ization, along with the problematicity of an external reality. It becomes clear that the death of the (unifying) subject, along with the crisis of common values about what is and must be, will be the cause of the for-mal *discontinuities* which have characterized literature since the begin-ning of the twentieth century. Realism may be dead, but let us not for-get that even in realism there was something of the hypothetical; the *description* of a given reality is never completely innocent, since one puts that reality in question by the very fact that one provides an an-swer. It is description which questions us, whereas later, things will get more formalized, more abstract.

When the fictional becomes problematological, the function of an-swers will be to emphasize the act of making the problematic explicit, even though, of course, not as such, an impossibility which can only be expressed fictionally. The more the discourse bears on the problem, the more it problematizes itself as pretending to be a solution, conse-quently the more it is a solution which itself raises a problem, that is, which makes the problematicity of discourse its own problematic. The more a text voices itself literally as a question, the less it suggests a uni-vocal interpretation, except through the assertion of this plurivocity. This is a problematological assertion though unable to express itself as such, able, therefore, to be fiction only regarding a literal stance of the problematological (which is beyond saying, according to propositional-ism). But the more a text is problematical, the less likely it will be to re-ceive an interpretation other than that which, rhetorically, states this problematicity. Kafka's "The Test" is not an isolated instance. Decon-struction is the propositional theorizing of one stage of problematologi-cal differentiation, one that sees discourse as more enigmatic than ever, as something that problematizes the very status of discourse. In reality, an evolution like the one which leads to deconstruction falls within the requirement of problematological differentiation. That differentiation is imposed by the strong problematization that addresses the obvious necessity of the real. Deconstructionism prevails only as a (brief) stage, and only as an effect of the application of the problematological differ-ence, an effect which has nonetheless remained unperceived (and thus autonomized) of that internal and historical unfolding of the problemo-tological difference through time, an effect which has been taken as a general solution.

The more problematological a text, the more the solution which is expressed in the text consists of stating this problematicity. This produces a plurality of interpretations which correspond to the variety of possible responses. It explains the greater degree of competition among interpretations of a single text, and also the theoretical fall-back position which leads to the denial of the possibility of interpretation. What has been called a greater symbolization is nothing other than accrued enigmatization. Let us be aware that narratives by their vicissitudes and their open and surprising alternatives continue to present both problems and solutions, which gives the narratives both appeal and durability. To be sure, there remains the solution which consists of affirming a text's problematicity and, above all, of specifying *the* problems at play in this particular text. There is a trap here: if any text deconstructs its meaning, and if meaning is identified as something beyond its own literal content, all the enigmatic texts would be forcibly reduced to *one single* meaning, namely their problematicity. This has been called a "trace" by propositionalism, which is unable to withstand problematicity as such, which sees in this artificial and indescribable presence the impossible unity of textual diversity. Deconstruction would suggest that each text says the same thing, something which nevertheless is neither *a* "thing" nor the same thing.

There remains but one point to make precise, and that is the difference between the discourse of fiction and that of referential language, the crime story versus the actual police reports, resemblance versus truth. Is there not, in both cases, a textuality, a rhetoric, an intrigue? But there is also a great difference, which is due to the process of autocontextualization. We can easily imagine that the actual procedures of the police have no need of making explicit their contextual elements which they can thus presume acquired by the reader. As a result, the solution is presented neither as a conclusion nor as a resolution of an intrigue, all because of context.

This analysis of literary rhetoric has allowed us to emphasize the inferential nature of reading, that is, the process of interpretation. The kind of inference that results appears to be of the same nature as a contextual reading of dual meaning, of argumentation seen in all its general applicability.

With that, we close our investigation of the *logos*.

S_{even}

On Scientific Knowledge

After our study of the *logos*, why do need we try to investigate how science accomplishes its own constitution?

We may begin by recalling the debate between logical empiricism and nihilism. Nihilism could say only that all discourse had become impossible. But our "Meditation on the Logos" allowed us to answer this charge and account for the uses of language. Therein we articulated a unified concept of meaning, of dialogue, of interpretation, and even an approach to literature. For nihilism, science was as much under attack as any other type of discourse. Logical empiricism, for its part, answered that only science, using known criteria like mathematical logic and experimentation, could resolve the questions which confront humanity and in that way give meaning to discourse.

Caught between the false claim that it was able to serve as the last refuge of rationality, and the completely contrary assurance that it could play a monopolistic role, science badly misunderstood its own nature and function.

The questions which we face are clear: we need to consider the status and the implications of scientific rationality. To do so, we need to understand the rationality of experience and causal logic as they are specifically involved in science and, above all, to be able to relate them to global rationality as a questioning process. It will no longer do to isolate these questions; they must be related to one another. The defeat of both nihilism and logical empiricism makes clear that the impossibility of articulating philosophy, language, and science is due to ignoring their common underlying interrogativity.

1. The Classical Conception of Episteme

Modern science, as it has existed since the end of the Renaissance, had its earliest expression in the thought of Descartes and Locke. Descartes' ideas about the nature of knowledge have their origins in Plato,

with whom Descartes shared a belief in the mathematical ideal. Apodicity, that is, the fact that a proposition excludes all doubt, was the result of the abandonment of problematicity, which is the noncognitive
par excellence. The analytic permits the acquisition of certainty, because its propositional character does not have to account for the impossible leap from the problematical to the nonproblematical. The analytic
is beyond such a categorization, which is how it transcends problematicity. This means it is resolutional; it resolves a problem by making
the problem disappear. How better to make it disappear than by not
speaking about it, or perhaps even better, by actively preventing oneself from thinking about it, which still is one way of *assuming* it as an implicit requirement? This is obviously a paradoxical approach; hence the
paradox of the *Meno* recurs time and again. Even if it does not acknowledge it, in fact analysis functions quite well as a *resolutional* device, as in
the assertoric resolution set forth by Plato. Aristotle cut analysis off
from the dialectical roots that Plato had failed to rule out. Yet Aristotle
could not provide any foundation for the necessity of such a cleavage
to safeguard the very autonomy of the propositional order. Later,
Descartes will attempt to establish the self-evident nature of this
propositional order by basing it on a positive intellectual process which
demonstrates the necessity of the order of assertion. Thus, we can see
that the presupposition which, ever since Plato, has allowed both reason and discourse to be made assertoric rather than problematological is
the ontologization of the *logos*. In that step, a new order was created, a
new level defined, one which freed thought from anything which could
relate this new order to something else. The focus on answers, which is
what will allow the problematic to be bypassed, will be accomplished
by eliminating the problematic by means of ontology. The shift toward
ontology, which separates Plato from Socrates, consists of referring
questioning as well as answering to Being. It renders their difference
inconsequential in view of the Essential, which subsequently will
no longer have anything to do with either. Aristotle, radicalizing the
rupture between dialectics and science, was obliged all the more to
work toward a more global ontology. In so doing, he also radicalized the
tension between ontology and epistemology, a tension which quickly
proved to be irresolvable.

When all is said and done, how will we assess knowledge? Will we
use ontological criteria, or will we rely on the conditions of cognitive
analysis? The question is unanswerable given the understanding of
knowledge we have inherited from the Greeks. Science and cognition
are nothing but modes of answering to which Socrates objected to by
his aporetic method, but an answering process which results from the
fact that asking oneself about something is tantamount to asking one-

self what the thing *is*, as answering is equivalent to telling what the thing is. Knowledge consists of this kind of specification, which is ontological; the two concepts refer to one another. What is absent from this relationship is problematicity, and for good reason. For it is in the suppression of problematicity that we find the concept of knowledge as suppressing any alternative, that is, of imposing as settled knowledge the exclusion of either term. It conceives the truth of the propositional as *the* answer, a necessity which of course depends on the exclusion of all other alternatives, of the *possible* of the problem. In fact, truth *cannot* fail to triumph: it has on its side those twin virtues of evidence and necessity, so dear to Descartes. Foundation and justification in univocal necessity become identical, and this identity is going to determine both the nature and the ordering of knowledge. Knowledge is born from a concern for answers, but since answers are unable to declare themselves as answers, science has become merely an accessory to the ontology which made it possible. Only because we ask what X *is*, when we are asking about X, do we know that the answer says *what* X is. Knowing X's essence, which is implicated in both question and answer, is the goal of science. Ontology allows discourse to emerge, rather than perpetuating itself in an aporetic process which is doomed from its inception to stop discourse from progressing, or even from existing. Yet, and it is here that the problem appears unsolvable, the primacy of ontology is no more acceptable than that of epistemology, because each has emerged to solve the other's difficulties. Indeed, even if we subordinate to being or to ontology all possible discursiveness, both reason and thought in its general sense, we shall still need knowledge to speak. Access to being will have to be had by way of a discourse which itself will have to be accounted for or explained. All of this brings us back to the epistemological problem. In this case, we call on intuition, or on a privileged mode of access, or an impossible discourse which can never state what it means to say, a noncircular circularity, and so on. The difficulty remains. How can we justify discourse that is at once noncognitive yet allows us to know, which is circular but not viciously so, a discourse whose propositional structure eschews the laws of propositionalism, which it nevertheless follows?

On the other hand, an epistemology which asserts its own priority will also find itself in difficulty. Epistemology involves concepts of truth, of correspondence to what *is*, and of justification, all of which make its content necessary; yet it is unable at the same time to articulate the problematological nature of those concepts and their contents, from which all interrogativity has been purged. Born out of silence in regard to interrogativity, a silence assimilated to a resolution which no longer had to describe itself as such (since this still would have rooted the *logos* in the unavoidable questioning process), science cannot account for itself. It cannot recognize itself as stemming from the interrogativity of the mind and still affirm its position as ensuing from mechanisms which are dedicated to *eradicating* rather than *explaining* questioning. Thus science needs ontology to make sense of its search after the *true*, its discussion of the *real* when it speaks of *what it is* as necessarily so because of *laws of nature* and *laws of society*. This is the source of the idealization of mathematization as a way of truly deciphering "the great book of Nature."

But the scientific ideal still proves to be apodictic assertoricity, as shown in the Cartesian method, where it is at least more workable than in the mysterious dialectic of Platonic Ideas. Analysis, by a process of elimination, creates a *justification* which provides access to the *true* proposition. And since it produces only propositions of this nature, it links them together in a justificatory order. It is clear enough that the proceedings which separate the alternatives, which put them in terms of truth and falsity, come back to what we are accustomed to call a problem. But this cannot be perceived as being a problem; in this analysis, the only thing left is its justificatory aspect, its results. On that basis, science will be seen as a continuing, irreversible accumulation (or progression) of established truths. As we have seen, for Descartes the analytic of knowledge could only emerge from the resolutional strength of the *Cogito*, which is not only the model for any possible answer (hence the link with *method*), but *is* the primary solution, the indubitable choice when everything else is called into doubt. It works as a rhetorical device which reduces discourse to an a priori certainty by conferring a priori apodicity to analysis, which therefore becomes wholly propositional. Self-consciousness is the a priori in every answer, of any answering which, in an analytical sense, comes back to itself. There would really be no analysis which leads to truth if the *Cogito* did not act as its point of support.

One could ponder the meaning of this "a priori-ism": if the *Cogito* is *the* answer among all answers, then all solutions are present in our consciousness before we even find them. This is radical innateness. "As to the fact that nothing can exist in the mind, in so far as it is a thinking thing, of which it is not aware, this seems to me to be self-evident . . . : we cannot have any thought of which we are not aware at the very moment when it is in us."[1] Contrast this with the following passage from the *Third Set of Replies (Tenth Objection):* "When I say that an idea

---

1. Descartes, *Fourth Set of Replies*, in *Philosophical Writings*, vol. 2, p. 171.

is innate in us, we do not mean that it is always there before us. This would mean that no idea was innate. We simply mean that we have within ourselves the faculty of summoning up the idea." The difference can be explained by the following dilemma. Either all answers are already known because the mind is what does the answering, making all questions rhetorical because of preexisting knowledge of which it is the measure, or else there is a possible external source for knowledge, and the mind is no more than a formal criterion. This is the opposition between form and matter which Kant used to make synthesis possible and which expressed itself with Descartes, as with Aristotle, in the distinction between a faculty and actual knowledge. Problematization must in any event be reduced by the *Cogito*, by self-consciousness as the analytical criterion of an a priori eradication of the problematical. But as Descartes well knew, the idea of the *Cogito* as a formal power of a knowledge which could only be virtual was hardly acceptable either. An a priori eradication of all possible problematicity presupposes that one already has the answer, not just the power or the faculty of finding the answer. Hence, his theory of innate ideas. If the *Cogito* contains all the answers, learning becomes impossible, hence Descartes' rejection of a solution based solely on a continuous self-conscious thought. Such a rejection, however, compels our philosopher to admit that certain questions are only excluded formally, or rhetorically, and that, from a material viewpoint, solutions are not to be found analytically in our mind, but require at least some experience. Will the *Cogito* then cease to be both the source and the measuring criterion for *all* possible responses? Do we need to look elsewhere than in the innermost reaches of our consciousness for the knowledge we seek? If this is the case, is the *Cogito* still the doubt-free answer which underlies every question and, therefore, every response? This cleavage of form from matter preserves for the *Cogito* its universal function while still allowing it to depart from it at another level. An answer is obtained outside the mind even if the mind *shapes* the answering by the responsorial structure of those answers. Kantian transcendence shows us the way; in Descartes, this double position is contradictory, even if its own goal was to confront the paradox of the *Meno*. Our consciousness knows, without having the material of knowledge. That means that radical rationalism cannot be assumed, since at least some minimal account must be taken of the material element, which suggests at least a minimal empiricism. Kant understood this well when he saw critical philosophy as surpassing both rationalism and empiricism.

Let us consider the matter carefully: the *Cogito* is an analytic principle; it emerges from analysis even as it governs it. Analysis assumes that there is a given which is the material for analysis. These data are present prior to any decomposition, prior to any resolution. What is the origin of these data? If they were self-produced by the mind, the latter would not be analytical but synthetical; moreover, there would be no need at all for analysis. That is why Descartes refused to adopt radical innateness, and why he felt constrained to reduce his a priorism to admitting an analytical faculty. This is so even though, because of the equivalence of analysis and synthesis so important to geometricians, he saw nothing contradictory in simultaneously postulating the innateness of content. It did not deter him that analysis comes back to data, to something that is already there, outside of analysis itself. And if knowledge has to be analytical, or not be at all, it is also necessary to admit precisely the notion that empirical relationships deal with a subject matter, precisely to analyze it.

Because analysis is incapable of producing what it resolves without ceasing to be, and because the very principle which underlies this analysis, itself discovered analytically, is immanent consciousness (that of the *Cogito*), empiricism is possible. Still, it is possible only on the condition that belief in radical innateness is destroyed, because it supports the idea of responsorial self-production. It makes consciousness something more than simply an analytical principle; somewhat contradictorily, it goes beyond the idea of mind as analytical. It is contradictory because the mind becomes aware of *itself* as capable of generating non-analytical answers in an *analytical* procedure: is the mind not also a substance (*res*)? There is no way out. Locke's *Essay Concerning Human Understanding* opens with a critique of innate knowledge which is perfectly logical as a point of departure. This is because the analytical principle which is consciousness necessarily comes back to some sort of matter about which the mind can reason and to which it applies itself to justify or show what is supposedly resolved and what is still in question. One makes assumptions and proceeds regressively. From that perspective, radical innateness is impossible, because it flows from the demand for an absolute rhetorical function for the answering process, originating in consciousness as the answer for all answers (whatever the question).

Locke denies this innateness in full conformity with the philosophy of consciousness which Descartes himself had developed, although only under pressure.

For Locke, experience is a necessity for the mind, because for him it is impossible to think or to know without an appeal to experience. It is not a question of thus finding again what one already knows without knowing it, because that would be contradictory, as Locke reminds us (*Essay Concerning Human Understanding* 1, II, 5), but rather of learning that of which one is truly ignorant (1, II, 23). Therefore, ". . . all reasoning is search . . ." (1, II, 10), and not simply the elaboration of a given which, paradoxically, would itself be produced, or at least retrieved, simultaneously with (and due to) this process of elaboration. A consideration of what analysis is compelled Descartes to make it something innate, something prior to one's becoming aware of it. Locke, even more rigorous on this point, denied that one could prove the existence of the innate, since nothing in the process of analyzing a given obliges one to identify anything as preexisting in the mind at all. On the contrary, if one believes that consciousness means self-consciousness, it is hard to see how there could be anything in consciousness of which one could be unaware. Thus, the action of consciousness by which one acquires knowledge cannot simply be a matter of recollection, for that would suggest that there were ideas within one's consciousness of which one was not aware. In that sense, the ideas of which one becomes aware have their origins not within us, but outside of us. "It being impossible, that any truth which is innate, (if there were any such) should be unknown . . . there being nothing a truth in the mind, that it has never thought on" (1, II, 26). Since the mind is nothing but consciousness, there cannot be innate principles which it would find later on. If it acquires knowledge, that proves that it was ignorant of that which it learned, and therefore the thing learned could not have existed within itself.

> To say a notion is imprinted on the mind, and yet at the same time to say, that the mind is ignorant of it, and never yet took notice of it, is to make this impression nothing. No proposition can be said to be in the mind which it never yet knew, which it was never conscious of . . . So that to be in the understanding, and, not to be understood; to be in the mind, and never to be perceived, is all one, as to say any thing is, and is not, in the mind or understanding. (1, II, 5; see also 2, i, 11)

Locke is here more authentically Cartesian than Descartes himself, or at least more consistently so. This consistency will have major consequences for the very destiny of empiricism, and through that, for Western thought. The reflexivity of consciousness suggests that the mind never knows anything other than ideas: Berkeley's idealism therefore becomes an inevitable consequence, as does Hume's skepticism. In opening an analysis onto the world, in making it dependent on the sense experience which provides the material of science, the question which is going to forcefully impose itself, according to the logic of the propositionalist model of *epistemē*, is that of *necessity*, that is, of the apodicity of experiential knowledge. This is what Kant will call a priori synthetic judgments. Indeed, if deduction produces necessary propositions, nonproblematical because of the simultaneous eradication of the opposites it implies, then the necessity for experience itself seems less clear, because things can always be other than what they are, even though at the same time they are just what they are and nothing else. Ontology, therefore, must make up for the epistemological deficiencies of empiricism, even if empiricism itself is an ontology, just as all the theories of knowledge have been since Plato. Therefore, we speak of the necessity of facts to indicate that they are unavoidable; the world is knowable because one can know it, and if one can know it, that shows that it is knowable. In any event, it is empiricism which surrenders knowledge to the apodictic rupture, and as a result, it can only reflect that rupture (and this results in skepticism). The way leads from Locke to Berkeley, but also to Hume and to Kant. How can we know through experience? Isn't this a concept of discovery, which suggests a psychological origin, rather than propositional justification and validity? We know that up to the twentieth century, empiricism, now called "logical positivism," continuously, if unsuccessfully, addressed these questions.[2] But all of these problems only make sense when measured against the logic of a propositional model focused on justification or, more precisely, on the self-justification of the true by way of evidence, on the elimination of alternatives deemed "false" from the single perspective of univocal discourse and rationality. Experience is not apodictic; it is indeed here that we find the difficulty of understanding modern science, which has been produced by the destruction of a purely a priori Cartesianism, which was more mathematical than physical.

For Locke, ideas and perceptions are one and the same (*Essay Concerning Human Understanding* 2, I, 9) to the extent that the ensemble of analytical entities which we call ideas rests on a given, which is analytically, atomically, the source of sensation (2, II, 3). Locke speaks of an *internal sense* well before Kant, as a characteristic of what he calls reflection, which is entirely empirical, in response to the constraints of a well-understood analysis. These same constraints determine the famous distinction between *primary qualities* and *secondary qualities*, which Locke took from Descartes (*Third Meditation*), but he bypassed the mathematicism which was not well adapted to the experimental

---

2. On this topic, see Michel Meyer, *Découverte et justification en science* (Paris: Klincksieck, 1979). See also *Revue Internationale de Philosophie* 144–45 (1983), which was devoted to logical empiricism.

science of his day (that of Boyle, for example). Analysis assumes that
sensible material can be decomposed; for Locke the apodictic nature of
knowledge is saved, and thereby knowledge itself, if one accepts the
idea that, even if things could occur otherwise, certain qualities would
still remain, the very ones which are the true objects of science. Since
ideas are produced by the stimulus of the sensible, it follows that there
will therefore be an awareness of the real, due to the so-called primary qualities. On the other hand, secondary qualities, which are all
subjective, are devoid of any sense of necessity because they do not
correspond to any reality in the object, that is, to the identity of a propositional subject, which should remain itself beyond any possible alternative which could be presented. If the subject of a proposition might
be A and non-A, if A can be something other than itself, it is not a subject, and therefore it is not an object:

> Take a grain of wheat, divide it into two parts; each part still has
> *solidity, extension, figure, and mobility;* divide it again, and it retains
> the same qualities; and so divide it on, till the parts become in-
> sensible; they must retain still each of them all of those qualities.
> For division . . . can never take away either solidity, extension, fig-
> ure, or mobility from any body . . . These I call *original* or *primary*
> *qualities* of body, which I think we may observe to produce simple
> ideas in us, viz. solidity, extension, figure, motion or rest, and
> number. 2dly such *qualities,* which in truth are nothing in the ob-
> jects themselves, but powers to produce various sensations in us
> by their *primary qualities* . . . (2, VIII, 9 and 10)

Thus color is a subjective datum, since depending on the lighting, the
same object can *appear* brighter or duller, etc.; likewise size, when seen
as a product of figure and movement, since a thing can appear smaller
or larger if we are distant from it or close to it. This is why secondary
qualities do not resemble objects as do the other qualities (2, VIII, 5),
but rather we attribute these qualities to objects as a result of their subjective action, their impact *on us.* Thus, to use an example from Locke,
we know that the snow that burns us is white, and that the pain, unlike
the whiteness, is not in the substance of the snow as such, regardless of
its power over our sensations. The *idea of warmth* would be produced in
us by the fire, but the idea of pain is not itself in the fire. "The particular Bulk, Number, Figure and Motion of the parts of Fire, or Snow, are
really in them, whether any one's Senses perceive them or no: and
therefore they may be called real Qualities, because they really exist in
those bodies. But *Light, Heat, Whiteness, or Coldness are no more really in
them than Sickness or Pain is in* Manna" (2, VIII, 17).

What we must understand in reading these texts is the passage from an analytic of consciousness to a reflection on the atomicity of the real, resulting in the ontologization of analysis. This ontologization derives logically from the empiricization of analysis which follows from the established fact that an analysis founded on radical innateness would destroy itself for intrinsic and internal reasons. Analysis, under these conditions, necessarily leads to primary qualities as the essential nature, the sine qua non, of an object, that which resists the introduction of any alternatives and which prevents those alternatives from becoming reality. Apodicticity is saved, although only temporarily. For rather quickly, in Berkeley, the distinction between primary and secondary qualities will no longer hold, based on the same presumption which Locke adopted regarding *consciousness* and *ideas*. Consciousness relates to ideas and not to reality itself, an independent. All ideas are on the same level, since they are indifferently within the consciousness as being its sole objects. Because consciousness is reflexive, that is, self-consciousness, it can have no possible object except ideas. Berkeley indeed radicalized Locke's empiricism, pushing it to its ultimate consequences. ". . . if all we can ever experience directly are ideas and if we can never look behind the curtain of ideas to observe the physical objects which cause our ideas, how can we ever know anything about the 'qualities' of such objects or even know that they exist at all?"[3] How, then, could consciousness distinguish those ideas which relate to primary qualities from any others? Is that difference really not an ontological one, born of necessity, of ontologized apodicticity, in conformity with the historically determined nature of knowledge as based on the requirement of having apodictic judgments? Since perception is the contemplation of our ideas, which are related to the real, and since analysis always refers to the external, perception and being conform, are identical: *esse = percipi*.

Let us consult the texts. Consciousness simply refers to itself, for, as Locke also believed, it contains no "matter," only ideas. Berkeley writes: "When we do our utmost to conceive the existence of external bodies, we are all the while only contemplating our own ideas" (*Principles* I, 23). It is because we pay no attention to ourselves, even as we perceive, that we have the illusion, however unconscious, of being thrust into the object, whereas the life of consciousness can proceed without interruption. Berkeley, in stating *esse est percipi*, did not deny that things exist, since we have an idea of them. He only rejected the *idea* that they could exist without our perception of them, for such an *idea*, insofar as it is an *idea*, presupposes a mind that can be aware of it.

3. D. J. O'Connor, *John Locke* (New York: Dover Books, 1967), p. 65.

"That the things I see with mine eyes and touch with my hands do exist, really exist, I make not the least question. The only thing whose existence we deny, is that which the philosophers call Matter or corporeal substance" (I, 35). Ideas suffice for themselves and suffice to make us aware of what is without our having to attribute to them a substrate, a substance supporting primary qualities. "Hence it is evident the supposition of external bodies is not necessary for producing our ideas: since it is granted they are produced sometimes, and might possibly be produced always in the same order we see them in at present, without their concurrence" (I, 18). "In short, if there were external bodies, it is impossible we should ever come to know it; and if there were not, we might have the very same reasons to think there were that we have now" (I, 20). Indeed, "though it were possible that solid, figured, moveable substances may exist without the mind, corresponding to the ideas we have of bodies, yet how is it possible for us to know this?" (I, 18). How can we get outside of ourselves to *say* that matter exists, when it is unknowable, in that it is precisely the *what* which exists independently of us, beyond our knowledge and our discourse? All that, however, does not prevent us from talking about it.

The origin of this somewhat radical idealism, which has always been attractive to the English, is the difference between primary qualities, which define matter, the external body; and secondary qualities, which are only affections of the internal senses and which are, therefore, lacking in objective counterparts. For Berkeley, such a distinction suggests a nonempiricist conception of knowledge, an empiricism which contradicts apodicticity, which is necessitated by a distinction which is purely Cartesian at its base.

> Some there are who make a distinction betwixt *primary* and *secondary* qualities: by the former, they mean extension, figure, motion, rest, solidity or impenetrability and number: by the latter they denote all other sensible qualities, as colours, sounds, tastes, and so forth. The ideas we have of these they acknowledge not to be the resemblances of any thing existing without the mind or unperceived; but they will have our ideas of the primary qualities to be patterns or images of things which exist without the mind . . . (I, 9)

But this is impossible: an idea is an idea, and any idea of an idea remains an idea. What each idea presents is indistinctly identical; for us, ideas based on their primary qualities cannot be distinguished from others. To do this would be to attribute to the mind the power to go beyond its own powers, which is self-contradictory. Ideas do indeed come from the senses, and thus there cannot be an idea of an unperceived matter. Berkeley's argument even relies on the *a contrario:* in the same way that we prove that these ideas of secondary qualities are within the mind, we can develop the same line of reasoning concerning primary qualities. For if a color is only an affection of the mind, it must be the same for movement, for example, which is related to the primary qualities. "Now why may we not as well argue that figure and extension are not patterns or resemblances of qualities existing in matter, because to the same eye at different stations, or eyes of a different texture at the same station, they appear various . . ." (I, 14). A movement will appear slower or faster to one person or another, one figure rounder, one object more solid, etc. Not only does the mind perceive only ideas and not matter, but the ideas arise from the sensible realm and not from a non-sensible substratum. As a consequence, there is no alternative which cannot happen. Sugar can become bitter, or something cloudy can become clear, and so on.

Quite clearly, Berkeley's idealism can be seen as a radicalization of empiricism. The causality of objects-qualities-ideas is broken; the only things that still exist are ideas, which *are* the "things" we perceive. They can present themselves to us each time, and look different, so that there is no more necessity in "things." Science is therefore a construct, one that does not simply reflect the real as it *is*, as Locke tries to show with his causal theory of perception. A consistent Locke, as we have seen, is achieved in Berkeley. For Berkeley did no more than to push to its fullest extent Locke's reflexive Cartesianism, a Cartesianism whose specificity comes from the "empiricalness" which must be attached to analysis: the given exists, thus only my idea-sensations exist. Berkeley has simply expelled science from empiricism.

The inevitable consequence of Berkeley will be Hume, with his famous critique of the rationality of causality. This critique consisted of making the regularity of the cause-effect relationship a product of subjective habit, due to the lack of another more constraining regularity. For Hume, even more than for Berkeley, science escapes from empiricism's constraints, strictly taken, because science depends on a principle of causality which is rooted in *subjective* regularities. These regularities are all weakened at their base by the inductive paradox: there is no reason why A, which precedes B and seems always to be associated with it, and why B, which always follows A, are *necessarily* linked. Thus, each morning I rise and observe that the sun is coming up in the east. Is this enough to *prove* that it will always happen that way? Does this constitute a causal explanation of the phenomenon in question? And yet, causality, which is a relationship characterized by necessity, in the last analysis rests on purely *subjective* associations like these, which could well fail to occur. In any case, the fact that they occur does not *logically* exclude the contrary possibility. This would seem to suggest that the scientific link thought to be rational par excellence is in fact irrational because of its lack of a foundation in necessity. We certainly can doubt that it is possible for a human being to fly by its own power. We have never seen it happen, and our physical structure prevents it, but it is not *logically* impossible; forming such a thought is not contradictory. What, then, is the nature of this causal necessity which seems not to be very necessary at all, because it is only empirical, so that contrary things are not inconceivable but simply either unobserved or unobservable? In short, regularity of occurrence is a *good reason* to infer from cause to effect, but still it is not a demonstration, a proof, or a *necessary* relationship.

Empiricism, as can clearly be seen, is a true subjectivism which radicalizes itself as it evolves, from Locke to Hume via Berkeley. And the subject which opens itself to experience gives itself over to a knowledge whose nature no longer has anything to do with apodicticity. Because the nature of knowledge has always been the exclusion of a propositional opposite, and the a priori possibility of arriving there is guaranteed by the propositional order of reason, therefore empiricism results in the skepticism and irrationality of science. With Locke, science had become possible; for Berkeley, it becomes merely a semiotic convention, an alternative way of discussing ideas, of expressing some unity from among diverse points of view, of saying the "same thing" in different ways thanks to language symbols estranged from common sense. But whatever is not an "idea-thing" is a construct, a fiction, like matter, and is recourse to it not a form of instrumentalism and conventionalism?

This discussion allows us to see the thrust of the role which Hume attributes to imagination, the associationist and subjective game which underlies experience. Experience is, ontologically, that which can always be something other than what it is: it is not knowledge, but extension of knowledge, novation. And that which in a human subject corresponds to such a synthesis is imagination, that which allows us to think about an object that is present as though it were absent, and an absent one as though it were present. It is the very faculty which allows us to think possible the changes of human experience. Further, through imagination we learn to expect the repetition of a similar event even though it has not yet occurred. Of course, since otherness is possible, the nonoccurrence of that event is equally possible. But if a given "that" fails to occur, we can still *expect* its reappearance, even if there is nothing necessary about its occurrence, which indeed could turn out to be its nonoccurrence. The alternative relies on a continuity for which it is precisely "the other."

We know what happened to the idea of imagination with Kant: made the ruler of understanding in the first edition of the *Critique of Pure Reason*, made its subordinate in the second, yet it occupied no less central a role, even if it is "transcendentalized," given the Humean role of guaranteeing synthesis *in* the mind, if not *of* the mind. At base, Kant arrived at a way of reintegrating experience into the realm of knowledge, and, as a result, of "deempiricizing" the subject, which becomes transcendental. Indeed, is that not the only really adequate conception of (universal) subjectivity? Within a purely *analytical* ontology, the subject becomes no more than an unconnected bundle of atomistic mental events, a fabric of perceptions; maybe a thing, or an idea among things, or an idea among ideas. We may also add that this corpuscular and analytical ontology, which gains momentum with the strengthening of empiricism (one could even call it the analytical breakup of reality), is going to give birth to a reversal of questioning about the necessity of causation in experience and become the question of *synthesis*. Analysis is now judged inadequate to respond to diversity in its connections, since it can only grasp that which is disconnected within that diversity. For as early as Berkeley, the idea of substance or substrate is abandoned because, empirically, human subjectivity can only have ideas aroused by sensations, and beyond that there is nothing except by some twist of language. The human subject is thus in the hands of its impressions and connections, which it imposes at the whim of its passions and its imagination.

But are there a priori synthetic judgments? Today, the answer imposes itself clearly as negative, despite the reawakening of interest in Kant which gave rise to neopositivism. Can there really be a causal relationship which links B to A without any alternatives, and which is found neither in A nor in B? It is essential to think about the issue of necessity in the apodictic or propositional model, its role of justification or verification of knowledge, for it is necessity which characterizes cognitive judgment. On the other hand, as empiricism has clearly shown, whether we want it or not, things can always happen differently, even if it is the mental and ontological role of causality to prevent the occurrence of alternatives. As a consequence, a synthetic judgment cannot be a priori, since it can always be refuted by experience, by an ever-possible alternative; yet it must be able to be a priori if it is a valid judgment, one of knowledge, because of the way knowledge is defined in this model. The pincers thus closed on propositionalism, which had been driven to find some deproblematizing necessity ever since; with

Berkeley, it had become clear that such a necessity was an illusion. Kant, nevertheless, raised the basic question of knowing how to justify our "intuition" or, if not that, our concepts of necessity and causality. For there are explanations, chains of inferences, and a process of eradication of alternatives, not, however, due to the nature of the objects considered, as empiricism rightly claims. But, unlike Kant, let us accept the view that it is not the subject which can make a necessity of what cannot be necessary in the object itself. Otherwise we would have to assume that there is a thing-in-itself behind the possibly contradictory multiplicity of phenomena. Clearly, the (necessary) foundation of necessity is beyond the scope of any propositionalist theory, even if transcendental. Necessity must therefore rely on ontology, on what is called "the determinism of nature," just as it pertains to the essence of subjects to categorize a priori. A solution which imposes necessity on empirical judgments, which must have it if they are to provide a *real knowledge* of experience, even while searching for it elsewhere than in experience, itself will surely be a weak solution. It will always wind up attributing to judgments characteristics which are not naturally theirs, yet which require explanation of their "somewhat apodictic characteristic."

It is this necessity, this causality, and these relationships to experience which must be considered. But to do this, we must abandon the classical model of knowledge. Let us summarize it: what exactly does it include? In its most basic version it may be summarized in the following way: There is no disruption between individual knowledge and science. Science is developed on a basis of knowledge, without the very nature of the type of knowledge employed being fundamentally altered. The progress is from sensation to reflection, in a pyramidal manner, from simple to complex ideas, and from them to propositional relationships which are themselves linked together in a complex manner. This view is what empiricism produced as a refinement of the classical, propositional model of knowledge which one could have found anywhere from Plato to Descartes. Hume, for example, follows Locke on this point. There is sensation, and there is reflection in Locke (*Essay Concerning Human Understanding* 2, I, 4); and there are impressions, and there are simple and complex ideas in Hume (*Treatise* I, 1, 1). This is the same general construct which begins with an individual point and ultimately reaches complex scientific conceptualizations. What was Hume saying, if not that this transition is impossible, because this is the truly profound sense of the problem of induction and the irrationality of causality? How can the latter be unjustifiable? Just because we have accumulated a number of individual observations, that does not, in general, constitute a *reason* for generalization. That demonstrates the basic gap between observation and reason. And it is not one that can be healed, being intrinsic. Unity cannot flow from scattered elements; it is unity which they clearly lack when they present themselves as individual elements, even where they are successive or contiguous ones.

There would be no difficulty with induction if it did not begin with an individual and with that individual's own perceptions, which must be placed in some sort of hierarchy or somehow put together so that one's knowledge becomes scientific. The problem arises from the impossibility of justifying what is universal as distinct from the particular. An observation coming from a subject will never be able to present itself as scientific. But would such a difficulty exist if we did not start from individual perception, and if we were not trying to understand science on such a narrow basis? In essence, doesn't the inductive paradox suggest rather that it is incumbent on us to reject this theoretical presupposition? Science becomes irrational only if one tries to explain things by starting from individual "knowledge," which can present only individualized judgments, built up one by one, and rooted in some analytical consciousness. Finally, it is not scientific knowledge that has wandered from the domain of reason, rather it is empiricism which, when it seeks refuge in the unavoidable anapodicticity of experience, places itself beyond the realm of justification which defines *epistemē*. Contrary to what a mere superficial reading might suggest, empiricism is not cut off from the classical model of *epistemē* because it does not find apodicticity in experience. It assumes apodicticity as a norm, as Berkeley's criticisms, or especially Hume's analysis of the problem of induction, have shown. The difficulty only emerges because there is a quest for justification and verification, which no experience, no matter how often repeated, can provide. Despite all that, empiricism rests on the classic idea of science: any knowledge which is *real* knowledge is rooted in the apodicticity of the *Cogito*, of *what* we perceive and *how* we perceive it, a certainty which analytically (by definition) *must* relate our mind to sense-experience.

Kant confirmed this empiricist victory. A strict foundation of the propositional order requires an empirical relationship whose necessity will be transferred—in a Kantian fashion to be sure—from the "I think" to the "what I think as I think it." Empiricism, like Kantianism, represents an ineluctable generalization of propositionalism. The Kantian triumph consists of the reconciliation, *at least at the level of intentions*, of the apodicticity of knowledge with experience. Is this to say that empirical knowledge is not actually knowledge? To the extent that self-consciousness includes external sense, it is cognitive. But empiricism as such cannot envision the transfer of this certitude, or any ontological a priorism, as the defeat of Locke at the hands of his successors clearly showed. Empiricism does indeed relate to experience, but not to that part of it which would stand out as its cognitive constraints. It does not see the subject, but operates based on it, which is not the same thing. Experience has the evidence of knowledge which empiricism can neither reflect nor express because the force of evidence is not itself an empirical datum. It goes without saying that experience teaches; therefore, it seems useless to inquire why it does so. Hume quite clearly reflected this limitation, and we understand why Kant was "awakened" by it. Why does experience teach? The answer to this question is not in experience, nor can it be deduced from experience. Kant never denied the role of experience; he assumed it even more than the empiricists. But they viewed it dogmatically, as a self-evident source of knowledge, whereas nothing in it is enough to compel reasoning to any conclusion. Nothing else is left but individual perceptual knowledge, and Kant would rebuild the bridge between this kind of knowledge and global scientific knowledge. The *necessity* of experience indeed exists but is not a fact; it is not itself empirical, even though it is the base of all possible experience. Kant's basic objection against the empiricists was that they had not thought through their true place in the classical model of the *epistemē*, where the necessity of a proposition conditions its truth, since it makes error impossible by excluding it. Kant claimed to be the real thinker about experience and empirical knowledge, more than the empiricists could ever be, since he could conceptualize necessity as stemming from the subject, something that pure empiricism never could achieve. Empiricism failed to value its own wealth: from Locke to Hume, it was rapidly squandered without even reflection, since that would have required looking outside of itself, at a place where the point of view ceases to be empirical.

Experience, like causality, has, in empiricism, this characteristic: the fulfillment of a noteworthy ontological function. "*This is*" means "*this is provable* through observation or experimentation." However, there can be a contrary state of affairs which arises or else which never does come up; but, it is uncontestable that once such a situation *does* arise, one cannot fail to take account of it; it simply *is*. Thus, it is essential to separate matters of fact from the simple formal relationships which exist between ideas. It is not quite true that Hume in this way would have anticipated the analytic-synthetic distinction drawn by Kant (since the synthetic could be necessary, as well as the converse). Rather, it is a matter of attributing a kind of constraint to facts, *a constraint which is nonlogical,* since the contrary is conceivable without a contradiction. There is no logical contradiction in imagining a man flying, using his arms as wings, but it is nevertheless an impossible thing if we are speaking empirically, considering the *physical* (nonlogical) constraints which limit human beings.

At any rate, experience is felt to allow the resolution of a matter without the necessity of having thereby to rethink what is resolutional. Although the problematicity which comes from experience appears to be only logical, that does not make it any less real; that is why Locke was just as indispensable to propositionalism as was Descartes. Nonetheless, the power of experience is conceded: it decides or distinguishes, even if not in an incontrovertible fashion; it avoids the hypothetical (*"hypotheses non fingo,"* as Newton put it) by immediately confronting one with the evidence, which is factual. It proceeds from facts, not from (transcendental) consciousness; just because what *is* certainly can be something else doesn't make it any less what it is.

The tyranny of experience, which demanded that it be used as a sole criterion, partakes both of an unthematized analytic of consciousness and a desire to reduce our opening to the world as made up of alternatives (that is, problems) to a decisional process for which facts are decisive. Thus, experience itself exists as the very ontologization of an analytic that cannot succeed in re-Socratizing itself. It is not strictly a matter of conducting an examination of the ontological texture of the matter ("What is the world made of?"), but rather of understanding that experience has an ontological role despite its lack of purely logical necessity. When experience, in and of itself, is made the absolute and universal criterion, the result is the circularity of the enterprise as we have discussed it here. Experience imposes itself as incontestable because facts are facts, and one doesn't debate facts. It is vain to imagine their contrary. They are what they are, and that is never going to be put in question. Experience takes on the force of law without being law. This is what produces the skepticism which is associated with it and which collides with reason, because it is necessary to accept or reject without really having the justification to do so. We are what we are because we borrow from experience. And yet this is as indisputable as the neces-sity of experience is itself disputable.

The scene is thus set for what has been called the *philosophy of science,* and the framework for its questions established. It is a matter of focusing attention on scientific judgment and, proving its nature, of verifying that it accords with experience and observation. It is also to see what is theoretical rather than observational, what is susceptible of confirmation or refutation, to determine its necessity, its being a law, and, finally, to establish its possible epistemological (therefore theoretical) superiority over rival types of judgments. And when we think of scientific theories, we understand the groupings of such judgments which they include; but theories do not fundamentally change the scientific validity or the scientific worth of the judgments that compose them. All these questions are even more pressing in that they come from an internal and well-defined subfield within philosophy. This subfield probably emerged because of the bankruptcy of the Kantian a priori synthesis. Viewed as self-contradictory, the synthetic a priori reawakened questioning about scientific laws and their necessity or their synthetic nature, that is to say, their innovational character. Neopositivism did indeed have a Kantian inspiration, but it lost the Kantian view of causality. Causality must depend on experience because it is characteristic of it. It is useless to search into structures of the mind, immanent but apparently hidden, for what belongs to the experiential realm. The Kantian solution falls apart, which suggests that causality, no longer apodictic, will create a new problem for the classical idea of knowledge. This is the basis for the launching of the nomological-deductive model suggested by both Hempel and Popper.

The philosophy of science, in the positivist sense of the term, is a product of this crisis of Kantianism. From the outset, its goal was to confront the challenge produced by the position that things must be what science says they are, which made central issues of questions of explanation and prediction. In the last analysis, the primacy of justification will be found in the positivist ambition. This was already the case in Hume's position on induction, with the underlying idea that perception, the basis of knowledge, is not a logical relationship, hence not marked by necessity. Confronted with the idea of *justification*, positivism is going to create a straw man called *discovery*, which is a type of process for the acquisition of knowledge just as irrational as induction. We can see in this propositionalist shift a denial of the problematological difference; I call this a "shift" and a negation, because discovery cannot simply overlap the questions, any more than justifying *is* answering, even if questions and answers are joined together. Induction will quite clearly be rejected by neopositivism in the name of its own deductivism, which positivism holds to be the sole source of necessity in and for discourse.

Independent of these philosophical questions focused on the kind of scientific judgment that the perpetuation of the classical model assures, there are many other difficulties which the model presents. I have addressed these at length in my book *Découverte et justification en science*.

If experience and progress through experience are allowed to become the basic criteria of scientificity, then it becomes necessary to explain how that empirical relationship is guaranteed. We suppose facts, a given, an observable world, but also a theoretical world, which exists independently and by itself, and to which theories must each time be able to be referred. It is obvious that general laws do not meet this requirement, since it would be necessary to be able to verify an infinite number of possible cases before being able to accept a universal proposition as scientific. Even as elementary an assertion as "All men are mortal" presupposes, to be valid, that we examine every man, past, present, and future. That, of course, is impossible. Thus there remains Popper's criterion of falsification, which posits that any one contrary case suffices to set aside the rule in question. Such a test, as simple as it might be, is really quite insufficient, especially when we realize that experience can always be reinterpreted to make it lose its "apparent" contradictoriness and be integrated into a rule by adding ad hoc hypotheses to the "disproved" theory. This brings us back to the matter of knowing why, when, and how a questionable theory is to be either preserved or abandoned. The only remaining criteria are sociological in nature. They find their worth in their ability to withstand the attacks carried out in the professional community by some new elite or, on the contrary, by conservative elements. And at this point we pass from Popper to Kuhn.

At the fundamental level, what is at issue here is the dichotomy between the theoretical and the observational in scientific discourse. Referentialism in science rests on the postulate that facts exist and one can observe them as facts. From that point, we pass from an individual standpoint to a more complex theoretical level; this is a reworked version of Locke's views on reflection and of Hume's on ideas. In any event, there always will be two levels: the empirical, which is contingent, and the demonstrative; contingency is no more than an empty space for logic, but not for the individual who cannot but believe in the evidence of the senses. In empiricism we see born again the opposition, as part of knowledge, between the observable and the conceptual, which stems from it. Such a dichotomy does not eliminate the posing of unsolvable problems, and not only because of the reification of observation and experience. The specificity of science gets lost in the reduction to the individual's knowledge and the isolated judgments, however cognitive, which are its results. It is as though science began with the naive observation of a given, prior to any theorization. The result is that the types of questions are predetermined, but they are also impossible to answer. One cannot help but remark on the number of scientific judgments which have no direct relationship with reality, which have significance only as they relate to other theories. One cannot help but fall back on paradoxes which affect the very nature of confirmation in science and which are purely logical.[4] One cannot help but think that science, rather than moving forward by adding up results which are justified, instead evolves by dealing with the very questions which it poses. This is a thought we attribute to Popper, but it is already spoken of by Bachelard:

> The scientific approach forbids us to have an opinion on a question which we do not fully understand, on questions which we do not know how to clearly ask. Whatever we may say, in the world of science, questions are not asked just like that, coming from nowhere. In fact, it is exactly *the sense for questioning* that characterizes the true scientific mind. For, in a scientific mind, all knowledge is the answer to a question. If there had been no question, there would be no scientific knowledge.[5]

Thus one cannot help but question the global link between data and theory in experience, as being a nonfixed, nonhistorical relationship between two established and autonomous ontological spheres. And finally one cannot help but think about apodicticity and experimental language, thus about causality in general.

Rather than following Bachelard and Popper, is it perhaps necessary to give up on starting from problems themselves and to adopt instead a theory of experience, if one can be developed independently from questions? The great temptation in this would be to give in to the history of science and to limit oneself to it. Scientists themselves frequently urge us to do so.

Such a historicist effort leads back to the question of its own possibility, never really posed but always resolved in the name of factualism. There is no way to read a history of science which can escape the task of telling us what a scientific inquiry is and which can serve as the *substitute* for such a philosophical quest. This implies that the history of science, which was never as neutral as Hume perceived it, is strictly an auxiliary enterprise and not a driving force. Few scientists comprehend that and are willing to admit that they are not philosophers. If they excel in science, why would they not think they are, *by the same token*, philosophers of their science? We can agree to a dependence on the history of science, but not on a simply random (even if unique) excellence in one discipline which ignores the diversity embodied in other types of

---

4. See Meyer, *Découverte*, pp. 207 et seq.
5. G. Bachelard, *La formation de l'esprit scientifique* (Paris: Vrin, 1969), p. 14 [author's translation].

research. We can disagree and refuse to believe that one can find in such historical factualities the whole quintessence and nature of questioning—even though questioning itself is absent—about science in general.

There remain all of those problems we have spoken about and which oblige us to begin our inquiry not from individual judgment, nor from logical deduction, nor from reified relationships to observational data, but with *factual problems*, with empirical interrogativity, and to clear up what it is that makes a questioning process scientific, that is, what makes theories what they are.

2. Experience, Causation, and Questioning: Beyond the Synthetic A Priori

Before we can tell if facts exist independent of their perception, we must ask what constitutes experience. For empiricism, it was a matter of ontology. What we observe here is a true reification of experience as an in-itself, which made us lose sight of what experience is above all: it is *a* method for the resolution of problems, but surely not *the* method. Experience, in the end, has meaning only in reference to questions. Nothing prevents answers from being something other than what they are, but because they resolve questions, they necessarily exclude other alternatives. An alternative is a problem, and a response is what solves it. That takes full account of necessity without producing contradictions. The notion of necessity is a purely apocritical one: it characterizes an answer to the extent that an answer which resolves a question must exclude other, alternative terms. This is a priori true of any sort of answer. What *could* have been something other is the answer, not the fact that if it is the answer, then all other statements are excluded as solutions. In regard to a question, an answer as such is not necessary, but the *statement* that emerges as an answer will necessarily *be* an answer by excluding the opposite statement from the right to be an answer, due to the very fact it is an answer. If we place this into the matter of problematological indifference, we cannot escape the difficulties of the *synthetic* a priori: since it bears on experience, it is resolutional; because it *is* an answer, it is a priori necessary, but, referring to a question, there is no a priori necessity that it be the solution. Once having become an answer, an apocritical statement cannot *not* exclude all alternative answers to the question posed. This is true, to be sure, only if one is able to reduce that question to a question with mutually exclusive responses. We will return to this point. If everything is reduced to the propositional, it will truly be necessary that the synthetic a priori has to be a shared property of scientific judgments, whereas, if one takes account of the fact that necessity involved something pertaining to answering, beyond all empirical content, then one can avoid that contradiction.

Experience which is reified, made autonomous and reduced to the very stuff of facts, confirms the impression that it is not just a resolutional mode, but the very substance of reality, of "things," as we may say. Indeed, we often pose as opposites observation, which is passive, and experience, which is active, without clearly seeing that we are reinforcing the postulate that experience is the portal of access to facts which would exist in themselves, separate from all questioning. Really, there is no more observational passivity than there is experiential activity. Neither can one read a piece of data that would be utterly transparent, nor can one gain access to it by successive built-up stages. Such a piece of data doesn't exist. That which is real truly exists, and experience is an interrogative method for discovering it. Observation is also interrogative; no reality can avoid being put forward as a response and, because of this, refers, even if only for an instant, to an underlying question.

3. Characteristics of the Scientific Process

The question which now presents itself is to discover, specifically, the process for constituting scientific knowledge. That involves determining how experience, causality, and theoretization articulate with one another. As for observation, it does not exist in its own right, because reality is not a given that is simply received; rather, it is an object we seek. It can turn out to be an "other" because of the constant problematization which it requires from us. Once put forth as an answer, given the repression of answering, *what* was in question appears to be what it is, and, not being anything other *than* that, it appears as not being able to be other *than* what it is. This is the origin of the impression of evidence and of the necessity of reality. This appearing becomes only an appearance if we lose sight of the questioning process which produced it. That is exactly what can happen if we surrender to the propositionalist tradition, which, being unable to conceive of questioning, theorizes only about its effects. The positivity of facts, with their ontological independence affirmed (with all the difficulties of conceptualization and formulation that implies, as Berkeley emphasized), emerges as the apparently static result of a nonexistent and undiscoverable process, at least in terms of this model.

Is this to say that problematology rejects all factualization? Not at all. Instead of thinking of factuality as simply evidence—as an unexplained given as empiricism saw it, or as something to be connected to various a priori categories, which, through a pure, analytical subjectivity that constructs for itself the necessity of this empirical given at the level of a purely passive sensible receptivity—problematology tries instead to retrace the path of factuality's emergence and explain what gave the impression of its autonomy. We know that answers make themselves autonomous in relation to what was in question, thus suppressing all reference to the question and all problematological reflexivity. Later, what we know enables us to give meaning to further questions, to a knowledge that "problematologizes" itself again. Thus, facts present themselves in constant reinterpretation in relation to the questions that are raised to reach such and such a goal. In this regard those facts function as premises—independent and supposedly well-known premises. By the factuality of facts, I mean what is generally understood by the notion that facts are self-prescriptive, that we have to comply with them, and that they are what they are *for us* but *without us*. This factuality must be understood in its problematological relationship in order not to engender conflict. As nonthematized responses, as the results of some antecedent other questioning process, facts set themselves forth as independent, as given; the given which they come to represent places them automatically within the confines of a questioning process that arises or is ongoing, and they provide a resolutional point of anchorage. Observation and the facts that are observed represent a bedrock experience, an out-of-the question par excellence. The duality of the apocritical and the problematological allows us to *state*, and thus to conceive, that what is observable is also a result, that it no longer is analyzed other than in terms of the positivity of its result, that it has a meaning for us. It is important for us to note that it is *we* who affirm its status as a result, that it is what it is because of an accessibility which seems to abolish, by the same token, the autonomy and the independence it has in itself. But if we propositionalize what has just been stated, then this apocritical-problematological duality collapses into a state of in-difference, simultaneously leaving the observable to be dependent on its observation to exist (*esse est percipi*), and distinct from observation as the *objective* correlate of the process.

A static view of referentialism, put forth as an autonomous theory, is indefensible. After all, we know that there is no such thing as pure reference, a fact-in-itself, because, as everyday life certainly confirms for us, facts appear to us only as already charged with meaning. The dichotomization of the referential and the interpretive is nevertheless fully admitted, because answers are not themselves their own objects. The *what* in question is in no way distinguishable from the question itself. If I wonder about your arrival at some place, for example, your arrival is what creates the problem; it *is* the problem. Thus, no one reasonably can distinguish a fact in question from the question. Questions have a factualizing function, one of phenomenonalization of their objects: they play a transitive role.

When one says, in the example mentioned above, that your arrival poses or creates a problem, that statement can be understood in two ways which are related and far from arbitrary. They both clarify phenomenonalization, observation, and the way facts are found and analyzed. So if I say that your arrival poses a problem, I can in fact be intending to say two different things: either that the fact itself, the eventuality of your arrival, is in question—you might arrive or not, but I'd like to know; or else I might be saying that your arrival is already an established fact, but that the event suggests another question, another problem. Thus I might quite well say, "The question of your arrival at the meeting is going to be rather embarrassing for our friends," or I might say, "The question of your arrival (last night) is not clear to me," which would suggest that the questioner wants an explanation of an admitted fact. The fact of your arrival in itself poses no problem because either you have arrived, or you will do so (as in the first example), but questions can arise about this fact; the arrival itself being no answer, something else is requested. It is a little like saying that Marx failed to resolve the question of the progress of history. The speaker doesn't deny that there is history, nor that Marx grappled with its factuality. As another example, one could say that an electrical problem has been poorly solved by one's neighbor. This statement assumes that at least he has electricity at his house. But if I say that the problem of the completeness of arithmetic is worth our study, that could well suggest that I am putting into doubt the existence of such a completeness.

In summary, all this seems to be leading to two apparently opposite readings. What is certain is that we have moved far from the conception of questioning according to ontology. The "What is X?" question is not seeking to learn what X *is* by supposing *that* X is, by supposing that what it is implies it has a Being of some sort or other, to be supplied in and by the answer, that is, its essence. An essence derived from that question would close the question, would give it an a priori orientation, and would thereby compel the answer to be of an ontological nature. What our questioner would then be asking, by his double reading of X, would be the being of X, which abolishes and then reabsorbs X in some "X-ity."

Let us take up our two cases. If I wonder if you are coming to a certain place, for example, it is the fact itself which is in question, and the

answer, being a declarative sentence, either asserts or denies the assertion (a denial would still be an assertion). The decision bears then on
another assertion: is it the answer or not? "You are coming": is that the
answer or not? In the other case, the question is not about the fact,
which is admitted, but about something completely different. There is
something out-of-the-question, namely A, and the question is "whether
B" or, on the contrary, "whether not B." At any rate, we are looking for
a B which will mean that A (the given) no longer poses a problem. A is a
given about which one poses questions and yet whose factual status one
never denies. To say that the question of history remained unresolved
by Marx means that Marx's explanation of history failed to satisfy our
speaker-questioner. He is looking for an answer, or a set of answers, that
explains a fact or an event, which in this case is change and evolution
among human societies. Let us imagine that another question was put:
"Marx has poorly handled the issue of intellectuals." Does this mean
that Marx wrote about intellectuals, and the speaker is rejecting Marx's
answer, or does it mean that Marx just didn't say much about this issue?
Or we could look at the following statement: "As to the topic of
progress in history, the question is far from clear." Here again two readings are possible: (1) progress in history is not denied, but its explanation is unclear; or (2) no explanation is asked for because, quite simply,
the speaker refuses to recognize that historical progress is a fact in itself
out-of-the-question, that is, that history progresses.

The two readings immediately above are quite evidently reconstruc-
tions of questions which in themselves contain a double reading. It is
often difficult to know if one or the other reading is to be preferred.
Moreover, one can challenge the first reading in the latter two examples, the one which admits the fact and maintains that the question
is about something else. For if we are really asking about that something else, why not do so directly, if the facts themselves are in no sense
in question? In reality, the two readings are more inextricably linked
than has been apparent up to this point.

Interrogativity is constitutive of our relationship to reality: one can
only find there what is sought; one can only see there what one makes
an effort to see; one can only find there what exists in relation to the
problems which impelled the inquiry. A "that" can only emerge in reference to a "which," to become a "that which" I see or a "that which" I
feel. "That which" is an answer to a question which disappears in the
appearing of what was in question but has now become an answer, an
answer that is no longer problematological, because only its own object
remains present.

Suppose I say that the question of elliptical orbits was posed by

Kepler. If I do not put into question the fact that orbits follow an elliptical path, then I admit it; I accept the proposition: "Heavenly bodies
follow elliptical trajectories." I am not questioning the basic fact, but I
am questioning *about* it; another question is put because the first one is
already answered. If there is a question, and if it is a fact that the elliptical orbit is not in issue, then the question must be something else
because of the problematological difference, which holds that the question differs from its answers; otherwise there is circularity and nonreso-
lution of the problem. Because the question divides itself and calls for a
response to the first (problematological) response, there is an inference;
here, there is an explanation. What the questioner is seeking is a proposition which relies on the question of the elliptical orbits of heavenly
bodies; that is to say, since the latter is admitted, something is sought
which explains or provides justification for *the fact in question.* That
which literally is *in question* is that which indicates *why* the phenomenon
occurs as it does and not another way. The fact connected to a proposition which explains it will give its *cause,* or at least an explanatory reason
for it.

If, on the other hand, what is literally in question is the factuality of
whether or not orbits are elliptical, nothing more is asked than to establish the matter. *Therefore, it ceases to be a fact because it is the very object of the
question.* This shows clearly that facts are facts only when they are unquestioned. This means that facts cannot be questioned in themselves,
that is, independent of their explanation, without ceasing to be facts,
denied that status by being questioned. The very idea of fact recalls
that of justification, an interpretive justification because the fact *questioned* is in that way linked to an *answer;* therefore to the problematic,
which gives it a theoretical meaning. Facts, and questions of fact, rest
on a prior conceptualization which allows their autonomization when
questioning about them, but they *cannot* be totally disassociated from
that questioning.

Yet we can say that all of this seems to indicate that facts can be
questioned in themselves, that it can *practically* be achieved, and if
done, that the reading of facts can be disassociated from their explanation. Such an empiricist view, rooted in common sense, can only be circular, and viciously circular at that. It gives as an answer precisely what
was in question; having resolved nothing, it claims to have resolved
everything.

Let us return to one of the earlier examples. I wonder about a given
fact, your arrival; that constitutes my problem. That matter arises in the
guise of a question. It is presented as possible and therefore contains
the possibility of its nonoccurrence. Further, this fact is *also* what will

resolve our question. Given that what is in question presents itself as an answer, one must not only conclude that the fact in question is independent with respect to the questioning process (which, nevertheless, is what made those facts come to our attention), but one must also say that one admits the existence of a fact when one asks about it, precisely *because* one asks questions about it. I admit that your arrival constitutes a fact simply in virtue of my asking myself if it is indeed a fact. We might well say that it is necessary to distinguish a fact from its occurrence, which will be called an "event" to comply with the problematological difference. Still, one must convince oneself that facts exist even beyond their occurrence. I certainly have the right to accept facts for themselves in the questioning process, but I must not forget that I am not thereby putting the fact itself in question but, still and always, another thing. Or, more precisely, I must not forget that I am asking about facts through the intermediary of a questioning process which includes those very facts within it and give it meaning. To speak about facts, it is necessary to locate them by implicit definitions which serve as reference points for questioning and which themselves are no longer questioned. Distinguish facts from their occurrence, and you no longer are questioning the facts; call forth a fact, and it will be questioned as being out-of-the-question. It is impossible to thematize a fact, to call forth a question about it, and still hold that it is a pure fact, that is, one without a prior response which had allowed its categorization as a fact. That common sense nevertheless proceeds in this fashion suggests that it is operating on the basis of presuppositions which it suppresses and of which it is unaware. In reality, the two readings mentioned here are always intermixed. This is the source of the ambiguity which allows such a double reading, the one conditioning the other, and vice versa. Since the link between the two readings is an *interrogative inference*, if the role of the questioning is denied, the link is lost, and each of the readings can claim to be able to make itself autonomous with respect to the other. The result would be to fall again into an unrelenting circularity which marks the factualization of reality, when factualization is considered as a self-sustaining process embedded in reality itself.

It is clear, for example, that I may study the French Revolution as much as I want and tell myself that I am studying this important fact in its pure phenomenological character as an event, but my enterprise still will not escape having a thematization based on what this Revolution factually is, reflected by a particular question, which expresses an approach that is affected by the various questions to be resolved. If the Revolution is seen as an historical rupture due to class struggle, as the advent of a new age which is not tied to what preceded it, then it will be explained, as a fact, just as it will be explained quite differently if, on the other hand, it is seen as a stage in the strengthening of the role of the state, or as an example of temporarily stalled activities of the elites by inadequate and unadapted political structures. Facts themselves would be thought of differently; the taking of the Bastille would be inconsequential, certainly accidental in relation to the actions of the nobility and aristocracy which preceded the event. The beginning of a fact, its establishment as fact, its very factual texture, changes with its meaning. One cannot inquire into the French Revolution and seek to explain it without knowing what facts were in issue in it. In delimiting these, one has already passed into answer, because one is thus presupposing what is to be explained. There is already an implicit definition of the nature of the problematic phenomenon. If I define the Revolution as a radical breakup, I am implicitly resolving the question of its continuity with the Ancien Régime. I can contest, a priori, the possibility of such a continuity, which is a circular means of providing a solution due to the type of questioning adopted. On the other hand, if the Revolution is described as the arrival of "new men" at the heart of government, there is just as clearly an implicit answer to the question of the French Revolution. I see it then as a regulative process in regard to a preexisting situation; and I explain it differently, because the issues I must account for in my explanation present themselves in a different way.

In seeing a fact as *this* rather than *that*, a whole group of prior conclusions is implied without being justified. The circularity used when such facts are singled out within theoretical frameworks meant to account for them would be destructive if it limited itself to an empirical observation, as common sense does. But science doesn't work that way. First of all, science puts its factualization to the test by applying to other facts the explanation which it assumes for "basic facts." It does so for those facts which result from other theoretizations and which therefore are relatively autonomous, due to their origin. It explains the double reading or division within problematization. And it does so for those facts which must be explained because they are part of the same factual domain, or for those facts which were not even expected to be accounted for by the same theory. The goal of simplicity, therefore, responds to the integration of facts to which at first sight they were not expected to be possibly linked. Systemization through unified theory corresponds to the requirement of verification of an initial hypothesis. If there is a question in regard to basic facts, it is because there has been a circular approach which, to be thwarted, requires that factualization be put into question. Such questioning, by its very nature, presupposes the existence of alternatives. It demands that the explanation which underlies the conceptualization of basic facts not be simply ad hoc, that is, one that includes only *those* specific facts. The more facts it explains, the more a theory can be called general. The more it is explanatory, the more it enhances the possibility that it will overcome a rival theory. To defeat a rival theory, there is a referral to facts already explained and already known by that previous or other theory which the theorist seeks to replace. There is reference also to facts outside of the theoretical realm as conceded (sexuality, for example, which Freud "debiologized" to turn into "psychology"); and, finally, there is the determination of new facts, which will become autonomous in relation to the inquiry which brought them to light (failed actions, to continue with the Freudian example).

The major difference between common sense and science is that common sense, which is circular, proceeds from the evidence of results acquired from elsewhere that it does not have to establish afresh, being to a greater or lesser extent verified analytically by a sort of local, pragmatic efficiency. Science, for its part, is bound to the conclusion that *any* perspective on facts is a hypothetical one. Thus, to verify a hypothesis which it factualizes, it must consider the hypothesis to be a question, which will not produce an inference of the pragmatic and circumstantial type, but rather, an inference which is directed at the hypothesis itself, so that the hypothesis can attain the status of being an answer. It is the very thing that common sense postulates to be a given, as granted. Therefore, since factuality is for science hypothetical, science will require other answers than those which come from factual circularity, making theory inevitable. The implications have to be drawn at the level of discourse rather than being limited to specific acts of theoretization. Facts beyond those which constitute the "basic facts" must be explained theoretically. The circularity which would limit itself to these *basic facts* would imply that the problematization (or singling out) of facts, while nevertheless quite real, is already considered to be a solution; therefore, one need go no further. Problematization can be forgotten when we have attained that real, empirical evidence: facts speak for themselves. They exist with all their strength and with all their evidentiary weight. But despite this necessity, they possess nothing of the nature of the necessary. Such a view includes no relationship to a reality which is developed by problematization; instead, one combines observations and experiences as empirical factual statements that grow in parallel with the complexity of the theory involved. This epistemological atomization goes on, from common sense to science, by aggregating the interactions of experimental and observational statements as well as the factual results which occur, under the effect of inspiration, of chance, of genius sometimes, always beginning from individual initiatives. This reading of the facts can be taken as a simple comprehension of an earlier ontological given, but accessible to everyone because of the "objectivity" it seems to have, since this given is quite literally the basis of science. If we fail to understand that there are no isolated facts, that facts emerge from theories before becoming autonomous, then we provide as answers that which necessarily results from the questioning process, but without understanding that process as a questioning one. The result is the problem of induction, as well as all the other difficulties which this epistemological atomism, propositionalism's concept of science, is heir to, and which is totally preoccupied with proving hypotheses, a problem which cannot be posed analytically. As Duhem put it:

> Contrary to what we have made every effort to establish, it is generally accepted that each hypothesis of physics may be separated from the group and subjected in isolation to experimental testing. Of course, from this erroneous principle false consequences are deduced concerning the method by which physics should be taught. People would like the professor to arrange all the hypotheses of physics in a certain order, to take the first one, enunciate it, expound its experimental verifications, and then, when the latter have been recognized as sufficient, declare the hypothesis accepted. Better still, people would like for him to formulate this first hypothesis by inductive generalization from a purely experimental law; he would begin this operation again on the second hypothesis, on the third, and so on until all of physics was constituted . . . Nothing which is not drawn from facts or immediately justified by facts would be promulgated.[6]

If one actually went from fact to fact, one would be going from truth to truth without any possibility of error. One would not have any more hypotheses (*hypotheses non fingo* would be true), nor would there be theories which could not be corroborated, proposition by proposition, by external facts, and it would make all conventional ad hoc accommodation impossible. Finally, there would be a *continuum* from individual experience to science, which would only consist of added and enriched individual experience. All of these ideas have been trite for some time. But it is this very framing of questions-without-answers that we must

---

6. Pierre Duhem, *The Aim and Structure of Physical Theory* (New York: Atheneum, 1962), p. 200.

reject and not keep on returning to. A problematization of facts requires above all a *theory* of facts, from which they emerge as facts, with their empirical positivity as a result, since they are answers. For them to be answers, the initial factualization must have been proved by other propositions, themselves generative of theoretical discourse. When questioning is denied its constitutive role in regard to facts themselves, we must concede the primacy of isolated facts, put one after another in a process of discovery perceived as a mere psychological episode, without reaching the level of logico-experimental proof or justification. The process of discovery so conceived orients the choice of facts that will be organized into a logico-experimental order, something which confers scientificity on propositions thus piled up.

The reality of the scientific process is quite different, for one does not proceed from facts individually presented, but rather from interrelated factualizations whose content emerges from a synthetic problematic. The presentation (in the preceding chapters) of an analytic, partial, and local rationality, meant to stand for what rationality should be as a whole, a rationality that cannot state itself as such, lest it should destroy itself in its own claims, underlines a different aspect of scientificity. It is not simply opposed to common sense, but it is also limited to a given sphere of application. Greater descriptiveness means a reduction of its power of explanation; but even where a scientific theory succeeds in increasing explanation, it is still always only a partial explanation. That is not to say that such a theory is constructed in a partial way, proceeding from purely singular observations, built up by successive collections of facts. Therefore, we should avoid confusing the analytical nature of scientific reasoning with the fact that it is not rooted in isolated experiences of individuals who would therefore be scientists.

The problematization which reveals factuality to our understanding produces answering, an inference, the goal of which is to validate the reading of the factual as an answer. This makes the irreducible reality of the factual a result which, possibly in later theories, can be considered as acquired independently, *a fortiori*, without any necessary reference to the interrogative process from which it originated and which gave it validity. Circularity, in this instance, would only consist of the mere transformation of questions into solutions, which common sense does. On the other hand, science must consider what it questions as problems and make assertoric, as a hypothesis, what it says to arrive at an answer which suppresses the interrogativity of the initial and hypothetical assertion. Thus, in the example about elliptical orbits, the question is as much if it is true as it is the reason they are elliptical and not, for example, circular. The answer to one of the questions is the answer to the

other, because the first question brings us back to the other, and because it is only when we have the answers that they can be disassociated from the original questions and, therefore, made autonomous as
results. Common sense works like constituted science, because both of
them deal with questions only once they are resolved; clearly, it is systemization which makes the difference.

Aristotle completely accounted for this link in his theory of science
when he wrote:

> Is it [the moon] eclipsed? [means] Is there some explanation or
> not? . . . For in all these cases it is evident that what it is and why
> it is are the same. What is an eclipse? Privation of light from the
> moon by the earth's screening. Why is there an eclipse? Or why is
> the moon eclipsed? Because the light leaves it when the earth
> screens it . . . So, as we say, to know what it is, is the same as to
> know why it is . . .[7]

Facts only can be characterized theoretically, through responses which
give them their identity. It is because the two questions have been separated that we have an inference. Aristotle saw there only the causation-
process of the real, because he was only familiar with propositions
which were linked by a logical relationship which becomes causal by its
ontological adequacy. But he was correct in seeing the initial question
as a single one, as divisible only in terms of results, or for Aristotle, of
propositions. This single question consists of inferring an answer, which
in turn gives reality to that answer, independent of its being an answer.
The relationship between the two is inferential; *once so constituted* they
present themselves as having a rational link. This implies further that
when one begins from facts, admitting that they already exist and do
not need reinterpretation, then they can be used immediately in a
causal way. They are already constituted; they need no further confirmation of their undeniable positivity. We say that they are established. And the double reading of factual questions has a fully justified
origin without its being legitimate to *totally* separate them.

The principle of reason, at base, is nothing more than the product of
the problematological difference which originates in the refutation of
circularity. The question about the French Revolution presumes that
the *fact* itself is this rather than that; but the question, instead of being
posed as an answer, demands, in turn, an answer which can justify the

---

7. *Posterior Analytics* II, 2, 90a, 8–32, trans. Jonathan Barnes, in *The Complete
Works of Aristotle*, ed. Jonathan Barnes (Princeton, N.J.: Princeton University Press,
1984), vol. 1, p. 148.

choice of one proposition over another. The Revolution would thus become the fact that is described in this particular reading. The problematological difference, which cannot be ignored if we want to avoid the vicious circle, is born of the presupposition of an *immediate factual*. I recall that the determination of the problematic is already an answer, and if one cannot see that this determination is *only* problematic, a problematological answer, then he will fall into the trap of confusion with the apocritical. To resolve a question about something, there must therefore be an answer other than the problematical made assertorical. Inference is the link between the two entities. If one begins from facts, the link will even be causal. This is not a constraint to the extent that the required answer must not itself be a matter of experience and be, for example, a law or an equation, something that does not have to be factualized.

What is reasonable to expect from such an answer? It is a *secondary* answer, if a factual question is singled out by a distinct problematological answer, problematological to preserve its status as a hypothesis, a question. It is also just an answer, if one takes the question as a question, because (for example) it is impossible to isolate the factual, since it is not established *from another point* in an independent fashion, as being an *answer* by itself.

4. Constructing Alternatives: From Causality to Relevance as an Experimental Criterion

We must be wary of any ad hoc theorizing which makes facts conform to problematical determination. The real cannot be found to be simply as it was supposed to be in the basic approach which has heretofore been used. We must not confuse the nature of a problem with what must characterize a solution. It is necessary that one take the *facts* in question as *questions*, providing the need to find a response, which, if it proves "correct," will transform those facts into an independent answer. We will have responded to the facts themselves only through deriving authority from a reading which allows the dichotomization of the facts which come from that reading. This leads us to the idea of truth as adequacy. If facts are what was in question in the first place, the answer that is required will be no less than a justification for the method of factualization, a response to these facts as made by a particularized assertion. A good explanation of the French Revolution also provides a justification for seeing its facts one way rather than another, and in this way works to question the facts themselves, but does not cease being problematical until the explanation is validated.

But how to validate it?

To answer, let us return to the question of the elliptical orbits of the planets. When I ask for its explanation, I am admitting the fact that the orbits *have* an elliptical trajectory. I am only asking for an explanation to establish the fact which the explanation assumes. For this is a matter of assumptions, as when I raise the question about your arrival, meaning that I am seeking an explanation, since your arrival has *already* taken place. It is not really your arrival which is in question, but it is the question which the issue of your arrival raises.

If we do not separate the two readings involved in any factualization, which can now be considered as interrogative, we would seem to be going in a circle. Hence their disassociation cannot be made complete, but must be placed at the very heart of the questioning process, considered generally. Both questions refer to one another: a first question is posed as answered, but, in fact, it will be answered only by a second one. Here, one begins with an answer, thereby a purely hypothetical one, which tells us what the facts are, and one then proceeds to an inference, whose goal is to justify the first reading of the facts, a reading upon which we have at first relied. Answering this initial questioning of the factual is the same as justifying one's grasp of the factual, and it is done by giving oneself a priori that "justification," even if only hypothetically. The question is still posed by a theoretization which must then be independently proved to be considered as an answer to the hypothetical reading of the initial facts. It is the theoretization which has become a question, and the autonomization of one of the readings of the question of the elliptical nature of orbits then arises.

Because there are questions, we are compelled to examine alternative answers. We want to know what is going to happen "in the opposite case." Theory B, which explains factuality A, assumes from the start that it will be tested problematically: B or non-B? It could be B, for example, which would mean that A is admitted. If B implies A, and B is agreed to, then A must be agreed to as well. To justify the problematical thesis B, one proceeds in the same way as if one began from A and worked toward B, to return again afterwards, in the manner of synthesis. This two-way movement covers the same field as the dialectic method of Plato, the only differences being that it is dealing with questions rather than propositions and that it is not limited strictly to a self-contained round trip. Indeed, one begins from fact A, and one suggests B *so that* B explains A. It is a perfect circle, hence, the problematicity of the "result." In reality, we are saying that B is no more compatible with the contrary of A than A is able to imply B *and* non-B. A must be linked to B, as non-A to non-B; if not, one will have, at best, only one explanatory factor and not the whole justification of A. If the test turns out positive, then one has "if A, then B," with B as justifying A, thereby autonomizing it as an independent fact. To break the circle, as we have shown, it will be necessary that B find an external validation, that it explain something other than A. Let us suppose this to be C: given B, C follows. Therefore, if there is no B, there is no C. The process is the same each time; it is repetitive in its structure. The effort is to *answer* either B or non-B, in checking whether one can *answer* C rather than non-C, or the reverse. Experience, as a new or external factuality, but one already known nonetheless, will be invoked if C is an event. It is B because C, if C is an observed fact, allows B to be posited as independent from A. In reinforcing itself, a theory fills itself out at the same time that it factualizes itself: A, C, and then E, G, and so on, for example. The empirical grounding is enriched, providing the basis for the analytical construction of the factual required by the synthetical nature of science, which cannot limit its part to circumscribing the realm of objects which it began with.

Let us take up the well-known example of Semmelweis, who discovered the cause of puerperal (or childbed) fever. What could have been the explanation of a series of deaths which took the lives of pregnant women at the Maternity Hospital in Vienna in 1844? One explanation offered at the time was that the priest, in going to administer last rites, was causing a shock to the future mothers when they saw him pass by their windows. Semmelweis asked him to change his itinerary but found that the death toll in the maternity wing remained unchanged. Semmelweis had also found that even women who gave birth in the street, all other things being equal, had a higher chance of not contracting the disease in question. It was only in 1847, well after a number of hypotheses had been offered, that Semmelweis, after observing the death of a fellow physician who cut his finger during an autopsy and developed a kind of puerperal fever, presented a new hypothesis: that the infection must be coming from dead tissues which were contaminating the blood. He then required that no one return to the maternity room without washing his hands with an adequate chemical solution, and the death toll fell dramatically.

The malady is the problem here: it is the fact in question. Knowing what it *is* comes back to knowing the *causes* of the matter. Theoretization is a matter of questioning. If the fact is a psychological trauma, caused, for example, by the priest's passing by, then the nonpassing of the priest should produce the nonoccurrence of the result. If the priest changes his route, the two facts should be linked, but they are not: there is B, interpreting A, which becomes non-B, without A's being altered. It must be B and A, and non-B and non-A, so that the explanation B can be retained. Fact C happens, which is interpreted, let us say, by D. It can be seen that non-C and non-A, and C and A, are linked by the intermediary of D. The death of the doctor and the puerperal fever have in common their origin from contact with infected, in this example necrosed, tissue. If D is the true explanation for the fact A, then puerperal fever becomes a certain type of infection (rather than another type or, for example, rather than there being a psychological origin for the problem, as in the priestly hypothesis). Then, if D is justification for the fact A, that which gives it meaning, there must be an observable fact E which will buttress the thesis, and the "birth in the streets" example illustrates that question. The less perilous birth which faces those mothers outside the hospital is explained by the absence of the microbial contamination found in the maternity-ward patients. Experience, represented here by birth in the streets, confirms the explanation that is put forward and resolves the question represented by the explanatory hypothesis. The question of a lower rate of mortality as linked to this kind of childbirth finds its solution in the answer which the explanation offers.

Here, it is important to do justice to a particular view of science which mistakes science's conjectural nature. Clearly, if B implies A, and B is confirmed by C, it is necessary to admit that A is factually true. One can certainly interpret C other than through B, and one can easily imagine a plurality of theories as answers to the same question X. Does that make each of the theories about X problematic? At any rate, however, one answers by theory, and theory answers to the facts so analyzed, too. That is not contradictory, because one depends each time on intratheoretical factualizations which are the products of experiments and have a goal of facilitating explanatory models. One never stops posing questions without going so far as to eliminate the possibility of inadequate or superficial answers.

Experience, which empiricism raises to the level of an ideal, consists, at its most basic, of asking something, the asking being based on something else. What can we say of B, given A? Can the question B be resolved beginning from question A? The formulation of question A remains something imposed, a circularity which literally has implications for subsequent questions, for example, B. Experience can always be put in question again, as can its interpretation and its result, at least at the level of the premises which result from this reading. But one answers facts by articulating them, by explaining them; that connects them with other facts. Despite everything, truth is reached, truth as the answer which is an answer to the facts, an answer which constitutes those facts in their very independence in regard to questioning. Experience doesn't describe reality any more than it *is* reality, but it does allow us to answer based on reality and to shape a picture of it. That picture or idea is called truth, at least in science, where it is the way results are obtained. The sum of all the processes of factualization does not prevent each factualization from being something other than it is. But one must still be able to fall back on factual answers which theory reaches, even if they have no other necessity than that which comes from their status as answers, exclusive even of contrary propositions just because they are answers and not questions. This gives them the positivity of experience as one usually thinks of experience, and which Hume made paradoxical by his failure to differentiate between the problematological and the apocritical, between questions and answers, grouping them without distinguishing what sets each apart from the other.

Causality embodies a principle which says more or less this: that if A is the cause of B, then each time that A occurs, B must follow. Same cause, same effect. And if not A, then not B. As we have seen, the reason causality is as it is, is that, at its foundation, it is interrogative. It is because one would not answer A by B if non-B were obtained with A (or non-A with B); no other combination but AB is admissible. Suppose that B might be an answer at one time, and non-B at another. In this case a question "B?" would never be resolved because the responses are inconsistent alternatives. And if B and non-B exist with A, whereas A should allow for the resolution of question "B?" it would have to be concluded that A does not explain B, because completely contrary answers would exist for the same A. This implies that A is not the question which should be posed to resolve B.

When we speak of cause and effect, we say no more than this: the resolution of one question suggests the resolution of another; the two questions are mutually *relevant.* The one can only be resolved through the other; causality is reinforced until it reaches the point which logicians would denominate as being necessary and sufficient. That matters little here. The whole problem is in knowing why we need one question to resolve another. This is truly the secret of causality. Why use such an answering process? The reader already knows the reason why, because that reader will recall the scientific requirements which we analyzed earlier. Science relies on an indirect way of putting questions and on answers which are proved by and through alternatives. One question in science is resolved by another in the pursuit of propositions and then of facts which emerge from these answers and which depend on other facts to be factualized in turn. In short, one always resolves one question by another, if one wants to avoid the trap of ad hoc, circular "explanation." It might be recalled, for example, what was said earlier about the question of the French Revolution, whose interpretation, as a question of fact, depends on the resolution of other questions which allow a reversal in the direction of questions, ultimately returning to the first question. Science needs an inferential mechanism like that which has just been described under the name of the principle of causality. And there is more.

To resolve a scientific question, answers must be tested, not one by one, but one must be able to settle question B if, for example, one begins from A. To do this, it is necessary to be able to decide what would happen if there were no A or no B. Experience is nothing more than this decision-making process. At its most basic, experimentation consists of developing one's problems in such a way that the problems can be resolved by considering alternative proposals. Experience thus serves to justify a proposition whose contrary might be true, which shows quite clearly, as Hume pointed out, that experience is not apodictic. But *should* it be? After all, if one conceives of experience as reality itself, and scientific decision-making, thus causality, as adequate to this reality, there is an inevitable difficulty. On the other hand, if one realizes that experience is a method of resolution because it puts into play a certain type of inference and makes it possible, the problem Hume identifies disappears. Experience is meant for answering, and one presumes that the answering has a causal structure. An answer can be other than what it is. But once we have it, it cannot be changed into its opposite, because then the answer would cease to be what it is, and the question, rather than being resolved, would still be posed in an identical fashion. Because a scientific question requires a causal treatment, experience must be able to lead us to an answer. Causality and experimentation thus are linked, but not, as had earlier been believed, in an ontological way. Experimentation is a mode of resolution, and resolution is here built on an empirical base. Our relationship to the factual is, in an underlying way, an interrogative one, and the only necessity which can be found there is part of the interrogative structure of inference.

It often happens that scientific questions are not stated in terms of alternatives; the genius of *methodology* consists of finding the right formulation for the initial question by posing alternative questions which are themselves decidable. Such alternatives, if formulated, will lead to justification as their only end.[8] This is what leads to the link that is

8. A question which seeks to explain progress in history admits that there is such progress and no longer inquires into *what* it is trying to prove. One assumes the existence of a fact the moment one tries to explain it.

often made between scientificity and justification: no result or response is really scientific until it is justified. Through the process of justification, a *proposed* answer can be accepted in a nonproblematical fashion. Science justifies its answers so that they can be answers. Nevertheless, we often hear it said that science is problematical and does not provide justification, that it continuously produces competing theories for the same set of facts. In reality, science answers without being immune to the problematization of its initial framework of problematization, of its own frame of conceptualization, that is, of its presuppositions, or better, of its basic factualization, upon which it still operates back through indirect confirmation, therefore through inference. The metatheoretical argument, which Kuhn calls the "scientific revolution," is an answer *upon* these questions and the very formulations which are given them. But it is quite clear that, at the end, some justification is needed and given; thus, we can find in Aristotle's *Physics* a kind of justification which "sticks" close to observation. Philosophy, on the other hand, can engender its questions without their ever being completely eliminated, thereby continually renewing philosophical questioning in its full radicality, at least at the onset.

The problematicity which is attributed to science derives, in the last analysis, from the theoretical assumptions already present in the integration of facts into any theory. One can test the answer to facts by other facts or by the presentation of logical consequences which will make apparent unsuspected connections; but those "new facts" are, even if independently so, theorized and discovered by problematization.

Experience, like causality, is an instance of questioning at large. Science seems to have accorded a privileged status to specific forms of questioning, due to its own privileged role in our culture since the classical age, the age par excellence of mechanism. But inference is neither necessarily causal nor observable, by experience or experimentation. Not even in science can one surrender to such a limitation.

Relevance is the key term here, for it is relevance which characterizes the relationship between problems. It is inference which links question and answer. Causality only appears as an empirical positivization of answers in this inferential link, for example, when applied to events, to the relations between substances as in mechanics (the "bodies"), to phenomena, or even to things. But it is relevance which is determinative, since without it one would have to conclude that A has nothing to do with B, given that A and non-A coexist with B (and with non-B). Such independence would prevent the linkage of question A and question B.

If a physicist, for example, conducts experiments to turn problematological answers into apocritical ones (which could always later find their problematological character actualized within some *other* interrogative process), we could note that inferentiality *in general* would obey the rules of questioning that are part of that process; so would mathematics, surprisingly enough. What is this mathematical language "of X" if not that of problematization? When one puts a theory into mathematical terms, one imposes thereon an interrogative structure. One links two variables, for example, X and Y, and then one assumes "all other things being equal," in order to be able to solve the equation $Y = f(X)$. But what does this phrase "all other things being equal" imply? What conditions the possibility of learning something about Y through the variable X, rather than through anything else? It simply means that factors other than X will have no substantial effect on Y, and that if X varies, Y also varies. In reality, it could be that X could be developed also as a function of Z, and if so, the effect would be different. In canceling all factors other than X, the relationship between Y and X can be analyzed and observed; we may see what in X determines Y. The relevance of X to the effect Y is typical of inference in the sense that problematology has allowed us to redefine it. Pertinence, or relevance, defines inferentiality as an interrogative relationship. It can be tested by the interplay of variables, of a continuing series of alternatives where one asks, "What would happen if . . . ?" So here, mathematical rationality adheres to the problematological model of scientificity which requires the experience of various other contingencies to confirm its results. And those results are always susceptible of being reproblematized later on, at another level.

Scientific revolutions, as Kuhn tells us, truly are crises of relevance, of pertinence, whereas (intra)paradigmatic developments work within admitted inferential relationships where one still seeks validation through experimentation applied to consequences. And that, as I have said, reinforces the initial model, since any question will seek to justify its assumptions by putting various alternatives to the test. Such a research process postulates that one will consider consequences of the model other than those which, in an immediate if not ad hoc way, arise from the initial problematization. We must not lose sight of the fact that there must be a *given*, for example, a fact, to test. To answer, there must be something that is out-of-the-question (which, being indirectly problematized, is so by the fact that it is a hypothesis), since any *logos* always respects and presupposes the problematological difference. The idea of a *given* allowed a belief that the empirical was self-evident, at least up until Kant, who began with a passive sensibility entirely made up of receptivity. Readers of Kant would have been able to recognize in the *presence* of such a given, in the *repetition* of the causal link A-B, and in the claim of *necessity*, the *synthesis of apprehension*, *of reproduction*, and *of recognition*, the latter permitting us to find a result, as an effect of that which we already know as being what must happen. Kant could see in this triad of articulations of (transcendental) consciousness only *critical* imperatives, not *apocritical* ones.

But little by little causality stopped being the paradigm of scientificity. It was replaced by probability, and the human sciences emerged as well. The calculus of probabilities, at the level of fundamental conceptualization, aims at developing an assessment of the schemes of relevance. In the human sciences, the rigidity of the causal as explanatory collapses. Human beings often do not obey the constraining regularity of unidirectional laws like "if A, then (necessarily) B." Relationships rely on many factors, and the relevance of those factors, which is no longer of the "necessary and sufficient" type, is more fluid. Inferentiality changes its appearance and reemerges as a form of opposition: explanation versus comprehension. Comprehension becomes part of the understanding of human action, an effort to understand what a particular individual could have intended when he did such and such a thing, whereas explanation continues to rely on some sort of causal functioning, as before. In reality, there is no more an explanation without comprehension of what has been justified than there is understanding without some explanation. It is hard to imagine, for example, that understanding Hitler's rise to power would not serve as an explanation of that rise, or that an explanation of Newton's laws would not allow for an understanding of how the forces of nature work. There is, however, at least one difference between them which still remains (is it an inexplicable or incomprehensible one?). Comprehension puts theory at the level of dealing with alternatives, where explanation takes them as already resolved. The more problematization imposed itself as something to be theorized, as is the case in history, for instance, the more it was necessary to disassociate it (although in a nonproblematological way) according to the requirement imposed by the problematological difference.

Let us examine this in a more concrete context, using the remarkable work of Paul Veyne on history: ". . . the king made war and was conquered; these are, indeed, things that happen. Let us further extend the explanation: through love of glory, a very natural thing, the king made war and was conquered by reason of his numerical inferiority, for, with some exceptions, it is usual for small battalions to retreat before big ones."[9] Grouchy could have arrived in time, and the king in this

9. Paul Veyne, *Writing History* (Middletown, Conn.: Wesleyan University Press, 1984), p. 87.

example could have had a dislike for glory, failed to reach the battle-field, and to crown it all, been outnumbered. Comprehension consists of perceiving within problematicity the action or the fact which has prevailed. Certainly Grouchy could have arrived in time, and if I understand that, then I must also understand that the reverse was possible. Comprehending means understanding an alternative and what ensued from it. Explaining, on the other hand, means relating a result to something that it is the result *of*, rather than to the opposite, which did not occur even though we understand that it could have. "Napoleon lost the battle, what is more natural? These are misfortunes that happen, and we ask nothing more; there is no gap in the narration. Napoleon was too ambitious; any man is free to be so—in fact, that explains the Empire . . ."[10] Veyne adds that one could have included the role of the bourgeoisie and thereby have shifted the *problem*. In that way, "[t]he historian explains plots."[11] Agreed, but why? The reason is simple, after all. Inferences are made more flexible in relation to a causal system which is a strict one. The relationship A-B is more problematic: A, just as B, could have turned out not to exist. We speak of comprehension without being able to limit it in relation to explanation, as I have pointed out. What the dichotomy really evokes is a more important problematicity which must be able to be expressed, but clearly not as such. Adds Veyne, quite correctly, "The problem of causality in history is a survival of the paleoepistemological era; men have continued to suppose that the historian gave the causes of the war between Anthony and Octavius in the same way that the physicist was presumed to give those of falling bodies."[12] In reality, we must see that the concept of causality corresponds to an ontological fundamentalism which no longer prevails. The principle of causality, like experience, needs to be rethought in problematological terms as a particularized mode of questioning. History involves a differential relationship, not a causality which goes back to a type of original foundation through a particular event or first mover. Historical inference seeks correlations and tests them as in any other scientific discipline and with the same essential problem, their factualization. "The conflict between town and country," writes Veyne, "does not explain the crisis of the third century as one event explains another; this crisis is interpreted in a certain manner . . ."[13] It is a matter of interpreting the plot, of putting it together, and then of verifying the adequacy of its level of understanding. Here

10. Ibid., p. 93.
11. Ibid., p. 88.
12. Ibid., p. 91.
13. Ibid., p. 118.

again, preferring a particular problematization, one which factualizes and groups specific events into an overall pattern, obliges a *scientific* questioner to verify their effects and also their consequences for other facts and theories.

As for the notion of a differential relationship, it allows us to avoid the idea of "a cause of a cause of a cause . . ." because it locates events in an evolution-based relationship: A develops in relation to B in a variable way, allowing, for example, B to emerge eventually. The relationship A/B reproduces this association, with which is also associated the classical interpretation of causality. This idea implies the principle of economy, or simplicity, which we have already described. For example, if, like Max Weber, one were to link the appearance of capitalism to Protestantism, the question of knowing whether an ideology can or cannot be the "cause" of a given mode of production appears unsolvable. The two phenomena are undeniably correlated. But certainly there are exceptions, such as Flanders and Italy, which saw the development of capitalism without adopting the Protestant ethic or ideology. They didn't need it, since in these areas at the fringes of empires, centralized power was weak, and there was little need to fight it to allow for social advancement. That suggests that Protestantism is not the explanatory factor, that it is itself a derived cause. The principle of economy implies that one must find another explanation. The struggle against centralized power seems to be the decisive factor, for such a struggle presupposes the existence of an ideology, and Protestantism indeed played that role, either in the service of princes or of the "bourgeoisie," who were able to justify themselves in their struggle against a king or emperor and his ecclesiastical servants.

What is important here is to see that the differential relationship, which refers us back to continuity, and which excludes the idea of a self-structured foundationalism of causes-in-themselves, adheres to the rules of scientific method outlined above. There are no more first causes but only relationships among events which interact with each other without a single force of origin. Given that, history can be read by starting each time from a "free" pattern of interpretation without its being antiscientific. With a differential reading, one would know if indeed the more that central power strengthened itself (or was weakened) in relation to an already relatively strong nobility, for example, the more the Reformation spread. Or one would know if an already well-established bourgeoisie, one which had through an earlier process of centralization risen at the expense of other social groups, became more Protestant or not in this context, developing itself consistently with its own interests, that is, in an increasingly capitalistic way. The differential technique is a way to reask questions without falling into what Paul Veyne aptly termed a "paleoepistemology" in the search for causes. What matters is the ability to correlate a large number of phenomena, with the formula "the more X, then the more Y" as their links, without prejudging, without even asking, if the links suggest "true causes" or "historical motives," rather than relationships of relevance that are what really count and for which it is better to reject the old ontologized version, which tried to "positivize" them into active entities, into so-called deep causes.

Conclusion

Can Metaphysics Survive?

The death of Man as Subject has meant the disappearance of an important conception of the foundational, and even of Man. This does not imply in the slightest that the subject has disappeared or that man has stopped being a focus of analysis. On the contrary, it is precisely because Man has lost ontological dignity (his status as exception) that he can be studied for his own sake. And it will be no real surprise to see the subject reemerge as omnipresent, in fields from linguistics to psychoanalysis. But if it is objectified, then it is no longer foundational, in the sense of its being the free and conscious source of discourse and of values, of knowledge—conceived as the extended concatenation of individual propositions that would make up science—and of behavior. There is no question of all this anymore, precisely because the subject has even more firmly established itself as a question, that is, questioning about itself, indeed, about *the* "self."

Man is truly an irreducible problem, one for which the only answer, far from suppressing the question, reproduces it endlessly. We could call that life. For answers still to have some meaning as answers, living Man can be divided into the conscious and the unconscious, self-forgetting and therefore forgetting irreducible interrogation by displacing itself into numerous answerable questions, problematological despite all their human reality. Being alive, we think because we question, and communicate because of an insatiable need for others, whom we ask to be our answer. Thus we love. This need is the opposite of dialogue, where I put to another a limited question, which that person will resolve by the answer that I ask of him and which will at the same time eliminate the question that was asked. All that I can say or do is, in the last analysis, the denied problematological expression of my own questioning-existence. Far from grounding questioning, mankind is "defined" by it, as the subject *of* questioning, a term which we will need to understand in both meanings of the preposition "of."

303

Failure to grasp this emphasis on the problematological originary—because there would no longer be any originary, therefore no metaphysics—would lead philosophy down an erroneous path. It would confirm the senselessness of the whole enterprise, which, after all, can only be radical questioning. But what could be more radical in this questioning than questioning itself? However, by renouncing the quest for the fundamental, which seems to reflect a certain kind of modernity, one is inevitably, in the best of cases, forced to abandon oneself to a series of purely descriptive or "phenomenological" concerns, if not simply arbitrary issues, opposable as such to any other. For one can state everything without having to base one's statement on anything, such a foundational request being rejected as not "postmodern" enough.

Bringing to light the matter of a problematological originary should not be confused with some sort of return to the traditional conception of metaphysics, despite the fact that, for problematology, it really is a matter of undertaking a foundational approach appropriate to the *philosophia perennis*. Indeed, if we look closely at what the impulse was for this metaphysic, we can see that it was born of the need to develop an anhypothetical foundation, as Plato labeled it, an unshakable certainty for apodictic knowledge, reflecting an order of things that was itself necessary. Descartes sought to do this as well when he put this congruence into an ultimate context with a God-foundation, before Kant's transcendental man came to guarantee this very possibility, at least at the level of knowledge. Be that as it may, the same idea has persisted: that it is important to be able to depend on, and to ground subsequent thought in, an ontologized or ontological foundation, a necessary entity, as knowledge, which becomes a point of departure from which all else can proceed.

Because such an undertaking has become philosophically impossible, there has been a too hasty leap to the conclusion that philosophy must renounce itself in favor of nihilism or scientism, condemning itself to dispersion, disorder, and fragmentation. But what problematology seeks to demonstrate is that an interrogative grounding requires neither an ontological foundation nor the necessity of any absolute, not even knowledge conceived as a network of apodictic propositionality. To say that the foundation is questioning is ultimately to say that only questions can be originary. Hence we recognize the pluralistic opening of answers which, while originating themselves in questioning in multiple ways, detach and free themselves in sui generis areas. The mechanism of problematological deduction, that is, the problematological prerogative, is in no way a constraining deduction, in the sense that one could find in it a necessary, apodictic knowledge. Then, exactly what is it that makes up inference? Let us recall that. An answer is derived from the question itself; it is the question which makes us see and understand. It is a synthesis in its very formulation. Knowledge, contrary to what we have been taught since Plato, can be associated with the problematic, thanks to the existence of problematological answers. As to answers that come from the questions themselves, their only necessity *is* this link; other answers, just as necessary, and not arbitrary, are thus possible de jure. The plurality of philosophies includes another point of confusion. Instead of providing absolute justification and thus rendering anything necessary, problematology substitutes for this necessity the idea of some resolutional method of its own, so that the concept of "justification" takes on another meaning. It can be seen as a strong link, all the way to strict causation, a meaning coming from the question-answer relationship, so that the answer is justified by the question which gave rise to it, needing only to show their relationship. The necessity is that of understanding the problematic and not that of solutions which, considered as proceeding from themselves and without reference to anything other than themselves, have generated nothing but difficulties for philosophers, from Hume and Kant down to our time.

A certain type of "foundational metaphysics" is dead, thanks to Nietzsche, among others. Will philosophy become science, or a simple game, for example, a linguistic one? Will we have to renounce two thousand years of the philosophical quest and, with Heidegger, proclaim its end? Or will we be able to see in philosophy the only effective answer to our intellectual crisis, and will we be able to think of this answer literally and not merely metaphorically? Then, the only way out will be to question thought, inasmuch as it is always engaged in answering, even when all signs suggest that it is not answering but asserting propositions. Problematology is the challenge which the philosophical tradition takes up when confronted with its own dissolution, or (and this amounts to the same thing) with an exclusive cult of the past.

Like all thought, knowledge progresses by developing alternatives to currently held theories. Only two things can happen. Either the theory resolves the alternative, or the alternative becomes a competing theory. The interrogativity of alternatives is what defines thought, because synthesis, the creation of questions, demands that those to whom the questions are addressed answer them, stimulating the mind by the incitement of implied questioning. Questions, whether we find them in science or in literature, make us think through that which they ask but do not provide; and by the putting into question of our very selves that they imply when taken at their most profound level, questions oblige us to defend ourselves, to give reasons, to assemble something coherent which will assure the existential identity of what we are and what we want to be. One who thinks is one who asks questions, because he is required to answer, and therefore to understand, to link elements together, to do what used to be called "exercising one's judgment."

From science to common sense, from language to literature, the problematical constantly requires us to be active and committed questioners.

He who pretends to have answers without their having been questioned, without having questioned them himself, should be quite shaken by all of this. He is a one who will obey, even if asked to sign his own death warrant. He is a creature of complete acceptance, one comfortable in hierarchies, the type of person in whom all Authority rejoices. Dedicated to being manipulated, he will also, if he can, turn the questioner into the prey for his weakness-become-strength. He will even seek revenge against the questioner he cannot be, recognizing in that questioner what puts him in question, in a vitally existential way. I fear this man above all, for he is the enemy of culture; he will become the intellectual of oppression. Socrates' trial is thus inevitable, the same Socrates with whom we began to philosophize, and without whom we could not conclude, if a conclusion is to have any meaning here.

Index